*Sociological Theory*

# SOCIOLOGICAL

## by Nicholas S. Timasheff

PROFESSOR EMERITUS OF SOCIOLOGY, FORDHAM UNIVERSITY

THIRD EDITION

# THEORY
## Its Nature *and*
## Growth

Random House | *New York*

To TANIA

# PREFACE

Ten years have passed since the second edition of this book appeared. For many sciences and for many decades, nothing spectacular could be reported; this is not so for sociology. Sociology is a science that is rapidly developing and expanding. At the present time, there are a great many sociological theories fighting each other. Beginners in the field of sociology cannot see their way clear through the mass of conflicting opinions and they need guidance. Good, objectively-minded instructors can help them, but students must have before them something even more tangible than the regularly appearing teachers; what they need is a book offering them a survey of theory corresponding to the sociology of today, as well as of the major steps made by our predecessors.

The task of writing such a survey implies a difficult solution, and one cannot deny that the personal opinions of the author of this survey influenced him. Numerous works as good as those selected for formulation in the present work had to be omitted to make the book readable and to avoid turning it into a poor man's encyclopedia. None of the authors of the omitted works should feel offended by the present author's choices.

One general remark is necessary. Expanding, sociology has extended upon more and more neighboring fields, very closely connected yet, in this author's opinion, outside the scope of sociological theory in the strict sense. Thus, the author of this survey had to be especially conscious of his task. At the present time, such fields are mathematical sociology, statistical sociology, the theory of the small groups (microsociology), and philosophical sociology. Mathematical sociology does not yet impose itself on the authors of surveys like the present one, since the results are meager and comprehensible only to students well trained in higher mathematics. Statistical sociology produces reliable data, but only relative to scattered phenomena (for example, in the year *NN*, in the city of *X*, such and such situations could be found); a few similar observations could help, but still not offer a basis for the formulation of generalized propositions about some aspects of society. Small-group theory suffers from the fact that its topic is also the object of psychology and, as explained in Chapter 19, deals with units which could scarcely be considered as *real* social groups. These three fields are sociologies of the future. Philosophical sociology is in danger because its objects of observations coincide with those of the philosophers; knowledge of the corresponding philosophical theories is necessary, but cannot be provided without discussing these theories. Therefore, the author of this book has preferred to use the rule *non multa sed multum*.

Many of the statements above will be denied by other sociologists, not to speak of philosophers. Only time can solve the debates.

To conclude, I wish to thank again those persons to whom I expressed my gratitude in the Preface to the second edition, particularly to Professor Charles H. Page, now Provost of the Adlai E. Stevenson College of the University of California, Santa Cruz. My gratitude goes also to Dr. Gertrud Neuwirth of Temple University, to Professor Joseph Scheuer of Fordham University, and to my daughter Mrs. Tania Bobrinskoy, who collected much of the material necessary to bring this book up to date and assisted me in all aspects of the preparation of the text.

*Nicholas S. Timasheff*

# CONTENTS

### Part Six  *Conclusion*

# PART ONE

# Introduction

# CHAPTER 1

# THE STUDY
# OF SOCIOLOGICAL THEORIES

Sociological activity in the United States from about World War I until recently de-emphasized *theory*. Instructor and teacher and researcher were largely concerned with teaching or learning or digging up factual information about this or that aspect of society, especially American society, and were often prone to identify "theory" with philosophy and even idle speculation. Empirically established facts, they sometimes seemed to say, speak for themselves and—if we gather enough of them—their voices will constitute a sociological science.

But science demands more than facts, more than careful description. Thus, as sociology matures, the former orientation is rapidly being replaced by widespread recognition of the indispensability of theory. As we shall see, theoretical considerations and theoretical concepts, implicitly or explicitly, have an essential role in shaping the direction of research, in directing observation, in guiding description itself. Today almost all sociologists agree that these functions of theory should be *explicit*.

However, if theory is to be used wisely and with sharp awareness we require knowledge of its nature and of its varieties. We need to know its concepts and the diverse terminological forms they take, and, conversely, the different concepts that are frequently expressed by the same terms. Moreover, we should be familiar with the history of sociological theoretical endeavor—with its changing emphases, its successes and failures, its promise for the future. These questions constitute the subject matter of this volume.

We begin with a definition of sociology in contradistinction to related disciplines and with an explanation of the meaning of theory in the context of scientific enterprise.

## What Is Sociology?

Auguste Comte first conceived the word *sociology* in 1839. He had intended to name the new science social physics; but he rejected this term after a Belgian scholar, Adolphe Quételet, began to make involved statistical studies of society and to call his area of endeavor social physics. Though the word sociology is a barbaric combination of Latin and Greek, its two component parts aptly describe what the new science wants to achieve. *Logy* connotes study on a high level (for instance, bio*logy* and psycho*logy*—high level study of life and mind respectively); *socio* points to society. Thus, etymologically, sociology means the study of society on a highly generalized or abstract level.

This definition presupposes that a person knows what society is. Actually, somewhat conflicting explanations of the nature of society are offered by different sociological theories; many of these will be met and reviewed in later discussion. A kind of vicious circle thus seems to arise: sociology is defined as the science of society, and society must be defined by sociology. Such a situation as this often occurs at the initial steps of scientific inquiry. The problem can be solved by giving to the object of study a working definition, an approximation sufficient for the present purposes. So, in a preliminary way, society may be defined as men (human beings) in interdependence. Men in interdependence therefore may be taken as the subject matter of sociology.

With this start, a boundary can be traced between sociology and the other sciences which study men as individuals or as collections of individuals with no regard to their interdependence. Human anatomy and physiology study the structure and functioning of human beings, that which is repeated in every man. Physical anthropology studies the variability of the body structure of these beings and classifies the variations, making nominal or statistical groups out of men displaying similar hereditary and externally recognizable traits. Psychology (except a hybrid branch called social psychology) studies the mental processes going on in individual minds, telling us how an individual human being sees, hears, feels, reacts to sensations, and so on.

Sociology is not interested in man's body structure or the functioning of his organs or in his mental processes as such. It is interested in what happens when man meets man; when human beings form masses or groups; when they cooperate, fight, dominate one another, persuade or imitate others, develop or destroy culture. The unit of sociological study is never an individual, but always at least two individuals somehow related to one another.

However, though the subject matter of sociological study is men in interdependence, the province of sociology does not embrace every type of study of men in interdependence. The same matter is also studied in other disciplines, such as social philosophy, history, and the concrete social sciences. What is the difference between these disciplines and sociology?

*Social philosophy* is a much older discipline than sociology. Well developed in ancient Greece and cultivated in the Middle Ages, social philosophy blossomed in the eighteenth century, in the Age of the Enlightenment which immediately preceded the birth of sociology. In the works of older social philosophers, many propositions are found which easily could be restated in the terms of contemporary sociology. Nevertheless, social philosophy and sociology are two different endeavors of man's inquiring mind. The difference between the two is similar to what, in general, separates philosophy and empiric science, a difference in levels of abstraction and in procedure. Both are attempts to describe and explain reality. Both are based on observation of facts and on generalizations derived from these observations. But here the similarity between empiric science (including sociology) and philosophy (including social philosophy) ends.

In empiric science, the generalizations concerning a specified field of inquiry are drawn from facts observed in that field or in closely related fields. These generalizations are drawn without assuming (neither asserting nor denying) any knowledge on a level of higher abstraction concerning reality as a whole. All propositions that constitute any empiric science form a self-sufficient system. No proposition is allowed to play a role in the system if it contains knowledge which is not empiric, in other words which is not formulated under the limitations just stated.

On the contrary, philosophy is primarily an attempt to understand reality in its totality. From a multitude of observed facts, the philosopher proceeds to certain ultimate principles which, taken together, attempt to explain reality as a whole. How propositions about total reality are derived is a question not pursued in this volume. In that regard, various schools of philosophy significantly differ from one another. From the ultimate principles of total reality thus established, the philosopher draws certain postulates and axioms and then uses them to reinterpret the particular classes of objects which he distinguishes in the observed facts. Thus, whereas the sociologist explains society in terms of facts observed in society and, eventually, in related fields of empiric knowledge, the social philosopher explains society in terms of the explanation he gives to total reality. He can speak of first causes, supreme values, and ultimate ends; the sociologist is not entitled to do so.

In principle the difference between social philosophy and sociology is clear. In practice the line of demarcation is blurred, especially on the level of theories, the very subject matter of this book. In the development of sociology there has been much confusion between sociology and social philosophy. Many sociologists have trespassed the boundary between the two domains and have introduced concepts belonging to social philosophy, often of questionable brand. This situation will often be met in this book.

*History* is another science which seeks to understand men in interdependence, more exactly, in past configurations of that interdependence. Even a historical work of the biographical type cannot fail to tell the story of the relations between its hero and other men. What is then the difference between history and sociology, the latter, of course, being interested not only in present day but also in past configurations of men's interdependence?

In principle, the difference is not difficult to establish. History studies the human past as a sequence of concrete and unique events, situations, and processes. The historian tries to reconstruct the past with many empiric details, just as it happened. Take the American War of Independence, the French Revolution, the Communist Revolution in Russia, the New Deal in the United States. How did these events occur and what were the individual processes of which they consisted? Why did they happen? These and similar questions will never cease to interest mankind.

But the human mind does not stop at the reconstruction of unique, non-recurring events. Behind them in their singular, historical, time-space setting the human mind tries to discover patterns of recurrence, of repetition. There have been many wars. Is there or is there not a recurring pattern of their origin, their impact on the societies involved, and their outcome? There are continuous fluctuations of market prices. Is there or is there not a common pattern behind these fluctuations? Uncounted crimes are committed. Cannot more or less constant patterns be distinguished despite the concrete variability of crime? Recurring patterns observable in human interdependence are the subject matter of the social sciences of the type to which sociology belongs. These sciences are based on the postulate of order, the logical premise of every study going above the level of simple description.

Concrete sequences studied by the historians are unique and cannot be repeated. There never will be another War of 1812 or another October Victory of the Communists in Russia. But these concrete sequences may be analyzed into elements, and among these elements invariable and necessary relations, according to their nature, may be established.

An analogy with chemical study may be helpful here. One hundred and three elements are known to chemistry; they combine into millions of compounds. The chemist explains matter by analyzing the compounds into their elements and predicting the major part of the properties of the compounds on the basis of his knowledge of the invariable properties of the elements. In actual life, innumerable varieties of happenings occur. Underlying these happenings certain elements recur which, when perceived, give the events unity and meaning. The historian shows the variable; the sociologist emphasizes the constant and recurring. History describes the multitude of the concrete combinations in which interdependent men have found themselves; sociology analyzes the diversified combinations into their relatively few basic elements and formulates the laws governing their operation. The discovery of these laws, or statements about the necessary and invariant relations between a limited number of elements into which social reality can be analyzed, is the very objective of sociology, a counterpart of the objectives of physics, chemistry, biology, and psychology in their respective fields.

In practice, once again, the line of demarcation is blurred. Historians often contribute to the discovery of recurring patterns in social reality. This happens when their study of concrete developments leads them to try to understand them causally. Historical works such as Arnold Toynbee's *A Study of History* (1934 *et seq.*) conspicuously invade the field of sociology; while sociological studies such as Max Weber's *The Protestant Ethic and the Spirit of Capitalism* (1906) and Pitirim Sorokin's *Social and Cultural Dynamics* (1937–41) greatly contribute to the historical understanding of past configurations of human interdependence. These works bring out clearly the combination of uniqueness and variability in social phenomena. A certain overlapping is there, but this overlapping is to the advantage both of history and of sociology.

Finally sociology must be distinguished from the *concrete social sciences,* such as economics, government, and ethnology. All of them, as does sociology, study men in interdependence—not on the philosophical but on the empiric level. They not only study concrete and unique phenomena, such as the Constitution of the United States or the organization of foreign trade of the United States during the present day, but also seek to discover laws, those necessary and invariant relations between phenomena according to their nature. What is the difference between these concrete sciences and sociology? More specifically, what is sociology's task with respect to the other social sciences? To this question, four principal answers have been given by sociologists at different times during the history of the discipline:

Comte believed that sociology must take over and digest all the data studied by these concrete sciences and thus deprive them of their reason for existence.

Herbert Spencer thought that sociology was a superscience, not itself making observations of social phenomena, but unifying the observations and generalizations made by the other social sciences.

Georg Simmel, a German sociologist working at the end of the nineteenth century, insisted that the study of the content of human actions defined by their ends formed the subject matter of the concrete social sciences. Thus, economics, for example, studies actions aiming at the solution of material problems, that is, production, distribution, exchange, consumption; political science studies actions aiming at the acquisition and exertion of political power. But none of these sciences, Simmel believed, investigates the form of human actions in society, the form common to all types of endeavor, such as the formation or dissolution of human groups, competition, conflict. Simmel claimed this field, formal sociology, not yet occupied by any concrete social science, for sociology, the new discipline.

Pitirim Sorokin, a contemporary sociologist, has offered a line of demarcation which is considered generally correct even by sociologists who commonly oppose him for the content of his sociological views. Sorokin derives his definition of sociology from a statement made by a Russo-Polish scholar, Leo Petrazhitsky. According to the latter, if there are, within a class of phenomena, $n$ subclasses, there must be $n + 1$ disciplines to study them: $n$ to study each of the subclasses, and one more to study that which is common to all, as well as the correlation between the subclasses.[1] In developing this idea, Sorokin says that to each of the many classes of social phenomena—economic, political, religious, and many others—a particular social science must correspond. But, in addition to these sciences, a science (sociology) is necessary to study the characteristics common to all the classes of social phenomena and the interrelation between these classes, because these two tasks cannot be satisfactorily achieved by the particular social sciences. The question has been debated, for example, whether the economic phase of human coexistence determines moral and religious ideas (as asserted by Karl Marx), or whether moral ideas of religious origin give special impetus to economic development (as asserted by Max Weber), or whether the relationship is more complex than is assumed by either of the views just stated. Neither the economist nor the student of the history of moral and religious ideas is competent to solve the scientific problem because he sees it from one side only; it falls within the province of a science which stands above the division of social phenomena into classes. This science is sociology.

In principle Sorokin's view offers the best possible answer to the question: What is sociology? In practice, however, sociology has evolved the tendency of annexing those fields of social study which have not been occupied by the older social sciences, for instance the study of the family, and of applying its generalizations to those fields of social study in which the particular social sciences have confined themselves to description, classification, and comparison. Hence have evolved such branches of sociology as political sociology, the sociology of law, the sociology of religion, the sociology of art, and the like. Sociology, then, consists of a central core of knowledge, approximately corresponding to the definition given by Sorokin, and of a periphery consisting of diversified studies of various social areas not preempted by the well-established concrete sciences.

This situation is somewhat annoying to those who like complete harmony in the majestic building of science. Fortunately for this volume the problem does not present any signal difficulty, since theory is primarily concerned with the central core of sociology.

[1] Leo Petrazhitsky, *Introduction to the Study of Law and Morals* (in Russian, 1907), pp. 80–81.

There is only one scientific neighbor with which sociology lacks a precise boundary line, *ethnology*. Until recently ethnology was confined to the study, largely descriptive, of preliterate societies. At present, cultural anthropology, to use the currently popular designation, is inclined to take the role of the generalizing science of men in interdependence, leaving to sociology the study of men living in modern, complex society. Since there is no authority to resolve the conflict emerging from the incompatible claims of sociology and cultural anthropology, this work will consider contributions of leading anthropologists and ethnologists to sociological theory as well as of professional sociologists themselves.

### What Is Sociological Theory?

The preceding discussion suggests indirectly what sociological theory is. To face this question directly, we may begin by briefly reviewing the structure of any empiric science, independently of its subject matter.

The foundation of every empiric science is *observation*. The result of an individual observation is expressed in a singular proposition stating that, at a given time and place, this particular phenomenon has taken place. The acquisition of such statements is a necessary prerequisite for any science but it is never sufficient. Individual observations must be brought into order and the manners of arrangement are many. Individual observations may be compared; this is tantamount to establishing similarities and differences. They may be classified; this means that types or classes are formed, each unifying a number of similar observations. A good classification allows the location in it of the phenomena observed not only before its formulation but also later on. The individual observations may be counted and submitted to statistical treatment, resulting in frequency distributions, time series, coefficients of correlation, and other statistical formulations. The individual observations may be arranged in genetic sequences showing the gradual unfolding of certain processes, and genetic sequences may be compared with one another and similarities between them discovered.

*Generalization* drawn from the manners of arrangement may be expressed as laws of nature (in the field of social studies, social laws), asserting that, whenever specific conditions are present, a definite effect will follow. With certain precautions, generalizations of the statistical type (frequency distributions, time series) also can be transformed into social laws. And there are still further procedures conducive to the formulation of such laws.

Findings concerning classes of phenomena are generalizations. A generalization no longer refers to any fact in itself; it is based upon many facts and eventually may be used to predict facts likely to be established by further observation. Knowledge expressed in generalizations is of a higher level than that expressed in singular propositions. But such knowledge is not yet the highest level attainable in empiric science; the highest level is that of theory. By accumulated efforts of men of science specializing in a particular discipline, a large number of generalizations of various types are formulated. Scientists then feel the need of unifying the scattered results they have thus far attained. Unification is tentatively achieved by constructing a theory.

A *theory* is a set of propositions complying, ideally, with the following conditions: one, the propositions must be couched in terms of exactly defined concepts; two, they must be consistent with one another; three, they must be such that from them the existing generalizations could be deductively derived; four, they must be fruitful—show the way to further observations and generalizations increasing the scope of knowledge.

Theory cannot be derived from observations and generalizations merely by means of rigorous induction. The construction of a theory is a creative achievement, and therefore it is not surprising that few among those laboring in the field of a science are able to carry it out. There is always a jump beyond the evidence, a hunch, corresponding to the creative effort. But every theory thus obtained then must be subjected to *verification*. It is considered verified, in a preliminary way, if no known fact or generalization seems to contradict it. If there is contradiction, the tentative theory must be rejected or at least modified.

This test, however, is only a preliminary verification. For often two or more theories seem plausible explanations of the known facts and generalizations. When this occurs, a procedure called crucial experiment (or crucial observation) is used. The procedure involves the reasoned conception of a situation for which the competing theories would yield contradictory predictions; this situation must then be artificially created (in experiment) or found to exist in actuality. Observation will then decide which, if any, of the theories is compatible with the testing experience. Yet even this verification is not final, for facts may be discovered later, or generalizations drawn, which invalidate the victorious theory of today. In empiric science theory is never final.

In a mature science like physics or chemistry, commonly only one highly abstract theory or a set of interrelated and mutually complementary theories is held by the people working in the field. But this state of maturity is reached only after long and strenuous efforts during a period characterized by the coexistence of two or more conflicting theories—the condition still marking sociology. There exists no set of propositions commonly held by all sociologists, couched in identical or easily convertible terms and allowing them to present the known facts and generalizations as logical derivations of a few principles. On the contrary, the development of sociology has been characterized by the rise of an unusually high number of conflicting theories. Although this state of things has not yet been overcome the struggle is no longer so acute as it was at the end of the nineteenth century. Today, the majority of sociologists agree upon a number of propositions included in a comprehensive sociological theory, although they often state these propositions in divergent terminology. (The reader should be aware of the fact that there are alternative terms for the same concepts—the same ideas; and that, conversely, sometimes different concepts and even theories are expressed by the same language.) There has been a decline in the range of theoretical disagreement and an increase in the range of agreement, as this book will attempt to demonstrate.

Inspection of the sociological theories of the past and present shows that they revolve around a few problems, the most important of which are indicated by the following questions:

What is society and culture?

What are the basic units into which society and culture should be analyzed?

What is the relationship between society, culture, and personality?

What are the factors determining the state of a society and a culture, or change in society or culture?

What is sociology and what are its appropriate methods?

The study of the growth of sociological theory must be focused on the various answers to these questions. In the presentation of the individual theories one must, however, go beyond these questions, because many theories assume the existence of other basic problems not covered by the questions, or they are so expressed that it becomes necessary to touch upon other scientific problems more or less connected with those singled out above.

## How to Study Sociological Theories

This volume does not aim at a systematic display of the results of the scientific study of society; rather, it does aim at the historical unfolding of the thought system which is theoretical sociology. The author is not trying to construct and to impose a particular theory; he is attempting to visualize the process of the development of theory in sociology manifested in the appearance, struggle, and disappearance or survival of various theories. This book concerns itself principally with the history of the gradual penetration of sociologists into the reality of society. The purpose is to establish the filiation and opposition of ideas, to single out cases of parallel invention, to find out in the earlier theories germs or anticipations of the later, and to discover the advance of truth through the clash of opinions. Study of these matters should help to an understanding of the reasons behind the choices made by participants in the scientific process; it should warn against errors committed in the past; it may show promising ways of further advance.

There is abundant material available for this study. But the study is complicated by the fact that sociological theories have developed according to a pattern somewhat similar to that of the growth of a plant: some branches have shot ahead vigorously with many subbranches, while others have, sooner or later, withered away. The situation is further complicated by the fact that, in addition to the pattern of branching, the pattern of convergence and merger is also observable. While through branching one theory gives rise to two or more, through convergence and merger theories which have started as independent and allegedly incompatible explanations of social reality come closer to one another and sometimes coalesce into one. Therefore, to attempt a schematic genealogy of sociological theories would be exceedingly difficult and would obscure rather than reveal the principal contributions and trends.

The complexity of the subject under study requires selection and careful arrangement of the materials. Selection is always somewhat arbitrary, and because this book does not pretend to be a sociological encyclopedia many valuable works must remain outside its scope. At least three basic types of arrangement are possible. First, theories may be classified into a few schools, based on the types of theoretical solution of the basic problems. This is the approach used by Sorokin in his well-known work, *Contemporary Sociological Theories* (1928). Second, theories may be presented in the historical sequence of their appearance; this is approximately the method used by J. L. Lichtenberger in *The Development of Social Theory* (1923) and by F. N. House in *The Development of Sociology* (1936). Third, theories may be presented according to the geographic areas in which their authors reside; this plan has been used by G. Gurvitch and Wilbert Moore (editors) in *Twentieth Century Sociology* (1945) and by Harry Elmer Barnes (editor) in *An Introduction to the History of Sociology* (1948). For this book the author proposes to use a combination of the first and second approaches.

The survey of the growth of sociological theory will be divided into four periods. The first period, extending from the birth of sociology until about 1875, is the period of the pioneers and of largely unrelated efforts. The second period, roughly corresponding to the last quarter of the nineteenth century, is the period of the battle of the schools and simultaneously of the dominance of evolutionism, the battle largely concerned with the question of which factor (economic, geographical, racial, or some other) determines social evolution. The third period, covering the first quarter of the twentieth century, is a time of indecision, following the demolition of the evolutionary theory and a growing consciousness of the need to concentrate on empirical studies; during this period stress is laid on the psychological foundations of sociology. The fourth and present period is the period of the battle of frames of reference or of convergence. The present period is characterized by increasing awareness of the existence of a large body of empirically established propositions (hence, a period of convergence) and by competition of points of view considered most adequate to explain social reality in its totality.

For each of these four periods the most representative schools and most influential theories will be presented, and their interrelationships will be brought out. And for the entire range of growth, persistencies and accumulations, as well as theoretical rebirths, sometimes in new guises, will be emphasized.

# The Pioneers

# The Pioneers

# CHAPTER 2

# AUGUSTE COMTE

Since this volume is concerned with the study of sociological theories and not with the history of social thought in general, it will begin with Auguste Comte, who was the first major figure to assert and then prove by deed that a science of society, both empiric and theoretical, was possible and desirable. But to make Comte understandable the intellectual climate of France early in the nineteenth century must be presented.

## France in the Early Nineteenth Century

The intellectual climate of a society is formed by the ideas taken for granted by the contemporary intellectuals, the problems commonly discussed by them, and the methods of discussion. This climate may be more or less integrated; in other words, the intellectuals may or may not be divided into factions each possessing a preferred set of ideas, a particular set of problems, and a peculiar method of discussion.

In the early nineteenth century the intellectual climate of France was well integrated. There was pride based on the achievements of mathematics and the natural sciences, and confidence in the omnipotence of methods. In regard to human affairs the climate included belief in the existence of social laws similar to those established in the natural sciences. Among these laws the dominant position was ascribed to the law of progress or the necessary development of human societies toward higher and better stages.

This set of ideas may be traced back to Blaise Pascal (1623–62) who suggested that the continuity of human generations be likened to an individual who lives forever and constantly accumulates knowledge. Charles Montesquieu (1689–1755), in the first sentence of his famous *Spirit of Laws* (1748), offered a definition of laws of nature which received common acceptance. Laws in the broadest significance of the term, he said, were necessary relations derived from the nature of things.

The idea of progress was developed by Jacques Turgot (1727–81). In an address delivered in 1750 and in a short *Discourse on Universal History* he tried to show that the advance of man's knowledge of nature was accompanied by a gradual emancipation of his mind from anthropomorphic concepts. This process, in his opinion, passed through three stages. First, men supposed that natural phenomena were produced by intelligent beings, invisible but resembling themselves. Second, men began to explain these phenomena by abstract expressions, such as essence and faculty. Third, by observing the reciprocal mechanical action of bodies, men formulated hypotheses which could be developed by mathematics and verified by experiment.

Another protagonist of the idea of progress, Marquis de Condorcet (1743–94), expressed his views in a work entitled *Historical Essay on the Progress of Human Reason,* written in prison shortly before his execution which he knew to be inevitable. Condorcet traced human progress in outline throughout the ages and conceived the possibility of a science which might foresee the future progress of mankind and thereby accelerate and direct it. To establish laws which can enable men to predict the future, history must cease to be a history of individuals and become a history of human masses. If and when this change is accomplished, prediction of the future will become possible, being based on knowledge of necessary and invariant laws. There are no reasons to believe that there are no such laws governing human affairs. Most of these laws are still unknown, but on the basis of historical observation one can assert that progress is necessary and uninterrupted, depending on the succession of anthropomorphic, metaphysical, and scientific explanations of natural phenomena.

### The Life of Comte

Comte (1798–1857) was born in Montpellier, France. At the age of sixteen the man who was to become the founding father of sociology enrolled in the *École Polytechnique,* the most distinguished school in France at that time. Its professors, mostly scholars in mathematics and physics, had little interest in the study of human affairs and society. But the young Comte had. Like many of the philosophers of his period, especially the social philosophers L. G. Bonald and Joseph de Maistre, he was startled by the destructive effects of the French Revolution, by the disorder created through the forcible destruction of social groups intermediate between the family and the state. Therefore the improvement of society early became Comte's main preoccupation, the very goal of his life. But he believed that to improve society one needed a theoretical science of society. Since this science was not available, he set about creating it. In his opinion this new science depended on other sciences; therefore, he decided to study the whole series of theoretical sciences which he identified with positive philosophy. From the results of such study Comte sought to formulate a system of laws governing society so that he could postulate a cure for society on the basis of these laws.

Comte's achievements, even the formulation of his gigantic enterprise, were greatly stimulated by the fact that, at the age of nineteen and when still a student of the *École Polytechnique,* he became secretary to the Comte Henri de Saint-Simon (1760–1825). Though a member of the French aristocracy, Saint-Simon became one of the earliest and most prominent Utopian socialists, one of the social thinkers, perhaps social dreamers, who believed that the problems of the society of their time could be best solved by reorganizing economic production, thereby depriving the proprietary class of the means of production of economic freedom, a foremost value of the time. In a pamphlet published in 1813, Saint-Simon expressed these ideas:

Morals and politics will become "positive" sciences.

The trend from many laws particular to individual sciences toward a single and all-embracing law will be completed.

Science will become the new spiritual power.

Society must, therefore, be reorganized and, in this way, humanity will enter the third great period of its history, the first, or preliminary, having ended with Socrates, and the second, or conjectural, having persisted until the time of Saint-Simon's writings.

From 1817 to 1823 Comte and Saint-Simon collaborated so closely that it is impossible to distinguish the contributions of the two. This collaboration is especially marked in the work *Plan of the Scientific Operations Necessary for the Reorganization of Society.* In later years Comte called this work "the great discovery of the year 1822." In this publication the joint authors asserted that politics must become social physics, a branch of physiology; that each branch of knowledge must pass through three stages, the theological, the metaphysical, and the positive; and that the object of social physics was to discover the natural and immutable laws of progress which are as necessary as the law of gravity. Thus the program of a new science (later to be renamed sociology) was clearly stated and the leading proposition of Comte's sociological theory was proclaimed— the law of the three stages.

Soon after that publication, Comte and Saint-Simon dissolved their partnership and began bitterly to attack each other. Comte never again found a stable and remunerative position, living by coaching and examining in mathematics and by other expedients. Personal disappointment and quarrels with others were frequent and his social isolation steadily increased. Nevertheless, a small group of admirers invited him to deliver a series of private lectures on positive philosophy. Comte agreed to the lectures and the lecture notes were gradually published between 1830 and 1842, forming his voluminous masterwork, *Course of Positive Philosophy,* in six volumes. While working on this project, Comte discovered the principle of cerebral hygiene. This discovery, in application to his life, meant that he stopped reading in order to keep his mind uncontaminated by the thoughts of others. In his later years, between 1851 and 1854, he wrote a treatise entitled *System of Positive Politics*, in four volumes, in which he applied the findings of theoretical sociology to the solution of the social problems of his time. Thus he accomplished his initial goal, the improvement of society, but in doing so he partly deviated from positivism and made an attempt to construct a religion of humanity. Nevertheless, one finds in the work a number of interesting and important additions to Comte's earlier *Positive Philosophy*.

### Basic Premises

The sociological theory of Comte forms a system at the center of which one finds two correlated propositions: the law of the three stages, and the theorem that the theoretical sciences form a hierarchy in which sociology occupies the summit.

Sciences, Comte asserted in the second of these propositions, were either theoretical or practical (applied). The theoretical could be further divided into descriptive (concrete) and abstract, the first dealing with concrete phenomena, and the second striving for the discovery of the laws of nature governing these phenomena, determining their coexistence and succession. The abstract theoretical sciences form a series, or hierarchy, in which every higher link depends on the preceding one because it deals with more concrete and complex phenomena. The base of the hierarchy is occupied by mathematics, which deals with abstract aspects of all phenomena. Next in rank is mechanics, which Comte almost identified with astronomy, a science which, in his day, was making spectacular advances. Mechanics is followed by physics, chemistry, and biology. And above them all was to be erected the new science of social physics or sociology.

The law of the three stages means, first of all, that each field of knowledge passes through three periods of growth: theological, metaphysical, and positive. But the individual sciences do not move simultaneously; the higher a science stands in the hierarchy, the later it shifts from one stage to another. It could not have been otherwise, for the simpler sciences had to develop first, the more complex later. Comte believed that all fields of knowledge but one had reached the positive stage; with the rise of sociology the series would be completed.

In Comte's system, however, the law of the three stages is much more than a principle governing the advance of knowledge. The development and education of the individual also must pass through the three stages, as well as the development of human society itself. Positive social development and organization depend on scientific, that is, sociological, knowledge of social phenomena. In other words, "the great discovery of the year 1822," in Comte's mind, was to become the directive idea for the re-organization of the society that had been shaken by the French Revolution.

Comte was so firmly convinced of the correctness of his views that he sent a copy of his *Positive Philosophy* to Emperor Nicholas I of Russia, writing him a letter in which he took it for granted that the autocratic ruler (who, interestingly, was well trained in mathematics) would initiate reforms elevating Russia to a positive society. Comte's pretensions, like those of many innovators, and as this incident illustrates, were at times ridiculous.

But the basic premises of his sociological theory deserve respectful consideration. Comte's list of abstract sciences is incomplete. He omitted psychology, which he took to be a branch of physiology, and the relationship between the individual sciences is more complex than he believed it to be. His general division of sciences, however, has proven to be generally sound. Comte's law of the three stages in the meaning ascribed to it by its inventor is clearly invalid. Yet early explanations of nature and men have often been religious and have been followed by philosophical explanations and later by empiric science. Yet neither of the later approaches wholly supersedes the religious approach; rather, there has been accumulation and often admixture of the three. Even with this correction, of course, Comte's law of the three stages could not stand the test of facts known today. Nevertheless in a greatly modified form it may be perceived in one of the most ambitious theories of the present day, that of Sorokin (see Chap. 20).

## The Science of Sociology

The meaning of sociology for Comte is suggested by its very location in the system of sciences: sociology is the abstract theoretical science of social phenomena. In 1822 when he (with Saint-Simon) conceived the necessity of this new science, he wrote: "We possess now a celestial physics, a terrestrial physics, either mechanical or chemical, a vegetable physics and an animal physics; we still want one more and last one, social physics, to complete the system of our knowledge of nature. I understand by social physics the science which has for its subject the study of social phenomena considered in the same spirit as astronomical, physical, chemical or physiological phenomena, that is, subject to natural invariable laws, the discovery of which is the special object of investigation." More precisely, the aim was "to discover through what fixed series of successive transformations the human race, starting from a state not superior to that of the societies of the great apes, gradually led to the point at which civilized Europe finds itself today."[1] Very reluctantly Comte changed the name of the new science from social physics to sociology. In the latter

[1] Reprinted in *Positive Politics*, vol. IV, appendix, pp. 149–50.

part of his *Positive Philosophy* he explained that he had invented a new name because the old one had been usurped by a Belgian scientist who chose it as the title for a work devoted to so base a matter as simple statistics. The work he referred to was Quételet's *An Essay on Social Physics* (see Chap. 4), one of the most influential contributions made to the social sciences in the nineteenth century.

In *Positive Politics,* Comte attempted to give more flesh and blood to the rather formal definition of sociology implied in *Positive Philosophy*. At one place, he seemed to identify sociology with the study of the totality of the phenomena of the human intellect and the resulting actions of men. Elsewhere, he qualified this position by stating that sociology was not the study of the intellect as such but of the cumulative results of the exercise of intellect. Since, beyond doubt, he did not abandon his conception of sociology as a theoretical science of social phenomena, the sum total of the latter was now identified by him with the cumulative results of the exercise of the intellect. This conception of social phenomena is similar to the concept of culture frequently employed by contemporary sociologists, who took it over from cultural anthropology. In germ, this conception of culture was already present in Comte's work long before it came to be viewed as of strategic significance by modern anthropologists and sociologists.

## Methodology

Comte believed that the discussion of methods could not be separated from the study of the phenomena investigated by these methods. Therefore, his methodological views can be reconstructed only by bringing together statements dispersed through his treatises.

To begin with, sociology must use the *positive* method—this was ingrained in the very program of the new science and derived from Comte's basic premises. But what was the positive method? In answer, Comte said little more than that it demanded the subordination of concepts to facts and the acceptance of the idea that social phenomena are subject to general laws; otherwise, no abstract theoretical science concerning these phenomena could be constructed. In accordance with his understanding of the hierarchy of the sciences, Comte recognized that the system formed by social laws was less rigid than the system of biological laws which, in their turn, were less rigid than physical laws.

Despite his advanced training in mathematics, Comte denied that the positive method could be identified with the use of mathematics and statistics. "The proposal to treat social science as an application of mathematics to render it positive had its origin in the physicists' prejudice that outside of mathematics there was no certainty. This prejudice was natural at the time when everything that was positive belonged to the domain of applied mathematics and when in consequence all that this did not embrace was vague and conjectural. But since the formation of the two great positive sciences, chemistry and physiology, in which mathematical analysis plays no role, and which are recognized as not less certain than the others, such a prejudice would be absolutely inexcusable." [2] On one occasion, Comte pointed to the "vain attempts of several geometricians to carry out a positive study of society by applying to it the delusive theory of chances (probability)." Once again he had in view Quételet's work. It is noteworthy that, in the present day, there exists a neopositive school (see Chap. 15) which sees in quantification the ideal of every science, including sociology. In this regard, neopositivism is hardly consistent with the ideas of the founder of positivism. [3]

How then was positive knowledge to be gained in Comte's view? Comte mentions four procedures: observation, experiment, comparison, and historical method.

Observation or use of the physical senses, as Comte correctly stressed, could be carried out fruitfully only when guided by theory. Of the modes of observation, Comte held in little esteem introspection, that is, observation of the phenomena going on in the observer's mind. Some of his statements in this connection anticipate those of the contemporary behaviorists. He himself looked in another direction and believed that phrenology [4] could best explain the variations of human behavior. Actual experiment, Comte knew, was almost impossible in the study of society. But in the French language *experiment* often connotes controlled observation. Fruitful comparison, he maintained, could be carried out between human and animal societies, between coexisting societies, and between social classes in the same society.

By historical method Comte meant the search for general laws of the continuous variation of human opinion, a view which reflects the dominant role of ideas apparent in the law of the three stages. Comte's historical method has little in common with the methods used by historians who emphasize causal relations between concrete facts and only incidentally formulate general laws. However, Comte only pointed to what ought to be done; he did not show how it could be done. Throughout his treatises he offers a number of inferences from historical facts; but these inferences are rarely convincing and seem to have been arrived at by deduction from the law of the three stages rather than by actual inference.

Two further points of methodological significance should be mentioned. First, in Comte's opinion, society is in one respect like an organism

[2] Comte, *Positive Politics*, vol. IV, appendix, pp. 123–24.
[3] See, however, George Lundberg's counterclaim in *Foundations of Sociology* (New York: Macmillan, 1939), pp. vii–viii.
[4] Phrenology is a pseudo-scientific theory offered by F. H. Gall (1758–1828) according to whom man's mental faculties are closely correlated with the peculiarities of his skull.

in that the whole is better known than the parts.[5] From this proposition he drew the somewhat inconsistent conclusion that such specialized studies as economics are misleading because no social fact taken as an isolated phenomenon should ever be introduced into science. Moreover, he scored economists of his time for their unwillingness to acknowledge the possibility of any order in society except an order which establishes itself automatically. Comte believed that, in addition to this spontaneous order, there could be planned order established on the basis of knowledge of social laws and their rational application to concrete problems and situations.

Second, in Comte's work there is a suggestion which anticipates by more than fifty years an outstanding contribution of Max Weber (see Chap. 14). Comte took social types to be "limits to which social reality approaches closer and closer without being ever able to reach them." In this statement, one perceives the influence of Comte's mathematical training, but also, in rudimentary form, Max Weber's ideal type, an excellent logical tool for sociological analysis. This affinity is corroborated by a statement of Comte, suggesting how to use these types in studying social phenomena. Intermediate cases, that is, cases not coinciding with any ideal type, he pointed out, must be studied under the influence of an exact analysis of the two extreme cases or types. This means that an intermediate case can be best understood by establishing how much of the one and how much of the other, or opposite, type are embodied in it.

### Static and Dynamic Sociology

Comte's sociology is divided into two major parts, statics and dynamics. This is a division taken over from biology (which in Comte's day was known as physiology) and therefore was in accordance with his stress on the hierarchy of sciences and of their possession of common features.

*Statics* involves the study of the conditions of the existence of society, while *dynamics* requires study of its continuous movement, or of the laws of the succession of the individual stages. The main fact of statics is order; the main fact of dynamics is progress. More explicitly, statics is a theory of order which is tantamount to harmony between the conditions of man's existence in society, while dynamics is a theory of social progress which is tantamount to the fundamental development, or evolution, of society. But order and progress are closely interrelated: no real social order can be established if it is incompatible with progress, and no durable progress is possible if it is not consolidated in order. The study of the two must be

---

[5] Relative to an organism, the proposition is correct: even without any special training, one understands the behavior of a man, a dog, a cat; while the understanding of the operation of the parts, or organs, requires some study. The proposition is, however, hardly tenable relative to society.

separated for analytical purposes only. Static and dynamic laws must be tied together throughout the system. In the present day, this optimistic identification of statics with order and of dynamics with progress is no longer accepted. But Comte's basic division of sociology continues in use, though expressed in different terms, such as social structure and social change, categories familiar to undergraduate students.

## STATICS: CONSENSUS

In Comte's view, the total social order establishes itself according to the laws of nature. Each particular order may contain many, sometimes serious deficiencies, but this situation can be rectified by rational intervention of human beings. This conception is in full accordance with Comte's ideas on the relative flexibility of social laws. Order, however, is possible only on the basis of a certain community of ideas held by those forming a society; therefore, no complete liberty of opinion should be granted.

The basic fact of social order is *consensus universalis,* the necessary correlation between the elements of a society. Such a consensus exists in all realms of life but reaches its climax in human society. There is consensus among the sciences, between the sciences and the arts, within political institutions, between civil and political society, between mores and ideas. It is claimed, at times, that Comte was unable to identify necessary or required institutional compatibilities and interconnections. This claim is somewhat misleading, for, when presenting the details of his law of the three stages, Comte brings out a number of points concerning these correlations.

*Consensus universalis* to Comte is the very foundation of solidarity as well as the basis for the division of social labor. The latter shows that society is once again analogous to an organism. Here and there specific functions are performed by specific but always solidary organs. Here as elsewhere Comte utilized the organismic analogy, though he never identified society and biological organism. There is a great difference between the two, he insisted: organisms are essentially immutable, while society is capable of immense improvement if guided according to scientific principles. This statement reflects both Comte's faith in progress and his conviction that human society can be improved only on the basis of positive social science.

The division of social labor, continues Comte, is the fundamental cause of the growing complexity of society; therefore, solidarity and cooperation must be carefully studied. Hence his emphasis upon altruism, another word that he coined. It was not until very late in the nineteenth century that the advice of the father of sociology to study social solidarity was heeded, when another great sociologist, Emile Durkheim, analyzed this phenomenon in a series of important works (see Chap. 9).

## STATICS: SOCIAL STRUCTURE

In society, Comte distinguished three levels: the individual, the family, and social combinations, the highest of which is humanity itself. However, he eliminated the individual from sociological study because a system must consist only of homogeneous elements. Therefore the basic social unit is not the individual but the family.

Nevertheless, he faced up to the persistent sociological problem of the relationship between society and the individual. In society, he noted, continuous and regular convergence of the activities of innumerable individuals is observed. Each individual lives his own life, to be sure, but he also has a spontaneous disposition to participate in the development common to all—without consulting others and while he believes that he simply obeys his own impulses. Fundamentally, then, individual and society are inseparable; they are distinguished for purposes of abstract analysis.

Comte made a number of interesting statements about the basic social unit, the family. For instance, he pointed out that the family possesses a particular degree of unity, a moral character which makes it different from other social units. In family life, he observed, there is not much reflection; needs are promptly satisfied on the basis of sympathy. Families may exist in the state of isolation, but commonly they do not. Through their coordination social combinations arise, such as social classes and cities, based on conscious cooperation. Of the many social combinations Comte considered carefully only the political type or states. He deplored the fact that groups intermediate between the family and the state had been destroyed by the French Revolution and hoped for their restoration.

Concerning the state, Comte did not add much to the already established conclusions of political philosophers. The political order, he pointed out, is somewhat artificial; but, on the other hand, it is a modification of the natural order toward which all human societies tend. The political order is natural because no society can exist without government, and government is possible because of the widespread desire to command and also because of the fact that many persons wish to be alleviated of the burden of making for themselves the necessary decisions.

## DYNAMICS: EVOLUTION AND PROGRESS

Social dynamics is presented by Comte as history without the names of men and of peoples. Here the task is the discovery of an abstract order in which the major changes of human civilization have followed one another. Throughout the movement, solidarity must be preserved; otherwise the movement would result in a complete decomposition of the social system. Therefore, no isolated development of individual aspects of social life can take place and be studied as such. This conception is based on Comte's general methodological views and his ideas about the *consensus universalis*.

Social dynamics must begin with the study of development as such. But thereafter the question may be asked whether development is the equivalent of progress. The increase of the population and the growth of the mental abilities seem to show that the latter is the case. Comte shared the prevalent opinion that young savages could not develop as far as children born in advanced societies. His optimistic view of progress was strengthened by his acceptance of the theory that traits acquired by an individual during his lifetime could be biologically transmitted to progeny, a viewpoint stressed by the physiologist Chevalier de Lamarck (1744–1829). Contemporary biology, except in a curious Soviet Russian version, denies this possibility of the inheritance of acquired characteristics.

Progressive development, Comte understood, does not follow a straight line. Not only do oscillations occur but the speed of progress can be modified by human interference.

Social evolution, he taught, is a continuation of the general progression beginning in the realm of plants. The great social series corresponds to the great organic series, not to the succession of the ages of a simple organism. This proposition is an essential element in a thought system emphasizing continuous progress, since the curve corresponding to the ages of an organism shows descent as well as growth.

In the course of social evolution human nature has been developed, but no new human faculties have been added to the original ones. As a corollary, the study of evolution should start from notions established in physiology concerning primitive men, though Comte made very little actual use of such material.

In the course of social evolution, said Comte (repeating one of the favorite ideas of Saint-Simon), a basic antagonism between the instincts of innovation and conservatism is conspicuous. This conception anticipates Vilfredo Pareto's doctrine of the circulation of the elites (see Chap. 13).

Finally, Comte put forward a view that underlies a good deal of the work of the later evolutionists. The study of progress, he stressed, was greatly facilitated by the fact that the development of all societies is governed by the same laws, so that the development of general principles may begin with the study of the advances made by the vanguard of humanity. For Comte, this vanguard was evidently France.

## DYNAMICS: THE FACTORS OF PROGRESS

Comte's sociological theory regarding the factors of progress is introduced by a statement that progress is observable in all aspects of society. Progress is physical, moral (toward more generous and nobler sentiments), intellectual, political. The intellectual phase, however, is fundamental and most conspicuous—history is dominated by the development of ideas—and, therefore, the history of philosophy is of paramount importance. Men often seem to be preoccupied primarily with the satisfaction of material needs and, in actuality, to be sure, progress is apparent in dominance over the forces of nature. But, Comte maintained, intellectual development brings about and stimulates material development.

Comte's analysis of the factors of progress leads him to the study of factors on which intellectual development depends. This question, however, is left largely unanswered. The main factors of intellectual progress are supposed to be boredom (producing an effort toward innovation) and fear of death. But when discussing the factors of progress in general (not merely intellectual progress), Comte emphasizes the increase of the density of the population which brings about greater specialization in the division of social labor. Consequently, individuals are pushed to carry out greater efforts to secure subsistence, and society is compelled to regulate more energetically situations deriving from increasing differences between individuals.

Finally Comte discussed the problem of the differential velocity of progress. Here he was aware of the insufficiency of his evidence and the tentative nature of his conclusions: the differential endowment of the races and, presumably, white superiority; the role of climatic differences, with the conditions in the Mediterranean basin being the most favorable for progress; and the view that political action may eventually accelerate or retard progress. He did not deny the role of geniuses in historical development but believed that they were agents of predetermined movements.

## DYNAMICS: THE STAGES OF PROGRESS

The basic stages of progress were described in the propositions which Comte designated as "the great discovery of the year 1822." Comte believed, however, that a further philosophical explanation of the law of the three stages was necessary, one which would reduce the law to human nature. This could be easily done, he believed, since individual development passes through the same three stages that social development does.

In the course of the lengthy discussion of the development of the vanguard of humanity, the most advanced societies, Comte established correlations between the basic, intellectual stages and stages in the development of man's material life, types of social units, types of social order, and prevailing sentiments. These correlations appear as follows:

| Intellectual phase | Material phase | Type of social unit | Type of order | Prevailing sentiment |
|---|---|---|---|---|
| Theological | Military | The family | Domestic | Attachment |
| Metaphysical | Legalistic | The state | Collective | Veneration |
| Positive | Industrial | Race (humanity) | Universal | Benevolence |

Comte submitted the first stage, the theological, to a more detailed study than the other two, probably because the positive was just beginning while the metaphysical had lasted for a much shorter period of time than the first. He subdivided the theological stage into five substages each of which was supposed to have made definite contributions to progress. The substages and their social contributions he outlined as follows:

| | |
|---|---|
| Fetishism | The family |
| Polytheism (Oriental empires) | The state, landed property |
| Intellectual polytheism (Greece) | Intellectual contributions |
| Social monotheism (Rome) | The fatherland |
| Defensive monotheism (the Catholic world) | Emancipation of women and workers |

## Comte in Retrospect

In the present day it is fashionable to minimize the role of Comte in the growth of sociological theory. On the one hand, it is commonly asserted that Comte made very few original contributions: almost all of his ideas can be traced back to numerous predecessors. On the other hand, it is often stated that Comte merely elaborated a program of sociology and did not construct a sociological theory. This assertion is somewhat unjust to Comte. It is true that a large part of Comte's statements reproduces, in modified form, ideas scattered through the bimillenial history of social philosophy. But he recombined them in a manner which gave the signal to a rapid and most fruitful development of knowledge relating to interpersonal relations, social groups, culture, social structure and change. Every sociologist knows, moreover, that all inventions—and the creation of a new science called sociology was a cultural invention— are primarily a recombination of elements already present in culture.

In Comte's work, an attentive reader finds an enormous wealth of ideas anticipating the majority of trends observable in the history of sociology up to the present, as well as large numbers of propositions concerning the scope and method of sociology. Very often these propositions have been rediscovered by later sociologists, sometimes with reference to the founding father of their science, more frequently without such reference. Moreover, Comte has shown the way toward the modern definition of sociology and its basic divisions. Under the influence of Spencer, to be sure, sociology deviated from the conception formulated by Comte and became a concrete (genetic) science describing a unique process, that of the evolution of human society. With the decline of evolutionism, however, sociology (at least, its central core) returned, though with modifications, to Comte's view about its subject matter.

It is true that contemporary sociology does not simply repeat Comte's definition. That proved to be too broad, including the theoretical parts of the special social sciences (economics, government, jurisprudence, and so on). On the other hand, sociology has not limited itself to the formulation of theoretical propositions; it has expanded into the realm of practical activity, becoming the counselor of men of good will desirous to ameliorate human society. (Comte invented his new science as a necessary instrument of social reform.) Finally, sociology has also performed a good deal of descriptive work, whenever no other science was present to accomplish the task of description of specific social phenomena. But these various developments are meaningfully integrated only in terms of theoretical sociology, and this type of sociology is gradually becoming what Comte wished it to be.

More specifically, Comte suggested solutions to the major problems of the sociological quest. He never defined society, but one can easily see that for him society consisted of families and social combinations which culminate in nations and humanity. He came quite close to the formulation of the contemporary notion of culture as the sum total of the achievements of interacting human minds. He did not single out any social unit for analysis since he believed that, relative to society, the whole was better known than the parts. He correctly understood the ever-present reciprocal influence between individual and society. He believed in the existence of a prepotent factor in social change—the development of ideas; therefore, he could be considered as one of the ideological determinists. But he understood also the impact of the growth of population and of its density. He defined sociology by locating it in his hierarchy of the abstract theoretical sciences: sociology was the abstract theoretical science of society. He used predominantly what he called the historical method, which in actuality was mainly an arrangement of selected historical facts in the light of his view of social evolution. For a long time this was to be the method of sociology. Of course, this method was faulty. So was the basic premise of his theory, the faith in evolution toward progress.

Comte's evolutionism, however, was not of the necessitarian type asserted a few years later by Spencer and logically conducive to strict adherence to the principle of *laissez faire*. On the contrary, he believed that progress could be accelerated and facilitated through political action based on positive knowledge. In this regard he prepared the way for the idea of *social telesis* subsequently developed by Lester Ward, who fully acknowledged his indebtedness to Comte.

Many of Comte's assertions and guesses have proven to be wrong. He was a poor metaphysician largely because he believed that he had annihilated the very possibility of metaphysics; he was a poor religious thinker though he firmly believed that religion was one of the pillars of society. As to his sociological theory, it may be considered as a premature jump from the level of observation and inferences directly based on them to the level of "theory."

Comte's work remained unnoticed in his lifetime in France. British students, especially John Stuart Mill (1806–73), were the first to become interested in his views and in Comte the person; yet Spencer rejected him with disdain. Through English authors Comte's ideas penetrated into Germany and from Germany returned to France. There the greatest of the sociologists of the late nineteenth century, Emile Durkheim, gave to sociology a new impetus in which many Comtean ideas are discernible. Comte's work has also exerted great influence on Russian sociology (Kovalevsky, Sorokin) and on American sociology (especially Ward).

It is noteworthy that a book which appeared in the United States in 1953 attempts to revive Comte's sociology: *The Nature and Elements of Sociology* by MacQuilkin DeGrange. Comte's ideas on society expressed in *Positive Politics* are combined with relatively recent acquisitions of sociological theory, especially with the understanding of the role of culture (collective cumulations) and with the shift from the organic analogy to the systematic approach.

# CHAPTER 3

# HERBERT SPENCER

Herbert Spencer (1820–1903), the second founding father of sociology, was born of a middle-class family. He never went to a conventional school; he was taught at home and for short periods in small private schools. His training, as he acknowledges in his autobiography, was first rate only in mathematics. He did not study systematically such subjects as the natural sciences, literature, or history, an astonishing fact considering that he wrote outstanding treatises on biology and psychology.

When still quite young, Spencer entered business in the railroad engineering field. Thereafter he shifted to journalism and became an editor of the *Economist,* one of the greatest English publications. After a few years he resigned this position and decided to earn his living as an independent writer. He never suffered from poverty, but neither did his work enrich him. His major treatises were published in installments, the continuous appearance of which, at least in the beginning, was precarious, since the income depended upon maintaining numerous subscribers, most of whom were Americans.

### The Works of Spencer

Spencer's literary career began by a series of articles published in 1842 in *The Nonconformist,* with the first entitled "The Proper Sphere of Government." There he expressed the view that man's adaptation of his social functions best develops when his relations to society are not artificially interfered with. This doctrine of *laissez faire* remained a motif of his sociological and political writings. In 1850 his first book, *Social Statics,* appeared. In it he presented a preview of his sociological theory: both in organisms and in society, progress is development from conditions in which like parts perform like functions to conditions in which unlike parts perform unlike functions, that is, from the uniform to the multiform. Some reviewers expressed the opinion that the title of the work had been borrowed from Comte. Spencer angrily rejoined that at the time of the writing of the work Comte was for him merely a name and that the original title of the book had been *Demostatics*.

In the years following the publication of *Social Statics*, Spencer came across some of the outstanding contributions to the biological theory of the times, pointing to the fact that the development of an organism was marked by change from homogeneity or uniformity of structure to heterogeneity or multiformity. In the middle 1850's, as he notes in his autobiography, he had an inspiration. He perceived that the advance from homogeneity to heterogeneity was the universal law of progress, whether in the inorganic, organic, or superorganic (social) orders.

A few years later a new perception gave Spencer insight into the causal background of this tendency: the instability of the homogeneous. This insight allowed him to make a decisive step toward what he called a completely deductive stage of his inquiry, in other words, toward the formulation of a theory. This theory from the beginning was grounded on physical science.

In 1859, Charles Darwin published his *The Origin of Species*. Spencer readily assimilated the new Darwinian concepts. They were akin to his own teachings and, characteristically, he remarked that he had been the first to discover them, referring to two of his articles published in 1852 in the *Westminster Review*. There he had written: "Some division of the species will become slightly more heterogeneous. In the absence of successive change in conditions, natural selection would affect comparatively little." These are, of course, anticipations of Darwin's views. In Spencer's later works one can find such expressions as "survival of the fittest," and such assertions as the conquest of one people over another has been in the main the conquest of the social over the antisocial, or of the more adapted over the less adapted.

About 1860 Spencer embarked on an almost superhuman enterprise: the writing of a system of synthetic philosophy, unifying all the theoretical sciences of his day. The first volume, entitled *First Principles*, appeared in 1862. The next part, on inorganic evolution, was skipped, as Spencer relates in his autobiography, in solicitude lest he find himself without enough time to finish the remaining and more important parts of his enterprise. These included *Principles of Biology* (1864–67), *Principles of Psychology* (1870–72),[1] *Principles of Sociology* (1876–96), and *Principles of Ethics* (1879–93). The publication of *Principles of Sociology* was preceded by an independent book entitled *The Study of Sociology* (1873), the most readable of Spencer's sociological treatises.

In *First Principles* Spencer dismissed theology as the science of the

[1] Written originally in the 1850's and completely revised to become part of *Synthetic Philosophy*.

ultimately unknowable. (This phrase, incidentally, satisfied both the religious-minded men and the atheists.) The volume dealt primarily with physical phenomena. Nevertheless, in this work Spencer's sociological system was almost complete, the later *Principles of Sociology* being essentially an elaboration of views published in 1862. This is why Spencer must be treated as one of the early sociologists.

Following the publication of *First Principles*, new perceptions arose in Spencer's mind concerning the connection between the increasing integration of matter and the concomitant dissipation of motion. By 1867 his thought system was complete, and it never changed thereafter. His new insights were incorporated in revised editions of *First Principles* and *Social Statics*.

## The Evolutionary Doctrine

The very foundation of Spencerism is the evolutionary doctrine. In *First Principles* three basic laws were formulated: first, the law of the persistence of force, which means the existence and persistence of some ultimate cause which transcends knowledge; second, the law of the indestructibility of matter (this was one of the recent physical discoveries of Spencer's time, invalidated in the present day); and third, the law of the continuity of motion, which means that energy passes from one form to another but always persists. Four secondary propositions were added: persistence of the relationship between the forces or the uniformity of law; transformation and equivalence of forces; the tendency of everything to move along the line of least resistance and greatest attraction; and, finally, the principle of the alternation, or rhythm, of motion. Several of these propositions were taken over from the physics of Spencer's day.

Spencer had stated seven laws and realized that he should express their joint product. The tendency of the time was to reduce the multitude of different laws to some general forms. Spencer believed that the joint product of these seven laws could be stated as the *law of evolution*, which in his mind was the supreme law of every becoming. Spencer's formulation of this law was a very cumbersome definition. "Evolution," he said, "is an integration of matter and concomitant dissipation of motion; during which matter passes from an indefinite, incoherent homogeneity to a definite, coherent heterogeneity; and during which the retained motion undergoes a parallel transformation." [2]

The important part of this conception is the one which already had been stated in *Social Statics*, namely, the tendency of the homogeneous or uniform to become heterogeneous or multiform. Was this tendency a necessity? Spencer believed that it was. He explained that the homogeneous is inherently unstable, that it cannot remain in this state because the different effects of persistent forces upon various parts of the

[2] Herbert Spencer, *First Principles*, p. 407.

homogeneous must cause differences to arise in the future development.

Spencer tried to demonstrate his evolutionary formula in the synthetic order, synthetic in the sense of integrating all of the sciences. He tried to show that there was redistribution of matter and motion, resulting in change from the uniform to the multiform in all worlds of being, in celestial bodies, in organisms, and in societies, though he acknowledged that this process took place in diverse ways. To strengthen the argument Spencer offered a number of illustrations. Societies, he argued, continuously adjust their populations to the means of existence; he had read Malthus and was very much impressed by his *Essay on Population* (1798). Supply and demand are usually adjusted. Political institutions fall into harmony with the desires of the people. A business partnership in practice becomes a union in which the authority of one partner is tacitly recognized as greater than that of the other.

Study of Spencer's writings inevitably raises the question of whether he believed that evolution, which was the law of becoming, was directed toward progress, indeed, of whether evolution was actually the law of all becoming. Spencer sometimes denied this interpretation. In the fourth edition of his *First Principles,* published in 1880, he wrote: "The doctrine of evolution is erroneously supposed to imply some intrinsic proclivity in every species towards a higher form. Similarly many make the erroneous assumption that the transformation which constitutes evolution implies an intrinsic tendency to go through those changes which the formula of evolution expresses." [3] But, he said, the progress of evolution is not necessary; it depends on certain conditions. The frequent occurrence of dissolution, a process opposed to evolution, the movement of the multiform to the uniform, shows that, where essential conditions are not maintained, the reverse process quite as readily takes place. The progress of a social organism toward more heterogeneous and more definite structures continues only as long as the actions which produce these effects continue in play. On the basis of these statements, one would be justified in concluding that Spencer was not guilty of claiming the ever-presence of evolution or that it was leading toward progress. But let us consider some of his other statements.

In *The Study of Sociology* Spencer said: "No more in this than in other things will evolution alter its general direction; it will continue along the same lines as hitherto." [4] In another place he stated: "The seeds of civilization existing in the aboriginal man and distributed over the earth were certain in the lapse of time to fall here and there into circumstances fit for their development." [5] In other words, at this point he believed that man by his nature was predestined to progress.

These contradictions (brought out clearly by a comparison of state-

---

[3] *Ibid.,* p. 481.
[4] Herbert Spencer, *The Study of Sociology,* p. 309.
[5] Herbert Spencer, *Social Statics,* rev. ed., p. 238.

ments from *First Principles* in its later editions with assertions from *The Study of Sociology* and *Social Statics*) can perhaps be reconciled. In principle, conditions may occur which direct the process of change toward dissolution, contrary to evolution (from the multiform to the uniform), but in fact conditions have prevailed which directed the process toward progress. However the sociological work of Spencer is dominated by the idea that throughout all times there actually has been social evolution, and that this evolution has been moving steadily from the uniform to the multiform, that is, to always more and more progressive forms. There seems little doubt that Spencer was a leading apostle of unilinear evolution toward progress.

### The Science of Sociology

Like Comte, whose work he read in his later years and severely criticized, Spencer recognized the possibility of a science of sociology, a term he reluctantly admitted he had taken over from the French master. Why is a science of society possible? In society, says Spencer, there is order of coexistence and progress. If there is order, then the corresponding phenomena may form the subject of a science which, as he said, could be reduced to the deductive form, in other words, a theoretical science. But, he added, the subject matter of sociology is very peculiar. The social process being unique, sociology is a science which must explain the present state of society by concentrating on the initial stages of evolution and applying to them the laws of evolution. He hoped to explain the known present by means of the unknown and conjectural past. This position was derived from Spencer's general view that evolution was the supreme law of every becoming.

It is interesting that though Spencer wrote several treatises on sociology—*Social Statics, The Study of Sociology,* and *Principles of Sociology*—and that much of *First Principles* is an introduction to sociology, he never presented a formal definition of the discipline. For him, sociology was the science of superorganic phenomena, more exactly, of superorganic evolution.

Spencer's conception of the *superorganic* (a term still used by a few writers) is that there has been continuity in evolution: first, evolution in the inorganic world of matter without life, then evolution in the organic or living world, and finally evolution among combinations of living organisms into societies. Superorganic evolution is a beautiful term, but it has meaning only if it denotes a clear conception of the nature of society—a matter that unfortunately Spencer never clarified.

Nor did Spencer define exactly the relationship between sociology and other sciences. He believed that sociology should make use of the generalizations of the particular sciences, such as economics, government, and ethnology. He also pointed out that sociology differed from history.

History was a narration of events in the lives of societies; sociology studied their evolution. Occasionally Spencer remarked that sociology, as it is ordinarily conceived, is concerned exclusively with the phenomena resulting from the cooperations of citizens. He hardly intended these remarks to be a formal definition of sociology. Nor do they apply to Spencer's own voluminous sociological works.

What methods should sociologists employ? To this question Spencer answered: "We must learn, by inspection, the relations of coexistence and sequence in which social phenomena stand to one another. By comparing societies of different kinds and societies in different stages, we must ascertain what traits of size, structure, function, are associated with one another." [6] This principle, however, did not guide his own procedures. As material he used mainly illustrations from ethnology, depending on the hypothesis that primitive man shows retarded stages of evolution. By observing retarded contemporaries, he assumed, one is enabled to reconstruct the series of transformations which brought about the advanced society of today. The importance Spencer assigned to ethnology is manifest in the fact that the first half of the first volume of *Principles of Sociology* is entitled "Data of Ethnology," and is almost entirely devoted to a conjectural reconstruction of the physical, emotional, intellectual, and, especially, religious life of primitive man.

Spencer, in fact, selected materials from most diversified cultures, widely separated in time and in space. He picked up facts here and there and brought them together in such a way as to support his evolutionary hypothesis; the materials combined in this arbitrary manner were used to confirm his hypothesis. Such a procedure, of course, is entirely out of keeping with rules of logic and principles of scientific method.

### The Organic Analogy

The foundation of Spencer's sociological theory was the evolutionary doctrine. However, he presented a secondary doctrine which also played a large part in his thought system—the organic analogy, that is, the identification, for certain purposes, of society with a biological organism. Spencer explicitly asserted in the revised edition of *Social Statics* that the recognition of parallelism between generalizations concerning organisms and those concerning societies was the first step toward the general doctrine of evolution.

The organic analogy was formulated by Spencer as follows: "So completely is society organized on the same system as an individual being that we may perceive something more than analogy between them; the same definition of life applies to both. Only when one sees that the transformation passed through during the growth, maturity, and decay of a society, conforms to the same principles as do the transformations passed

[6] Herbert Spencer, *Principles of Sociology*, 3rd ed., vol. I, p. 442.

through by aggregates of all orders, inorganic and organic, is there reached the concept of sociology as a science." More specifically, he noted several similarities between biological and social organisms:

First, both society and organisms are distinguished from inorganic matter by visible growth during the greater part of their existence. A baby grows up to be a man; a tiny community becomes a metropolitan area; a small state becomes an empire.

Second, as both societies and organisms grow in size they also increase in complexity of structure. Here Spencer had in mind not so much the comparison of the development of a society with the growth of an individual organism as the affinity of social development and the assumed evolutionary sequence of organic life. Primitive organisms are simple, whereas the highest organisms are very complex.

Third, in societies and in organisms progressive differentiation of structure is accompanied by progressive differentiation of functions. This is almost a tautological proposition: If there is an organism that has complex organs, each organ performs a specified function; if there is a society subdivided into many different organizations, these have different functions.

Fourth, evolution establishes for both societies and organisms differences in structure and function that make each other possible.

Fifth, just as a living organism may be regarded as a nation of units that live individually, so a nation of human beings may be regarded as an organism. Spencer pursued this peculiar line of reasoning to a further similarity: In organisms and in society alike the life of the aggregate may be destroyed, but the units will continue to live for at least a while.

Spencer was an individualist, a condition difficult to reconcile with organicism, and he recognized important differences between societies and organisms. The first difference is that in an organism the parts form a concrete whole; in a society, the parts are free and more or less dispersed. The second difference is that in an organism consciousness is concentrated in a small part of the aggregate; in a society it is diffused throughout the individual members. And the third difference: in an organism the parts exist for the benefit of the whole; in a society the whole exists merely for the benefit of the individual. (Here is an important example of Spencer's individualism.)

In spite of this elaborate effort to establish the similarities and differences between organic and social life, and in spite of his use of the organic analogy as the central theme of the second part of his *Principles of Sociology*, Spencer denied that he held to this doctrine. Replying to critics he made statements such as the following: "I have used the analogies, but only as a scaffolding to help in building up a coherent body of sociological induction. Let us take away the scaffolding: the inductions will stand by themselves." [7] Unfortunately, however, he consistently and conspicuously

[7] *Ibid.*, vol. I, pp. 592–93.

used the terminology of organicism. Moreover, one chapter of *Principles of Sociology* is entitled "Society Is an Organism."

Of course Spencer was not the originator of the organic analogy. Ancient philosophers used it, and it was also often represented in German philosophy and political science, especially during the first half of the nineteenth century. But Spencer was the first to give to that analogy the value of scientific theory, and he was very definitely taken prisoner by the ghost he had evoked. He understood that actually society was not an organism, since there were substantial differences between the two, and yet he retained that analogical thesis. He asserted that the analogy was merely a scaffold, but when constructing his theory, he proceeded as if the scaffold were the real building.

Today the source of Spencer's difficulties has become clear, and sociology has worked its way out of the fallacies which beset the human mind in the use of the organic analogy. Present-day sociology asserts that society is a *system* and understands that an organism is also a system. This concept of system is one of the key concepts used in science. System is spoken of in relation to many diversified things—the stellar system, of which the sun is a part, the solar system of which Mother Earth and the planets are parts. The atom is a system consisting of the nucleus and electrons. And there is a system in ideas: the system of Plato's philosophy, the system of Roman law, the system of Newtonian physics. The word system designates everything that may be conceived as a whole, consisting of interdependent and semi-autonomous parts. This is true of society and of organism to the extent that both are wholes, consisting of interdependent parts, each of which is semi-autonomous, possessing some being and becoming of its own—and to that extent the analogy is valid. But it is improper to transfer without empirical evidence any biological proposition into sociology, because organism and society alike are systems. No more should any proposition from subatomic physics be taken over by sociology on the same ground of systematic similarity. In sociology, the question of social system has been most suggestively posed by the Italian sociologist Vilfredo Pareto, whose views will be discussed in Chapter 13.

## Society and the Steps of Evolution

Spencer's preoccupation with the evolutionary doctrine and the organic analogy played an important role in preventing him from answering satisfactorily the basic question, What is society? There was perhaps an additional reason for his neglect of the problem of the nature of society. Spencer was an extreme individualist. In keeping with this position, he postulated that the characteristics of the component parts, the individuals, completely determined the characteristics of the whole, a view he developed explicitly in *Social Statics* and in *The Study of Sociology*. But here too he deviated from that position and once more inconsistency appeared.

In the first volume of *Principles of Sociology,* for example, Spencer notes quite incidentally that there arises in the social organism a life of the whole quite unlike the lives of the units, though it is a life produced by them.

If Spencer had nothing very definite to say about the nature of society, he nevertheless expressed very definite views about the advancement of social evolution. On this matter Spencer's work contains two lines of reasoning, one of which is logically related to his basic concept of evolution more effectively than the other. The first line of reasoning develops the thesis that the main fact of evolution was the movement from simple societies to various levels of compound societies. By the aggregation of some simple societies, compound societies arose; through further aggregation of compound societies, doubly compound societies arose; by aggregation of doubly compound societies, trebly compound societies arose. A simple society consists of families, a compound society of families unified into clans, a doubly compound society finds clans unified into tribes, and the trebly compound societies, such as our own, are those in which tribes have been brought together into nations or states. With increase in size, structure increases, as well as differences in power and in the occupations of the members. Simultaneously, functions are differentiated. This is the main line of Spencer's evolutionary scheme, as presented in *First Principles* and again in *Principles of Sociology.*

The second line of reasoning develops the thesis that a somewhat different type of evolution also has occurred, namely, from military to industrial society (Comte had previously proposed a similar thesis). The two types are distinguished on the basis of the predominance of compulsory cooperation in the military society and voluntary cooperation in the industrial type.

It is worth noting in this connection that Franklin H. Giddings, an American sociologist active in the late nineteenth and early twentieth century (see Chaps. 6 and 11) who was to a large extent a follower of Spencer although he belonged to another sect of the cult of evolutionism, must be held responsible for widespread misunderstanding of Spencer's evolutionism. Giddings, in a statement concerning Spencer's ideas, neglected the main line of Spencer's thought, concentrating exclusively on the transition from military society to industrial society. He submitted this document to Spencer, who was then about eighty years old, and receiving the latter's endorsement, Giddings published it in one of his own works with a reference to Spencer's letter. Subsequently, Giddings' formulation was accepted as official in many presentations of Spencer's evolutionary views.

Spencer occasionally stated that societies need not necessarily pass through the identical stages of evolution or become exactly one like the other, as the vulgarizers of his ideas believed. He maintained that there were differences between individual societies due to disturbances which interfered with the straight line of evolution. *Principles of Sociology* cites five possible disturbances: first, a somewhat different original endowment of the races; second, the effect due to the impact of the immediately preceding stage of evolution; third, peculiarities of habit; fourth, the position of a given society in the framework of a larger community of societies (whether, for example, a society is surrounded by friendly or antagonistic nations); and fifth, the impact of the mixture of races. Concerning this last point it should be noted that the anthropology available to Spencer had not yet established the relative unimportance of race mixture and the paramount importance of culture contact in the theory of social change. If this necessary correction is made, Spencer's point on race mixture is well taken.

### The Principle of Noninterference

Although Spencer's treatment of sociology was primarily theoretical, the discipline in his mind should also serve the purpose of providing principles of social policy. It will be remembered that Comte fathered sociology to guide men in the construction of a better society; Spencer, in contrast, wanted sociology to demonstrate that men should not interfere with the natural processes going on in society. He believed in the existence of an innate instinct of freedom and that every interference with that instinct produced harmful reactions. He believed, too, that nature was endowed with a providential tendency to get rid of the unfit and to make room for the better. Who are the better? Spencer said that they were not the morally superior but, primarily, those who are healthier and more intelligent. He who loses his life because of stupidity, vice, or idleness, according to Spencer, is in the same class as the victims of sickness or malformed limbs. The sick and crippled, indeed, should not be protected.

The theory of progress disclosed by the study of sociology, Spencer added, is one which greatly moderates the hopes and fears of the extreme parties. So far as a doctrine can influence general conduct, the doctrine of evolution is calculated to produce a steadying effect on thought and action. The men of the higher type may see how little can be done and yet find it worth while to do that little. He emphasized that one should combine philanthropic energy and philosophical calm.

For Spencer, the state was a joint-stock company for the mutual protection of individuals. He specified many activities to be prohibited to the state, including education, sanitary measures, regulation and coining of money, postal service, provision of lighthouses, improvement of harbors. When government initiated activity in one of these areas, he wrote to an editor (his letters were published because of his fame) denouncing the stupidity of a government which interfered with natural evolution. He believed that nature is more intelligent than man; nature knows where it goes and prepares a better future for man.

In Spencer's mind the final stage of evolution was not yet achieved, although to a large extent his theory was a kind of Victorian eschatology, taking the Victorian *laissez faire* type society to be the climax. He believed, however, that there would be some further development, and with it the little residue of coercion which was still present would disappear. The final stage of evolution, he seemed to believe, was to be a kind of anarchy. However, in 1884 he published an article in which he admitted that though this conception was far in advance of his age it could perhaps be used by future sociologists.

### Spencer in Retrospect

What were the solutions given by Spencer to the basic problems of sociological theory as formulated in the first chapter? For Spencer, society was a superorganism, arising from the combination of individual organisms. The modern conception of culture as of a system of interrelated ways of acting and thinking was absent in his writing, as is to be expected. Yet this present-day concept of culture would have led him to see the inadequacies of his method. One of the most important corollaries of that concept is that every cultural item must be viewed in its context, that it cannot be understood in isolation. In contrast to this principle Spencer persistently removed culture items from their contexts and fitted them into his own preconceived patterns.

The problem of the relationship between man and society was solved by Spencer along the line of extreme individualism: the individual was paramount; society should not interfere with men; the individual has to act and, acting, will do the best for himself and society.

Spencer was not a sociological monist. He did not single out some one factor that pushes society ahead through the various phases of its evolution. The whole evolutionary process, for Spencer, was the prime force, the motive power which explains everything, an unknowable and impersonal force, determining every becoming in all realms of being. But his ideas about disturbances, ideas which he did not develop extensively, show that he was inclined to believe that there was no single determining factor in change.

The method of investigating society and its changes that Spencer purported to use was partly comparative, partly functional. The investigator using this method first compares societies; then the individual items brought to light in comparative study are explained in terms of their significance for the whole of evolution. But, in fact, Spencer proceeded by deduction. He began with an evolutionary scheme itself arrived at deductively; from that scheme he derived the necessity of certain phases, and then he gave flesh and blood to these abstract phases by the method of illustration, by selecting examples from here and there which seemed to fit his system.

Spencer presents his main types of society—simple, compound, doubly compound, and trebly compound—with subdivisions concerning the forms of leadership, on the one hand, and concerning nomadic, semi-settled, or settled type of living, on the other. After having located various societies of which he knew from library research, he presumably could have ascertained whether societies which were, say, doubly compound, were marked by similarities in politics, religion, law, arts, and so on. It is certain, however, that he would not have achieved any positive results because, as it appears in his classification, the same type of society, say the doubly compound type, may lack leadership, have unstable leadership, or have most stable leadership, which means the greatest possible difference in its politics. The people may be nomads, semisettled, or settled, which means again a great variation in economic arrangements.

Spencer should have realized that societies which are at the same stage of evolution, according to the principle of the differentiation of social structure, do not necessarily possess similarities in politics, religion, morals, art, and other cultural features and that, contrariwise, similar types of government and forms of religion are found among different structural types of society. But Spencer did not make the empiric test essential to scientific procedure.

Spencer's theory, in contradistinction to that of Comte, was not sociological theory as it is understood today. Comte had formulated a basic theory which explained the social segment of reality, and tried to describe and explain social facts in terms of that limited theory. But Spencer's ambition was higher. He formulated an integral theory of all reality. His law of evolution is a cosmic law. His theory is therefore essentially philosophical, not sociological, and, strictly speaking, philosophers should check its validity. However, it may be noted that Spencer's philosophy was basically a sublimation of the physics of his time, itself in a state of transition. Physicists of today have rejected many of the nineteenth century's views. Since Spencer's theory was built on the latter, it is understandable that much of his system has dropped into the discard. This is always the danger when a system of empiric science is built on the basis of a philosophical theory, itself rooted in temporary empiric conclusions reached by men at a certain time.

Nevertheless, unlike those of Comte, Spencer's views found enormous acceptance in his lifetime. They dominated the minds of many scholars and others from 1865 to 1895. In the course of three decades it was almost impossible for an intellectual to admit that he had not read Spencer. He had adversaries, to be sure, but everyone had to take him into account. This was the case especially in England, in the United States, and, peculiarly, in Russia. His influence was less felt in France and Germany.

Spencer's appeal was strong because his theories responded to two needs of the time: the desire for unifying knowledge (Spencer acknowledged this himself in his autobiography), and the need for a scientific justification for the *laissez faire* principle, the dominant note in the ideological climate of the time in England and the United States. In Russia the theory appealed because it emphasized freedom, and in those days Russia was struggling for freedom.

Spencer reached the peak of his popularity in 1882 when he visited the United States. He was received here with much acclaim and frequently was declared the greatest man of the time by the ranking captains of industry, because he justified their activities. After this trip of triumph, his popularity steadily declined. New ideas came over the horizon. Many men began to think that there should be some rational and political control of society. Furthermore, pragmatic philosophy was beginning its ascendancy and it soon replaced the somewhat naïve naturalistic philosophy of Spencer. In his old age Spencer was aware that the currents of the times were running against his teaching. He died a sad man, it has been recorded, feeling that his lifework had not achieved the goal of his expectations.

# CHAPTER 4

# OTHER PIONEERS

At the same time that the founding fathers of sociology were presenting their views, a number of scholars and social philosophers were formulating theories which today are recognized as also having pushed ahead sociological inquiry in various directions. These writers did not call themselves sociologists, but without knowledge of their contributions an adequate understanding of the development of sociological theory would be impossible.

Although the contributions of the individual authors presented in this chapter are almost unrelated, their theories may be distributed among three groups: those of Quételet and Le Play made important advances in research methods; the views of Marx, Morgan, Gobineau, and Buckle are outstanding instances of monistic theories, that is, of theories explaining social becoming by the unfolding of one particular factor; the theory of Danilevsky may be interpreted as an early alternative to evolutionism.

## Quételet: The Statistical Approach

Adolphe Quételet (1796–1874), a Belgian statistician, was a very precocious youth. At the age of seventeen he was teaching mathematics at a private school; at nineteen he was instructor of mathematics at the University of Ghent; at twenty-one he was appointed professor at the Athenaeum in Brussels. His original interest in literature and poetry gradually shifted to mathematics and its application to social phenomena, under the influence of the famous astronomer Laplace who introduced Quételet to the then novel theory of probability. In an essay published in 1829 and later in his major work, *On Man and the Development of Human Faculties: An Essay on Social Physics* (1835), Quételet emphasized regularity in the realm of social events, especially in phenomena commonly assumed to reflect free will.

On the basis of numerous calculations performed by himself and by others, such as the measurement of the stature of the soldiers of a regiment, Quételet came to the conclusion that, in social phenomena, the normal curve of distribution commonly obtains. In other words, cases close to the average of a series, by necessity, occur much more frequently than cases presenting significant deviations from it. Hence the concept of the average man which, in his theory, occupies a central position. But Quételet mistakenly identified the average with the desirable. He did not take into account the fact that identical averages may be derived from two or more quite different situations, depending on differences in distribution. Thus, for instance, two societies may have the same average income per capita, but in one situation most of the people may have incomes close to the average while in the other large numbers with very low income would be balanced by a small minority with very high income.

Despite these shortcomings, Quételet's contribution to the social sciences, including sociology, was highly important. He was the first to show the possibility of using statistics as a tool for the understanding of social phenomena. In one of his works he presented the view that we can judge of the perfection of a science by the facility with which it may be approached by calculation. This statement has become a *Leitmotif* of present-day neopositivism (see Chap. 15).

Quételet, unlike certain other scholars of his day, was a man of considerable prestige. He was an honorary member of many academies of sciences; royalty asked him to give instruction to its youngsters. But, for quite a time, sociologists ignored or spurned his views, as if nursing the indignation which Quételet's efforts had provoked in Comte (see Chap. 2). It was only in the late nineteenth century that sociology began to employ the statistical method, and only in the twentieth century that quantification-oriented neopositivism emerged.

### Le Play: Early Case Study

Like Comte, Fréderic Le Play (1806–82) was concerned with contemporary social disorganization, the consequence, so they believed, of the French Revolution. Both of these scholars pursued the question of how to integrate or how to restabilize the social order. And both sought answers based on empiric knowledge.

Le Play was born in Honfleur, a small French seaport village. His father died when he was five years of age, his mother a woman of strong character and deep religious conviction taking over the family responsibilities. Young Le Play studied at the *Collège du Havre;* in 1825 he entered the *École Polytechnique* and in 1827 the *École des Mines.* Here he met professors who disparaged national customs and considered the development of the mind to be the supreme purpose of civilization. These ideas were repellent to Le Play and, it seems, served to strengthen his interest in traditional customs and values. During his recovery from a serious injury suffered in 1830, another revolution occurred in France. Le Play vowed to give the rest of his life to the establishment of social peace in his country.

In 1833, at the request of the Spanish government, Le Play made a geological survey in a province of that country. The publication of his observations gave him the opportunity to make similar expeditions to Germany, where he had traveled in earlier years, Belgium, England, and Russia. He was appointed professor at the *École des Mines* in 1840. By 1855 he had completed and published his magnum opus, *The European Workers,* in six volumes, a work that not only brought him immediate fame but also enabled him to devote the rest of his life to the study of society. At the insistence of Emperor Napoleon III, he wrote three volumes on *Social Reform in France* (1864); he subsequently completed *Organization of the Family* (1871) and *Organization of Labor* (1872). Shortly before his death he prepared a volume entitled *Essential Constitution of Humanity* (1881).

Although Le Play's early training was primarily in mathematics and engineering, he was a diligent student of the works of Rousseau and Comte. More importantly, he was a keen observer of people and their ideas. In his writings he laid stress on the laboring classes (a term he introduced) and social authorities (the local leaders, but also religious and political leaders). He aimed at a sound reconstruction of ideas in general and the conservation of the mores.

Le Play's principal method of study consisted of careful observation of social phenomena in terms of a unitary scheme. This scheme, in its essentials, was completed in 1833. This approach incorporated what is known today as the case-study method—and here is one of Le Play's outstanding contributions to social-science methodology. Agreeing with Comte that the family is the basic social unit, he utilized the family budget as a quantitative expression of family life and as a basis for the quantitative analysis of social facts. One of the primary functions of the family is that of obtaining subsistence for its members through work and, he contended, the mode of that is determined by place, that is, by geographical conditions. Hence Le Play's well-known emphasis on place-work-family as the triadic focus of sociological study.

When selecting a family for observation, Le Play, with the help of social authorities, sought one whose habitat and like conditions approached the average for the locality; sometimes he did not know the local language, but by living with the family he gained a basic understanding of their way of life. In this way Le Play inaugurated a social-research technique known today as participant observation. Le Play was well aware of the fact that systematic observation is only the first step in scientific investigation. The true social sciences, he realized, must use not only a precise method but intelligence as well.

On the basis of his numerous and careful observations, Le Play formulated a conception of prosperity and sufferings which contains the beginnings, at least, of a general theory of social structure. "Everywhere," he said, "happiness consists in the satisfaction of the two principal needs imposed by the nature of men, daily bread (material things) and the essential mores (the nonmaterial things)." When these needs are assured by the existing social structure, the race [he used the term to mean society, perhaps ethnic group] is prosperous; when they are not, there is suffering. Social structures inducing prosperity and preventing suffering, he believed, were composed of seven elements divided into three classes: first, the two fundamentals of universal moral law and parental authority; second, the two cements of religion and government; and third, the three materials of community property, individual property, and patronage. From the first two classes were to come the essential mores; from the third, man's daily bread.

Le Play did not believe in evolution, still less in progress. His view of social change was essentially cyclical: simplicity, complication, corruption, and finally reform or ruin—this constitutes the vicious circle from which to this day no civilized race has been able to extricate itself. He was especially interested in the declining phase of change, from prosperity to suffering. He cited several reasons for the decline of the society of his time: the revolutionary spirit and its contempt for national customs; the destruction of the influence of social authorities; the incessant extension of bureaucracy; the abnormal influence of the *literati;* the corruption of the language, especially of such terms as liberty, equality, and democracy; the belief that prosperity depends upon some particular form of government. As contributions to the growth of sociology Le Play's conclusions concerning these matters, though often full of insight and provocative, hardly match his development of useful research methods.

### Marx: Economic Determinism

Karl Marx (1818–83) is most famous, of course, as the original leader of the revolutionary labor movement now divided into the two principal branches of socialism and communism. While a large part of Marx's writings were devoted to the propagation of this movement, some of his doctrines were, in the modern sense, sociological.

Marx's philosophy was materialistic—and materialism forms the basis of his sociology. According to Marx, only matter exists, consciousness being an epiphenomenon, a manifestation of motion in brain cells. This view reflects the influence on Marx of Ludwig Feuerbach (1804–72), a left-wing Hegelian philosopher. As sociological theory, Marxism is reducible to two basic postulates and a few corollaries.

The first postulate is the one of economic determinism, namely, the view that the economic factor is the fundamental determinant of the structure and development of society. This factor, consisting essentially of the technological means of production, determines the social organization of production, namely, the relations into which men must and do enter to produce goods more effectively than they could if working separately. These relations, according to Marx, develop independently of human will. Moreover, the organization of production (called by Marx "the economic substructure of society") not only limits but also, in the final analysis, shapes the whole superstructure: political organization, law, religion, philosophy, art, literature, science, and morality itself.

The second postulate of Marxist sociology concerns the mechanism of change. According to this view, social change must be understood in terms of its three ever-present phases. This is the dialectical scheme borrowed by Marx from the German idealistic philosopher Georg Hegel (1770–1831), whom he was proud to have turned upside down (by applying the scheme not to fundamental spirit, as Hegel did, but to matter). Everything in the world, including society itself, passes by a kind of dialectical necessity through the three stages of affirmation or thesis, negation or antithesis, and reconciliation of opposites or synthesis. On this higher level of synthesis the dialectical process continues with new conflicts and accommodations always marking the historical process.

A combination of the two fundamental Marxist propositions yields certain corollaries. Every system of economic production begins by being an affirmation, the best or most adequate of the orders possible at that time. But any system, once it is socially entrenched, becomes an obstacle to the application of new technological inventions and the use of newly discovered markets and supplies of raw material. Historical development cannot stop at this stage; therefore, the entrenched order must be overcome by a social revolution which creates a new order of production, a synthesis of the old and the new.

In every society there are two basic classes, one representing the obsolescent system of production, the other the nascent order. Society evolves from one stage to another by means of struggle between these classes. The emerging class is ultimately victorious in this struggle and establishes a new order of production; within this order, in turn, are contained the seeds of its own destruction, the dialectical process once more.

Marx and his followers used this dialectical scheme in their analysis of contemporary Western society, which they called capitalist. In this society, they said, the social organization of production that came into being with the industrial revolution is expressed in the existence of two classes:

the bourgeoisie or owners of the means of production, and the proletariat or the laborers. Struggle is inevitable between the two classes and will result, as class consciousness and militant class action develop, in the overthrow of the existing system. Capitalism's heir will be the socialist order characterized by the collective ownership of the means of production and ultimately by a classless and, indeed, stateless society—a Utopian goal long held by pre-Marxian and, according to Marx himself, nonscientific socialists.

The sociological theory of Marx presented here in very brief outline must be criticized on several grounds. In the first place, strict correlations between the economic basis of society and the superstructure were not demonstrated by Marx—nor can they be. On the contrary, as it has been pointed out frequently, essentially the same capitalist economic system has coexisted with various political institutions, including absolute monarchy and democracy. Similarly, throughout the era of the dominance of the capitalist order, philosophy, the arts, and other cultural phenomena have been highly diversified. In the second place, historically viewed, change from one type of social organization of production to another is not necessarily the consequence of the victory of the exploited class. In European history, for example, the destruction of feudalism was much more the work of the relatively small and powerful bourgeoisie than of the serfs. In the third place, Marx's predictions, such as the waning of the middle class and the initial triumph of socialism in nations most developed industrially (and hence having the most advanced proletariat), run counter to the actual historical events.

Marxist theory, however, has sociological significance. Like the doctrines of Comte and Spencer, it is an evolutionary theory, stated twenty-five years after Comte's "discovery of the year 1822," but almost fifteen years before the publication of Spencer's *First Principles*. It is noteworthy that whereas Marx's sociological theory could have been constructed independently of its philosophical premises, on the basis of empirical study, such was not its genesis. Although Marx spent many years documenting his theory with historical illustrations, his conception of social structure and social change was essentially a logically necessary premise for the demonstration of the proposition that socialism must inevitably triumph in the modern world.

Marx's writings, moreover, contain several insights into social and social-psychological problem areas that not only concerned writers of his day, but are of great interest to sociologists and others currently. One of the most important of these is the phenomenon of *alienation*, generally conceived as the social and psychological isolation of human beings in the very midst of many other men, or as it was later expressed, the "mass." Marx, in keeping with his fundamental postulates (and as especially brought out in his earlier writings), stressed the alienation of workers from the means of production resulting, more generally, in the "alienated *power of humanity."* [1] A second problem area of continuing sociological interest, similarly reflecting his basic orientation, is the field of study known in more recent years as the *sociology of knowledge,* a field of which Marx was the major founder. This relatively new discipline emphasizes the dependency of ideologies and other human thought forms prevailing at a given time and place upon the structure and composition of the society in which their development occurs. We shall return to the problem of the social roots of knowledge when discussing the contributions of Emile Durkheim, Charles H. Cooley, and especially Karl Mannheim, whose views were strongly influenced by Marx.

In the development of sociology, Marxist thought is important as an attempt to achieve a systematic theory of social structure and change. More significantly, it stands as the first and perhaps the most forceful theory emphasizing a single, determining factor in social change. Later on there emerged many other theories of the same monistic type, differing from Marxism in the choice of the basic determinant, to be sure, but sharing the monistic approach. Here it is merely pointed out that such theories, although they often have the positive function of calling attention to hitherto neglected social facts—and this was true of Marxism—oversimplify and often distort both the complex process of social change and the complex nature of the social structure and cultural patterns.

## Tylor and Morgan: The Impact of Technology

Edward B. Tylor (1832–1917), a British anthropologist, believed in the existence of distinct stages in the development of man's culture; he did not however use the term evolution. Experience, he claimed, leads the student of ethnology to expect and to find the same phenomena of culture resulting from similar causes—whenever and wherever the latter are present. Tylor sought to find a means to measure this development. The principal criteria of cultural growth, he believed, were the development of industrial arts, the extent of scientific knowledge, the nature of religion, and the degree of social and political organization. Throughout his work he investigated human advance along these lines. But he did not believe that progress in cultural growth was necessary; on the contrary, he quoted with approval statements of the pessimistic French philosopher `de Maistre on this subject.

Tylor's most lasting contribution to sociological theory was his definition of culture which appears on the very first page of his major work, *Primitive Culture* (1871): "Culture or civilization . . . is that complex whole which includes knowledge, belief, art, morals, law, custom and any other capabilities and habits acquired by man as a member of society." However, not until about fifty years later did sociologists begin to make

[1] See T. B. Bottomore and Maximilian Ruben, *Karl Marx, Selected Writings in Sociology and Social Philosophy* (London: Watts & Co., 1956), pp. 167–77.

common use of this concept of culture. In recent decades Tylor's view of culture has become not only an almost standardized conceptual tool for many sociologists, but also an important place to depict systematically the complexities, functional interconnections, and changes in man's social and cultural world.

Lewis Henry Morgan (1818–81), an early American anthropologist, formulated a theory of social evolution which had a measure of influence in sociological circles for several years. His theory stressed the key significance of technological factors in society and its changes. He developed this view in a series of special studies published in the 1860's and 1870's, which were brought together in the volume *Ancient Society* (1877). Morgan believed in the existence of definite stages of evolution through which men must pass everywhere. The experience of mankind, he argued, has run in nearly uniform channels; human necessities under similar conditions have been essentially the same; and the operation of the human mentality is uniform throughout the various human societies.

Morgan distinguished three main stages of cultural advance: savagery, barbarism, and civilization. He subdivided each of the first two into three substages. Each stage and substage was assumed to have been initiated by a major technological invention. Thus, the second stage of savagery was brought into being by the arts of making fire and catching fish, the third by the bow and arrow. Barbarism began with the invention of pottery-making; the second stage was characterized by the domestication of animals and the third by the technology of melting iron. Civilization was heralded by the invention of the phonetic alphabet. Each of these stages of technical evolution, according to Morgan, was correlated with characteristic developments in religion, the family, political organization, and property arrangements.

Morgan's *Ancient Society* made a strong impression on Marx and his co-worker, Friedrich Engels (1820–95). The latter, following Marx's advice, published in 1884 *The Origin of the Family, Private Property and the State,* a volume making extensive use of Morgan's theories and of his illustrations, taken largely from observations of American Indian societies. In this way Morgan's work became a part of Marxian sociology and, in some measure, continues to play a role in Soviet Russia.

### Gobineau: Racial Determinism

Comte, Marx, and Spencer were exponents of the doctrine of progress. Arthur de Gobineau (1816–82), in contrast, deplored what he considered the conspicuous retrogression of the France of his day and sought to discover its cause. The results of his meditations were offered in the four volumes of *Essay on the Inequality of Human Races* (1853–55), which may be considered as the mainspring of racial theory in sociology. As a representative of the French aristocracy, the author was proud of

being a descendant of the Teutonic conquerors of the Gauls. He considered Germans racially inferior to Frenchmen because of the former's
greater biological mixture—itself a highly questionable proposition. The
truly superior race, he argued, had been best preserved in England.
Gobineau's views were influenced in some measure by the famous historian Augustin Thierry (1795–1856) [2] who, in turn, owed some of his
ideas to Comte.

The significance of the racial factor in social development was established by Gobineau through arbitrary elimination of other hypotheses. In
answer to the question of why nations decline, Gobineau states that neither religious fanaticism, religious decay, luxury, licentiousness, corruption, nor cruelty explains such decline, for many nations continue to
flourish despite the presence of one or more of these conditions. The
essential causal variable, he claimed, is racial composition. Racial circumstances, his argument ran, dominate all major problems of history.

Inequality of races, then, is sufficient to explain the destinies of peoples: superior races are capable of substantial progress while others, such
as the American Indians, are socially and culturally limited by their racial
inheritance. Thus, all of the principal civilizations have been the achievement of Aryans (not in fact a racial division), who formed the highest
branch of the white race.

Gobineau never stated explicitly what constituted a race, and he
badly confused race as a biological division of mankind with an ethnic
group consisting of men integrated by their common acceptance of a
specified culture. Speaking in terms of race, he asserted that conquest of
one people by another of a superior race is followed by improvement
proportionate to the hereditary quality of the conquerors, provided that
racial purity is preserved. But conquerors commonly mix with the conquered; racial decay and cultural decline follow. Therefore, human history can be summarized as a sequence of the ages of gods, of heroes, and
of confusion and mediocrity during which human societies degenerate
into mere herds. This was the theory of retrogression, the opposite of that
of progress.

Gobineau's theory is in error anthropologically: there are no superior
and inferior races. In other words, man's innate capacities are not determined by race. And the theory is wrong sociologically: racial mixture as
well as interpenetration of cultures often result in a blossoming of culture.
At the time Gobineau published his work, anthropology and sociology did
not yet possess these facts, now available, so that its scientific weakness
could not be convincingly demonstrated; on the contrary, the theory
could have fascinated the imagination of many. Nevertheless, Gobineau's
racial theory was largely unnoticed during his lifetime, especially in
France. This happened because his theory flatly contradicted the view

[2] Author of *Considerations on the History of France* (1840).

then commonly held, namely Turgot's, Condorcet's, and Comte's doctrine of unlimited progress.

At the end of the nineteenth century his theories were introduced into Germany largely through the work of Houston Stuart Chamberlain (1855–1927). Chamberlain published in German *The Foundations of the Nineteenth Century* (1899), a work which deeply influenced Emperor William II and many men around him. Though following the main lines of Gobineau's theory, Chamberlain assumed that racial mixture was not always culturally detrimental; there could be favorable mixtures which in fact should be preserved. These racist doctrines were taken over subsequently by National Socialism, the Nazism of Hitler. They also helped to bring about Anglo-Saxonism, a fairly widespread viewpoint in the United States in the late nineteenth- and early twentieth-century period, and one that played a role in shaping the restrictive immigration law of 1924 (the basic provisions of which were reenacted in the law of 1952, although greatly modified by later laws).

## Buckle: Geographical Determinism

Henry T. Buckle (1821–62), the son of a wealthy London merchant, traveled extensively and devoted his life to literary and scientific pursuits. In the latter capacity he played a role in bringing a form of geographical determinism into nineteenth century sociological thought. *The History of Civilization in England* (1857–61), Buckle's principal work, was left incomplete because of his early death.

Buckle's basic idea was that social and historical processes result from the action of external phenomena upon the mind and from the action of the mind upon these phenomena. Only the first part of this theory was developed in Buckle's published writings. Cultural progress, he asserted, depends on the rise of a leisure class, a development which is possible only when production grows greater than consumption. Such a surplus is essentially the consequence of a favorable combination of conditions of climate, soil, and available food. In early history the creation of a surplus of food depends on the energy and regularity of human labor on the one hand, and nature's nature or the natural environment on the other. The quality of labor is determined by climate; temperate climate invigorates, hot climate debilitates; in frigid areas desultory habits emerge; while the productivity of human labor depends on the fertility of the soil. Buckle "tested" these hypotheses by his general observations of the geographical and social conditions in Ireland, India, Egypt, Central America, and Peru, coming to the conclusion that his observations supported his theory.

Buckle also ascribed some sociological significance to the visual aspect of nature: if the natural environment is sublime or terrifying, it overdevelops the imagination; if it is less formidable, intelligence prevails.

He attempted to demonstrate this theorem by contrasting the civilizations of India and Greece.

Buckle believed that the influence of geographical environment was most direct and therefore strongest upon primitive people and that it declined with cultural advance. Had he completed his work he probably would have attempted to show how, in later historical periods, increasing human control of external natural phenomena took place.

The study of the influence of geographical conditions was undertaken many times by writers who predated Buckle. Among his predecessors were Aristotle, Montesquieu, and several German geographers. But Buckle expressed the thesis with exceptional force; for a few decades, his *The History of Civilization in England* was widely read and influential in intellectual circles. And frequently Buckle's views have been restated in the form of one-sided geographical determinism. This doctrine is no longer acceptable, for today it is known that geography limits rather than determines social and cultural development. The presence of natural resources, for example, does not guarantee that they will be exploited by man, but in their absence numerous developments are precluded. This established view, unfortunately, is challenged by an occasional geographical determinist even today.

### Danilevsky: An Early Alternative to Evolutionism

Nicholas Danilevsky (1822–85) was a Russian naturalist deeply interested in political affairs. In 1869 he published, in installments appearing in a Russian monthly, a work entitled *Russia and Europe* in which he tried to answer the question: Why does Europe hate Russia? In the course of his discussion of this question, he set forth a theory of the development of human societies at variance with evolutionary theory. In fact Danilevsky's theory of societal growth provided a kind of model which in subsequent years became a substitute for evolutionism.

Danilevsky's starting point was the observation that it is unscientific to view universal history as a continuous development of the European experience, ignoring or treating residually developments in other parts of the world. Rather, historical recurrences should be studied within the framework of cultural historical types or civilizations. On the basis of available evidence, he claimed, one may establish thirteen more or less complete and independent or semi-independent civilizations: Egyptian, Chinese, Ancient Semitic, Indian, Iranian, Hebrew, Greek, Roman, Arabic, Germano-Romanic, Slavic, Mexican, and Peruvian. Each of these civilizations passes through a cycle analogous to that of organic growth: infancy, youth, maturity, decay. Some civilizations, for example the Mexican and Peruvian, were arrested in early stages; while the Slavic at the time was just reaching the age of maturity and the Germano-Romanic was already in the process of decay.

Not all tribes or peoples ascend toward civilization, in Danilevsky's view, but only those which are mentally and spiritually capable of doing so. Moreover, civilizational development is not confined to a single tribe or people; it takes place in a group of tribes or peoples linguistically affiliated with one another. The indispensable condition for growth is political independence of at least one of these peoples, permitting the formation of a cultural historical type. There are also groups whose activities negate civilizational formation, such as the Huns, the Tatars, the Turks; while the remaining peoples form a kind of residue which Danilevsky referred to as ethnographic material.

Every civilization, according to Danilevsky, develops its particular style, which is especially evident at the age of maturity. More precisely, each civilization excels in one or a few realms of human activity. Thus, the Greeks accented beauty; the Romans specialized in law and political organization; Semitic civilization emphasized religion. In more recent times, Germano-Romanic societies excel in the political, technological, and esthetic fields, while Slavic civilization shows great promise in *all* fields.

As wholes, civilizations are impenetrable and intransmissible. But their individual traits can be borrowed, especially scientific and technological achievements. Moreover, civilizations may be diffused by colonization and, less efficiently, by "grafting"—the latter illustrated by the flowering of Hellenic civilization on the Egyptian stem and the growth of Roman culture on the Celtic tree. Commonly, stem or tree civilizations die out in the process of grafting. All civilizations, however, have a limited life span, though Danilevsky did not claim to know the time limit of the cycle of growth and decay. But he assumed that, sooner or later, civilizations die by a kind of inner necessity. At this stage the peoples themselves return to the state of ethnographic material, though at some future time they may become the bearers of new civilizations.

At the time of its appearance Danilevsky's work was largely unnoticed. But in the late 1880's it suddenly attracted attention in Russia, so that two new editions of *Russia and Europe* appeared, followed in 1890 by an abridged French translation. Probably this volume was an important source of inspiration for Oswald Spengler's *Decline of the West* (see Chap. 20), a treatise which for a few years was widely influential, a half century after the appearance of its obscure predecessor. Danilevsky's theory of civilizational growth and decline was untimely, opposing as it did the popular doctrine of unilinear evolution toward progress. And of course, the fact that his work was written in Russian and remained untranslated until 1890 was also an obstacle against recognition. Yet Danilevsky contributed to the cumulative growth of the sociological theory, especially to the study of social and cultural change. Some of his ideas will be met in the works of Toynbee and Sorokin, whose theories will be considered in Chapter 20.

# CONCLUSION TO | *Part Two*

In the course of half a century there were a number of starts made in the social sciences; after some time they converged and thereby contributed to the body of sociological theory. But in this first period these starts were only loosely related to one another. Spencer, for example, knew Comte's work and even borrowed the term sociology; but otherwise he was not influenced by the French master's contributions. Le Play was familiar with Comte's work, and Gobineau was influenced by the historian Thierry who had been impressed by Comte's remarks about the significance of race. Quételet grew up in the same intellectual climate as Comte. Tylor acknowledged that no author made a deeper impression on him than Quételet; he also quoted Comte. Morgan was familiar with Spencer's writings, but his use of the term evolution was incidental to his main arguments. The original version of Marxism stands apart from other early sociological exploration (though it had connections with the disparate intellectual streams of Hegelian philosophy, Utopian socialism, and, ultimately, British political economy), but, in a later work, Engels incorporated a number of Morgan's ideas. Buckle's and Danilevsky's writings seem to have been entirely unrelated to those of their contemporary sociologists.

The majority of the contributions thus far surveyed were written in the firm belief that evolution was the supreme law of becoming. Spencer's evolutionism was cosmic; Comte's evolutionism was pluralistic but with emphasis on the ideological and demographic factors; Marx's evolutionism was economic; Morgan's evolutionism was technological. In opposition to the ideas of these authors Danilevsky put forward a cyclical theory of social change, dismissing the dogma of unilinear evolution toward progress. Tylor, Gobineau, and Le Play also rejected the assumption of progressive development in human society.

One of the major preoccupations of the early evolutionists was the explanation of what they called progress or, translated into contemporary language, the determinants of social change. The tendency was toward monism, affirmation of one factor as basic or at least prepotent. In addition to the ideological, demographic, economic, and technological factors stressed by the evolutionists, the racial and geographical factors were emphasized respectively by Gobineau and Buckle.

Two of these early starts were important from the point of view of methodology. Quételet showed how to apply statistical methods to the study of social phenomena, and Le Play carried out excellent work by a method which, later on, became known as case study. It is noteworthy that, relative to both methods, the phenomenon of delayed action took place. Not until the end of the nineteenth century was the statistical method applied in specialized social studies, first in the field of criminology. And not until the 1920's did the idea of making sociology a quantitative science gain impressive momentum. Le Play's method, on the other hand, was used from the beginning by his followers in the limited field of family studies. But it was not until the second decade of the twentieth century that, rather independently of Le Play's lead, American sociologists discovered the case-study method and made it a rival of statistical research.

The majority of the works surveyed were not intended by their authors to be works in *sociology*. Only Comte and Spencer and, to a less extent, Le Play were aware that they were building up a new science. Quételet was preoccupied with statistics; Marx, Gobineau, Buckle, and Danilevsky would have classified their works as philosophy of history; Tylor and Morgan were contributing to ethnology. It is therefore understandable that during the period of the pioneers sociology itself remained a vague concept. The scientific problems forming the central core of sociological theory were more often posed than answered. Methodology, except in Quételet's and Le Play's work, remained amateurish. But there were many brilliant insights in these early years which provoked thought and bore scientific fruit in the course of the succeeding decades.

# PART THREE

# The Emergence
# of Competing Schools

# CHAPTER 5

# SOCIAL DARWINISM

The last quarter of the nineteenth century approximately delimits the second period in the history of sociology. On the one hand, it may be viewed as the period of the battle of the schools. In contrast to the situation that obtained during the earlier period, scholars in the field of sociology were familiar with the diverse theories and emphasized, often overemphasized, the differences among them. In consequence, a large part of their activity consisted of efforts to demolish rival theories. On the other hand, inasmuch as it was dominated by the evolutionary doctrine, the period had a certain unity. What the sociologists were mainly debating was the most adequate interpretation of evolution, and, more often than not, debate centered on identification of the dominant factor responsible for the evolution of society.

It should be noted, however, that the dominance of evolutionism was not absolute. At a time when evolutionism by its very nature was tending to reduce sociology to the study of social dynamics and to explain the structure and functioning of any society solely in terms of the evolutionary phase that had brought it about, a few sociologists arose to pursue the line initiated by Comte in his statements on social statics. Through their activity developed a new approach to sociology which could be called analytical or systematic, emphasizing the study of the structure and operation of society and devoting relatively little discussion to the stages through which society has passed. Some of the pioneers of analytical sociology believed in evolution, but evolution played a rather insignificant part in their theories.

Foremost among the many schools into which the dominant evolutionist theory was divided was social Darwinism. It is noteworthy that Charles Darwin, author of *The Origin of Species* (1859) and of *The Descent of Man* (1871) and inventor of the modern theory of biological evolution, was not a social Darwinist. He did not discuss problems of social philosophy and was inclined to emphasize the contrast between the processes of biological and social evolution.

### Bagehot

The first author to attempt to formulate a sociological theory by applying the principles of natural selection and variability to political society was Walter Bagehot (1826–77). He belonged to a middle-class English family, studied at Oxford, and later entered the banking business. From 1860 he was the editor of the *Economist*. He first presented his views in a series of articles published in *The Fortnightly Review* (1867); later these articles appeared in book form under the title *Physics and Politics* (1872).

In this work Bagehot tries to establish the essential character of group struggle. The main feature, he holds, is that such struggle is conducted by groups of cooperating men, not by individuals. The superiority of compact groups over the loosely knit ones is obvious. The difference between uncivilized and civilized men, says Bagehot, is like that between wild and tame animals. He maintained that the taming process for men is the same as that for animals, which is a curious statement indeed in view of the obvious dissimilarities of the two processes. The most docile tribes survived; subsequently the nations with the most compact family systems have come to possess the earth. This conception is a sublimation on the sociological level of the survival of the fittest.

Since group cohesion is so important in the evolutionary process, the group-making factor must be established. To Bagehot this factor is "the cake of custom" or the tendency of descendants to resemble their progenitors not only biologically but also mentally. A question then arises: What are the forces that maintain the customs? Bagehot answers this question by citing three forces. First there is the religion of fear endowed with terrible sanctions against violators. Second there is a persecuting tendency or a propensity for punishing deviations from the established order, which supports customs. No barbarian, Bagehot believes, can bear to see one of his nation deviate from the old customs and usages of his tribe. Third there is man's proclivity to imitate what is before him. Imitation is not conscious; it is contagious and is strongest among children and savages. Imitation accounts for the amazing sameness in savage society and for the fact that savages are quicker and better copiers. (Modern social science knows of course that these traits do not necessarily mark "savage" society.) In this emphasis upon imitation Bagehot anticipated Gabriel Tarde, one of the creators of analytical sociology, who contributed significantly to the decline of evolutionism in sociology (see Chap. 8).

Bagehot's discussion of custom, just outlined, was undertaken to clarify the assertion that group cohesion is the main prerequisite for victory in group struggle. As another factor making possible the survival of the fittest, Bagehot took over from Darwin the idea of variability. Without variability, the struggle for existence would be meaningless, resulting in no improvement of the biological or social organization. Like Spencer, Bagehot believed in progress, explaining its possibility by positing, in addition to the tendency to imitate, the opposite tendency of descendants to differ from their progenitors. Progress is possible, he believed, only if the force of legality based on imitation is powerful enough to bind the nation together, but not so strong that it kills all variation and thwarts nature's perpetual tendency to change. Those groups survive in which a balancing of these forces secures the greatest group efficiency. This balance, in his opinion, is distinctive of societies that are marked by government by discussion: in such societies, the door is open for innovations and progress.

### Gumplowicz

Bagehot's ideas never gained especially wide recognition; in fact, his work was largely ignored. This cannot be said of another representative of social Darwinism, Ludwig Gumplowicz (1838–1909), a Polish Jew. Gumplowicz entered upon an academic career in the Austro-Hungarian monarchy where anti-Semitism was strong and inter-ethnic conflict dominated the political scene. Throughout his life he suffered from an inferiority complex, and tragedy marked his last years. In 1894 his son committed suicide; in 1909 Gumplowicz put an end to his own life after having killed his wife. The gloom surrounding his life was lightened but not dispelled by a visit, in 1903, from the American sociologist Lester F. Ward (see Chap. 6), a highly optimistic man. As the result of that visit Gumplowicz was granted the opportunity to publish an article in *The American Journal of Sociology* (Volume 9). There, contrary to his earlier teaching, he admitted that the iron laws of the natural processes could be modified by human intellect, itself a natural force.

Gumplowicz's academic career was confined to the provincial University of Graz where he was at first a lecturer and, after 1882, a professor. His first acquaintance with the field of sociology came through the writings of Comte and Spencer. His own major volumes are *Race and State* (1875), *Race Struggle* (1883), and especially *Outline of Sociology* (1885). He wrote many other works which added little of importance to the ideas expressed in the *Outline of Sociology*.

In all these writings Gumplowicz, though emphasizing the necessity of relating sociology to the general field of science, maintains that social phenomena constitute a unique category distinguished from all other phenomena by several fundamental traits. In his opinion sociology is the science of human society and of social laws. Therefore it is the basis of all other social sciences, which are devoted to particular manifestations of social life.

In Gumplowicz's opinion social and cultural evolution is wholly a product of the struggle between social groups. This struggle, analogous to the struggle for existence and the survival of the fittest among individuals, replaces individual struggle in his theory of evolution. Only the group is important, for the individual is a group product. Only an insignificant minority of men continue their education by receiving impressions originating outside their own social groups. It is the community that thinks, for the notion that man thinks as an individual is an illusion.

Why, however, must groups fight? Gumplowicz offers two basic hypotheses: one, the polygenetic hypothesis, asserting that the species man evolved from various older types at many different times and in many different places, so that between the races there is no blood bond; and two, the hypothesis that an unsurmountable hatred exists between different groups and races. Both assumptions were reached deductively and confirmed by good authority. The further back we go, says Gumplowicz, the larger the number of small social groups we find, hordes characterized by sexual promiscuity and equality of social position. Conflict (war) between them was directly caused by the desire for improved economic conditions. (Here, as in many other places, the teaching of Gumplowicz shows a Marxian flavor.) In earliest times, war resulted in the extermination of the defeated group. Later men found it more advantageous to enslave the conquered and to exploit them economically. In this process of the superimposition of one group upon another Gumplowicz saw the origin of the state. This theory was accepted, though reluctantly, by many sociologists, including scholars in the United States, in the absence, at that time, of other plausible hypotheses.

After the formation of the state, group struggle bifurcates: wars between states driven by the implacable urge for conquest continue but, in addition, class struggle arises within states. Although the struggling classes and their goals change throughout history, the class in power always realizes that it can most easily maintain and extend its dominance by establishing legal and political institutions. All these ideas concerning the state have affinity with Marxism.

Like many German thinkers of the time Gumplowicz was inclined to contrast state and society. For him society was the sum total of conflicting groups, each group being centered around one or more common interests. Everywhere men feeling themselves closely bound by common interests endeavor to function together as units in the struggle for domination. Thus groups are formed, and the struggle between them is relentless.

Contrary to other evolutionists Gumplowicz was pessimistic about progress. He could not accept the idea of the evolution of mankind as a whole because there was for him no such thing as mankind. His polygenetic view precluded the possibility of a unitary evolution. Evolution in each group, he believed, has been rather sporadic and interrupted by setbacks. In every state partial evolution and progress have taken place; but always there have been barbarians awaiting the signal to begin the work of destruction. Although it is certain that Gumplowicz did not borrow from Danilevsky, there is some parallelism here with the latter's view (see Chap. 4) on the rise of particular cultures (not of humanity-wide culture) and on the existence of negative or destructive forces. The fall of many a powerful state before the assault of rather small barbarian hordes, Gumplowicz continues in an interesting anticipation of Toynbee's views, cannot be comprehended unless the existence of domestic social enemies is recognized.

To sum up, there is neither progress nor retrogression in the course of history as a whole; progress can be observed only in particular periods and particular countries. Gumplowicz's view on this subject is much closer to the common opinion of the present day than were the views of his optimistic contemporaries.

### Ratzenhofer

Social Darwinism appears in a much milder form in the work of an Austrian sociologist, Gustav Ratzenhofer (1842–1904). Born in humble circumstances, this man, who became a cadet at the age of sixteen, fought numerous duels, and saw distinguished service in war, in 1878 was put in charge of the army archives, a position that gave him ample opportunity for reading and stimulated the urge to write. In 1898 he was promoted to the rank of field marshal and appointed president of the supreme military court of Austria. He retired from the army in 1903. Intellectually, he was a self-made man, influenced by reading Comte, Spencer, John Stuart Mill, and Gumplowicz. His main works include *Nature and End of Politics* (1893), *Sociological Studies* (1898), and *Sociology* (1908, posthumous). He died on board ship on a return trip from the United States, where he had lectured with great success.

In Ratzenhofer's opinion, sociology is the science of the reciprocal relations of human beings. Its task is to discover the fundamental tendencies of social evolution and the conditions of the general welfare of human beings. The fundamental problem of sociology is to establish the unique character of social regularity and to distinguish it from the regularity of the world of phenomena in general. Sociology must discover the underlying principle that governs all social affairs and, with this guide, help to solve all social problems.

This governing principle, the driving force, *Urkraft*, is *interest*. Interest is the key that unlocks the treasure house of sociology. Social life, according to Ratzenhofer, is a bundle of interests rooted in the very nature of men. Interest is the expression of a need through the awareness of its necessity. Needs as such are innate or instinctive, but to become interests they must be perceived by human minds and understood to be necessary.

Ratzenhofer classified interests as follows: procreative, physiological (nutrition), individual (self-assertion), social (based on consanguinity, directed to group welfare), and transcendental (religion). These five types of interests are the real forces behind individual and group action. Society exists only in the social process, which is the sum total of social relationships existing between men; but these relationships in turn are based on interest-seeking behavior which motivates all social action.

As was perhaps natural for an old-school military man, Ratzenhofer believed that conflict predominates in group action. The social order is the organization of the struggle for existence. Conflict predominates because of man's innate disposition both to obey his primary impulses and to hate all his fellow men. This disposition is limited with the increase of population. Then, as subjugation by rulers becomes necessary, the beginning of social articulation and of the state appear. Further expansion leads to the conquest of some states by others, a process conducive to increasing complexity and differentiation. Struggle and war generally consolidate social structures, while culture and commerce weaken the social bond.

### Small

Albion W. Small (1854–1926), without having been an especially original thinker, contributed perhaps more than anyone else to the academic advance of American sociology.

Small was born in Maine, studied at Colby College and the Newton Theological Seminary, and later spent two years at the universities of Berlin and Leipzig where he gained a thorough knowledge of German social science. For ten years he was professor of history and economics at Colby College and for three years he was its president. In 1892 he was appointed head of the newly created department of sociology at the University of Chicago, the first in this field to be established anywhere. He occupied this position until his death, playing a major role in the training of a whole generation of sociologists. In 1894, in cooperation with George E. Vincent, he published the first introductory textbook in sociology. The following year he founded *The American Journal of Sociology*, which he edited until his death. In 1905 his masterwork, *General Sociology*, was published. In teaching and writing he familiarized his fellow countrymen with European thought and promoted the recognition of American sociology in Europe, in itself full justification of his presidency of the International Institute of Sociology in 1913.

Though influenced by Ratzenhofer, Small mitigated the latter's mild social Darwinism, reducing it to a theory of interests and their conflicts. This theory was congenial with his earlier conception of desires as the mainsprings of human action in society, an idea probably borrowed from Ward. In *General Sociology* Small defined interest as "an unsatisfied capacity corresponding to an unrealized condition." This formula, he said, was an attempt to express something back of consciousness. The vagueness of this statement is unfortunately characteristic of Small's works in general.

Interest is the pivot of Small's sociological theory. Interests are the simplest modes of motion which can be traced in the conduct of human beings; living itself is the process of developing, adjusting, and satisfying interests. The latter fall into six classes: health, wealth, sociability, knowledge, beauty, rightness. Subjectively viewed, interests are desires; objectively, they are wants.

Interests dominate both individual and social life. The individual at any time is the product of a persistent struggle of his interests; and similarly society is the consequence of the myriad efforts of individuals to fulfill their interests. Small stresses the interdependent relationship of individual and social aspects of the struggle of interests and says, "Individual and society are not means to each other, but phases of each other. A society is a combining of the activities of persons. A person is a center of conscious impulses which realize themselves fully only in society."

In this context, Small used the term society, though earlier in his work he had repudiated it in favor of association, insisting that the change was not merely verbal. Society suggests a rather static view on social facts, he claimed, while association connotes a dynamic view. Small wished to study the *process* of human association. And in this process he saw conflict as the primary pattern, involving the collision of interests. In keeping with his own ethical preferences, however, he went on to assert that conflict resolves itself into cooperation through socialization.

Despite Small's personal influence, his work has neither persisted nor influenced American sociology to any large degree. One reason is clear: formulated at the turn of the century, Small's views belonged to a kind of sociology which, at that time, was already waning. Although, in contradistinction to the majority of his contemporaries, Small did not arrange his ideas around the concept of evolution, he nevertheless assumed the validity of the evolutionary doctrine on the whole. He conceived of evolution toward progress as expressed in the movement from original conflict to pacification through socialization, and believed that the social process, by inner necessity, produced more and more dissimilar men, a view in line with Spencer's evolutionary formula.

But Small's explanation of the relationship between sociology, the other social sciences, and psychology was consistent with much present-day thinking. He insisted on the unity of the social sciences, especially in *The Meaning of the Social Sciences* (1910), and noted that each science gives primary attention to certain fragments or aspects of the one thing. Of sociology and psychology he wrote: "A psychologist takes association as the known and fixed fact, to pursue the investigation of the mechanisms of the individual actors. The sociologist, on the contrary, takes the individual for granted and pursues the investigation of the association." It is regrettable, in the author's opinion, that later sociologists did not follow this excellent advice more frequently.


### Sumner

A special variety of social Darwinism emerges in the work of one of the most important American sociologists, William Graham Sumner (1840–1910). Born in Paterson, New Jersey, Sumner was the son of an English immigrant who had left his native country because his trade had been ruined by the advance of the industrial revolution. In spite of this background, the son became one of the strongest champions of the *laissez faire* principle which was, in part, a reflection of the industrial revolution in the world of ideas.

When he was in his middle twenties, Sumner spent several years at Oxford. Reports that have been preserved about conversations held there show that the main problem under discussion was the possibility of a science of society, where such a science should begin, and how it should be built up. Philosophy of history in the style of Buckle was often considered to be the starting point; but social science must be an inductive science, and no one could see how the mass of material was to be collected and so arranged that induction could actually be performed.

In 1868, after his return to the United States from England, Sumner was appointed tutor at Yale University. While occupying that position he read Spencer's *First Principles* and *Social Statics,* but these works made no great impression on him. In 1869 he was ordained in the Episcopal ministry. When he came to write sermons he found that he was primarily interested in subjects within the area of social science and political economy. About that time he read Spencer's *The Study of Sociology* and found there the lead he wanted. He was promoted to the professorial rank at Yale at the same time he was being converted to evolutionism. When he required his students to read Spencer he was almost dismissed from the university under the suspicion of atheism. However, he retained his chair, which he occupied until his death. During the last two years of his life he was president of the American Sociological Society, succeeding Ward, who had been its first president.

Sumner's principal work is *Folkways* (1906). In spite of the date of publication, Sumner's views belong with nineteenth-century sociology because his book was based on lectures delivered in the course of many years. *Folkways* was conceived as an advance section of a monumental work, *The Science of Society,* which Sumner had begun in 1872 but which he did not complete. Sumner's faithful disciple Albert G. Keller finished and published it in 1927 under their joint signatures. Many of the ideas expressed in *Folkways* Sumner had stated in numerous essays published in the 1880's and 1890's. A posthumous collection of *Essays* (1934) testifies to the persistence of interest in Sumner's work many years after his death.

Sumner viewed society as a system of forces subject to laws which it is the task of science to investigate. Men must respond to social laws as they respond to physical laws: these laws are to be learned and obeyed. Hence Sumner's unconditional acceptance of the liberal doctrine expressed in the very title of one of his essays, *The Absurd Effort to Make the World Over* (1894). The basic law was, for Sumner, the law of evolution, a spontaneous, unilinear, and irreversible process which cannot be changed by social effort. Evolution is pushed ahead by the struggle for existence, a contest pitting man against nature and man against man with no one to be blamed for the hardships men impose on one another. The survival of the industrious and the frugal is the survival of the fittest; this is the law of civilization. The only alternative is the survival of the "unfittest," the law of uncivilization. No other possibilities exist. It is equally impossible to bind the social forces which produce monopoly, wars, and social classes and their struggles. These forces are first of all the pressure of population and of economic conditions; the role of moral forces is secondary. Class struggle has marked all historical development; the main objective of this struggle is domination of the state.

Sumner's teaching combined a good deal of economic determinism with the use of biological concepts; and he was firmly convinced of the preeminent value of the data of ethnology. He was little influenced by or even acquainted with nonevolutionary theory in American and European sociology. According to Keller, Sumner's successor at Yale, the latter's principal method was to assemble a large body of verified facts and let them tell their own story, under the application of trained and organized common sense. This is the judgment of an admirer. More exactly, Sumner used an enormous quantity of material, but his organization of it was rather weak.

*Folkways* is an attempt in the style of social Darwinism to explain the evolutionary origin, nature, function, and persistence of group habits (customs). Since the first task of life is to live, men begin with acts, not with thoughts. By trial and error, from various ways of acting, the best and the fittest under the particular conditions are selected. These methods are repeated and their repetition produces habit in the individual and custom in the group. Thus folkways, that is, the ways of doing things that are commonly accepted in a society, develop unconsciously. They arise no one knows whence or how, and grow as if by the play of internal life-energy.

Sumner was never quite clear about the force producing the folkways. He attempted three different explanations: interest (under the influence of Small); pain and pleasure (the hedonist pair); and the four motives of hunger, sex, vanity, and fear (an anticipation of W. I. Thomas' four wishes). The folkways can be modified, but only to a limited extent, by the purposeful effort of man. In time they may lose their power, decline and die or be transformed. Sumner never investigated the conditions under which folkways become transformed or lose their impact on men. Therefore he could never formulate approximations of social laws.

When they are vigorous, the folkways largely control individual and social undertakings and produce and nourish ideas of world philosophy and life policy. When elementary views on truth and right are developed into doctrines of welfare, the folkways involved become *mores*. Sumner's terminology is somewhat inconsistent. Sometimes he opposes mores to folkways, but on other occasions he uses the term folkways to designate all commonly accepted ways of acting, including the mores. Sumner ascribed supreme importance to the folkways and mores. The folkways dominate social life; the life of society consists in making folkways and applying them. Laws reflect the mores, and to be strong they must always be consistent with them. When folkways and mores become institutions or laws, however, they change their character.

Sumner's discussion of institutions anticipated the teaching of the institutional school (see Chap. 21), an approach based on a philosophy entirely at variance with Sumner's Darwinist leanings. "An institution consists of a concept (idea, notion, doctrine, interest) and a structure. The structure is a framework, an apparatus, or perhaps only a number of functionaries set to cooperate in prescribed ways at a certain conjuncture. The structure holds the concept and furnishes instrumentalities for bringing it into the world of facts and action in a way to serve the interests of men." [1] Since laws and institutions appear only at a high level of development, after mores have evolved from mere folkways, Sumner seems to have believed that the irrational mode of development of folkways is gradually replaced by a highly rational mechanism which creates structures or organizations with the objective of embodying specified ideas. However, he never explored this line of investigation.

Sumner's theory is evolutionist. But his discussion of the folkways and mores (terms in common use among contemporary sociologists) may be seen as a contribution to analytical sociology, to the understanding of the structure and the mode of operation of social groups. Sumner also gave to analytical sociology the distinction between we-groups and they-groups. He emphasized the opposition between ourselves, the we-group or in-group, and all others, the they-group or out-group. Each group nourishes its pride and vanity, boasts of its own superiority, exalts its own divinities, and looks with contempt on outsiders. Each group thinks its own folkways to be the only right ones, so that the folkways of other

[1] William Graham Sumner, *Folkways* (1906), p. 54.

groups excite disapproval and epithets of contempt and abomination. Whereas the members of an in-group are bound in a relationship of peace, order, and law, their relationship to all outsiders is one of hostility. To attitudes of superiority concerning the folkways of one's in-group and of invidious comparison to those of out-groups, Sumner gave the name *ethnocentrism,* a term now commonly used.

Sumner also maintained that a correlation exists between ethnocentrism and the growth of group solidarity. "The exigencies of war with outsiders are what make peace inside . . . Loyalty to the group, sacrifice for it, hatred and contempt for outsiders; brotherhood within, warlikeness without—all grow together, common products of the same situation." [2] Bagehot and others had made similar observations many years before but only after Sumner's work did these views gain wide acceptance.

An equally important and related aspect of Sumner's work is that he originated the normative (or institutional, in Parsons' terms; see Chap. 18) approach to social phenomena. In other words, he initiated the study of the origin and functions of social norms. To be sure Spencer and early ethnologists had treated the customs and usages of various societies; but they had merely described them, with little or no analysis of their functions in society. Sumner, however, did not stop at this point. In the introduction to *Folkways* he stated that he had intended to write a book about sociology, but that in this attempt he had deviated by inner necessity into the study of the sociological importance of usages, manners, customs, mores, and morals. *Ethology,* he noted, would be a convenient term for such a study. This term is derived from the Greek word *ethos,* applied by the Greeks to the usages, ideas, standards, and codes by which one group is differentiated from others and individualized in character. Ethics, things pertaining to the *ethos,* are the standards of right. In Sumner's opinion it was a strange fact that modern nations had lost these terms and have overlooked the significant suggestions that inhere in them. His work was therefore to be an attempt, only partly successful, to enrich the study of social life by focusing upon commonly accepted standards of right.

His contributions to analytical sociology are more important than Sumner's conception of the origin and persistence of folkways. His theory of the survival of the fittest or the most adequate folkways is refuted by the existence of harmful customs that are often conducive to the decay or even destruction of groups adhering to them.[3] His view that folkways are forces independent of men is also untenable: it is now known that the phenomena of the rise, persistence, modification, and decay of customs are reducible to complex systems of human action and interaction. And it is known that under certain conditions law can greatly alter the mores themselves.

[2] *Ibid.,* p. 12.
[3] It is a surprising fact that he was aware of the existence of such customs—and still held the thesis that the fittest customs survive!

### Social Darwinism in Retrospect

Spencer saw in evolution a universal law of becoming. He derived both organic (biological) and superorganic (social) evolution from one cosmic law. The social Darwinists reasoned differently. They were familiar with the Darwinian theory of biological evolution and believed that this theory could be carried into sociology by substituting social groups for organisms. On the basis of this belief they built up their own sociology. Society was for them a rather vague universe of social groups in conflict. Bagehot, the first of the social Darwinists, did not specify what type of groups these were. Gumplowicz and Ratzenhofer identified them with racial groups; Sumner, in an important advance, with ethnic or cultural groups. Gumplowicz, strongly influenced by Marxism, also identified social classes among the basic groups in conflict; in this respect, he was followed by Sumner. None of these men brought out the nature of culture, though Bagehot and Sumner, when emphasizing customs (folkways in Sumner's terminology), came close to the concept. No basic unity for analysis may be singled out in the works of Bagehot and Gumplowicz. For Ratzenhofer, interest was such a unit; for Sumner, folkways.

The social Darwinists held divergent views on the relationship between society and the individual. Bagehot and Gumplowicz viewed the individual as completely immersed in society. Ratzenhofer, on the contrary, saw society as merely a network of interpersonal relations, a view not too far removed from Spencerian individualism. Sumner's position was rather ambiguous. Through folkways and mores society could be assumed to dominate completely human life, yet Sumner remained a strong advocate of extreme individualism.

For all of these writers the basic determinant of social change, and implicitly of social conditions in general, was biological. Selection and survival of the fittest group were stressed by Bagehot, Gumplowicz, and Ratzenhofer, while the fittest folkways determined the state of a society according to Sumner.

The necessity of making sociology scientific was emphasized by Gumplowicz and Ratzenhofer. This meant that the methodological models to be applied in sociology must be those prevailing in the natural sciences. Since these models also were identified with the evolutionary scheme, however, this attempt to make sociology truly scientific was abortive. The methodology of the social Darwinists did not differ greatly from Spencer's; historical and ethnological facts were used essentially to illustrate propositions derived from their theory of evolution and, on this basis, these propositions were declared to be proved.

In the history of sociological theory, social Darwinism may be thought of as the exploration of a possibility. Today it is known that this exploration led largely into a blind alley. In the late nineteenth century, however, the path seemed promising.

Yet, it should be acknowledged that not everything in the teaching of the social Darwinists was waste. They started to build a theory of social conflict, identified some of the groups most likely to oppose one another, and established the correlation between intergroup conflict and intragroup solidarity. Bagehot glimpsed the sociological significance of imitation. Gumplowicz well understood the vulnerability of the doctrine of progress and, independently of Danilevsky, saw progress confined to segments of humanity, not marking human change as a whole. Sumner brought a new perspective into sociological study in emphasizing the normative aspect of social life. Although the principal emphases of social Darwinism, like those of evolutionism in general, proved to be fruitless, some of its by-products were genuine contributions to sociological theory.

# CHAPTER 6

# PSYCHOLOGICAL EVOLUTIONISM:
Ward and Giddings

The evolutionism of Spencer was cosmic. Evolution, the supreme law of all becoming, included the becoming of human society. The human mind with its ability to deliberate and to choose was therefore not a factor in evolution; in fact, its interference with evolution was rather harmful. In the middle 1880's a new brand of evolutionism arose which, contrary to the theory of Spencer, ascribed to human mentality an important role in evolution. The founder of psychological evolutionism was the American sociologist Lester F. Ward. His theory was developed further by Franklin H. Giddings. The views and works of both men will be presented in this chapter.

### The Life and Works of Ward

Lester F. Ward (1841–1913) was born in Illinois of people in humble circumstances. Though he received little formal schooling on the elementary level, his personal desire for knowledge led him to study biology and foreign languages at night, after exhausting and uninspiring work during the day. He did enter a preparatory school, but this schooling was interrupted by the outbreak of the Civil War. He joined the Union Army in 1863 and was severely wounded. After the war Ward held a clerical position in the United States Treasury Department and combined with this job study at Columbian University (now George Washington University). He majored in botany and law and received the master of arts degree in 1872. In 1881 Ward was appointed assistant, and in 1883, chief paleontologist in the United States Geological Survey where he pursued original research in geology and paleobotany.

Ward's interest in the field of sociology was awakened as a result of his reading Comte and Spencer. He came under the spell of the majestic systems of the two founding fathers of the new science and largely agreed with Spencer's cosmic evolutionism. But he could not accept the conclusions drawn by the English master from the postulate of an impersonal, selfwinding evolution. Ward's own humble origin and the suffering he had observed around him prompted him to introduce into the Spencerian scheme a principle that would make both desirable and scientifically justifiable conscious human interference with evolution. The germ of this principle he found in the work of Comte. Was not Comte's system oriented toward social reform on the foundation of social laws to be discovered by the new science? In human society, Ward decided, there was, in addition to impersonal evolution, purposive action, itself a product of the evolutionary process.

This idea of purpose in human affairs was the moving spring behind twelve years of work on Ward's two-volume masterpiece, *Dynamic Sociology* (1883). For some time this work remained almost unnoticed. The United States was going through a period of rapid advance under the banner of the principle of noninterference; and at such a time a work attacking the leading principle of visible progress seemed backward and even detrimental. However, in 1890 Albion Small, then president of Colby College, recognized the great merits of *Dynamic Sociology*. Small's interest and soon that of other scholars encouraged Ward to write further volumes: *Psychic Factors of Civilization* (1893), *Outline of Sociology* (1898), *Pure Sociology* (1903), and *Applied Sociology* (1906). For the most part these works expand, restate, and modify in minor respects the earlier magnum opus. In *Pure Sociology*, however, is a section reflecting the impact of Ward's contact with the two Austrian social Darwinists, Gumplowicz and Ratzenhofer. (As noted in the preceding chapter Ward, in his turn, brought about certain changes in the views of Gumplowicz.) Other new influences are noticeable in *Pure Sociology*, especially that of Tarde, a French sociologist who underscored independently of Ward the importance of the psychic factor in social reality and consequently liberated himself almost completely from evolutionism (see Chap. 8). In general, during the twenty years which passed between the publication of *Dynamic Sociology* and that of *Pure Sociology*, sociology had been rapidly developing. Using his knowledge of French, Ward avidly read the major works in the field. In 1902 he enumerated the principal systems of sociology and wrote a critical essay on them.[1]

About the time of the publication of his last works, Ward was enjoying wide fame not only in the United States but also throughout the scientific world. In 1903 he was elected president of the International Institute of Sociology. He became the first president of the American Sociological Society in 1906. In the same year he resigned his position with the government and began teaching sociology at Brown University; prior to that

[1] Published in *The American Journal of Sociology*, vol. 7 (1902).

time, he had taught only a few summer courses, mainly at the University of Chicago. The position at Brown he held until his death.

### Basic Postulates

Lester Ward's sociological theory can be arranged around four postulates. The first is the law of evolution, understood to have approximately the same meaning as in Spencer's work. In *Dynamic Sociology* Ward preferred to speak of the law of the aggregation of matter, but he did not retain this verbal innovation in his later works. A comprehensive view of evolution appears only in *Dynamic Sociology,* where the total process of evolution is divided into the stages of cosmogeny, biogeny, anthropogeny, and sociogeny. These terms illustrate Ward's predilection for neologisms based on classical languages.

A second postulate of Ward's theory is the bifurcation of evolution after the stage of anthropogeny. Accompanying spontaneous evolution, caused by blind forces which Ward called *genesis,* appears *telesis* or man's purposive action based on knowledge and anticipation of the consequences of his acts.

Third, Ward postulates that every science is a systematic study of a particular group of forces. For Ward social forces were clearly psychic forces, but they were limited to feeling, as the motive power behind social phenomena, while "the thinking faculty is not a force." Ward worked at length on the problem of the classification of social forces. His final classification appeared in *Pure Sociology* where he divided forces into the ontogenic: one positive, seeking pleasure, another negative, avoiding pain; the philogenic: one direct, sexual, another indirect, affection based on consanguinity; and the sociogenic: a triad of moral force (seeking the safe and the good), esthetic force (seeking the beautiful), and intellectual force (seeking the true and the useful). If one wonders how Ward could include the intellectual among the social forces and hold at the same time that ideas are not forces, the seeming paradox can be resolved by stating that the intellectual force is not truth as such but love of truth, which is a feeling.

Fourth, Ward postulates the principle of creative synthesis or synergy. This principle, not made explicit in *Dynamic Sociology,* is the very backbone of *Pure Sociology.* It is a universal principle operating in every department of nature, and at every stage of evolution the transition from one stage to another is achieved through synergy. Social energy, says Ward in *Pure Sociology,* where he seems to regret having earlier used the term force instead of energy, surges through society in all directions; and like a storm or a flood, it is ruthless. The innate interests of men work at cross-purposes, often to no purpose. This situation holds throughout nature. Many forces conflict and collide, but since no motion can be lost a partial equilibration is achieved from which more or less stable structures are created. These structures collide again and the process is repeated, generating higher and higher structures in all realms of being. Everywhere the structures thus created by synergy contain more than the sum of the factors taken independently. In formulating the principle of synergy, Ward acknowledged a partial indebtedness to Wilhelm Wundt (1832–1920), a famous German philosopher of that day.[2] Elsewhere Ward stated that creative synthesis is "the cosmological expression of the Hegelian trilogy." [3]

## Sociology: Its Division and Method

Ward never felt it necessary to offer a formal definition of sociology. In *Pure Sociology* he wrote that sociology is the science of human achievement. Sociology moreover, Ward claims, is a true science since it covers a definite field of phenomena occurring in a regular order, as the effect of natural causes or forces.

He distinguished sociology from anthropology, holding sociology to be a science dealing mainly with the historical races which have built up civilization. The relationship between sociology and the special social sciences he explains by means of the principle of synergy. Sociology is a compound generated by the creative synthesis of the special social sciences.

Ward was also concerned with the problem of the proper divisions within sociology. First, he distinguished pure from applied sociology. Pure sociology is a treatment of the phenomena and laws of society as it exists. An etiological diagnosis is thus reached, excluding questions of therapeutic treatment and all ethical considerations. This is to say that the questions of pure sociology are these: What, why, how? Applied sociology, on the other hand, must answer the question: What for? It is concerned with social ideals and with ethical considerations and its object is to propose man-made improvements of social conditions. Nevertheless, applied sociology is a science, not an art, since it offers for guidance certain substantiated general principles.

Although he distinguished carefully between pure and applied sociology, Ward insisted that knowledge of social laws gained in pure sociology could and should be used to improve human society. He had to fight for this view against the majority of his contemporaries, especially against Spencer and Sumner who did not believe in planned social action. The social laws are indeed unalterable, Ward agrees, but men can utilize them to achieve their ends, just as they utilize physical laws.[4] How can

[2] Wilhelm Wundt, *Logik*, vol. II (1895), pp. 267–81.
[3] Lester F. Ward, *Pure Sociology* (1903), p. 175. The subsequent references are also to this volume.
[4] This position was stated in numerous papers, collected in six volumes under the title *Glimpses of the Cosmos* (1913–18).

men do this? His answer is found in his development of the doctrine of telesis.

Pure sociology was divided by Ward into two parts, genetic and telic (in accordance with the second of his postulates). This classification proved to be scientifically inadequate, for Ward was never able to distinguish clearly between genetic and telic phenomena and was often forced to consider particular phenomena in both the genetic and the telic divisions of his system, sometimes even contradicting himself.

That part of sociology which is devoted to genetics Ward further divided into statics and dynamics, terms made familiar by Comte's and Spencer's works. But Ward gave to this distinction a precision that was lacking in the works of his predecessors. He polemicized against those who contended statics should be confined to the study of social structures, while dynamics should be concerned with their functioning. Function, argued Ward, is that which structures do. Statics covers both structure and function; dynamics is the study of change in structures.

Ward was not preoccupied with the method of sociology, a favorite subject for many of his contemporaries. He believed that the main method should be generalization, that is, the grouping of phenomena and the treatment of the groups as units. This procedure is very vague indeed. Actually Ward introduced most of his sociological concepts and theorems with evolutionary statements concerning the realms of astronomy, physics, chemistry, biology, and anthropology. Through the author's creative effort, these materials then become arguments in favor of propositions about social phenomena, which are assumed to be part of the same cosmic evolution. Ward usually reached his sociological propositions by intuition and sometimes by keen observation of events and situations of his day. For such an achievement, no articulate methodology can be formulated, which is perhaps the reason Ward had so little to say on the subject.

In one respect, however, Ward was very firm and explicit about method: he rejected the idea, then gaining momentum, that sociology should rely upon mathematics. "It does not always follow," he wrote in *Pure Sociology*, "that because the phenomena embraced by a science are subject to uniform laws they can always be reduced to mathematical formulas. Uniform laws or processes are the essentials of a science. Their mathematical expression is not essential."

## Genesis and Telesis

Ward, whose major interest in pure sociology concerned dynamics, pictured statics as a kind of snapshot of the continuous activity that constitutes the functioning of social structures. Since social forces are psychic in nature, the fundamental law of social statics must have the same quality. Therefore the basic rule of social statics is the law of parsimony, the law of least effort. "In this law," wrote Ward, "we seem to reach the maximum stage of generalization." Ward does not, however, make quite clear the meaning of this law. Most probably it refers to the functioning of social structures which reveal an algebraic sum of pleasures and pains; in other words, functioning results in excess of pleasure over pain.

Ward distinguishes laws, which are statements about uniform sequences, from principles, which explain their mode of operation. He cites but one principle of social statics: synergy, through which the clashing social forces are checked, equilibrated, and molded into structures which, once developed, persist and serve as dynamos of social power.

Ward's principal interest, social dynamics, focuses upon change in social structures. While static phenomena are controlled by a single principle, there are three dynamic principles: first, difference of societal potential, manifested chiefly in the crossing of cultures; second, innovation based on invention; and third, conation, or social effort through which social energy is applied to material things, resulting in human achievement. It is perplexing to read that all three of these principles are unconscious agencies working for social progress.

That progress was being achieved was for Ward a self-evident proposition. He could not understand how anyone could read history without seeing progress. In his opinion, it is superfluous to enumerate examples of the superiority of modern civilizations to earlier ones. *Pure Sociology* treats progress by reference to synergy. Ward said that progress results from the fusion of unlike elements; this is creative because from it results a third element which is new and superior to either. In *Dynamic Sociology*, written before the principle of synergy was evolved, the inner necessity of progress is demonstrated in a peculiar, quasi-geometrical manner. Six definitions and five theorems all linked together and including one of his favorite ideas, salvation through education, are presented. Ward's definitions are at least consistent with his basic propositions: happiness is excess of pleasure over pain; progress is success in harmonizing natural phenomena with human advantage; dynamic action is the employment of the indirect method of conation; dynamic opinion is a correct view of the relations of men to the universe; knowledge is acquaintance with the environment; education is the universal distribution of extant knowledge. The theorems assert that each subsequent item on the list is a direct means to the one immediately preceding it and an indirect means to the other items. Accordingly, progress is the direct means to happiness, while knowledge and education are indirect means to progress and happiness. These theorems are not, and could not be, demonstrated. In place of demonstration, Ward offers very eloquent pleas addressed to the feelings of the readers. Nevertheless, in *Dynamic Sociology* Ward's psychological evolutionism, emphasizing knowledge and anticipation, appears in purer form than in *Pure Sociology*, where progress is discussed within the framework of genetics, not telics.

In his study of dynamics, Ward makes use of the concept of telesis, the second agent of social change. He brings out the difference and relationship between genesis and telesis: the great agents of society are the dynamic and the directive. Social forces (the dynamic agent) are natural forces and obey mechanical laws. They are blind impulses. This is true even of spiritual forces. The directive agent (appearing in telesis) is indifferent sensation, or idea. It is not a force, and still its influence is immense. The mind is able to form ideals of perfection. This is creative imagination. The mind cannot make something of nothing. But with these materials it not only can reconstruct, but it can construct.[5]

The rational faculty of man is also stressed: "The directive agent is a final cause . . . A final cause is always more or less remote from the end . . . The end is seen [known] by the mind. Some natural property or force is also known to exist and its action upon the material things . . . is understood. [The body adjusts] to be moved in such a manner that the known natural force will impel it to the perceived end."[6] Despite the misuse of philosophical terminology, this statement is a reasonable, common-sense formulation of the way in which ideas (knowledge) influence human activity in society. It is, however, difficult to see how Ward could consider such principles as innovation based on invention, conation, or social effort to be genetic, not telic. This conclusion is probably due in part to the faulty psychology of the late nineteenth century, which tended to compartmentalize the mind. Therefore, ideas, among them ideals of perfection so important in telesis, could not be brought to work in the same system as feelings and conations. This conception unnecessarily complicated and even weakened Ward's system.

Ward was perhaps more fortunate in expression and classification when, in *Dynamic Sociology*, he distinguished between direct and indirect conation. Direct conation refers to the use of the muscular strength of the organism; its laws are identical with those of motion. When conation is indirect, interposed barriers are evaded by circuitous approaches (on the basis of knowledge). Direct conation is barren of results; indirect conation is much more efficacious. Ward believed that there was a signal advance in the field of government from the methods of direct to those of indirect conation. Compulsory legislation, the expression of brute government force, tends to give way to attractive legislation in which rewards are promised for the performance of acts that the state believes beneficial. Since indirect conation is based on knowledge, education renders indirect conation easier and more frequent. Therefore, Ward insists, education must be compulsory and universal.

In his discussion of telesis, Ward came very close to viewing culture as a major object of sociological study. He saw sociology as the study of social achievement. The sum total of human achievement in the cumula-

---

[5] Lester F. Ward, *Dynamic Sociology* (1883), p. 82.
[6] *Ibid.*, p. 467.

tive light of knowledge he called civilization, rejecting the term culture, which he believed to connote the humanities. To him achievement implied continuity, so that he could speak of products of achievement, among which he cited material goods, military systems, political systems, legal systems, industrial systems, and institutions. Here, though in rudimentary form, are some of the basic traits which today are called culture. To this extent Ward anticipated one of the outstanding developments of sociology in the twentieth century, namely, the emphasis on culture.

## Ward in Retrospect

Ward's answers to the fundamental questions of sociological theory may be briefly summarized:

First, he never formulated a definition of society, apparently taking it for granted that everybody agrees on this matter. He made a number of pertinent observations concerning culture, using the term civilization, which was for him the cumulative and durable achievement of the human mind.

Second, his unit for sociological analysis was social force, which he identified with feeling as the producer of motive power. He also emphasized another unit, the individual act of creative imagination. Through a combination of dynamic action, based on feeling, and creative imagination, social structures arise and change.

Third, for Ward, as for other consistent evolutionists, the state of society at a given time and the direction of social change were determined by its stage of evolution. This proposition is, however, not as firmly conceived in Ward's writings as in other sociological systems of the evolutionary type, because of his emphasis on creative synthesis, the primary power of evolution, and because of the existence of psychic factors of civilization that characterize the later stages of cosmic evolution.

Fourth, the problem of the relationship of personality to society and culture was never explicitly posed by Ward. Man is immersed in the genetic process, but at the same time man influences that process through telesis. "The environment transforms the animal, while man transforms the environment." [7]

Fifth, for Ward, sociology is the science of sciences, a creative synthesis of all sciences. The diffuse content of his sociological treatises is in conformity with this view.

What is the significance of Ward's sociology in historical perspective? Ward himself considered the following innovations as his principal contributions: the law of aggregation, distinct from evolution; the theory of social forces; the contrast between social forces and the influence of the environment; the superiority of the telic over the genetic process; the demonstration of the necessity for equality of education. In the light of

[7] *Ibid.*, p. 16.

subsequent developments, a different listing of Ward's achievements may be outlined: the emphasis on the psychic element in interhuman relations, especially telic action; the stress on human achievement as the appropriate subject-matter for sociology; affirmation of the possibility of rational human progress through social planning and education; a number of suggestive formulations concerning pure and applied sociology, about the relationship of statics and dynamics (especially the relationship of structure and function); the denial that quantification is a requisite of science.

Ward's sociological theory was more philosophical than empiric in so far as he shared the popular belief of his time in cosmic evolution as the supreme law of social becoming and explained social phenomena on the basis of a theory about total reality. But this view was mitigated by his emphasis upon the unique characteristics of social evolution rooted in man's rational faculty. His theory of social forces incorporated the view that sociology can be developed upon the conception of a mechanical interplay of human actions caused by feeling, an unacceptable position today. His illuminating views of telesis were blurred by the faulty psychology of his day. He was often inconsistent and his treatises were rather badly organized. Nevertheless, because of their insight and frequent brilliance, and the wide erudition of their author, Ward's volumes remain more readable than almost any other sociological works written in the same period.

## The Basic Concepts of Giddings

Franklin H. Giddings (1855–1931) was born in Sherman, Connecticut. Although he studied engineering at Union College he began his gainful life as a journalist, an occupation that afforded him many insights into diversified social situations. In 1888 he was appointed lecturer (later professor) in politics at Bryn Mawr College and six years later he left this position to become professor of sociology at Columbia University.

The sociological contributions of Giddings are primarily two-fold. In his earlier works, he was essentially a psychological evolutionist. Without abandoning evolutionism his later writings accent quantification and behaviorism. In this way Giddings became one of the founding fathers of the neo-positivist trend in sociology which blossomed in the second quarter of the twentieth century. Only his earlier theory is to be considered at this point, particularly as expressed in his masterpiece, *Principles of Sociology* (1896), and ably abridged and somewhat modified in *Elements of Sociology* (1898).

Like so many social scientists of his time, Giddings accepted the evolutionary doctrine as self-evident truth. For him, as for Spencer and Ward, evolution was the supreme law of becoming in all realms of reality. He explicitly stated, with reference to Spencer's *First Principles*, that social evolution is a phase of cosmic evolution. Consequently Giddings believed it unnecessary to seek a new principle of objective interpretation; evolution through equilibration of energy should suffice. The impact of this view on Giddings' work is heavy. Like Spencer, he approaches the problems of social evolution from the fields of biology and ethnology and sees in these areas convincing evidence about social facts.

In contradistinction to Spencer, however, and in agreement with Ward, Giddings believed that society is essentially a psychic phenomenon, though the psychic process in its turn is conditioned and limited by a physical process. Thus social laws are, first, laws of a psychic process, but second, laws of social limitation by a physical process. This position renders Giddings' sociology rather complicated. He is forced to alternate continually between psychic laws and physical laws and to explain their interplay. That social laws exist and can be established with the same precision as laws of natural phenomena, Giddings took for granted.

However, he emphasizes the laws of the basic psychic process. Following Ward's lead, he believed that the key to the explanation of social phenomena is to be found in volition. He sought, moreover, a single motive or a principle characterizing the conscious individual as a social being and determining social relations in so far as they are volitional. Such an explanatory principle, he asserted, had not yet been discovered. Briefly surveying the contributions of his great contemporaries, Novicow, de Greef, Tarde, and Durkheim, he claimed that their explanations of society were either too narrow or too broad. Since contract (stressed by de Greef) [8] and alliance (emphasized by Novicow) are more special features of society, and imitation (Tarde's basic law) and impression (emphasized by Durkheim) [9] are phenomena more general than society, one must find a principle intermediary to these. This principle is *consciousness of kind,* a phrase coined by Giddings though he explicitly acknowledged his indebtedness for the idea to Adam Smith who, in his *Theory of Moral Sentiments* (1759), had noted the importance of reflective sympathy in social life.

Consciousness of kind, according to Giddings, is a state of consciousness in which any being recognizes another conscious being as of like kind. Consciousness of kind may be an effect of imitation or imposition (constraint). But it is not merely effect; it may initiate contact and alliance and other social phenomena as well. Therefore, consciousness of kind meets the requirements of the intermediary concept Giddings had been seeking. Furthermore, it fulfills the function of delineating *social* conduct from similar types of conduct, namely, economic, political, or religious.

Consciousness of kind is a pleasurable state of mind which includes organic (subconscious) sympathy, the perception of resemblance, reflec-

[8] Guillaume de Greef, a Belgian sociologist (1842–1924), author of *Introduction to Sociology* (1886).
[9] See Chaps. 7, 8, and 9.

tive sympathy, affection, and the desire for recognition. United through consciousness of kind, Giddings claims, individual minds play upon one another in such a way that they simultaneously feel the same emotions, arrive at the same judgments, and sometimes act in concert. By means of this interaction, social mind is generated.

The social mind, to Giddings, is not a mere abstraction or fiction but something concrete, though it exists only in individual minds. Social mind, he notes at one point, is the simultaneous mental activity of two or more individuals in communication with one another, the concert of the emotions, thought, and will of two or more communicating individuals.

Although Giddings seems to have been influenced by Durkheim (see Chap. 9), he did not give to social mind the dominant place that Durkheim assigned to collective consciousness. The social facts reported by Giddings under this heading are usually explained today by reference to culture as a stable system of standardized ways of thinking and acting, without recourse to the misleading concept of social mind. The notion of consciousness of kind, which was for several years very much in vogue, has also been abandoned. But in Giddings' theoretical work consciousness of kind was the central concept around which the system of sociology was to be built, taking for granted the underlying postulate of evolution.

### Sociology: Its Nature and Methods

Sociology for Giddings is not an abstract science. Since the first principles of evolution are concrete, the science that formulates them must be concrete. Sociology is a descriptive, historical, and explanatory account of society viewed as a concrete reality. Underlying these propositions is once more the belief of the evolutionists that evolution is one for mankind. Sociology is therefore the description of a unique, nonrecurrent process, though its elements may be recurring.

In defining sociology as a concrete science, Giddings followed Spencer. He differs however from Spencer in establishing the kind of relationship that exists between sociology and the other social sciences. Sociology for Giddings is a general science of the total class of social phenomena, studying those attributes which are common to all the subclasses. (This is a notable though incomplete anticipation of Sorokin's definition cited at the outset of this book.) As a general science sociology is the science of elements and first principles. This conception, as the reader may recall, is almost identical with our earlier formulation of sociological theory itself.

Giddings' formal definition provides little insight into what the science really does. The formal definition is supplemented by another: sociology is the interpretation of social phenomena in terms of psychic action, organic adjustment, natural selection, and the conservation of energy. Of the four elements cited here only the first is related to the psychic process which, according to Giddings, is basic in social life. The other three are related to the limiting physical process; two (the second and third) are couched in terms of social Darwinism, while the last recalls Spencer's views as expressed in *First Principles*.

Since sociology is primarily the study of the evolution of mankind from its origins into its present civilized state, sociology's main method is historical or retrospective. One serious problem of method is the question of how to determine approximately the characteristics of primitive men. This feat may be accomplished primarily by the assumption of a parallelism between primitives and present-day savages. Unlike many other evolutionists, however, Giddings understood that the problem was not a simple one, since he recognized substantial differences in conditions and the possibility that many contemporary primitive societies are in the process of decay. Therefore, historical retrospection must be supplemented by deduction, by close attention to psychic possibilities and to psychological synthesis. One of the methods used by Spencer, the organic analogy, Giddings explicitly rejects.

Giddings characteristically was concerned with the internal division of sociology. He joins Ward by rejecting the identification of social statics with structure and social dynamics with the functioning of human groupings. This functioning, argues Giddings, is another part of statics and could be called kinetics. Dynamics obtains only when function is modified or structure is transformed. These telling remarks could be addressed to a number of contemporary sociologists who use the phrase structural-functional analysis and are inclined to identify functioning with dynamics.

### Statics and Kinetics

Like most evolutionary sociologists, Giddings failed to elaborate a detailed theory of statics. He distinguished, however, social composition and social constitution, somewhat in the manner of Ferdinand Toennies' *Gemeinschaft und Gesellschaft* (see Chap. 8). Social composition is the natural product of the physiological and psychological activities of individuals, supplemented by natural selection. Groupings arise unconsciously. Their forms are established before the social mind begins to reflect upon them. Social constitution, on the other hand, is the organization of individual members of society into specialized associations for achieving various social ends. Giddings did not clearly work out this dichotomy. The simplest grouping included in the concept social composition is the family. Through combination of families, two broader types of groupings arise: one ethnic (based on actual or alleged kinship) such as the horde, the tribe, a folk; the other demotic, held together by habitual intercourse, mutual interests, and cooperation rather than kinship. Among demotic groupings are neighborhoods, local divisions like counties or cities, and states. But the state is also treated by Giddings as one of the most important manifestations of social constitution.

Giddings' theory of statics also embraces class divisions within society. Contrary to the view prevailing in his day, he believed that economic classes are secondary divisions in society, while classes (in the sense of categories rather than social groups) based on physical, mental, and moral differences between individuals are of primary importance. In his opinion there were four true societal classes: the social (corresponding to the elite), the nonsocial (the masses), the pseudosocial (those who depend on the assistance of others), and the antisocial (the criminals).

Giddings' views on tradition complete his theory of statics. He identifies tradition with social memory or inherited ideas and explains this phenomenon as the simultaneous occupation of the minds of many individuals with certain beliefs, precepts, maxims, and facts of knowledge that have been handed down by preceding generations. Like Ward, Giddings here was approaching the present-day conception of culture without using the term itself or clearly recognizing culture's properties. In the whole body of tradition he sees three great orders: economic, based on utilization; juridical, resting in toleration; and political, rooted in alliance and obedience. There are also secondary orders: personal (beliefs about body and soul), esthetic, and religious; and tertiary orders: theological, metaphysical, and scientific (which evolved later than the first two).

Giddings attempted, not very successfully, to systematize knowledge about what he called social kinetics. As was natural for a man living in the intellectual climate of social Darwinism, he believed that conflict is the universal mode of action. But antagonism is self-limiting; the majority of individuals are too nearly equal in strength for one to hope to vanquish another. The equilibrium of strength is nevertheless tested from time to time. But the test by necessity terminates in an equilibrium of toleration. Thus toleration and justice originate in force.

### Dynamics

Giddings developed more fully the dynamic aspect of his sociology, the study of social genetics. This study requires the development of generalizations concerning the modes and mechanisms of evolution and description of the concrete process of human evolution.

External life conditions, he points out, result in the formation of social aggregations. Within the aggregation, consciousness of kind appears in like individuals and develops into association, which reacts favorably on the pleasures and life chances of individuals. As individuals become aware of this favorable reaction, the volitional process begins. Individual and social choices become important. Among the scores of relations and activities that are attempted, some appeal and are selected. But here the physical process reappears. Since the selections may be foolish and harmful or wise and beneficial, in the struggle for existence many choices may not survive. Nature will reject harmful choices, sometimes through the extinction of a society. These views, again reflecting social Darwinism, are very similar to those of Sumner, except that Giddings insists on the conscious and volitional character of choices.

Since harmful choices are rejected through natural selection, the theory of social change may concentrate on wise choices. Here we have Giddings' law: A community endeavors to perfect its type in compliance with the prevailing conception of an ideal good. (In modern sociological language, this would mean that every large-scale group is influenced by the social ideal that it accepts.) Developing this law, Giddings stresses that the bases of rational social choices are social values, which he defines as social appraisals of certain satisfactions, relations, modes of activity, and forms of social organization. The supreme object of social values is kind itself. Giddings' use of the term social value is noteworthy; it had not yet gained general acceptance.

As has already been emphasized, the laws of social choice which belong to the psychic or volitional aspect of society are limited by the physical laws of natural selection and survival. The law of natural selection is expressed in terms of the survival of the fittest; social fitness is identified with the possession of intellectual and moral qualities, including sympathy and affection. The law of survival takes the following form: those values will survive which fit into a total of values that is becoming more and more complex and harmonious. This proposition is a reformulation of the Spencerian conception of evolution, with due regard to the volitional processes so important in Giddings' theory.

Giddings' writings on the concrete process of evolution are couched in terms reminiscent of Ward's neologisms. Society, prehuman and human, writes Giddings, has passed through the four basic stages of zoogeny, anthropogeny, ethnogeny, and demogeny. Zoogenic association is a primeval social intercourse which developed the forms of animal life; anthropogenic association is the more varied intercourse which created the human mind. Organized intercourse which creates a folk is named ethnogenic association, while demogenic association refers to intercourse, both varied and organized, which develops great civic peoples. Civilization, then, corresponds to the demogenic stage of human evolution. On the basis of various choices, three types of civilization arise in historical experiment: military-religious, liberal-legal, and economic-ethical. The economic-ethical civilization appears in one of two varieties: either tireless pursuit of material ends (a dangerous course) or the social predominance of moral and intellectual goals illustrated by democracy in earlier America.

In Giddings' opinion, as in Ward's, the fact of progress should not be questioned. Objectively, progress appears in the multiplication of relationships, the increase of material well-being, the growth of population, the evolution of rational conduct. Subjectively, it can be perceived in the expansion of moral and intellectual life. This view was congenial to the intellectual climate of the late nineteenth century, when optimistic belief in progress was rarely a challenged dogma.

Giddings' genetic sociology has here been condensed to a few propositions. He himself, essaying a detailed reconstruction of man's social past, piled conjecture upon conjecture, each a plausible guess but none of them capable of proof or refutation. He answers the question "How could it have happened?" rather than "What do we know about what did happen?" It must be acknowledged, however, that this deviation from the canon of science has not altogether disappeared even in the present day.

### Giddings in Retrospect

With reference to the basic problems outlined in the first chapter, the sociology of Giddings in its early phase (until about the turn of the century) can be formulated as follows:

First, society is any number of men united by the consciousness of kind. The interplay of minds thus united gives rise to social mind, a term that approximately signifies culture. This concept, however, is only incidentally discussed as tradition.

Second, in Giddings' sociology, the unit of investigation is the *socius,* or man related to other men through consciousness of kind.

Third, the main factor determining the state of a society and of change in society is psychic; but its impact is limited by the physical conditions of human existence, especially through the processes of selection and survival.

Fourth, the problem of the relationship between individual and society is not clearly posed. Emphasis on the psychic factor seems to secure for man the role of creating and molding society, although this role is limited by the biological processes just mentioned.

Fifth, sociology is defined as the most general of the social sciences; nevertheless, it is a concrete, not an abstract science. The chief method is historical reconstruction which, in Giddings' hands, is largely a procedure of almost unlimited conjecturing, based on little established knowledge on the one hand and common-sense psychology on the other.

In the general growth of sociological theory, Giddings must be classified as one of the ablest and most brilliant of the evolutionists. Since his theory is so deeply permeated with the postulate of evolution, very little remains of it if this postulate is refuted—which, according to many scholars, is the case.

Nevertheless, certain contributions of Giddings remain. First must be cited his emphasis on the psychic component of society and culture and his demonstration of the impossibility of reaching an understanding of human society and its achievement by analogy with mechanical or biological systems. In this regard, Giddings continued a line of thought begun by Ward and developed independently by Tarde. So this line of development, culminating in the writings of Charles H. Cooley, W. I. Thomas, and Talcott Parsons, among others, can be traced back at least in part to Giddings. Second, Giddings achieved a suggestive and, to many, acceptable definition of sociology and offered sound views on the division of the science into statics and dynamics. Third, Giddings was one of the first sociologists to bring out the significance of values in the social life of man.

# CHAPTER 7

# OTHER EVOLUTIONISMS
# AND ORGANICISM

Social Darwinism and psychological evolutionism were trends of conspic-uously Spencerian inspiration, in spite of the many differences between these two schools and Spencer's theory. But evolutionism did not spring from the mind of Spencer only. Comte and Marx were in their own ways evolutionists as to some extent were many other contributors to early soci-ology. With these influences it is not surprising that there emerged during the second period of the growth of sociological theory additional varieties of evolutionism.

### Loria: Economic Evolutionism

Economic evolutionism is represented in numerous works, the most important of which is Engels' *The Origin of the Family, Private Property and the State* (see page 52), and in numerous proponents, the most representative of which is the Italian economist Achille Loria (1857–1943). In his *Economic Foundations of Society* (1886) Loria attempts to establish the thesis that the gradual decrease of free land (land not yet appropriated) is the basic factor in social evolutionary development. Loria hoped with this argument to replace with a tangible and under-standable factor the mysterious and immanent force which, in the works of the Marxists, was supposed to push society ahead.

Loria's thesis is rooted in the assumption that ancient and medieval history repeated itself in the history of the colonies in America. In both cases so long as land was free there was no division of society into classes nor such restraining forces as morals, law, or religion. With the beginning of the appropriation of land, slavery became the dominant institution. The next stage, determined by the advance of the same appropriation process, was characterized by compulsory organization of labor—serfdom in rural areas, guilds and corporations in the city. When all or most of the land was appropriated capitalism emerged, marked by the institution of free labor. Loria recognizes the many differences between the mentalities of the ancient-medieval and colonial worlds. But he argues that these differences, not having affected social development, show that the influence of psychological factors is superficial.

Loria's volume contains many other questionable assertions. In his opinion, Dante's work reflected the social and economic status of the "old families" of the Florentine bourgeoisie, Petrarch's that of the "new families," Boccaccio's that of the plebs. The various stages in the development of religion, morals, law, and the state merely reflect different stages in land appropriation. Religion and morals functioned to hold down the slaves, and were supplemented by unorganized terrorism. The suppression of serfs and artisans required a system of dual morals: one for the oppressed classes, exhorted to disregard the misery and other evils of their earthly existence; another for the upper classes, taught only not to go too far lest there be mass revolt of the plebs. The stage of capitalism is characterized by a fuller development of law and the state and by the rise of one more restraining force, public opinion.

Loria's definition of sociology is closely related to these views. Sociology is a science intermediate between economics and the sciences of law, morals, and politics. Its main task is to establish correlations between changes in basic economic conditions and alterations in morals, law, and politics. While this conception helps to bring out frequently neglected or obscure interconnections between different aspects of society—always an important task of sociology—it nevertheless makes the mistake of identifying economic phenomena with *social* relations themselves. This unfortunate identification is found repeatedly in the writings of the economic evolutionists.

### Veblen: Technological Evolutionism

Technological evolutionism is a modification of economic evolutionism and is best represented in the work of Thorstein Veblen (1857–1929). Veblen was born in Wisconsin, studied at Johns Hopkins, Yale, and Cornell universities, held various teaching positions after 1892, and in 1899 published his first and best-known volume (though only one of the many he wrote), *The Theory of the Leisure Class*. Veblen's basic theoretical views may be presented briefly.

The great agencies of habituation and mental discipline in human life are the various kinds of work by which men live and the techniques associated with work. Veblen tried to demonstrate that human social relations and culture are thus shaped by technology. Man has certain constant instincts, but the habits to which these instincts give rise vary according to the changing opportunities for expression which are provided by the material environment. In a word, man is what he does.

The evolution of society then is essentially a process of mental adaptation by individuals under the stress of circumstances which no longer tolerate previously formed habits. Readjustment is made slowly and reluctantly under the coercion of new situations. Facility in adaptation depends on the degree to which individual members are exposed to the constraining forces of the environment. Any class of the society which is sheltered from the action of the environment will adapt its views more tardily to changing situations and so tend to retard the total transformation of society. The leisure class is just such a retarding segment of the social order.

Any society may be viewed as an industrial machine, the structural elements of which are its economic institutions. There is a close correspondence between culture and the underlying technology. The feudal order was a system of trained manpower organized on a plan of subordination of men to men. In the new order of industrial society, mechanical power takes over the place of manpower. The new technology destroys the old organization of society.

Veblen's conspicuous influence on other writers—especially sociologists, historians, and economists—has persisted and continues today. However, his technological evolutionism has been much less influential than his incisive and ironic depiction of leisure class behavior and of the competitive emulation of that class by most of the rest of society. Many writers have found suggestive leads in Veblen's systematic discussions of such economic institutions of capitalism as absentee ownership, and his insistence upon the basic contrast and conflict between the predatory (business, vested interests, kept classes) and the industrious (common man, working classes) classes of society. In Veblen's mind these divisions are rooted in technological conditions. His conception of technology as being in the vanguard and leading the way in the evolutionary process found expression in the notion of culture lag developed by William F. Ogburn (see Chap. 15) and popularized by such writers as Harry Elmer Barnes.

### Coste: Demographic Evolutionism

The demographic evolutionism of Adolphe Coste (1842–1901) was not of Marxian but of Comtean inspiration. In his early years, Coste was a member of the small group of positivists, avowed disciples of Comte; later he was influenced by Loria and Durkheim. His main works are *Principles of Objective Sociology* (1899) and the *Experiences of the Peoples* (1900).[1]

---

[1] The complete French title is *L'Expérience des peuples et les prévisions qu'elle autorise.*

Coste's main contention is that one factor only determines the evolution of society: the increasing density of population reflected in types of human agglomerations. Five consecutive evolutionary stages are depicted by Coste: the borough, the city, the metropolis, the capital city, and the capital of a federation. To each of these stages in the demographic evolution of mankind correspond definite stages in the development of government, economic production, property, and various types of human associations.

Coste understood, however, that his theory did not explain everything. So he made the bold scientific decision to separate from the bulk of social phenomena those types which could not be explained genetically, namely, religion, philosophy, literature, and the arts. These areas, not susceptible to sociological analysis, should be studied by the yet-undeveloped science of ideology. Sociology and ideology, Coste reasoned, investigate two distinct classes of phenomena. On the one hand, discoveries in the realm of abstract thought and creative acts in the arts occur almost at random; on the other hand, social organization develops independently of these discoveries and creative acts.

Coste's critics have often shown that the independence of the two realms is only relative, not absolute. Nevertheless, Coste brought to sociology an idea which was later to be explored by Alfred Weber and Robert M. MacIver, among others, who distinguish between the two realms of civilization and culture and postulate different principles to explain their development (see Chaps. 18 and 20).

### Kidd: Religious Evolutionism

While Coste considered religion and, in general, all intellectual and esthetic activities of mankind independent of the evolutionary process, the English social philosopher Benjamin Kidd (1858–1916) asserted that religion is the mainspring of evolution. Of course Kidd was not the first to state the thesis that religion is the paramount factor in history. For one, the great French historian Fustel de Coulanges (1830–89), author of the classic work *The Ancient City* (1864), contended that ideas, religious ideas above all, are the mainspring of social change. Kidd, however, combined an emphasis on the religious factor with the evolutionary doctrine. In evident opposition to Comte, Kidd in his *Social Evolution* (1894) declares that reason cannot be the basic cause of progress, since reason makes man individualistic and antisocial, while evolution has been primarily social, increasing social cohesion. The only force that can account for progress is religion, endowed with supranatural sanctions and fostering altruistic morals. It is religion that unifies the generations, holds together societies, and saves civilizations threatened by grave dangers. It was religion that prevented complete social disintegration in the early centuries of Christianity; it was upon a religious basis that the greatness of the later Middle Ages was built; it was again religion in the form of Protestantism that brought about political and economic freedom. Only religion will permit further social progress. Stress on religion as the basis of progress is the theme of some authors in all ages, illustrated today for example by the works of Arnold Toynbee (see Chap. 20).

### Novicow

This cursory survey of late nineteenth-century evolutionism concludes with the views of Jacques Novicow (1849–1912) [2] who was of Russian ancestry but who spent the major part of his life in France and wrote mainly in French. His theory is formulated with great precision in *The Struggles between Human Societies and Their Necessary Phases* (1893), a conspicuously evolutionist work. Novicow agreed with the social Darwinists that struggle for existence is the central mechanism of evolution; but, contrary to their views, he believed that the mechanism itself is subject to change. In that change, he observed four necessary stages (their necessity emphasized in the title of his major work). In the first, human struggle was chiefly physiological, resulting in the extermination of the enemy. Struggle became primarily economic in the second stage, though it remained combined with many phases of physical compulsion. In the third stage, conflict took on a predominantly political character: struggle for political dominance both within states and between states. Conflict of an intellectual nature marks the final stage, sometimes taking the form of religious wars or revolutionary activity, but remaining essentially a struggle for the dominance of ideas. It was Novicow's firm conviction that the cruder forms of social conflict are gradually disappearing and that, in the final account, struggle will be reduced to intellectual competition. The latter, he argued, must result in the increase of justice and sympathy and in the decrease of hatred. This scheme was clearly one more theory of unilinear evolution toward progress. Novicow even expressed the somewhat Spencerian idea that the four phases of social evolution merely continued the line of chemical, astronomical, and biological conflicts.

In contrast to most of the other authors considered in this chapter, Novicow defined society and sociology. He conceived of society as a certain number of individuals among whom vital relationships have been established and who are conscious of their reciprocal solidarity. At the time he expressed this view, emphasis on social solidarity was quite rare. Comte's formulations were almost forgotten and Durkheim's *The Division of Labor in Society* appeared simultaneously with Novicow's book. Novicow defined sociology as the general science of society of which the concrete social sciences form parts or chapters. With slight modification

---

[2] To a certain extent Novicow can be considered also to be a member of the organismic school, but his contributions to that school are of minor importance only.

this was a restatement of Comte's original contention that sociology would absorb the concrete social sciences.

## Versions of Organicism

While the evolutionistic theories surveyed above were mainly non-Spencerian, a group of organismic theories were Spencerian though not evolutionist. The authors of this organismic school were inspired by the analogy between society and an organism—the second postulate of Spencer's system.

Paul Lilienfeld (1829–1903) was a Russian citizen of German ancestry. For seventeen years he was governor of the province of Courland (now part of Latvia) and during the last years of his life he was a member of the Russian Senate, a high judicial and administrative body. In 1897 he was president of the International Institute of Sociology. His five-volume work is *Ideas about the Social Sciences of the Future* (1873–81).

Lilienfeld asserts that human society, like a natural organism, is a real being. Society is but a continuation of nature, a higher continuation of the same forces that lie at the basis of all natural phenomena, the highest and most developed of all organisms. Though recognizing that there are also significant differences between organisms and societies, Lilienfeld draws a number of detailed analogies. Cells of an organism correspond to individuals in a society, tissues to simpler voluntary groups, organs to the more complex organizations, intercellular substance to physical environment—including even telegraph wires! Economic, juridical, and political activities parallel the physiological, morphological, and unitary aspects of an organism. Merchandise in transition is tantamount to unassimilated food. Conquering races are male, the conquered are female; their struggle matches the struggle of spermatozoa around the ovum. Persons who go from one society to another are analogous to leucocytes.

These analogies became identities in Lilienfeld's theory. In society, he claims, one finds exactly the same structures, organs, and functions as in other organisms. Therefore the conclusion is reached that sociology can be built up in no other manner than on the foundation of biology.

A much more moderate organic theory was developed by Albert G. Schäffle (1831–1903). Born in Nürtingen, southwestern Germany, Schäffle studied theology at the University of Tübingen. In 1860, he became professor of economics at Tübingen, and in 1868, at Vienna, where he remained for three years. After a brief excursion into Austrian politics, he went to Stuttgart, where he devoted the remainder of his life to study and writing. His chief works in the field of sociology are *Structure and Life of the Social Body* (1875–78) in four volumes, and *Outline of Sociology* (posthumous, 1906).

Schäffle acknowledged that his views had been influenced significantly by Comte, Spencer, and Lilienfeld. Although he agreed with Spencer that society is not in fact an organism he, like Spencer, frequently moved from analogy to identification. He stated that the structure, life, and organization of social bodies (one of his favorite terms) closely resemble those of organic bodies. Although he ascribed to the organic analogy high heuristic value, he acknowledged that organic and social bodies are not identical. The social body was for him a living individuality of higher nature, the last most complex equilibrium of forces on our planet.

Schäffle's work, especially the first edition of *Structure and Life of the Social Body,* in spite of his moderate claims contains many questionable analogies: buildings and highways are the social body's skeleton; accumulated goods are intercellular substance; economics is nutrition; exchange of goods and persons is locomotion; the technical equipment is the muscular system; symbols and communications are the functioning of the nervous system; mining and colonization and propaganda correspond to the organism's self-assertion and growth.

Had Schäffle merely presented such analogies, his work would not merit our consideration. But he had much more to say. Under the fallacious guise of organicism he helped to initiate the analysis of society in terms of a *system.* Sociology, he claims, can produce valuable results only if it conceives the totality of social phenomena as an organic whole. Replace "organic whole" with "system," and the result is an important and commonly accepted proposition of present-day sociology.

In keeping with this basic idea, Schäffle focused his study upon the most developed of the social wholes, the peoples (or ethnic groups, in modern terminology) and their communities. A people is for him a durable mass of persons, mentally linked to one another, attached to a definite territory, and capable of developing a culture. He included in his concept of society the material possessions of a people, a view that probably reflects his preoccupation with the science of economics. The sum total of those peoples who are related by communication and contact, though individually reflecting different levels of evolution and growth and possessing geographic and ethnographic peculiarities, is, for Schäffle, society.

Schäffle was keenly interested in the question of the appropriate sociological method of inquiry. This is to be based on both external and inner experience (introspection). The task of sociology is to formulate empirically knowable causal relationships in social life. The main difficulty in carrying out this task is the interference of arbitrary acts of individuals. But every purposive action, he claims, is causally determined, individual motives playing the part of cause. Freedom should not be conceived as random behavior but rather as freedom of self-expression. This is the manner in which historians explain the problems they study, and historical cases should form the starting point for sociological inductions. On the basis of a sufficient number of inductions, deduction becomes possible. In this way, a unitary genetic law can be found explaining the rise of the higher civilizations. Schäffle himself never formulated such a law but accepted implicitly a modified version of evolutionism, emphasizing natural selection in the Spencerian manner.

Another member of the organismic school, Alfred Fouillée (1838–1912), a self-educated Frenchman who never attended a university, was for many years a teacher in provincial high schools and for three years professor at the *École Normale Supérieure* in Paris. His fame derives from a series of volumes in which he expounds the idea that society is an organism, though of a peculiar type, since society is contractual. His main works include *Contemporary Social Science* (1880), *The Evolution of Idea-Forces* (1890), and *The Psychology of Idea-Forces* (1893).

Fouillée's theory is definitely organicist. He found similarities between societies and organisms closely resembling those stressed by Spencer. But Fouillée underscored a basic difference: the unity of a society depends primarily on the willingness of the individuals composing it to share the collective necessities. There can be no society without inner accord between the members, without the representation of the whole to which the individuals belong. An implicit contract exists between the members of a society, and this contract is manifested in human conduct.

The representation of the whole is a fundamental idea-force. Idea-forces are engendered by society, to be sure, but they are located in individuals. These idea-forces have their own intellectual heredity; in other words, they develop according to immanent laws. In changing, however, they influence the society in which they were engendered, a process especially apparent in education.

Organicism appears in a mild form in Fouillée's work. The theoretical writing of his compatriot René Worms (1869–1920), however, champions its most extreme form. In his *Organism and Society* (1896), Worms conceived society as an enduring aggregation of living beings, exercising all their activities in common. He lists four similarities between societies and organisms: external structures are variable in time and irregular in form; internal structures undergo constant change through the process of assimilation-disintegration; there exists a coordinated differentiation between the parts; both organisms and societies reproduce themselves. Since the organic analogy is profound and close, sociological conceptions should be developed under the same headings as the biological ones. Nevertheless, it must be recognized that society is not only plastic, better able to replace the loss of its members than the organism, but also more complex —in fact, it is a superorganism. These differences, however, are not sufficiently important to force the abandonment of social analysis in the framework of organicism.

Worms modified his view in the seventh edition (1920) of his work: "Study, experience and reflection have taught us to qualify the approval we at first gave to the organismic analogy." Societies come into existence on the same level as organisms and at first function according to the same laws. But later they advance in a peculiar human way toward an ideal constructed by the mind (justice, freedom, enlightenment). In this process emerge equality and contractual solidarity.

## Summary

The doctrines surveyed in this chapter were not complete sociological theories. Those of the first group, representing various brands of evolutionism, were primarily efforts to answer but one question: What is the principal determinant of social change? The various answers were conspicuously inconsistent with one another. But all the writers in this group agreed that there is a basic cause of evolutionary development to which other alleged determinants can easily be reduced. Novicow's theory was somewhat less monistic than those of the other writers.

The second group of theories, various versions of organicism, are chiefly attempts to answer another question: What is society? The reply that society is an organism clearly confuses analogy with identity. The views of Lilienfeld and Worms represent the most radical position, while those of Schäffle and Fouillée indicate awareness of serious difficulties in the analogy and significant differences between social and organic life, which they try to explain. Fouillée's ideas were more original than those of Schäffle, but the latter came closer to a systematic theory of society of the type now current.

Today, except for the economic brand, evolutionism in its nineteenth-century form is dead although new and modified evolutionary doctrines have appeared in very recent decades, as we shall see in Chap. 19. But since death occurred during the succeeding period in the growth of sociological theory, the discussion of the causes and circumstances of the demise will be postponed to the next part of this book.

Crude organicism declined earlier than evolutionism—Schäffle and Worms themselves substantially qualified their organic views in their later years. The death of this approach has also been complete in almost all sociological circles, though its persistence is seen in the writings of twentieth-century Oswald Spengler and a few others. In an entirely new form and in keeping with the canons of empirical science, modern functional theory (see Chap. 17) utilizes but does not rest upon the organic analogy.

This chapter, then, has dealt with two blind alleys. In the history of ideas, there have been many such dead ends. One must know the major ones to avoid mistakes already corrected.

# CHAPTER 8

# EARLY ANALYTICAL SOCIOLOGY

At the same time that evolutionism blossomed, a new analytical approach to sociology emerged. In the last quarter of the nineteenth century, four men made outstanding contributions to this trend. One among them, Durkheim, was also an outspoken evolutionist and therefore his views must be treated separately (see Chap. 9). The other three pioneers of analytical sociology were Ferdinand Toennies, Georg Simmel, and Gabriel Tarde.

### Toennies

Ferdinand Toennies (1855–1936) was born in Schleswig, the northernmost province of Germany, and spent all his academic life at the University of Kiel in the same province. In addition to outstanding contributions to sociological theory, he performed a number of excellent field studies and wrote brilliant reports about them. (In this connection, he suggested that descriptive sociology be called sociography; though the term did not win common acceptance, it is now used fairly widely to refer to a special type of quantitative field study.)

His first and most important work was *Gemeinschaft und Gesellschaft*, originally published in 1887 and subsequently in six other editions, a rare event for a study in sociological theory. In it his main contribution to theory is to be found. His later volumes (the last, *Introduction to Sociology*, appeared in the year of his death) contain many excellent ideas, but none of them has had the influence of *Gemeinschaft und Gesellschaft*. (An English translation of this book was published in 1940 under the title *Fundamental Concepts of Sociology*; this translation included a few essays from later works of Toennies.) Like many theoretical treatises by German authors, *Gemeinschaft und Gesellschaft* seems unnecessarily complicated. Its basic ideas, however, may be readily summarized.

All social relations are creations of human will, of which there are two types. The first is essential will: the basic, instinctive, organic tendency which drives human activity as from behind. The second is arbitrary will: the deliberative, purposive form of volition which determines human activity with regard to the future. Essential will, Toennies stresses, dominates the life of peasants and artisans or "common" people, while arbitrary will characterizes the activities of businessmen, scientists, persons of authority, and members of the upper class. Women and youth are inclined to display essential will, men and older people the arbitrary type.

These two modes of will explain the existence of two basic types of social groups. A social group may be willed into being because sympathy among the members makes them feel that this relationship is a value in itself. On the other hand, a social group may arise as an instrument to attain some definite end. The first type of group, the expression of essential will, Toennies called *Gemeinschaft*, the arbitrarily willed group *Gesellschaft*. In this distinction one may see a development of Comte's contrast of union and social combination. (In current terminology, the concept of *Gemeinschaft* approximates community or communal group, while *Gesellschaft* refers to association or associational society.) Toennies, in his major work, studied the following instances of *Gemeinschaft*: family, neighborhood (in village or town), and friendship group; the two large cases of *Gesellschaft* he analyzed were the city and the state.

For Toennies, the concepts of *Gemeinschaft* and *Gesellschaft* refer not only to types of human grouping but also to genetic stages of growth. *Gesellschaft* emerges through the detachment of persons and services from the framework of *Gemeinschaft*, especially when goods and services come to be bought and sold on the free market. Since Toennies clearly expressed preference for the values associated with the *Gemeinschaft* type, some authors [1] have interpreted his views on historical growth as a theory of retrogression. Toennies denied taking such a position; people, he said, die from old age, but no physician would condemn old age. In his later works Toennies recognized the possibility of reversing this trend (attempted in a sense by Hitler's National Socialism), but not by the superficial methods of oratory and romanticization of the past.

Since *Gemeinschaft* and *Gesellschaft* correspond to types of will, social relations are treated by Toennies as manifestations of these. Human wills may enter into manifold relations, with emphasis on either preservation of social order or on its destruction; but only the former, relations of reciprocal affirmation, should be studied by sociologists. Reciprocal affirmation itself varies in intensity. Thus a social state exists if two persons will to be in a definite relationship; this relationship is commonly recognized also by others. When a social state obtains between more than two persons, there is a *circle*. If however individuals are regarded as forming a

[1] Especially H. Höffding, a Danish philosopher, and von Wiese.

unit because of common natural or psychic traits, they form a *collective*. Finally, if there is organization, assigning specific functions to definite persons, the social body becomes a *corporation*. According to Toennies, all these social formations may be based either on essential will or on arbitrary will. It is, however, hard to conceive how a collective could be a *Gesellschaft* or a corporation a *Gemeinschaft*.

Toennies also presented an original classification of social norms which, although superseded today, contains a number of significant insights. Law, he held, consists of those social norms which, according to their meaning, should be applied by the courts. Moral rules are those which, according to their meaning, should be applied by an ideal judge, whether personal or divine or abstract. Concord consists of these regulations which are based on relations of the *Gemeinschaft* type and are considered as natural or necessary. Mores (*Sitten*) are rules which are rooted in customs while conventions are based upon explicit or implicit agreement which, in turn, is founded upon common aims for which the rules are considered to be the correct means. This classification of social norms, clearly enough, is closely related to Toennies' fundamental distinction between types of social groups. Law and convention are characteristic of associations, morals, and concord of communities, while mores presumably pervade both types.

Toennies' chief contribution to sociology was the introduction of a suggestive typology of social groups and even of types of society. With modifications, the distinction between *Gemeinschaft* and *Gesellschaft* is similar in certain respects to dichotomies which were subsequently developed by other writers, for example, Henry Maine's status and contract and Durkheim's mechanical and organic social solidarity (see Chap. 9). Though the dichotomy is perhaps an oversimplification of the great variations that characterize man's group life, Toennies' formulation is still used in sociological analysis.

### Simmel

Georg Simmel (1858–1918) was a German of Jewish parentage (a fact that unfortunately handicapped his university career). He studied philosophy at the University of Berlin, spent many years as a *Privatdozent* at the same university, and concluded his academic career as professor at the University of Strassburg. He achieved fame among sociologists as a spectacular lecturer and through a series of brilliant articles, published in the 1890's, though his *Soziologie*, a collection of these articles, did not appear until 1908.

What is society? Simmel's answer to this fundamental question indicates his role as an innovator of ideas and theoretical leads. Society, he stressed, cannot be understood as a psychic entity independent of individual minds; this view is a kind of mysticism or conceptualism that ascribes reality to mere concepts. But it is equally incorrect to believe that only individuals really exist; individuals as such are not social atoms, that is, the matter of which society consists. Nor is it true that reality can be identified only with the smallest units of which wholes are composed. Reality is found not only in matter, but also in that which gives matter its form. Society, therefore, is much more than the individuals composing it; in fact, society's true significance is revealed in its contrast with the sum of individuals. Society (or a group—Simmel did not distinguish clearly between the two concepts) is an objective unity expressed in the *reciprocal* relations between its human elements.

Reciprocity among men arises either from specific impulsions, which may be, for example, erotic, religious, or associative, or because of special human purposes, such as defense or play. The social sciences, Simmel argued, have so far studied only a few types of reciprocal relations, chiefly economic and political; yet there are actually innumerable varieties of interactive relations, including such everyday phenomena as looking at one another, dining together, exchanging letters, helping others and being grateful for help. Society, then, refers to individuals in their manifold reciprocal relations; its understanding requires analysis of psychic interaction.

Many reciprocal relations may not persist in time, while others are crystallized as definable, consistent situations, such as the state, the church, or even a band of conspirators, a school, an economic association. Here and elsewhere Simmel displayed an unusual gift of bringing together instances that are seemingly so dissimilar that only a few minds could have grasped those common features which served him as the basis for theoretical abstraction.

Simmel was greatly preoccupied with the concept of sociology itself. He never wrote a systematic treatise on sociology, in the belief that such an effort would be premature. The new discipline, he maintained, was in the unfortunate position of establishing by deed its right to exist. But he added, the human mind tends to create superstructures while foundations are still insecure. With this apology he set out on the task of defining the new science.

Earlier attempts to create an independent sociology, Simmel claimed, were failures because their authors established no subject matter not already treated by the existing social sciences. This claim was misleading for, as he himself had pointed out, there are innumerable types of social relations which are not studied by the concrete social disciplines. But this inconsistency had rewarding results: it encouraged Simmel to come to a novel view on the appropriate material for sociological analysis.

To be a science, he proposed, sociology must have a well-defined subject matter which must be studied by scientific methods. Each science is

defined by a central abstract concept; the diversity of these concepts permits the differentiation of sciences and the division of labor among them.
On such conceptual bases are built political science, economics, and the
sciences of the various aspects of culture. There is not, he argued, a single
social science with several subdivisions, but a series of distinct sciences.
Accordingly, Simmel rejected the pretension of many of his contemporaries that sociology should be a kind of superscience.

Sociology's central defining concept was the *form* of society. By form
he meant that element of social life that is relatively stable, that is patterned, as distinct from content, which is conspicuously variable. Abstract
analysis of social forms is a legitimate undertaking because it requires
study of the actual structure of society. Similar forms of organization exist
with quite different contents oriented to diversified interests, while similar
social interests (contents) are found in quite dissimilar forms of social
organizations. Forms such as superiority-inferiority relations, competition,
division of labor, and the formation of parties are similar everywhere despite the infinite variations of content. For any such social form, therefore,
these questions may be asked: What does it mean in its pure state? Under
what conditions does it emerge? How does it develop? What accelerates
or retards its operation? If sociology is constructed along these lines, it
will provide a new approach to well-known facts. Sociology's study of social facts will perform a function similar to geometry's analysis of the facts
of the natural sciences, for geometrical forms, like the social, may be embodied in most diversified configurations of contents.

Simmel was eager to trace clear boundaries not only between sociology and the concrete social sciences, but also between sociology, on the
one hand, and psychology, social philosophy, and history, on the other.
The social situations studied by sociology, he said, are the result of specific psychological contents in the individuals involved in social situations.
Psychology analyzes these contents but does not go beyond the individual
existences. While the latter are the bearers of society, individual motivations in themselves are not in fact societal, and their study does not
belong to sociology. Social philosophy differs from sociology in that it
includes values and goals which are not accessible to sociology as an
empiric science.

History, on the other hand, approaches a sociological focus when it
seeks historical laws. Comte's theory falls into this category and is as
much history as sociology; the same may be said of investigations which
try to prove that there is a natural tendency of political power to disperse
gradually from one to a few and then to many, or of attempts to formulate inevitable stages of economic development. According to Simmel
such efforts are doomed to failure. For the existence of historical laws
cannot be substantiated; these laws are only precursors of scientific
knowledge. Sociology, however, must discover *social* laws, that is, regularities, concerning the forms of social organization. Its task may be

achieved by comparison of similar situations independent of time and space.

Simmel was aware of the highly abstract nature of his theoretical views; therefore he frequently introduced very illuminating illustrations. For example, to make clear the differences between the psychological, the sociological, and the economic approaches (the latter representative of the concrete social sciences), he utilized the situation in which a substantial number of hitherto steady workers do not appear at the workshops. The psychologist, according to Simmel, investigates the motives and emotions behind the decisions of the individual workers to stay away from the job. The sociologist analyzes the situation as one in which two (or more) forms of association are in conflict. The economist views the episode as a labor union on strike. However concrete his illustrations, Simmel was primarily concerned with establishing the tasks of sociology as the investigation of pure forms of association in abstraction from their material contents, to depict the different types of social forms, and to state the laws according to which the members of groups interact.

Simmel understood that sociology was committed to scientific methods. The principal method, as he saw it, was to be comparative, though in quite another meaning than that given to the term by such evolutionists as Spencer. The sociologist is not directly concerned with the concrete circumstances of the cases under study, but he should try to select for study cases in which contents or interests differ while forms of interaction are the same. Simmel offered no simple formula for the process of comparison. He knew also that this method sometimes lends itself to subjective and intuitive bias.

Simmel himself was a keen participant observer, a fact made apparent in his graphic and insightful essays on conflict, on superordination and subordination, on the role of the stranger, on the modern city, and even on such a subject as the change in the group membership from two to three members. Contrary to his admonition, he often plunged into the discussion of contests—and very concretely—in his writings.

Simmel's influence on sociology has been considerable; in some measure it continues to the present day. Early in the twentieth century his views, especially on conflict and social stratification, were reflected in the writings of the American sociologists E. A. Ross and Albion W. Small and, somewhat later, in those of the distinguished contemporary sociologists Florian Znaniecki (see Chap. 18) and Howard Becker. Lewis Coser's *The Functions of Social Conflict* (1956), inspired by Simmel's insightful observations, has provoked renewed interest in the latter's work. Few would agree today with Simmel's insistence upon confining sociology to the study of social forms—and Simmel himself was a conspicuous offender of this principle. Nevertheless the systematic study of social forms as such contributed significantly to the growth of abstract sociological theory.

## Tarde

Gabriel Tarde (1843–1904) was born in Sarlat in southern France. He attended a Jesuit college and studied law at Toulouse and Paris. For twenty-five years he was a *juge d'instruction*.[2] This position confronted him with many practical problems to investigate and also afforded him enough leisure to meditate and write. In the 1880's he began a series of stimulating articles. In 1894 he was called to Paris and in 1900 was appointed professor of moral philosophy at the Sorbonne. His main sociological works include *Laws of Imitation* (1890), *Social Logic* (1894), *Universal Opposition* (1897), and *Social Laws* (1898), a brief restatement of the three previous volumes.

Tarde's sociological theory is centered around the process of *imitation*. The importance of imitation in social life had been emphasized by Bagehot many years before Tarde; it seems however that the English author was unknown to Tarde. The latter acknowledged rather his indebtedness to the great French mathematician A. Cournot (1801–77), from whom he learned the significance of the recurrence of phenomena and the importance of measuring and counting them. In one of his works Cournot had asserted that in all phenomena of life there is a manifest tendency to imitation, repetition of similar acts. (Tarde did not mention a treatise which appeared three years before his own *Laws of Imitation*, Bourdier's *The Life of Societies*, where this phrase appears: "As diffusion in a gaseous mixture tends to equilibrate the volume of gases, so imitation tends to equilibrate the social environment.")

Throughout the domain of scientific inquiry, Tarde stressed, persist three great processes: repetition, opposition, adaptation. All resemblances are due to repetition which, for Tarde, is a cosmic law almost in the same meaning in which evolution was for Spencer. Repetition appears in various forms. In the physical world it is undulance; in the biological world it is heredity; and at the psychic and social level the form of repetition is imitation. All social phenomena can be reduced, ultimately, to the relation between two persons, one of whom exerts mental influence on the other. Society itself began when man first patterned his behavior on another's.

But why is one man another's model? Tarde answered by citing the stimulation of variation, the consequence of individual initiative or invention. Invention-imitation is the basic pattern of the social process. Invention always involves some element of change; usually it is a creative association of elements already existent or a fruitful combination of repetitions (or of imitations of former inventions); the latter case is however

[2] The *juge d'instruction*, or inquiring magistrate, performs approximately the same functions as the grand jury in this country.

reducible to the former. The tempo of inventions carried out in a society is affected by the relative difficulty of combining ideas, by the level of the innate mental ability of its members, and by social conditions which may be favorable or unfavorable to inventions. Imitation then is a process through which an invention becomes socially adopted. And society is a group of men who are able to imitate one another or at least are in the possession of common traits which are copies of the same model.

Tarde tried to bring out the importance of imitation by defining its nature in four areas: philosophically, imitation is an instance of the universal pattern of repetition; neurologically, imitation is a function of memory; psychologically, imitation is reducible to suggestion (at one place Tarde states that imitation is a kind of somnambulism); sociologically, the laws of imitation provide answers to such questions as why, for example, from among a hundred inventions, are ten adopted and the others ignored? Logical laws of imitation include the propositions that individuals imitate a certain model because they think it is more useful or more in accord with others previously established, and that the imitation of models spreads from the center to the periphery of a society, but that in this process the models are modified by the refraction of the media as are light rays going through water. Nonlogical laws include the following generalizations: subjective models (ideas) are imitated before objective ones; examples set by superior persons or groups prevail over inferior ones; sometimes the past and sometimes the present prevails as a model —which in present-day terminology amounts to the assertion that at times custom (imitation of the past), at other times fashion (imitation of novel models), is accented. Tarde's theory of imitation, as this instance suggests, contains elements that have become part of contemporary sociological theory. But some of his views are unacceptable today, especially the first of his nonlogical laws; and others must be qualified, as in the case of his claim that superior models are necessarily more influential than inferior ones.

Less suggestive is Tarde's analysis of opposition and adaptation. Once again, opposition appears to be a kind of cosmic law, alleged to be discernible in mathematics, physics, biology, psychology, and sociology. Opposition appears in two forms. Opposition of *conflict* is a meeting of antithetical waves of imitation, discernible in war, competition, and polemics. War, resorted to when opposition is complete, is tending to disappear—an optimistic viewpoint common in Tarde's day. Competition characterizes economic activity, while the verbal opposition of polemics prevails in religion, jurisprudence, and science. Opposition of *rhythm*, Tarde's second form, is the tendency of social phenomena to fluctuate periodically. It is illustrated by waves of immigration, crime, the alternation of prosperity and depression, the rise and fall of empires and civilizations. Tarde's depiction of conflict and rhythm as merely different forms of the single process of opposition is highly questionable, for these two aspects of social life appear to have very little in common.

Adaptation is manifested in the law of aggregation, in the discovery of a new balance after opposition. Adaptation is preceded by a prelogical and then a logical stage of affairs; during the former, inventions are unrelated and the situation is chaotic; during the latter, inventions contradict one another and either logical duels are fought or a union takes place between competing inventions. In any case, discordance is suppressed and a new system is built up. Every new adaptation is an invention so that the process continuously repeats itself. Here the influence of Hegel's dialectics is unmistakable. Adaptation is a movement that selects a small number of realizations from a large group of possibilities. It is a movement that, in general, cannot be reversed but has no visible goal. One trend, however, is apparent. The evolution of social facts—here Tarde bowed to the evolutionism of his day—consists in their gradual shift from a host of very small phenomena to a smaller number of greater ones. As the culmination of this process one can foresee the rise of a single all-embracing civilization.

The scientific implications of his theory of imitation were never realized by Tarde. In effect, he had constructed a tool for the demolition of evolutionism. For the evolutionists, it will be recalled, considered similarities among various societies to be a decisive argument for their theory. These similarities could now be explained by imitation; and principles of imitation could form the basis for the emergence of a comprehensive theory of culture diffusion (see Chap. 20).

Tarde influenced sociology in various ways. American sociology felt his impact through the writings of E. A. Ross and others. His teaching became part of modern ethnology, and from the latter it has returned to present-day sociology. His emphasis on imitation as an individual process brought him into opposition with Durkheim, who taught that social constraint was the basic aspect of social reality (his views are discussed in the following chapter).

### Early Analytical Theories in Retrospect

A review of the theories of the three pioneers of analytical sociology shows that each has contributed significantly to modern sociological theory. Toennies inaugurated the study of basic types of social groups and suggested a system for their classification. Simmel initiated the study of types of social processes as revealed in the interaction of individuals, and many of his formulations have not yet been surpassed. Tarde was the first to provide what, according to many thinkers, is a sound basis for a theory of social and cultural change.

Yet there was almost no awareness at the time of the significance of these efforts as preparing the way for systematic sociological theory based upon empirical investigation. The pioneers of analytical sociology, in fact, disregarded one another, as had the representatives of the various brands of evolutionism. The time was not yet ripe for the achievement of the task of building a general theory of society and social change.

# CHAPTER 9

# EMILE DURKHEIM

Emile Durkheim (1858–1917) was born in Epinal, Lorraine, on the northeastern frontier of France, of Jewish parentage. It is probable that his birth in the most nationalistic section of France, his early contacts with the disaster of the Franco-Prussian War, and his identification with the strongly cohesive Jewish minority all contributed to his interest in the study of group solidarity.

After graduating from the *Ecole Normale Supérieure* in Paris, Durkheim traveled in Germany studying economics, folklore, and cultural anthropology. He was appointed professor at the University of Bordeaux in 1887 and in 1902 he joined the faculty of the University of Paris. He founded the *Année sociologique* in 1896, for many years the leading journal of sociological thought and research in France.

Comte was Durkheim's acknowledged master. Durkheim took from Comte both the positivistic stress on empiricism and the emphasis on the significance of the group in the determination of human conduct.

## The Study of Social Facts

The core of Durkheim's approach is sometimes described as sociological realism, in the sense that he ascribed ultimate social reality to the group, not to the individual. In this respect, Durkheim's views were similar to those of Gumplowicz (although he was probably not familiar with the latter's works). His theory was diametrically opposed to Spencer's individualism and nominalism. For Durkheim maintains that social facts are irreducible to individual facts.

What then is a social fact? So to designate any event that is related to society or that has social relevance is to use the term without clarity or profit. In social life there are some facts, Durkheim finds, that are inexplicable in terms of physical or psychological analysis; there are ways of acting, thinking, and feeling which are external to the individual and are endowed with a power of coercion over him. Illustrations include maxims of public morality, family and religious observances, rules of professional behavior. These realities are Durkheim's social facts that constitute the proper domain of sociological study. Social facts exist as social currents even in the absence of any clearly defined social organization, as in the case of waves of enthusiasm and indignation that grip individuals in a crowd. Such currents are truly social, for they have objective reality and a constraining effect on the individual.

Social phenomena are rooted in the collective aspects of the beliefs and practices of a group. Universality is not the distinguishing mark of social facts; a thought that is in every individual consciousness does not for that reason become social. For an important distinction exists between the two orders of fact, individual and social: certain modes of acting and thinking, performed repeatedly, become crystallized as patterns distinguishable from the particular events which reflect them. Durkheim notes that these patterns (social facts) thus acquire a body, a tangible form, and constitute a reality in their own right, apart from their particular manifestations in individuals. The latter represent social phenomena in only a very restricted sense of the term social. Since individual manifestations, however, belong to both orders of fact they are properly referred to as socio-psychological. Individual events, such as a specific case of suicide as contrasted with the rate of suicide in a group, interest the sociologist only indirectly.

For Durkheim, then, sociology is a study of social facts. Moreover, it is a study the nature of which is determined in part by its subject matter. For social facts are discoverable in two ways: first, by their power of coercion over individuals, often evidenced in the sanctions attached to various types of behavior; and second, by their general diffusion within a group. Durkheim points out that imitation is not an actual social fact, as Tarde claimed, for imitation is an individual process which, although it has social consequences, nevertheless is located in the individual as such. Imitation has generality, to be sure, but is not obligatory and therefore not social. Institutions, on the other hand, when understood as beliefs and modes of conduct established by the collective life of the group, are real social facts since they have an external existence apart from the individual and constrain him. Sociology, therefore, Durkheim concludes, can be defined as the science of institutions, of their genesis and functioning.

Social facts, Durkheim claims, should be treated as things. He observes that previously sociology had dealt more or less exclusively with concepts, not with things. Comte and Spencer, for example, devoted large parts of their writings to discussions of the course of human progress; but progress is a mental conception and not a fact that can be verified by empirical research. For Durkheim, a thing differs from a conceptual idea in the same way as that which we know from without differs from that which we know from within. According to Durkheim, "Things include all objects of knowledge that cannot be conceived by purely mental activity, those that require for their conception data from outside the mind, from observations and experiments, those which are built up from the more external and immediately accessible characteristics to the less visible and more profound." [1]

Durkheim insists that the study of social facts cannot rely upon the questionable method of introspection. No one can be sure that ideas of things correspond with the things themselves. The sociologist must seek objectivity: when he studies society he must, like the natural scientist, assume that he may be entering a realm of the unknown and the unexplored. When his research is first under way, facts can be approached by observing those phenomena sufficiently external to be immediately visible, such as religious affiliation, marital status, suicide rate, economic occupation, and the like. But these readily discernible phenomena, Durkheim stresses (and sought to demonstrate in studies of suicide and religion, as will be brought out below), are shown with more penetrating analysis to be reflections of more fundamental social conditions. Thus, for example, suicide rates may reflect the degree of social solidarity in various types of groups.

Social facts are not a product of individual human wills and hence can not be ascertained by psychological investigation. Social facts are external to the individual and, at the same time, inevitably and significantly mold human actions. The facts of individual and of collective life are therefore interrelated; but they are not coterminous. Durkheim draws a parallel situation: a living cell consists of chemical elements, but the life characteristic of the cell is distinct from and external to these elements. So, too, in every human society: each is marked by social facts distinct from and external to its individual members. Social facts, therefore, differ qualitatively from psychological facts, and their study represents a different level of analysis—a point elaborated below in the discussion of Durkheim's methodology.

To understand Durkheim's position fully, one must take into consideration the state of psychology at the time when the great French scholar lived and worked. Psychology was then almost entirely introspective and most psychologists identified psychological phenomena with conscious process. Durkheim's "sociologistic" position was therefore in part a warning against succumbing to the temptation of explaining social processes by reference to decisions of such individuals as monarchs, ministers, and generals—a type of explanation of social phenomena still in vogue. Contemporary psychology is quite different. Without surrendering to the fallacy of integral behaviorism (see Chap. 15), today sociologists generally agree that human actions are largely determined by learned behavior tendencies which form the backbone of every social order. These tenden-

---

[1] Emile Durkheim, *The Rules of Sociological Method,* 2nd ed., p. xliii.

cies have been studied and interpreted by psychologists, and reference to their findings in sociology is not only permissible but mandatory.

## Collective Forces in Social Life

Durkheim's treatment of social facts is closely related to his several discussions of collective consciousness (translating the French term *conscience* as consciousness) or collective conscience (following the alternative translation). Some elements of both meanings, the mental and the moral, are apparent in his extensive efforts to clarify the functions of collective forces in social life. Some of Durkheim's interpreters have attributed to him the conception of a collective mind as an objective reality —an untenable position from the viewpoint of modern social science— and Durkheim's terminology and many of his assertions justify this interpretation. But others claim that this extreme form of social realism was not Durkheim's intention and that his analysis of collective mental and moral phenomena approaches in some respects the modern conception of the role of culture in social life. He pursued this analysis (as well as other problems) in all of his major works.

*The Division of Labor in Society* (1893), Durkheim's initial sociological volume, is a classic study of social solidarity. In the first part of this work social phenomena in general are treated as consequences of the division of labor in society, which is taken to be an independent variable. The study makes extensive use of material drawn from the law, the aspect of social life which Durkheim considered to be not only readily observable but also the most organized form of social constraint.

Comparing archaic and advanced societies, Durkheim finds the former to be characterized by *mechanical* and the latter by *organic* solidarity. Mechanical solidarity is rooted in the similarity of the individual members of a society, organic solidarity in their dissimilarity. This distinction is similar to Spencer's conception of evolution as change from homogeneity to heterogeneity. But evolution is not the focal point of Durkheim's volume. The contrast between the two types of society, mechanical and organic, serves as a background for the study of collective phenomena.

In societies where solidarity is mechanical, there are strong states of the collective *conscience*. The latter, in this early work, is defined as the sum total of beliefs and sentiments common to the average of the members of society, forming a system in its own right. The common *conscience* possesses a distinct reality, for it persists in time and so serves to unite the generations. The collective *conscience*, to be sure, lives in and through individuals, but since it is the product of human similarities its strength and independence are strongest when similarities among individuals in a society are most pronounced. This condition prevails in archaic society, marked by mechanical solidarity; the common *conscience* almost completely blankets individual mentality and morality. In every individual, however, there are two *consciences:* one shared with the group (that is, "society living in us," a conception very similar to the present-day view of the internalization of culture); another peculiar to the individual. But under conditions of mechanical solidarity, the superior strength of collective forces is indicated by drastic reactions against violations of group institutions. Here social constraint is expressed most decisively in repressive, severe, criminal law which serves to maintain mechanical solidarity.

Organic solidarity emerges with the growth of the division of social labor. Division of labor and the consequent dissimilarities among men bring about increasing interdependence in society, and interdependence is reflected in human mentality and morality and in the fact of organic solidarity itself. As the latter increases, the significance of the collective *conscience* lessens. Thus, criminal law supported by repressive sanctions tends to be replaced by civil and administrative law calling for restitution of rights rather than punishment. (On the basis of the evidence, this claim of Durkheim, following the evolutionary style, is highly questionable.) Advanced societies, more and more marked by organic solidarity, it follows, represent moral progress stressing the higher values of equality, liberty, fraternity, and justice. Contracts, for example, become paramount. But contracts, Durkheim points out, betoken no elimination of social constraint, for they contain predetermined elements which are not negotiated by the parties and which exist prior to and independently of the contractual agreements themselves. (Contemporary labor contracts provide a good illustration of Durkheim's point: to a large extent the law, not the contracting parties, decides questions of length of the working day, wages, and physical working conditions.) Even in societies based on organic solidarity, then, social constraint continues to play a major role. In this connection it should be noted that when *The Division of Labor in Society* was written, analysis of the social limitations on personal freedom was relatively undeveloped. This has been one of Durkheim's major contributions.

The second part of Durkheim's volume deals with the causes of the increasing division of labor, stressing the key role, as he viewed it, of the growing social density (not physical) of population. This discussion, now largely outmoded, contributes little to sociological theory, although it has recently been revised in the work of Leo F. Schnore.[2]

*The Rules of Sociological Method* (1895), Durkheim's subsequent principal work, introduces a new conception of the collective *conscience.* Here Durkheim emphasizes that the aggregation, interpenetration, and fusion of individual mentalities generate a kind of psychic unit together distinguishable from individuals themselves. This collective product should not be identified with the sum of its parts: the group thinks, feels,

[2] See L. F. Schnore, "Social Morphology and Human Ecology," *American Journal of Sociology*, 63 (May, 1958), 620–634.

and acts quite differently from the individuals who compose it. Therefore analysis of group behavior should begin with the study of collective phenomena, not individuals; it follows that there is no more continuity between psychology and sociology than between biology and psychology. Sociology has its own unique subject matter—the group, a reality *sui generis*—and hence its own methods.

Social facts cannot be explained on the basis of individual psychic processes because the latter do not by themselves produce collective representations, emotions, and other group tendencies. These collective phenomena, on the contrary, exert strong pressure on individuals; attributes common to the individual members of a group are the consequence of this pressure, which may not be apparent to the individuals themselves. This formulation appears in *The Rules of Sociological Method*, in one of its aspects, as a reversal of the position taken by Durkheim in *The Division of Social Labor*. There the collective *conscience* was said to be composed of the representations and sentiments of the average man who forms the majority of a group. In *The Rules of Sociological Method*, mental and emotional similarities of the majority are derived from the pressure exerted on each of them by the collective *conscience*.

Durkheim's large monograph on *Suicide* (1897) contains, at places in the sharpest possible form, the theory of *social constraint*, which is closely related to his views on the collective *conscience*. Accepting Quételet's suggestion that quantitative techniques are useful if not essential in social science, Durkheim investigated carefully (and with considerable statistical ingenuity, for his day) suicide rates in various segments of European population. His extensive statistical analysis is used for two purposes: first, to refute those theories which purport to explain group variations in the amount of suicide on the basis of psychological, biological ("racial"), genetic, climatic, or geographical factors—and in this effort he was eminently successful; second, to support with empirical evidence his own sociological, theoretical explanation.

In the latter effort Durkheim came to the conclusion that different rates of suicide (as distinct from individual cases—a problem for psychology) are the consequence of variations in social structure, especially of differences in degree and type of social solidarity. Thus egoistic suicide, a product of relatively weak group integration, is prevalent in those groups where lack of social cohesion is marked, for example, among the unmarried and Protestants; and anomic suicide, induced by a breakdown of social norms, is encouraged by sudden changes characteristic of modern times. Durkheim also made clear that social solidarity can induce suicide, illustrated by his third type, altruistic suicide, revealed, for example, by high rates in certain primitive societies and in some modern armies. This brief sketch of a few of his findings does little justice to *Suicide*, often cited as a monumental landmark study in which conceptual theory and empirical research are brought together in an imposing manner.

Unfortunately, however, in this same work Durkheim displays an extreme form of sociological realism. He speaks of suicidal currents as collective tendencies which dominate individuals and, so to speak, catch them (or rather some of them—the most susceptible) up in their sweep. Thus the act of suicide at times is interpreted as a product of these currents. The larger significance of *Suicide*, it should be remembered, lies in its demonstration of the function of sociological theory in empirical science.

*Collective and Individual Representations* (1899), in which the common *conscience* is viewed as essentially a socio-psychological product of human interaction, adds little to Durkheim's earlier discussions. However, this work suggests a new two-sided emphasis in Durkheim's thought that continued throughout his career: on the one hand, an increasingly idealistic conception of the social group; on the other, speculation about the social or group origin of morals, values, religion, and knowledge.

Both trends are evident in *Judgments of Reality and Judgments of Value* (1911). Here Durkheim relates the collective *conscience* to social ideals, holding that a reciprocal process connects the two—social ideals bring into being the collective *conscience* and the latter in turn generates social ideals. Ideals arise from reality, to be sure, but go far beyond it; man's conception of ideal society is part of social reality and therefore requires sociological study. Religion, law, morals, and economics—considered by Durkheim as the major social systems—are at once systems of values and of ideals. Social ideals constitute the collective *conscience* as it exists independently of individual conceptions, while values are manifestations of the common *conscience* in individuals themselves. These views illustrate the new phase in Durkheim's thinking. The collective *conscience* seems to be shifted from the level of group psychology to the world of ideas, supplying the very content of the ideas of individuals. In this work there is clearly the tone, if not the intention, of the idealistic, especially Hegelian, philosophy that had impressed Durkheim in his youth.

### Social Interpretation of Religion

In *Elementary Forms of the Religious Life* (1912), the last of his major works, Durkheim brings his analysis of collective or group forces to the study of religion in its most elementary manifestations. "In this book," he states at the outset, "we propose to study the most primitive and simple religion which is actually known . . . found in a society whose organization is surpassed by none in its simplicity." He selected for intense study, though through secondary sources, the Arunta, an Australian tribe. This choice was based in part on the assumption that the Arunta represent a remote stage of evolutionary development; but Durkheim also was eager to study a case in which the whole society could be grasped and in which the internal features and institutional interconnections are experimentally observable.

Others had sought the most elementary form of religion. Spencer and Tylor, for example, had found it in the *animism* or worship of ghosts in primitive societies; Max Müller (1823–1900) identified it with *naturism* or the worship of nature's forces. But Durkheim rejected these theories, as failing to explain the universal key distinction between the *sacred* and *profane* (a distinction developed below) and because they explain religion away by interpreting it as an illusion without foundation in the world of reality. Durkheim, in contrast, took *totemism* as prevailing in the Arunta as the simplest form of religion. Totemism refers to an implicit belief in a mysterious (or sacred) force or principle which provides sanctions for violations of taboos, inculcates moral responsibilities in the group, and animates the totem itself. The latter, in the form of an animal, plant, or natural object, is a symbol of both the sacred totemic principle and of the group (clan). The life of the Arunta was sharply divided into the secular pursuits of scattered small groups (uniform, languishing, and dull) and the sacred periodic collective gatherings of the clan marked by exaltation, group euphoria, and even the breaking of taboos. Durkheim sees these collective activities as the birthplace of religious sentiments and ideas.

From study of this elementary case, Durkheim develops his fundamental theses: that group life is the generating source or efficient cause of religion; that religious ideas and practices refer to or symbolize the social group; that the distinction between sacred and profane is found universally and has important implications for social life as a whole.

The sacred, for Durkheim, refers to things set apart by man, including religious beliefs, rites, deities, or anything socially defined as requiring special religious treatment. Durkheim says: "The circle of sacred objects cannot be determined, then, once for all. Its extent varies infinitely, according to the different religions." The significance of the sacred lies in the fact of its distinction from the profane: "the sacred thing is par excellence that which the profane should not touch and cannot touch with impunity." Man always draws this distinction, however diverse his designations of the two orders in different times and places. Participation in the sacred order, for example in rituals or ceremonies, gives a special social prestige, illustrating one of the social functions of religion. Religion itself may be defined as a unified system of beliefs and practices relating to sacred things. Sacred beliefs and practices unify people in a moral community (a church in the most general sense), a collective sharing of beliefs which in turn is essential for the development of religion.

"To what do the sacred symbols of religious belief and practice refer?" asks Durkheim. Noting that they distort empiric reality, he argues that they cannot refer to the external environment or to individual human nature but only to the moral reality of society. The source and object of religion are the collective life; the sacred is at bottom society personified. This secular sociological explanation of religion (in which Durkheim grossly neglects the nonempirical nature of religion) is supported by discussions of the similarity of man's attitudes toward God and society: both inspire the sensation of divinity; both possess moral authority and stimulate devotion, self-sacrifice, and exceptional individual behavior. The individual who feels dependent on some external moral power is not, therefore, a victim of hallucination but a member of and responding to society itself. Durkheim concludes that the substantial function of religion is the creation, reinforcement, and maintenance of social solidarity. So long as society persists so will religion.

*Elementary Forms of the Religious Life* includes, in addition to his analysis of religion, the beginnings of a similar explanation of the basic forms of classification and the fundamental categories of thought itself, in which Durkheim finds these collective representations also rooted in the group life. Durkheim's venture into the social determination of classification and categories cannot be pursued here, but it should be noted that this speculative exploration brought Durkheim squarely into the field of the sociology of knowledge, today an important division of sociological study.

### Contributions to Methodology

Durkheim was keenly aware that most of the earlier social theorists had largely neglected the problem of the appropriate method to be used in analyzing social phenomena. Comte, to be sure, had dealt with method but in quite general terms, stressing the necessity of his positivistic approach. And Spencer's *The Study of Sociology*, in bringing out the possibilities and difficulties of scientific sociology, was rather vague about the methods to be used by the new discipline.

In the treatment of collective forces in social life (see page 113) *The Rules of Sociological Method* was referred to. While this volume is concerned specifically with methodological problems, Durkheim's valuable contributions to this area are dispersed through all of his major works.

To a large extent Durkheim's methodology consists in the formulation of rules to help single out social facts. First of all, in observing social facts, preconceptions must be eradicated. The sociologist must emancipate himself from the fallacious ideas that dominate the thinking of the layman. As Durkheim says, "He must throw off, once and for all, the yoke of those empiric categories which from long-continued habit have become tyrannical." Second, the subject matter of every sociological investigation should comprise a group of phenomena defined in advance by certain common external characteristics. That is, the investigator should concern himself with social facts whose existence he can infer from their external aspects. Third, the investigator must consider social facts as independent of their individual manifestations. He must go beyond individual acts and seek the permanent basis of collective habits; he must study the norms as such—for example, legal rules, moral regulations, and social conventions —in their own permanent existence.

Durkheim's main rule is derived from this independence of social facts. Since all explanations of social facts in psychological terms fail to account for the fundamental constraining effect that real social phenomena exert over man's life, the explanation of social life must be sought in society itself. Society is not a mere sum of individuals, but a system formed by the association of individuals—a specific (and emergent) reality that has its own characteristics. Consequently, Durkheim concludes, whenever a social phenomenon is explained as a direct product of psychological processes, the explanation is a false one. The source of all obligation lies outside the individual: filial piety, love, religious devotion, marital loyalty. These and other sentiments arising from social living are too often taken as causes of social facts, whereas they actually result from the pressures of social facts upon individual consciousness. Since collective life is not derived from individual life, Durkheim believes that "the determining cause of a social fact should be sought among the social facts preceding it and not among the states of the individual consciousnesses."

In discussing rules for establishing sociological proofs, Durkheim says that indirect experiment (or the comparative method) is the only method suitable to sociology. Comte's notion of the historical method is of no use, for the mere sequence of progress in development gives no cue to causality. Causation is a necessary relation between a prior and a subsequent state of phenomena and can be determined only by a comparison of the two states. For Durkheim a given effect always has a single corresponding cause. If, for example, suicide is found to have more than one cause, then the evidence points to the existence of more than one type of suicide. To explain a more complex fact, such as the existence of an institution, in any one social species, the investigator must compare its different forms not only among groups of that species but in preceding species as well.

For Durkheim, comparative sociology is not a branch of the discipline: in so far as it ceases to be merely descriptive and seeks to account for social phenomena, it *is* sociology. Valid procedure requires, however, that societies must be compared at the same period in their evolutionary development. (Here Durkheim, notwithstanding his view of the insufficiency of their methodology, tests his own procedure in part on the assumption of progressive evolution of Comte and Spencer.) But Durkheim was even more concerned to argue the merits of studying what John Stuart Mill called concomitant variation, a method which holds that if a change in one variable (for example, the rate of suicide) is accompanied by a comparable change in another (for example, religious affiliation) the two changes may be causally related directly or linked through some basic social fact (for example, the degree of social solidarity in a group). Much of Durkheim's own empirical work sought to demonstrate causal relationships with this refinement of the comparative method.

But causal relationship between social facts is but one kind of important sociological quest, as Durkheim realized. Thus he also formulated a functional approach to the study of social phenomena, an approach of considerable interest to present-day sociologists (see Chap. 17). Durkheim's functionalism was an alternative to the teleological method, as illustrated in the writings of Comte and Spencer, that assumed that social facts are sufficiently explained when their usefulness in terms of meeting human desires is brought out. But desires themselves change, a fact requiring sociological explanation. And social facts frequently persist after their original utility has been lost. Therefore Durkheim holds that, in addition to the search for the efficient cause bringing about a social fact, sociology must seek the social function it fulfills. Here Durkheim borrows from biology by assigning to function the meaning of a relation of correspondence between the fact under consideration and the needs of the organism. In social terms, the function of a social phenomenon is the correspondence between it and some general need of the society. For example, the division of labor functions to integrate modern society, though clearly it was not brought into being to perform this role nor does the integrating function of the division of labor necessarily benefit the individual. The task of functional analysis, then, is to make clear how institutions and other social phenomena contribute to maintaining the social whole. The fulfillment of this methodological task, according to Durkheim and to many modern functionalists as well, is an essential one for understanding the persistencies and alterations of the social order.

### Social Typology

Durkheim was less successful in his attempts to build up a typology of human societies. His categories do not greatly differ from Spencer's. Between the myriad patterns of human societies and the conception of humanity stands the intermediary concept of the social species. Durkheim holds that these species or types of societies are formed in much the same way as biological species, as the results of various combinations of similar units. He sees, however, two important differences between social and biological species. First, there is no equivalent in the social species to reproduction in animal life. Social species have no internal force of heredity that maintains their form in the face of pressure from external stimuli. Second, social species are difficult to ascertain; the attempt to discover social types by eliminating all variants often results in a multiplicity of indeterminate forms.

Durkheim's classification of social species rests upon the postulate that societies are composed of parts which are themselves simpler societies.

This postulate is consistent with the view of both Comte and Spencer. Societies should be classified according to their degree of organization. The perfectly simple society is taken as the basis, a species in which individuals are in atomic juxtaposition. Once this conception of the horde or single-segment society has been formulated, a complete range of social types can then be developed. One step beyond the basic type are simple polysegmental societies, unions of hordes or clans, as in certain Iroquois tribes. Next in order of complexity are polysegmental societies simply compounded, aggregates such as the Iroquois confederation. There follow the polysegmental societies doubly compounded, for example, the city-states.

This venture into classifying types of societies, though representing a task still attempted by sociologists, has had little impact on modern scholars, which cannot be said of Durkheim's other contributions.

### Durkheim in Retrospect

Although Durkheim never wrote a treatise on sociology, his theory is fairly systematic and has been highly suggestive for his successors in France and elsewhere, including leading figures in the United States today. To the main problems in sociological theory he gave clear answers.

Durkheim defined sociology as the science of social facts and of social institutions. Social facts in turn were analyzed in their capacity as constraining forces in the determination of human conduct—or, in more modern terms, as part of the apparatus of social control. In this connection, his discussions of the collective *conscience*, in spite of their variations, call attention to the ways in which social interaction and relationships significantly influence individual attitudes, ideas, and sentiments. For Durkheim, the reality of society preceded the individual life.

Durkheim's work from the vantage point of today was marred by his acceptance of certain evolutionary doctrines. Evolutionism appears, for example, in his theory of growth from mechanical to organic solidarity, in the assumption of necessary stages in social organization, in the view that contemporary primitive societies represent earlier periods in evolutionary development. It must be stressed, however, that evolutionism did not dominate or obscure Durkheim's thought. Had Durkheim removed the evolutionary scaffold, the structure of his theory would have remained.

Durkheim's treatment of social facts and the collective *conscience* combines significant sociological truths with misleading if not fallacious views. It is certainly the case that attempts to explain social phenomena exclusively on the basis of individual actions and motivations must fail. To become social facts, individual actions are subject to a process analogous to the composition of forces, in which principles are involved that are irreducible to principles of individual psychology. For example, no one wants or plans a large-scale economic depression, but time and again depressions have resulted from the composition of numerous individual actions for which there are myriad motivations. Many unintended and unwanted phenomena—depression, war, political apathy, perhaps even growing rates of neurotic anxiety—require social, not psychological, interpretation. Durkheim taught this important lesson well. At the same time he frequently, especially in discussions of the collective *conscience*, reached a degree of sociological realism that seemed to deny altogether the social significance of individual volition or decision. Society is real, to be sure, but so is the individual and the two, it should be remembered, are always in *inter*action. Giving priority to one or the other is misleading in the long run.

But Durkheim's exaggerations no doubt played a positive role in his major contributions to sociological theory and method. He showed convincingly that social facts are facts *sui generis*. He brought out vividly the social and cultural importance of the division of labor. He analyzed the nature and many of the consequences of social solidarity. He indicated the role of social pressure in areas of human activity where it had previously escaped detection. With Max Weber (see Chap. 14) he brought the attention of sociologists to the significance of values and ideals in social life. And he faced up to complex methodological problems and demonstrated by deed the necessity of empirical research for a science of society.

# CHAPTER 10

# RUSSIAN SUBJECTIVISM

The development of Russian sociology illustrates a theorem of contemporary sociology: that scientific views themselves to a large extent reflect social and cultural circumstances. During the second half of the nineteenth century, the top level of Russian society was divided into two sectors: the ruling bureaucracy supported by the majority of the landed gentry; and the intelligentsia, consisting mainly of academic and professional men, but also including substantial minorities of liberal bureaucrats and social workers from among the gentry. The ruling bureaucracy shared a conservative ideology of which Danilevsky's views may be considered a sample (see Chap. 4), while the intelligentsia adhered to Western ideologies of liberalism or socialism. At the same time there was considerable pressure on each of these groups to justify its intellectual position on a theoretical level. One response to this pressure took the form of numerous sociological theories, most of which functioned to support political points of view. One type of sociological theory still warrants our attention, the subjective school, for many years the most popular among the Russian intelligentsia.

### Lavrov-Mirtov

The subjective school was founded by Peter L. Lavrov-Mirtov (1823–1900), nobleman, artillery officer, and professor of mathematics, who in 1868 was arrested for spreading subversive ideas, exiled to a remote province, and ultimately escaped to Paris. Lavrov-Mirtov's training in Hegelian philosophy is reflected in his formulation of a dialectical triad: solidarity-individuality-progress. He held that critical-minded individuals are the agents of progress. His main works include *Sketches of Critical Philosophy* (1860); *Historical Letters* (1870); *Essays in the History of Thought* (1876); and *The Problems of Understanding History* (1898).

Lavrov-Mirtov's main discovery was the subjective method. In sociology and history, he asserted, there are some truths as unalterable and absolute as the truths of the other sciences. But in sociology and history there are other truths which cannot be discovered before certain epochs come into being, because only in certain ages are the members of a society subjectively prepared to understand fundamental questions and formulate answers to them. History does not repeat itself; the process of historical evolution is progressive, but can be perceived only subjectively. Scientific subjectivism, then, is a selective tendency in history which must be related to ethics and ideals. Although sociology itself must be teleological, its goals cannot be postulated a priori; they must be derived from an inductive study of society. Whereas history seeks to understand progress in the process of evolution, sociology is the study of the solidarity of conscious individuals. The growth of solidarity and the growth of individuality are parallel processes. Solidarity arises in animal society. It appears in the relations between mother and children. Solidarity is perpetuated by imitation and gives rise to custom, which is one of its most important supports. Individuality, the antithesis of solidarity, is nevertheless closely bound up with it, so that these two elements can be separated only analytically. Conscious individuals are products of the social process, the individual receiving his motives, knowledge, and habits from society. Since, however, in the functioning of social aggregation only individuals wish, deliberate, and act, no development is possible without the critical thought of individuals. But critical-minded individuals are always a minority in comparison with the masses. Yet the force of thought and the energy of volition are agents of historical determination. History, then, is essentially a generalization of individual biographies. The decisive role of the personality that destiny has placed in the center of each epoch, whether monarch, demagogue, or prophet, must be recognized.

Progress is not necessarily a continuous movement, but participation in progress is a moral obligation imposed on an individual who has grasped its meaning. A theory of progress is necessary for the elaboration of a program of action. Since the growth of individuality and the growth of solidarity are both essential to progress, that society will be best in which all individuals will have like interests and convictions, live under equal conditions of culture, and forbid all struggle for existence. Progress is possible only when the individuals who form the advanced minority are aware that their interests are identical with the interests of the majority. Throughout history, minorities have seldom moved in that direction; but each generation is responsible for what it could have done but failed to do.

### Mikhailovsky

The foremost exponent of the school was Nicholas M. Mikhailovsky (1842–1904). Mikhailovsky graduated from a school of mining, began his literary career at the age of eighteen, becoming later the editor of one of the outstanding Russian monthlies. He was a radical positivist, influenced by Comte and Mill. For him as for others, the basic problem of the time was reconciliation of truth and justice. The solution of this problem, he believed, required that sociology be teleological, and that the subjective method as described by Lavrov-Mirtov be followed. Sociology, for Mikhailovsky, is the science of interpersonal and intergroup relations and of the relations between the group and the individual. Though he recognized that social phenomena form an independent class of events he held that sociology, which studies these phenomena, is closely related to other sciences.

The main goal of social activity, Mikhailovsky argued, should be the struggle for individuality. In conscious opposition to Spencer, he believed that progress consists in the gradual approximation to integral development of every individual and is expressed in the decrease of the division of social labor. Everything which retards movement toward personal integration is immoral and unjust. The struggle for individuality is inherent in the very situation nature has assigned to human beings; there is continuous struggle between the individual and society. Looking at his own time, Mikhailovsky wrote that the Western workingman is no longer an independent individual because he has been degraded by the bourgeois division of labor. The Russian people might be spared this degradation by the maintenance of the agrarian communities.

In Mikhailovsky's major work, *The Hero and the Mob* (1882), the hero is viewed not necessarily as a great man but as one whose example pushes the masses toward good or evil. Great men are products of the same environment that molds the mob. Men crave ideals and readily follow those who, in offering them ideals, exemplify heroism. Finally, the hero is the man who takes that first step that has been awaited and will now be imitated by the mob. Imitation, a general law of human behavior, is commonly unconscious. Since consciousness and will are usually weak, the tendency to imitate generally gains the upper hand.

Both Lavrov-Mirtov and Mikhailovsky employed the concept of objective possibility. The individual person in social life is always confronted with a number of objective possibilities with differential chances of realization. Which of the possibilities embedded in a concrete situation will materialize is determined by a complex combination of circumstances that only rarely can be fully understood. On many occasions light-minded confidence in the easy advent of the desired possibility induces men to remain inactive and to rely on the natural unfolding of events. Of course, Lavrov-Mirtov's critical-minded individuals and Mikhailovsky's heroes do not make this error.

### Yuzhakov and Kareyev

The ideas of these authors were criticized and modified by two other members of the subjective school, Sergei N. Yuzhakov (1849–1910) and

Nicholas I. Kareyev (1851–1930). In his *Sociological Studies* (1891), Yuzhakov declared that the subjective method itself was unsuitable for sociology. However, he maintained the necessity of evaluating social developments and processes on the basis of a social ideal (which he identified with moral philosophy); on this foundation, a scientific theory of society should be built up. Rather than establishing the necessity of a particular method, he claimed, the Russian school had demonstrated an important theorem: that social development is pushed forward by personalities. For sociology to ignore this theorem is a serious mistake. But since this theorem is a substantive proposition, not a matter of logical procedure, it does not form a suitable foundation for the construction of a particular method.

Kareyev was the only academic member of the subjective school, serving as professor at the universities of Warsaw and St. Petersburg. Like Yuzhakov, he claimed that his predecessors were in error in one important proposition: rather than espousing the subjective method they should have dealt with the subjective factor in society. Similarly, he stressed *The Role of the Individual in History* (the title of one of his major works, 1890). In 1897 Kareyev published a valuable *Introduction to Sociology* in which appears an exceedingly able systematic survey of the sociological theories of his time.

Sociology was for him a *nomothetic* science seeking general laws of social life, in contrast to history which, being limited to concrete phenomena and the explanation of specific events, is *idiographic*. Kareyev also emphasized that the individual is not a passive tool of history. Great men are those possessing the ability to plan complex activities and to induce others to execute these plans. He defined progress as evolution toward a social ideal; he defined social ideal as the gradual elevation of the standards of human life and the just division of labor among men.

### Subjectivism in Retrospect

The members of the Russian subjective school concentrated on one of the basic problems of sociological theory, the relationship between the individual and society. In explicit opposition to the Marxists and Spencer, these sociologists emphasized the significant functions of the individual in the social process. They ascribed to individuals, especially of the higher type, an active role which was identified with the obligation to contribute to progress. Progress for them was quite different from what it seemed to be to most of their fellow sociologists in the West. Material advance and social differentiation had little interest for them. Their common ideal was a society of equals allowing self-expression to each of its members.

In some ways these writers anticipated or developed ideas which became identified with the discoveries of other men. Thus Lavrov-Mirtov and Mikhailovsky emphasized the role of the individual in social life and social change, perhaps before Ward's treatment of this matter. Both stressed the importance of imitation many years before Tarde and dealt with the relation of imitation to custom at about the same time as Bagehot. Their chief handicap was the fact that they wrote in Russian, so that their interaction with non-Russian sociologists was one-sided. Although Russian scholars avidly read the works of their foreign colleagues, few sociologists outside Russia were familiar with Russian accomplishments.

This school was also handicapped by the misunderstanding about the so-called subjective method. Much time and energy were spent on an essentially terminological controversy before the method was clarified and corrected by the younger members of the school, especially Kareyev. Perhaps the main reason for the collapse of the school was that it made sociology dependent upon a social ideal and emphasized value judgments as an intrinsic part of sociology. Subjectivism could not prevail against the forceful demonstration of Durkheim (see Chap. 9) and Weber (see Chap. 14) that value judgments must not intrude in the development of theoretical sociology.

However, another feature of the school might have favorably impressed Western sociologists, namely, its view on objective possibilities. In the more sophisticated form of probability, this concept reappeared in the teaching of Weber and others.

The Russian subjective school, then, did not significantly influence the development of sociology. But much of what its members said about the role of the individual in history or in the social process has current relevance and value in the construction of sociological theory.

CONCLUSION TO | *Part Three*

During the last quarter of the nineteenth century sociology was almost hopelessly divided among a number of major and minor schools. The different sociologies seemed to have little or nothing in common. What views, for instance, were shared by Loria (for whom sociology was the science of the relationships between the economic substructure of society and the moral, legal, and political phases of its superstructure) and Simmel (for whom sociology was the science of the forms of human interaction)? In Simmel's view Loria's work would lie outside the scope of sociology. Today, however, both types of interest and many others are held to be legitimate aspects of sociological theory.

Still there was one doctrine, even a dogma, shared by most of the late nineteenth-century contributors to sociology—the idea of evolution. In the majority of the theories surveyed evolution was the key concept. Even those writers who were not primarily evolutionists did not as a rule reject the doctrine. The organicists Schäffle and Worms asserted it quite explicitly. Of the analytical sociologists, Toennies underscored evolution from *Gemeinschaft* to *Gesellschaft;* Tarde an evolution leading toward the unification of humanity through imitation; and Durkheim an evolution from mechanical to organic solidarity with all its consequences. Only Simmel was outside the dominant trend; he could be indifferent to evolution since he concentrated his attention on invariant forms of social interaction.

Though evolutionary doctrine was a common element in the large majority of the theories of the epoch, it did not serve to bring about any real unity. For in each particular school or trend, evolution was defined quite differently. Spencer was alive and active throughout this period, and so was his cosmic conception of evolution. A rival view was that of the social Darwinists who turned from the process of differentiation (basic in Spencer's thought) to stress the mechanisms of natural selection and survival of the fittest, whether individuals, groups, or social norms. An even more far-reaching departure was psychological evolutionism represented in Ward's telesis and Giddings' consciousness of kind. Economic determinism was vigorously emerging; technological evolutionism, begun by early anthropologists, was strikingly developed by Veblen; more or less casual remarks of Comte and Durkheim were expanded into a system of demographic evolutionism by Coste; and Novicow performed the *tour-de-force* of finding an evolutionary trend in the very mechanism of evolution itself. Still other types of evolutionism built upon the racialism of Gobineau and the geographical monism of Buckle.

In contrast to the earlier years of the pioneers, when divergent views simply coexisted, during this second period of sociological development the variant approaches were brought to bear upon one another. Unfortunately, this interaction between different views consisted mostly of destructive criticism. A large part of the effort of the sociologists of the period was devoted to attempts to demolish the ideas of the competitors. The social Darwinists could rejoice to see their belief in the basic importance of the struggle for existence so vividly manifested in sociology itself. This harsh antagonism was in part a consequence of the very nature of the evolutionary theories. Since the theories were predominantly monistic, asserting the paramount role of one factor in evolution, every author who wished to vindicate his choice of a fundamental factor sought to prove the absurdity of the evolutionary explanations offered by his rivals. Today almost all of these quarrels are forgotten, swallowed up in the decline of evolutionism in general.

Late nineteenth-century sociology was not exclusively concerned with the vindication of the evolutionary dogma. There were other trends. Two schools, the organismic and the Russian subjective, passed away as completely as evolutionism. But early analytical sociology has proved viable and fruitful. Contemporary sociology would not be what it is without the major contributions of Toennies, Simmel, Tarde, and Durkheim. Moreover, even the work of the deceased schools was not altogether wasted: valuable insights into material of sociological relevance were achieved as by-products of misdirected research.

Of the views on the nature of society, Simmel's identification of society with men in interaction has prevailed. So has Durkheim's theorem that social facts are facts *sui generis,* irreducible to biological or psychological proportions (though today this viewpoint is not entirely beyond controversy). Toennies' dichotomy of social groups contributed to the possibility of their scientific classification and of the identification of features common to all types of societies. As a contribution toward the understanding of the role of social and cultural forces in human conduct, Durkheim's persistent quest for the functions of collective *conscience* was, in fact, important spade work of a pioneer of present-day sociology.

In addition, Simmel's emphasis on human interaction as the basic unit for sociological research has persisted. Toennies and Durkheim contributed significantly to the understanding of cooperative interaction. The social Darwinists, although they exaggerated the role of conflict, laid the groundwork for a scientific theory of antagonistic interaction. Novicow's writings were helpful in the development of a theory of conflict; and Sumner called attention to the correlation between solidarity within a particular group and antagonism toward outside groups.

To Tarde belongs the honor of having realized the great importance of imitation in social life. However, at the time he wrote, his achievement was not fully realized, in part because of the explicit opposition of Giddings and Durkheim. It will be recalled also that some of Tarde's views on imitation had been anticipated by Bagehot and by the Russian subjectivists.

Starting from different premises Sumner, Toennies, and Durkheim took the first lengthy steps in the sociological study of the normative aspect of human interaction. Sumner put forward an explanation of the transpersonal aspect of social norms; Toennies outlined a method of classifying norms from a sociological point of view; and Durkheim, using the misleading language of social realism, sought to demonstrate the basic role of group norms in social life.

The second period in the history of sociological theory was highly productive of theories about the relationship between society and the individual. In their writings Ward, Giddings, Tarde, and the Russian subjectivists revolted against the dogma of impersonal social forces that impose themselves on individuals and that compel men to be spectators rather than actors in the social scene. However, the element of validity contained in sociological realism (the ascription to society of an independent reality) was ably presented by Gumplowicz, Sumner, particularly by Durkheim, and conspicuously by the organicists (of whose work Schäffle's contribution was the most important).

Few formal definitions of sociology were offered in this period. Simmel's definition of the new science was a distinct advance over earlier ones. But the problem of definition hardly existed for the majority of the evolutionists; for them, sociology was the science of social evolution as envisioned by Comte and Spencer.

Questions of method were hotly debated, but often fruitlessly: the method likely to be recommended would be merely the corollary of the sociologist's basic theorem about the fundamental determinant of social change. Simmel, one of the most thoughtful sociologists of the time, confessed that he had no definite method to offer. The Russians thought that they had invented a new method but, in the end, they had merely emphasized the role of personality in the social process. The quantitative and the case methods advocated by Quételet and Le Play during the first period remained largely unapplied in the main stream of sociological theory until fairly recently. Only Durkheim offered a well-developed methodology, stressing the requirements of an empiric science; but his significant contributions were partly vitiated by his adherence to the language and, at times, the substance of social realism.

In conclusion, one may say that the majority of the theories surveyed in this part were one-sided or answered only a few of the basic questions of sociological theory. The organicists and Simmel were primarily concerned with the nature of society; the various types of evolutionists were chiefly interested in the prepotent factor of social change; the Russian subjectivists devoted themselves to the relationship between society and the individual. Of the sociologists of the period, Durkheim came closest to developing a systematic sociological theory which remains useful today.

# PART FOUR

# The Vogue
# of Psychological Sociology

# CHAPTER 11

# THE DECLINE OF
# EVOLUTIONISM AND THE
# RISE OF NEO-POSITIVISM

On the eve of the twentieth century evolution was a commonly accepted dogma. Its dominance transcended the realm of sociology. Under the influence of Spencer and his disciples, a number of scientists sought to discover the necessary or pre-established stages of development of particular phases of social and cultural life. They asserted, for example, that evolution of the family began with sexual promiscuity, passed through the stages of the matriarchal family (clan) and the patriarchal family (gens), finally bringing about the small conjugal family of our day. Economists sometimes claimed that humanity had evolved through the successive stages of food-collecting, hunting, cattle-breeding, agriculture, and industry. Technology was said to have moved through the three or four "ages" of wood, stone, bronze, and iron. Evolution in the legal field was described as a movement from common to individual property, from status to contract. Such sequences as magic-animism-totemism-personal deities were announced as discernible stages in the development of religion. In the realm of politics, democracy was held to be the peak of a manifestly ascending line of development. There were doubts, of course, as to the exact stages and their sequences. But the evolutionists believed that these doubts could be resolved by further study. Some sociologists and other social scientists preferred different foundations on which to build their theoretical systems, yet more often than not even these writers paid lip service to the dogma which seemed to crown the edifice of the biological and social sciences.

### Late Evolutionary Thought: Kovalevsky, Keller, and Hobhouse

Gradually, however, difficulties accumulated. Facts were discovered which did not fit into the evolutionary scheme or which stimulated social scientists to try new approaches. But some scholars, considering evolutionism to be undefeated, attempted to amend the doctrine and to give it forms making it compatible with the advance of knowledge. The teaching of three of them is pertinent to this study.

Maxim M. Kovalevsky (1851–1916), though a Russian scholar, spent the most productive years of his life in western Europe and was keenly interested in its legal and economic history. As a sociologist, he stood apart from the Russian subjective school (some of whose members bitterly complained that he ignored their views). Therefore, Kovalevsky, president of the International Institute of Sociology in 1907, can properly be considered as a prominent representative of the late evolutionary thought of western Europe.

Kovalevsky was definitely an evolutionist, but more along Comte's lines than Spencer's. He sought to establish the stages through which societies must pass by inner necessity but was inclined neither to Spencer's cosmic view of evolution nor to the identification of social and biological evolution. His work represents that type of creative synthesis of the concrete social sciences which was proposed by Ward as the central task of sociology. Several volumes published in Russian, German, and French are devoted to the economic growth of western Europe, the origin of modern democracy, and the development from immediate to representative democracy.[1] On the foundation of these studies and of other original and borrowed materials, he published two volumes of *Sociology* (in Russian) in 1910.

This study is devoted largely to the problem of working out the essential stages of social evolution. More specifically, Kovalevsky tried to identify and to correlate stages in different areas of socio-cultural life. He avoided the careless conclusion that similarities between two or more concrete developments establish a relation of evolutionary necessity between them, recognizing the possibility of imitation and cultural diffusion. He emphatically denied the ascription of priority, or supremacy, to any particular factor in evolutionary development, although, in the earlier stages of evolution, he believed, changes in the density of population were of strategic significance in stimulating further changes. He acknowledged the existence of variations or deviations from the straight lines of evolution, but he believed that their study should be postponed until sociologists had succeeded in establishing social and cultural similarities and in

---

[1] Kovalevsky's major works along these lines are *The Economic Growth of Europe up to the Rise of Capitalism* (1898–1903), *The Origin of Modern Democracy* (1895–97), and *From Immediate to Representative Democracy* (1906).

reducing them to general laws. Finally, Kovalevsky indicated that contemporary primitive societies are *contemporary* and therefore do not necessarily represent earlier stages in evolutionary growth, a fact that even today sometimes is unrecognized.

Kovalevsky's writings stand in sharp contrast to those of Albert G. Keller (1874–1956), the outstanding American representative of late evolutionism. Keller was a student, colleague, and disciple of William Graham Sumner (see Chap. 5), whose chair at Yale he assumed after Sumner's death. The latter had not worked out the relationship between the development of the mores and organic evolution, the problem Keller set for himself in *Societal Evolution* (1915), his major independent contribution.

This work is an attempt to shift evolutionism from the Spencerian variety, regarded by Keller as philosophical rather than scientific, to a Darwinian basis—in his view a task the social Darwinists had mismanaged. Thus, for Spencer's formula of change from incoherent homogeneity to coherent heterogeneity are substituted "variation, selection, transmission, and adaptation," principles to be applied to the primarily mental process of societal evolution and to the societal raw material of the mores. *Variation* is the power that sets evolution in motion, although how and why this takes place is not made clear. But the fact that customs are nowhere identical indicates the ubiquity of variations in the mores, variations that reflect group differences in mental reaction to the environment. These reactions are selective, following the paths most agreeable to men. Keller finds three types of societal *selection:* automatic selection, involving no deliberate adaptation of means to conscious goals, and revealing itself in war, class struggle, and competition; rational selection, analogous to the breeder's art and thereby giving some scope to man's ability to control the direction of change (though this scope is greatly limited in Keller's view); and counterselection, which through such practices as war, low fertility in the "better classes," late marriage, celibacy, and modern industry, permits the survival of the biologically less fit. Societal *transmission*, Keller's third principle, in view of the fact that the mores are not biologically inheritable, refers to the role of automatic imitation and artificial education in preserving the traditions of society. The processes of variation, selection, and transmission make possible, finally, *adaptation* in the mores. Each custom or institution, however outmoded or inconsistent with others (and, it should be noted, Keller was one of the first to call attention to maladjustments produced by uneven rates of change in the mores), is the result of man's adaptation to environmental conditions.

This brief sketch of Keller's application of Darwinian concepts to social evolution does little justice to the skill with which he performed his task. But his was the final major effort of this type. Sociological knowledge has grown impressively since Keller's volume was published, but few if any advances have been made along the lines of *Societal Evolution*, which suggests at least that scientific growth lies elsewhere.

The third author to be considered is the English social philosopher and anthropologist Leonard T. Hobhouse (1864–1929). Hobhouse fully recognized the failure of extreme evolutionism, especially the Darwinian variety, but hoped to salvage whatever could be used effectively in modern sociology.

From the viewpoint of empirical sociology, the most important of his works is *Social Development* (1924). Here Hobhouse attempts to formulate objective criteria of the evolutionary advance of human societies. The criteria include size; efficiency, that is, the adequate coordination of functions in service of specific ends; freedom, which is taken to be the permissible scope of independence in thought, character, and imitation; and mutuality of service, or the organization of social relations in such a way that each who serves common ends also participates in their attainment. As a social philosopher Hobhouse rejected not only the tooth and claw conception of evolutionary development and extreme *laissez faire* doctrine but advocated a modified collectivism; he believed that social evolution itself increasingly rests upon conscious control. These convictions no doubt influenced his selection of criteria of evolutionary advance. However, the application of these standards to comparative ethnographic materials represents a major effort to test hypotheses objectively (a quality also apparent in his much earlier volume, *Morals and Evolution*, published in 1906). Although the findings in *Social Development* are largely inconclusive, they do indicate, as Hobhouse makes clear, that societies may retrogress as well as advance along one or more of the four lines indicated by the criteria of human evolution.

This conclusion is consistent with the evidence produced in *The Material Culture and Social Institutions of the Simpler Peoples* (1915), a cooperative work of Hobhouse, Morris Ginsberg, and Gerald T. Wheeler. Here the authors examined the evolutionary contention that the development of social institutions is correlated with changes in economic conditions. More than four hundred societies were studied and rough statistical techniques were used in classifying stages of advancement and political, familial, and military institutions, among others. While certain correlations are evident in the numerous tables in this volume (for example, between the "lower hunters" stage and nascent political institutions), no case is established—or claimed—for either the priority of economic conditions or the regularity of evolutionary growth.

## The Empirical Challenge to Evolutionism

The late evolutionists were waging a losing battle in their attempts to patch up evolutionism. Doubts concerning the doctrine had already arisen in the nineteenth century. And many of these doubts grew out of more or less empirical studies of specific evolutionary hypotheses.

For example, one of Hobhouse's colleagues, the Finno-Swedish scholar Edward A. Westermarck (1862–1939), spent many years examining ethnographic materials in an attempt to refute the postulation of sexual promiscuity as the earliest stage in the evolution of the human family. (This view had been held by many evolutionists, for example Morgan, though a few early anthropologists such as Tylor did not accept it.) Westermarck's findings were published in *The History of Human Marriage* (1891), in which he successfully demolished the hypothesis of original promiscuity and claimed, on the basis of evidence from the life of anthropoids as well as human societies, that man was originally monogamous and that the simple paternalistic family type is the most ancient and most universal. Although modern anthropologists have given up the search for origins of institutions and produced extensive evidence showing a large variety of family systems as culturally normal, they generally agree that sexual communism marks no stage or type of human society and that all family systems, however extended, involve combinations of the nuclear or conjugal family of parents and their children.

Westermarck's refutation of primitive promiscuity was paralleled by investigations of the economic evolutionary doctrine of an original primitive communism (as accepted, for example, by Engels). Again making use of ethnographic studies, it was demonstrated that, while common ownership of land is widespread among primitive peoples, rights of private property—in tools, weapons, clothing, and the like—are also a part of their institutions. The evolutionary view of a sequence of economic stages of growth, from hunting to cattle-breeding to agriculture, was shown to be inconsistent with the known facts, one scholar (Hahn[2]), for example, deducing that the early male pursuit of game coexisted with female gathering of the wild products of the earth. Instances were discovered in which agriculture had developed in the absence of the presumed intermediary stage of cattle-breeding, as among many American Indian societies.

Evolutionary views concerning the growth of political institutions were more persistent than these economic theories. But the events of the past few decades, it should be noted, have inflicted a deadly blow on political evolutionism.

Doubts arose also as to the soundness of the methods used by the evolutionists. The latter usually assumed that they were using the comparative method, though in fact their procedure was generally one of illustration. Evidence selected from very different cultures was often brought together to bear witness to evolutionary stages; phenomena which did not fit the evolutionary scheme were declared to be survivals of

[2] E. Hahn, *Die Hausthiere und ihre Beziehungen zur Wirtschaft des Menschen* (1896).

older stages, and individual items were so classified because they did not support this or that evolutionary theory. Therefore, the reasoning of the evolutionists was frequently circular. Moreover, much of their evidence was unreliable, being based on reports of travelers and missionaries rather than of scientists. Finally, contemporary primitive culture often was *assumed* to represent earlier stages of evolutionary growth.

Conceding these errors, the evolutionists still might have maintained a modified version of their doctrine, relying on their ability to explain surprising similarities of material tools and social institutions among peoples separated by vast distances. Their explanation, however, of these similarities was that they embody stages of evolution through which all human societies must pass. This line of reasoning was challenged by the spread of knowledge about culture diffusion based on imitation.

The distinguished German geographer Friedrich Ratzel (1844–1904) in his *Anthropogeographie* (1892) had already noted cultural similarities in societies markedly dissimilar in their environmental surroundings, similarities that therefore could be explained as a consequence of contact. The latter view was consistent with Tarde's *Laws of Imitation* (1890), in which the author sought to establish the process of imitation as the motive spring of social becoming. This theory was an exaggeration, but it did serve to bring out the important role of imitation in human contacts. Early in the twentieth century, the German ethnologist Fritz Graebner published a series of studies, culminating in *Methods of Ethnology* (1911), in which he denied that there had been many independent inventions and claimed that diffusion of inventions was a widespread phenomenon. His works as well as those of several of Graebner's followers are, to be sure, marked by exaggeration and unwarranted conjectures. But the diffusion hypothesis received considerable support from a number of archaeological findings which indicated that items of material culture at least had traveled from their place of origin to surprisingly distant areas in early periods of human history. For example, marine shells and fish bones, remains of the Old Stone (Paleolithic) Age, were found far from seashores, suggesting that commerce existed between reindeer hunters and coastal tribes. Flint produced in France in the New Stone (Neolithic) Age was found in Belgium; sea shells of the same age traveled to Germany and Czechoslovakia. Wheat grown in Denmark and sheep raised there in former ages were found to have been brought from elsewhere and not to be descendants of some wild species of northwestern Europe. Obsidian used in Egypt and Mesopotamia came from Armenia and Melos; lapis lazuli found in Iran had been used much earlier in Egypt and Sumer.[3] Such facts as these were not suspected by the classic evolutionists and their discovery deprived the school of one of its last lines of defense.

[3] These illustrations have been taken from V. Gordon Childe, "A Prehistorian's Interpretation of Diffusion," *Harvard Tercentenary Publications*, vol. III (1937).

This conclusion does not mean that nothing has survived the collapse of evolutionism. Certain of its contributions continue to be useful in the structure of contemporary sociology. The investigations of the evolutionists established partial parallelisms in particular customs, beliefs, and material objects. While they demonstrated no pre-established stages of advance in spite of their monumental efforts their studies corroborate the common-sense idea that certain things come first and others later. Societies with no differentiated political organization, for example, give rise to chieftains whose position is first based on personal traits but then tends to become hereditary. Tools are simple in the beginning and gradually become more complicated. Transportation is first by foot; later, more and more complex techniques are added. Summing up, one may say that the studies of the evolutionists have confirmed the conviction that there is order in social and cultural change and have indicated that a systematic theory of change must incorporate the conception of operating causes in the historical process.[4]

The validity of these contributions largely explains the persistence of some survivals of evolutionism until the present day.

## The Roots of Neo-Positivism

The decline of evolutionism was accompanied by the rise of a new trend, which was ultimately to be given the name of neo-positivism. During the period under study three elements of this development clearly appeared on the horizon and were combined with survival of evolutionism in the later writings of Giddings. The three elements were quantitativism, behaviorism, and positivistic epistemology.

*Quantitativism* emphasizes enumeration and measurement as the method of study essential in scientific investigation in any field, including sociology. It will be recalled that this emphasis was made by Quételet (see Chap. 4) in the first half of the nineteenth century, his influence reaching sociology through biology. Quantitativism received further and stronger support from Francis Galton (1822–1911). Galton's *Hereditary Genius* (1869) and *English Men of Science* (1874) were impressive studies, largely statistical in nature, of the transmission of family traits, which, he concluded, were primarily a matter of biological inheritance, though his data equally support the opposite view that the transmission of such qualities as inventiveness and outstanding accomplishment in various fields is essentially social in nature. Galton's follower, Karl Pearson (1857–1936), published a work entitled *The Grammar of Science* (1892) which became the gospel of neo-positivism, strongly supporting quantitativism and other elements of this approach.

[4] This summary reproduces in abridged form that offered by A. Goldenweiser, "Contributions of Anthropology" in H. E. Barnes and H. Becker, eds., *Contemporary Social Theory* (New York: Appleton-Century, 1940).

*Behaviorism* in germ is contained in Pearson's work. But behaviorism made headway especially after an American psychologist, John B. Watson (1878–1958) gave it a precise and radical form in a series of publications.[5] Developing and exaggerating the ideas of the famous Russian physiologist Ivan Pavlov (1849–1936), the discoverer of conditioned reflexes, Watson asserted that "consciousness" was objectively unknowable, that introspection could not be a source of scientific knowledge, and that consequently psychology and, by implication, sociology should study only observable behavior. All human behavior, claimed Watson, could be reduced to sets of conditioned reflexes. In these could be discerned stimulus situations (specified conditions under which behavior takes place) and responses (the content of behavior thus stimulated). From this viewpoint, a sufficiently refined analysis of stimulus situations and of responses would explain all aspects and forms of human conduct. In this formulation, verbal behavior may be considered both a stimulus (of another's action) and a response. But in his study of verbal behavior a consistent behaviorist cannot take into account the meaning of words because "meaning" involves introspective observation.

*Positivistic epistemology* has its roots in the pragmatic philosophy of William James (1842–1910), and John Dewey (1859–1952), and, later, Bertrand Russell (1872–    ). But, once again, Pearson's has been the strongest single influence on sociology. Pearson strictly limited the knowable to sense impressions and their sequences. The reality of a thing, he said, depends upon the possibility of its occurring in whole or in part as a group of sense impressions. That a certain sequence of sense impressions occurs is a matter of experience to which we give expression in the concept of causation. When we are able to establish regularities of sense impressions we speak of laws, which are merely statements of regularities or recurrences. Therefore law introduces no necessity into these sequences; necessity indeed is a human conception and is only illogically transferred into the world of perceptions.

### Evolutionism and Neo-Positivism Combined: The Later Giddings

Neo-positivism's three elements, especially quantitativism and, in certain respects, behaviorism, were blended in the later writings of Giddings. (See Chap. 6 for his earlier views.) As early as *Inductive Sociology* (1901), Giddings discussed the statistical method, which he believed to be a quantitative mode of the comparative and historical method. In this work, he advocated tabular analysis, which he viewed as inexact statistics, and here and there in this volume are mathematical formulae and statistical graphs. *Inductive Sociology* also introduces Giddings' treatment of con-

[5] His *Psychology from the Standpoint of a Behaviorist* appeared in 1919.

sciousness of kind by a general discussion of the response of nervous matter to external stimuli.

In the preface to his *Studies in the Theory of Human Society* (1922)
Giddings acknowledges the need to revise his earlier position. "Logic has
abandoned . . . classifications for frequency distributions"—the quantitative stress. "Psychology has become experimental and objective. It has
discriminated between reflex and conditioning" [6]—the behaviorist emphasis. Anthropology has discovered more variations of primitive society
than the earlier anthropologists had suspected—a recognition of the
breakdown of linear sequences, in which the evolutionists (including
Giddings himself) had believed. He did not, however, discard completely
evolutionism nor give up the study of "consciousness of kind," though it
was difficult to reconcile these tasks with behaviorism. One attempt at
reconciliation appears in *The Scientific Study of Human Society* (1924),
the last major work he published: "Consciousness . . . is a name for a
physiological phenomenon and not for an ontological mystery . . . [it] is
highly integrated awakeness and attentiveness of an organism." [7] It is by
no means certain that strict behaviorists would consider such a definition
as complying with their canon.

Quantitativism greatly impressed Giddings during his final years. Returning to ideas and procedures he had learned from Mayo-Smith [8] and
referring to the work of Quételet, Galton, and Pearson, Giddings declared: "Sociology [is] a science statistical in method" and held that "a
true and complete description of anything must include measurement of
it." [9] He hoped that statistics would be applied to the study of social evolution, especially to the determination of societal types and deviations
from them. Part of his *Scientific Study* outlines certain statistical techniques, among them calculation of the coefficient of correlation, and indicates their application to social data. Summaries of the findings of a few
of his own experiments in counting and measuring social phenomena
(which, from the viewpoint of modern statistics, are grossly inadequate)
are presented, and suggestions are made for further studies along similar
lines, for example, measuring social values by examining sacrifices and
estimating social pressures by analyzing the contents of laws.

Behaviorism largely replaced the volitional psychology of Giddings'
earlier works. He described sociology as the psychology of society and
held that its subject matter is pluralistic behavior, an expression which he
coined along with the plurel. The plurel is the behavioristic counterpart of

---

[6] Franklin H. Giddings, *Studies in the Theory of Human Society* (1922), p. vi.
[7] Franklin H. Giddings, *The Scientific Study of Human Society* (1924), p. 14,
footnote.
[8] From 1880 to 1899, Professor Richmond Mayo-Smith (1854–1901) taught at
Columbia University. He is often considered to have been the first man in the United
States to teach statistics on the scientific level. His *Statistics and Sociology* appeared
in 1895.
[9] Giddings, *Studies*, p. 252; Giddings, *Theory*, p. 189.

the group, while pluralistic behavior is the response of a plurel to a stimulus situation. Responses of individuals forming a plurel may be similar or dissimilar, but pluralistic behavior has its own conditions and forms, distinct from those of individual behavior. Sociology faces two tasks: first, it should break down stimulus situations into factors which provoke pluralistic behavior; second, it should explain the genesis, integration, differentiation, and functioning of pluralistic behavior. Giddings stated this program for sociology; he did not accomplish it. But the statement itself was a testament of the aging scholar to the coming generation of sociologists, among whom were many of his students at Columbia University.

Only incidentally did Giddings allow himself to make sweeping generalizations anticipating the results of the formidable work to be performed. He did declare, however, that the study of social phenomena by the statistical method had already demonstrated that the societal process was telic as well as physically evolutionist. And he asserted that evolution was leading to progress expressed in the increase of the individual's freedom, power, and happiness.

Evolutionism, as we have seen, was rapidly becoming an almost dead doctrine. But neo-positivism was destined to win the allegiance of many sociologists, some of whose views we will consider in Chapter 15.

# CHAPTER 12

# CHARLES H. COOLEY
# AND W. I. THOMAS

In the early twentieth century, while evolutionism was waging its losing battle and neo-positivism had scarcely begun to emerge, a main trend in sociology could be called psychological sociology. This trend was represented by outstanding scholars and perhaps the most durable achievements of the period. In the United States, Charles H. Cooley and William I. Thomas were the foremost exponents and most significant contributors to psychological sociology.

### Cooley

Charles H. Cooley (1864–1929) was born in Ann Arbor, Michigan. Except for short intervals, Cooley remained in Ann Arbor all his life, studying at the University of Michigan and teaching at his alma mater. As teacher and author, he left his mark on American social science—on sociology, social psychology, and institutional economics. But he avoided departures from his life of serene contemplation, refusing, for example, a professorship at Columbia University in the hectic "megalopolis" of New York though he served (reluctantly) as president of the American Sociological Society in 1918.

His relatively uneventful life in a middle-sized Midwestern community is well reflected in the style of his writings, which are characterized by poise and by manifest attachment to the value system of the comparatively stable American agrarian society which he had known before the turbulent years of industrialization.

Cooley's major works include *Human Nature and the Social Order* (1902), *Social Organization* (1909), and *Social Process* (1918); the last, to a large extent, is a restatement of the first two. After his death, a collection of his papers was published under the title *Sociological Theory and Social Research* (1930); despite the title, only one paper of importance for sociological theory, "The Roots of Social Knowledge," is to be found in it.

Cooley's thought system represents the merger of several trends. Greatly influenced by literary figures such as Emerson, Thoreau, and Goethe (Cooley spoke of sociology as an "artistic" science), perhaps the sociologist who impressed him most initially was Schäffle, a master of the organismic school (see Chap. 7). In any case, Cooley called his own view organic, though his organicism, as will be indicated below, is not that of Schäffle or other representatives of this school.

Second, as was natural for a person whose views took shape in the last quarter of the nineteenth century, Cooley was an evolutionist of a kind. The first of his major works opens with the phrase, "If we accept the evolutionary point of view . . ." And twenty years later, he began an article on heredity and environment [1] by noting: "We have come in recent years to look upon all questions from the evolutionary point of view." Notwithstanding these assertions, evolutionism in the strict meaning of the term is hardly to be found in Cooley's works. He was more concerned with the evolution of the individual social being, the social self, than with the growth of the total historical process. When he discusses history, it is with a view to its relation to the development of the social self, with no concern for identifying stages of social evolution. In the article cited above he states his views on history in this picturesque fashion: "History appears to flow in two rather distinct channels. Perhaps there is a stream and a road running along the bank, two lines of transmission. The stream is heredity or animal transmission; the road is communication or social transmission. One flows through the germ plasm; the other comes by way of language, intercourse and education. The road is more recent than the stream." This article was written in the mid-twenties, its author taking a position consistent with the cultural point of view which was then gaining momentum in American sociology.

Although he was disinterested in the study of the grand evolutionary sweep of history, Cooley shared the contemporary faith in the beneficent outcome of the on-going process. His belief in progress is implicit in all his writings and is frequently expressed explicitly as in the following passage: "The evolutionary point of view encourages us to believe that life is a creative process, that we are really building up something new . . . , and that the human will is a part of the creative energy that does this." [2]

Third, Cooley was influenced by the psychologically minded sociologists of his day. Although he did not cite Ward very often in his writings, Cooley's two lines of transmission—the genetic and cultural—could have

[1] Charles H. Cooley, "Heredity and Environment," *Journal of Applied Sociology*, X, 4 (March–April, 1926), 303–07.
[2] Charles H. Cooley, *Human Nature*, rev. ed. (1922), p. 50.

been derived from Ward's conception of genesis and telesis. Tarde, on the other hand, was quoted by Cooley at several points, and some of Tarde's views were painstakingly incorporated in *Social Organization,* though he decried Tarde's one-sided emphasis on imitation. Moreover, Cooley followed closely new developments in psychology, as is indicated by frequent references to the works of William James, James M. Baldwin, and J. Stanley Hall. Cooley explicitly rejected William MacDougall's instinctivism and gave little attention to Watson's behavioristic theory.

Fourth, in sharp contrast to the canons of emerging neo-positivism, Cooley thought and wrote as an idealist. He conceived of social reality as consisting of men's personal ideas of one another and construed the basic sociological task to be the study of social relationships as reflections of ideas, attitudes, and sentiments. This viewpoint is to be seen in his organic approach.

### Cooley's Organic Theory

The focal point of Cooley's sociology is his organic theory. In *Social Process,* he states without qualification that society is an organism. His organicism, however, is not Spencerian nor did he, like Schäffle and others, search for infinitely detailed organismic analogies. Society, for Cooley, is a living whole made up of differentiated segments, each of which has a special function. It may also be considered as a complex of forms or processes each of which is living and growing by interaction with the others, the whole being so unified that what takes place in one part affects all the rest.

Cooley's organic view stresses both the unity of the whole and the peculiar value of the individual, explaining each by the other. "A separate individual is an abstraction unknown to experience, and so likewise is society when regarded as something apart from individuals . . . Society and individuals do not denote separable phenomena, but are simply the collective and distributive aspects of the same thing" (*Human Nature,* pp. 36–37).

One of Cooley's major preoccupations was the resolution of what he viewed as pseudo-problems on the foundation of his organic theory. In his time, the question of the priority of heredity or environment in the determination of human behavior was sharply debated. Cooley answered: "When our individual life begins, the two elements of history, the hereditary and the social, merge in the new whole and cease to exist as separable forces . . . Heredity and environment . . . are, in fact, abstractions; the real thing is a total organic process" (*Human Nature,* p. 15). He considered discussion about the ultimate or relative importance of heredity or environment to be as futile as the debate concerning the dominance of mind over matter or vice versa. (He referred to social or public mind and seemed to believe that mind is an organic whole made up of cooperating individuals. This view is, of course, a dangerous approximation to the organismic theory.)

An organic theory of society, in Cooley's meaning, should bring out as clearly as possible the relationship between the individual and society. His writings concerning this relationship, a fundamental sociological problem, are somewhat disappointing (except for the discussion of primary groups, as noted below). Society, he says, is more than the sum total of individuals. The unity of society coincides with the unity of the social mind; the latter is constituted not by agreements among individuals but by organization. But in his attempt to explain the nature of organization, Cooley had little to add to the statement that it consists of "the differentiated unity of mental or social life." He believed it to be valueless to attempt a more elaborate definition: "We have only to open our eyes to see organization" (*Social Organization*, pp. 4–5).

Cooley returned to the question of organization in his discussion of institutions. Here again his treatment is rather vague. "An institution is simply a definite and established phase of the public mind. The various institutions are not separable entities, but organized attitudes of the public mind, and it is only by abstraction that we can regard them as things by themselves." At this point, however, Cooley reveals that his approach to society is not only organic but also psychological: "It is in men and nowhere else that the institution is to be found" (*Social Organization*, pp. 313–14).

Cooley's organic theory is, of course, incompatible with sociological monism, which involves the selection of a particular factor, social or nonsocial, as the basic determinant of the state or the development of society. His views on this subject are clearly expressed in a paper delivered in 1903:[3] "The organic view of history denies that any factor or factors are more ultimate than others. Indeed, it denies that mind, the various institutions, the psychic environment have any real existence apart from a total life in which all share in the same way that the members of a body share in the life of an animal organism."

## THE SELF, THE PRIMARY GROUP,
## CLASS AND CASTE

Cooley's organic theory and his psychological orientation are reflected clearly in his treatment of the development of human personality. He stressed the role of primary groups (discussed below) and social interaction, especially communication, in the genesis and growth of personality. Thus "self" develops within a context of social relationships: "Self

[3] As a rejoinder to Giddings' paper entitled "A Theory of Social Causation," *Publications of the American Economic Association*, Third Series, V, 2 (May, 1904), 182–87.

and other do not exist as mutually exclusive facts . . ." Self is *social*, Cooley emphasizes throughout his major works. In *Human Nature and the Social Order* he presented the influential concept of the reflected or "looking-glass" self, marked by three principal elements: the imagination of our appearance to the other person; the imagination of his judgment of that appearance; and some sort of self-feeling, such as pride or mortification.

This formulation and his more extensive discussions of the social nature of self indicate again Cooley's philosophical idealism—the "imaginations" we have of one another "are the solid facts of society"—and illustrate his extreme subjectivism. At the same time, his exploration of social self and of its dependence on social interaction represents an important anticipation of the present-day cultural approach to the study of personality.

Similarly, Cooley's analysis of the primary group is a major landmark in the growth of social science. Primary groups are characterized by intimate, face-to-face association, direct cooperation and conflict, a relatively free play of personality and of sentiment. The family, play group, and intimate neighborhood were of greatest interest to Cooley, but he recognized the ubiquity of primary (or, as it is often put today, informal) groups in all social organizations. These intimate collectivities are *primary*, he brought out, because they are the nursery of human nature, providing the individual with his earliest and most complete experience of social unity, and because this group experience gives rise to universally found social ideals, such as faith, the spirit of service, kindness, obedience to social norms, and also the ideal of freedom. Only through primary groups can these ideals develop, and as they spread through the greater society they become the marks of progress and democracy.

The latter view illustrates the intrusion of Cooley's personal convictions in his social analysis, a characteristic that is apparent in most of his work. Nevertheless his depiction of the nature and functions of primary groups not only opened up a new and important field of inquiry but represents a substantial contribution to the typology of social groups, an area first investigated by Toennies. But Cooley's distinction between primary and secondary groups was an independent innovation.

The most important of the more inclusive social groups for Cooley are social classes and castes. He recognized the universality of social stratification and its functional implications for society, stressing that inheritance and competition account for, respectively, the presence of some elements of caste and open class in all societies. In this connection, he anticipated the work of Robert E. Park and his present-day successors, especially W. L. Warner, by noting the "caste" aspects of ethnic group structure in the United States. His analysis of stratification, once more, is combined with his personal values: strong sympathy for the lower classes and faith in the increasing development of an open-class society.

SUMMARY AND PERSPECTIVE

Cooley's contributions and place in the history of sociological theory can be summarized as follows:

First, Cooley never offered a formal definition of society, but he insisted that society is both an organic whole and a psychic entity. He called his view organic, but today his basic theorem is one of the main premises of leading exponents of functional theory.

Second, he emphatically denied the existence of any single determinant of the state or development of society. He never singled out a specific unit of society, except the primary group, for sociological analysis. This is perhaps one of the major handicaps of his writings, which are attractive but rather vague.

Third, Cooley's treatment of the primary group remains an outstanding contribution to both sociology and social psychology. The primary group is today commonly a major category in classifications of types of social groups.

Fourth, although he stated his propositions in terms of an idealistic epistemology which verged on solipsism, Cooley's position on the problem of the relation between the group and the individual foreshadowed the view commonly accepted at the present time. Contrary to Spencer, who asserted that the individual is basic and the group only the sum total of its members, and contrary to Gumplowicz and Durkheim, who gave the group primacy over its individual members, Cooley maintained that neither the individual nor the group has primacy in sociological analysis, that there is rather an interactive process of mutual influence between group and individual.

Closely connected with this position, Cooley's insights into the nature of the social self, together with the similar conceptions of his contemporaries, James, Baldwin, and G. H. Mead,[4] suggest an important cumulative development in social science, since they are nearly akin to later theories of Dewey, Thomas (see below), MacIver, Willard Waller, and others. Moreover, Cooley's emphasis on the role of social interaction in personality formation foreshadowed such current views as the psychodynamic position in psychology and the culture-personality approach in anthropology.

Fifth, as we have seen, Cooley's treatment of class and caste also anticipated later large-scale developments in sociology. Though not as precise, his theory of institutions as the working out of permanent needs of human nature is very similar to later functional formulations. In the case of economic institutions, Cooley's discussion of their social and cul-

---

[4] Mead's analysis of "I," "me," and "other," which are similar to Cooley's discussions of the "social self," have had an especially strong and lasting influence and are reflected in what today is known as the "symbolic interaction" orientation in sociology and social psychology. See especially George H. Mead, *Mind, Self and Society* (Chicago: University of Chicago, 1934).

tural ramifications gave added force to the growth of the institutional economics of Veblen, Walton, Hamilton, and others.

Sixth and finally, as a methodologist Cooley advocated and practiced sympathetic understanding, holding that empathy is essential in any sociological investigation, a view somewhat similar to Max Weber's stress upon *verstehen* (understanding) (see Chap. 14). Although he was a keen observer of the group life around him, especially children's play groups, he was inclined to rely upon "just seeing things," grasping them by intuition. This practice, as we shall see, places Cooley, methodologically, close to the phenomenological school in modern sociology (Chap. 21). However invalid from the viewpoint of the requirements of empirical science, what Cooley "saw" he communicated to others, oftentimes with great skill.

## Thomas

William I. Thomas (1863–1947), the other leading exponent of psychological sociology, worked independently of Cooley. There seems little doubt that, of the two, Thomas has made a deeper impression on the thinking of the modern architects of sociological theory.

Born in Virginia, Thomas studied at the University of Tennessee and at the universities of Berlin and Göttingen, Germany. During these earlier student years he was not interested in the social sciences. But in 1893 he became a graduate student of sociology in the department of sociology newly established at the University of Chicago. The following year he began teaching at Chicago and continued his work there until 1918, when he resigned for personal reasons. From 1923 to 1928 he taught at the New School for Social Research in New York and, later, for one year (1936–37), he accepted the position of visiting professor at Harvard University. The intermediate years and the last years of his life were spent in independent research and writing.

Thomas' main works include *Source Book of Social Origins* (1909), which, considerably modified, was published again in 1937 under the title *Primitive Behavior; The Polish Peasant in Europe and America*, written in collaboration with Znaniecki (five volumes, 1918–21); *The Unadjusted Girl* (1923); and *The Child in America* (1928), in collaboration with his wife, Dorothy Swaine Thomas. After his death, the Social Science Research Council created a committee to collect Thomas' contributions to social theory and social research; the result was the publication of *Social Behavior and Personality* (1951), edited by Edmund H. Volkart.

### METHODOLOGY

"Thomas did not write a final synthesis presenting his ideas in a systematic manner." [5] Therefore, his theoretical system must be reconstructed

[5] E. H. Volkart, introduction to *Social Behavior and Personality* (New York:

from his mature work. This is not an easy task, since many of his views changed during the long years of his active life. He was responsive to new ideas when they appeared on the scientific horizon, although he never surrendered himself to any one of them. During one period he was under the spell of psychoanalysis, but subsequently he rejected Freudian formulations as being as fallacious as the theory of Nordic superiority.

Despite his changes in viewpoint, Thomas never doubted that social theory, a term he used to cover both sociology and social psychology, must be scientific. It was urgent, he said, to develop more exact and systematic study of human behavior on a scale and with a method comparable to those of the physical and biological sciences. This plea, of course, is not the same thing as advocating the adoption by social theory of generalizations or laws established by natural sciences, a position Thomas rejected. However, if sociology is to become scientific, he argued, it must apply the type of reasoning used in the natural sciences to social reality itself.

Since the quest for causal relationships between phenomena is paramount in all science, valid social theory must consist of laws demonstrating necessary relations between units of social reality. Such theory is essential for social analysis. This is the central theme of the famous study *The Polish Peasant,* in which Thomas argues that the fundamental units of social reality are attitudes and values (their nature and interrelationship will be discussed below).

As the years passed, Thomas became less and less confident in the possibility of finding social laws of this sort. In his later works he took the view that the sociologist should be satisfied with inferences of lower certainty than laws. Increasingly influenced by modern statistics (and probably by his wife, herself a prominent statistician), he substituted the goal of probabilities for laws, noting that when the total situation is complicated, the interrelations are numerous and measurement is necessary.

In one of his papers, Thomas took a position which, at face value, rejects altogether the causal approach to the study of social phenomena. It is essential, he said, to give up the idea of "causation" in favor of an approach which seeks specific consequences of specific antecedents. Thus he formulated the main question in the field of personality and culture: "Individuals differentiated in what ways and placed in what situations react in what patterns of behavior, and what behavioral changes follow what changes in situations?" (p. 296). Behind this statement, however, there seems to be a misunderstanding that has recurred in the history of empiric science, including sociology. This misunderstanding involves the unwarranted identification of the causal approach with the search for "the cause" of a given phenomenon. To find the cause, as Thomas stated, is im-

Social Science Research Council, 1951), p. 1. Unless otherwise indicated, the page references to Thomas' writings in the following paragraphs refer to quotations reproduced in this volume.

possible. But if the sociologist can formulate a system of propositions an-swering such questions as were posed by Thomas, these propositions will certainly have causal relevance.

In his late years, Thomas considered various techniques which would help the sociologist approximate scientific goals. Among diverse research procedures, he insisted on the necessity of using control groups in the study of the statistical frequency of social phenomena, for example, speci-fied factors in rates of criminal behavior. Today the use of control groups is common procedure, but it was not in the days when Thomas was press-ing for the adoption of this method in social research.

## THE SITUATIONAL APPROACH AND
## THE STUDY OF ACTION

Thomas' doubts about the applicability of the causal type of reason-ing arose, at least in part, because, in the construction of his own social theory, he chose one of the most difficult approaches, one focused on the action of the individual in a social situation. "The study of the situation," he wrote in 1931, "the behavior in the situation, the changes brought about in the situation, and the resulting change in behavior represent the nearest approach the social scientist is able to make to the use of experi-ment in social research . . ." (p. 88). Thomas selected the situational ap-proach only after pondering other possibilities.

On the one hand, he was impressed by the fact that experiment is the principal tool of advance in the natural sciences, and hoping for similar advance in social science he sought the best possible substitute for ex-periment. On the other hand, Thomas rejected many approaches used by sociologists of his day. In his formative years he had accepted, as did so many of his contemporaries, the evolutionary formula, but he soon aban-doned it. He had no use for racial theory or any theory purporting to ex-plain social facts in biological terms (though frequently he referred to the biological background of human action). He also rejected various particu-laristic approaches, including Tarde's imitation, Durkheim's social con-straint, and Giddings' consciousness of kind. But he was deeply impressed by behaviorism. Thomas often quoted Watson and used almost inter-changeably the terms situational approach and behavioral approach. Nevertheless, he never accepted the main contention of behaviorism, namely, that human action is scientifically explicable without reference to the minds of the actors on the social scene.

However, Thomas chose behavior, and later especially adjustive be-havior, as the central concern of his sociological theory. Action in a social situation, he held, is the social fact to be explained. The social situation (often referred to as the total situation) consists of three interrelated ele-ments: objective conditions, which include socially enforced rules of behavior; pre-existing attitudes of the individual and of the group; the definition of the situation by the actor himself, influenced, however, by the group.

In *The Polish Peasant*, the second of these elements is emphasized, since Thomas and his collaborator, Znaniecki, believed at the time that they were writing this work that causal relationships can be established between attitudes and values. Of the two concepts, that of value had already been developed, though along somewhat different lines, by Durkheim and Max Weber (see Chap. 14). But Thomas and Znaniecki attempted to refine the concept of value so that it would be more useful in social theory, and they brought into their theory the concept of attitude. In the frequently cited Methodological Note in *The Polish Peasant*, the two concepts are given rather cumbersome definitions: "By social value we understand any datum having an empirical content accessible to the members of some social group and a meaning with regard to which it is or may be an object of activity . . . By attitude we understand a process of individual consciousness which determines real or possible activity of the individual in the social world . . . The attitude is thus the individual counterpart of the social value; activity, in whatever form, is the bond between them" (pp. 49–50). In subsequent works, Thomas defined attitude and value more simply: attitude is the tendency to act, representing a drive or wish; value represents the actor's object or goal. Still later, Thomas combined the two concepts in the phrase attitude towards value.

Substitution of the later definitions for the earlier brings out clearly the views of the authors of *The Polish Peasant* about the causal relations between attitudes and values. Their main theorem is that the cause of an attitude or a value is never an attitude or a value alone, but always a combination of attitudes and values. This is why men do not react in the same way to the same influences. They illustrate this theorem (rather inadequately perhaps) by citing the case of two sons living under the tyrannical rule of their father but reacting differently. If for one son the value of solidarity is strong, the attitude of submissiveness may evolve; if the other holds individualistic values dear, the attitude of revolt may gain the upper hand.

Thomas never discarded entirely the concepts of attitude and value, but in his later works they do not have as prominent a part as in *The Polish Peasant*. But even there he did not study attitudes and values in isolation from the context of the total situation. The total situation, we have already noted, includes objective elements, of which values themselves are a crucial part. Among these are rules of behavior, that is, social norms by which the group maintains, regulates, and makes more general and frequent types of action defined as desirable. Established systems of such rules form social institutions, and the latter in turn make up social organization. Social organization, a normative system, is the proper subject matter of sociology. Sociology, focusing upon values, is thereby differentiated from social psychology, the general science of attitudes (or of the subjective side of culture). The two disciplines together are said to form "social theory."

Objective conditions, the first of the three elements of the total situation, in Thomas' view, were practically identical with the rules and institutions which mold a person's attitudes and, consequently, his definitions of situations. "The definition of the situation," noted Thomas in one study, "is begun by the parents, . . . is continued by the community . . . and is formally represented by the school, the law, the church" (p. 8). At the same time, however, the definition of the situation, as the point of view of an actor when coming to a decision to act, is also depicted as the third element of the total situation. The latter always contains subjective factors (attitudes). Behavior can be understood only when it is studied within its whole context—the situation not only as it exists in verifiable, objective form, but also as it *seems* to exist to the person himself. The latter subjective factor must never be discounted in social analysis since, to cite Thomas' well-known theorem, "if men define situations as real they are real in their consequences" (p. 81).

## INDIVIDUAL AND SOCIAL DISORGANIZATION

Analysis of human conduct is complicated by the fact that, in Thomas' theory, in addition to the personal definition of the situation, there exists, as we have seen, a culturally or socially defined situation, and the two definitions are in complex interaction. In stable society, the two are highly consistent and action is easily predictable. But in cases of crisis, which may be social or quite personal (based on new acquaintanceship, change in the environment, or other disruptions), the strength of social definitions is weakened.

In the case of individual behavior, two phases of this process may be observed: vagueness and indecision, followed by "crystallization" when the individual begins to control his new experience. When the influence of social rules upon individuals becomes weak, social disorganization takes place.

Social disorganization is by no means an exceptional phenomenon; in some measure, it is present in all societies at all times. But during periods of social stability incipient disorganization is largely neutralized by group activities which reinforce the power of existing rules. The stabilization of group institutions is thus a changing or dynamic equilibrium of processes of disorganization and reorganization. However, this equilibrium may be disturbed so drastically that attempts to reinforce the existing rules can no longer succeed. In this case, new norms of behavior and new institutions better adapted to the new demands must be developed: this is the process of social reconstruction. If reconstruction is to take place, it is essential that some of the members of the group do not become individually disorganized during the period of social disorganization.

This conception of disorganization and of the group as a dynamic equilibrium presented in *The Polish Peasant* is quite similar to some of the basic theorems of Pareto's *General Treatise on Sociology* (see Chap. 13), which had appeared a few years earlier. However, there is no reason to believe that Thomas and Znaniecki were influenced by the Italian sociologist, since the views outlined above were expressed in embryo by Thomas as early as 1906.

## THE FOUR WISHES, TYPES OF PERSONALITY, PERSONAL DOCUMENTS

Thomas' preoccupation with the subjective aspect of action in a social situation led him to introduce two additional sets of concepts and to suggest and to try a new technique for gathering sociologically relevant facts.

The first of these sets of concepts includes the four wishes, which, without valid reason, are sometimes thought of as a major or even essential part of Thomas' sociological theory. Thomas held that "every individual has a vast variety of wishes which can be satisfied only by his incorporation in society." He postulated as the four fundamental wishes, representing observable general patterns, the desires for new experience, for security, for recognition, and for mastery. This listing appears in *The Polish Peasant,* but in *The Unadjusted Girl* the wish for mastery is replaced, without explanation, by the wish for response.

Thomas never succeeded in formulating clearly the relationship of the four wishes to attitudes, nor did he incorporate the wishes into his general conceptual scheme. He describes the wishes as the motor element, the starting point of human activity in society, but this seems to be a function of attitudes as well. At one point Thomas holds that the wishes are neither exhaustive nor biologically instinctive, but he lets it be understood that the wishes correspond in general to the nervous mechanism. In any event, whether one wish or another tends to dominate behavior in this or that person is explicable on the basis of temperament which, in its turn, seems to be a chemical matter, dependent upon secretions of the glandular system. This line of reasoning, in certain respects similar to Pareto's theory of sentiments and residues (see Chap. 13), is, at least, inconsistent with Thomas' firm rejection of biological explanations of personality and of social phenomena and blurs his otherwise strong emphasis on the decisive influence on behavior of culture and personal life-experience.

The second set of additional concepts refers to three types of personality. Thomas depicts these three types as the philistine, the bohemian, and the creative personality. The philistine's attitudes are so stabilized that formation of new attitudes is almost precluded; he is the conformist. The bohemian's personality is characterized by unstable and unrelated attitudes that make the individual susceptible to a variety of influences; bohemians show a high degree of adaptability, but this adjustment is always provisional. The personality of the creative man is settled and organized, but involves the possibility and even necessity of growth, because his attitudes include the tendency to change implicit in planning of productive activity. Thomas explained that the three types do not exhaust the variations of human personality; they are ideal types (a term probably borrowed from Max Weber) and, in concrete fact, all individuals, though in different proportions, manifest traits of each of the three.

While, in general, personality is molded by life experience in the framework of the social definition of the situation (culture), the creative individual is able to influence culture by means of invention. Thomas did not, however, accept the great-man theory of invention. His view on this matter is illustrated by a statement taken from one of his earlier writings: "The individual mind cannot rise much above the level of group-mind [a term by which, at that time Thomas meant, roughly, culture], and the group-mind will be simple if the outside environmental conditions and the antecedent racial [6] experiences are simple. On this account it is just to attribute important movements and inventions to individuals only in a qualified sense" (p. 221). This position is now commonly accepted by theorists of social change.

The three types of personality and the four wishes were developed at some length in *The Polish Peasant,* but in later years they were more or less completely discarded by Thomas himself, though they continued to be utilized by a number of other authors in spite of this desertion by their original author. Thomas' introduction of a novel research technique, on the other hand, began a significant trend in social-science investigation.

The new technique involved the use of personal documents, such as letters, diaries, and especially life histories or autobiographies written at the request of an inquirer. (Recently documents of this type have been aptly called "biograms." [7]) A single life history constitutes a large part of one volume of *The Polish Peasant,* and other personal documents were employed extensively in this work. Thomas and Znaniecki explained that such documents give invaluable insight into the interplay of attitudes, values, and objective conditions in a social situation.

The significance of *The Polish Peasant* is not limited to the concepts, theorems, and procedural suggestions that we have reported. Equally important is the fact that this research represents the first large-scale attempt to apply general concepts of modern anthropology to the study of rapidly changing culture and social organization of advanced societies. Numerous

[6] In later works, Thomas would not have used the term "racial" in this context; he probably meant "group."

[7] See T. Abel, "The Nature and Use of Biograms," *American Journal of Sociology,* vol. 53 (1948).

works using a similar approach have enriched contemporary sociology, for example, the well-known *Middletown* volumes (1929, 1937) by R. L. and H. M. Lynd and the *Yankee City* Series by W. L. Warner and his associates. (See Chap. 17.)

But Thomas had a larger concern than illustrating how sociology can utilize the approach commonly employed in ethnology: the study of *total* cultures. The *Source Book on Social Origins* (1909) stresses the principle that, in analytical studies, no phenomenon can be completely understood when separated from the whole structure of which it is a part, and no culture can be comprehended when its elements are considered in isolation. In *The Polish Peasant* he emphasized the necessity of taking into account the whole life of a society in all social analysis. This viewpoint today, of course, is commonly held by cultural anthropology and sociology alike.

## SUMMARY AND APPRECIATION

Thomas' conceptual scheme and methodological theory attracted so much attention for many years among American sociologists that, in 1937 and 1938, an unusual event took place. A round table discussion of *The Polish Peasant* was arranged by the Social Science Research Council and the results were published as the Council's initial volume [8] in a series of studies of methodological problems.

The main critic, Herbert Blumer, pointed out that, although Thomas and Znaniecki had set out to establish laws, they had actually proposed very few; that the concepts of attitude and value are vague; that the two concepts overlap inasmuch as both include meaning, and therefore no causal relationship can be established between them; that the authors did not in fact use the methodology they had worked out; and that their interpretation of the personal documents employed in the study is subjective, not really scientific.

Thomas agreed that concrete material had not been adequately correlated with the methodological scheme, and that no social laws, but only statements of a high degree of probability, had been formulated. Thomas' admission was in conformity with the views he had acquired during the twenty years that had passed since *The Polish Peasant* was published. Znaniecki, moreover, acknowledged that the authors had treated attitudes and values as constant elements (which may be questioned) and that many years passed before he recognized this methodological error.

A summary of the round-table discussion by Read Bain brings out further evaluations of work. For example, the conceptual scheme consisting of attitude, value, wishes, personal types, and definition of the situation, according to some, is incapable of producing laws of social change.

[8] H. Blumer, *Critique of Research in the Social Sciences: I* (New York: Social Science Research Council, 1939).

The theoretical interpretations of the authors, it was noted, had not been derived from the personal documents or otherwise empirically supported. But it was acknowledged that some subsidiary theories, for example the view of social disorganization, have proven to be helpful in further research.

These criticisms of *The Polish Peasant* are well taken. But they do not, of course, offer a satisfactory explanation of the place of Thomas' writings in the growth of sociological theory. What were Thomas' answers to the fundamental problems of sociological theory as stated in Chapter 1? They may be summarized as follows:

First, Thomas never defined explicitly the nature of society. Instead, he held that social organization is composed of institutions, which, together, constitute a system of rules imposed by social groups on their members. He employed the term culture to designate the material and social values of any group of people.

Second, society and culture must be analyzed in terms of their fundamental unit, which, for Thomas, is social action. The latter consists of action of an individual in a social situation determined by the objective conditions, the attitudes and values of the actor acquired during his life experience, and his definition of the situation.

Third, the relationship between society and culture and personality is one of reciprocal influence, personality receiving from culture the major part of its attitudes and values within the framework of social organization, but also influencing culture and social organization. In this connection creative personalities play a prominent role; nevertheless, their influence is limited by the cultural conditions which they face.

Fourth, there is no prepotent determinant of the state of society and culture or of their changes. Differences in behavior and in culture are the result of differences in the life experience of various groups as well as of differences in psychological interpretation of such differences (the consequences of human definitions are real and important).

Fifth, sociology is defined as the science of institutions. But sociology must be supplemented by social psychology, the science of attitudes or the subjective aspect of culture. The methods of both sociology and social psychology must be scientific, based on the same logic as the natural sciences. The subject matter of sociology, however, is unique, as is the case of every science, and consequently particular procedures must be used. The most appropriate procedure is revealed in the situational approach, the analysis of conditions which determine the actions of individuals in total situations. More particularly, the combined effects of the differentiation of individuals and of situations, including changes in them, must be established; whenever possible, this method must involve measuring the impact of variations in factors and using control groups. To understand the integration of different factors in the individual's life, personal documents are invaluable.

These, then, are the principal elements in Thomas' theoretical writings. In historical perspective, which of them have contributed most to the growth of sociological theory? It may be too soon to undertake such an assessment, but the following points seem clear:

First, Thomas was one of the earliest sociologists to reject the evolutionary doctrine and, with Cooley, one of the most convinced and convincing opponents of monistic theories which interpret society, culture, and their changes on the basis of some one factor.

Second, concurrently with Pareto, but independently of him, and early neo-positivists, Thomas underscored the necessity of using scientific procedure in sociology. His own work illustrated both the possibilities and difficulties of empirical social research. The now commonly used method of comparing an experimental group with a control group is due in part to Thomas' suggestions.

Third, Thomas was one of the earliest promoters of a persistent trend in contemporary sociology which may be termed normativism. This trend stresses the central significance of norms or rules of conduct in society, norms which exert "moral pressure" on the actor. However, Sumner's work (see Chap. 5), containing the same emphasis, was already available to serve as a source of inspiration before Thomas' major writings appeared.

Fourth, Thomas enriched the theoretical treasury of sociology with several important concepts, among which social situation, definition of the situation, and social disorganization have proven to be durable acquisitions. The distinction between attitude and value, in spite of its lack of preciseness, illustrated the basic problem of treating both subjective and objective elements in the analysis of action, a problem reflected, for example, in MacIver's more recent discussions of attitude and interest (see Chap. 18). The latter concept is closely akin to Thomas' "value," which, in turn, has some affinity with value as dealt with earlier by Durkheim and Max Weber.

Fifth, Thomas was one of the earliest promoters of what may be called the principle of integration, that is, the insistence that social phenomena must be viewed in the context of total cultures. *The Polish Peasant* has shown the way to a number of studies of modern societies of this type. Today this principle is a central part of the functional approach in sociology and cultural anthropology.

Sixth and finally, Thomas called attention to the fundamental importance of the study of the relationship between personality and culture. He insisted that the main problem to be solved in social theory centered around the interdependence of the individual and social organization and culture. This problem continues to be of major concern to sociology, social psychology, and anthropology.

Notwithstanding these significant contributions, Thomas' views contain some dangerous elements, dangerous in their potentiality for leading sociology into a blind alley. In Thomas' formulation, the basic unit of sociological study is not interaction, but the action of the individual in a social situation. Thomas persistently emphasized that the social situation is in part objective in nature. But his emphasis on subjective factors (together with a trend originating with Max Weber, as will be seen in Chap. 14) has encouraged some contemporary American sociologists to overstep widely the conventional demarcation between sociology and psychology; they have identified social theory with the theory of action (or with part of that theory), whereas action heretofore has been one of the central themes of psychology. Thus, for some sociologists, their discipline has become primarily concerned with the motivation of human behavior. This concern results in a blurred objective for sociology, since there seems to be no tendency to abandon the long-standing problems of the field pertaining to socio-cultural structure and change.

As we have seen earlier, several of Thomas' formulations are subject to criticism. The four wishes, for example, though Thomas himself dropped the conception, became for a time in the hands of some authors a kind of stereotype to explain behavior, yet neither Thomas nor his followers could establish specific functions of the different wishes under specified conditions. Thomas' three personality types, which also have been carelessly used by a few writers, were essentially literary rather than scientific concepts. The distinction between attitude and value is not clear-cut in Thomas' treatment: each appears to be both personal and social, subjective and objective, preventing the establishment of causal relationships between them.

However, these weak points in Thomas' theory have been exposed largely on the basis of developments in social science which have taken place years after his own landmark work, especially *The Polish Peasant*, was published. Indeed, Thomas himself brought out some of these criticisms in his later years. They cannot be used as a yardstick for measuring the value of his accomplishments. For Thomas was a bold scientific explorer, with few peers in American sociology. Sociological theory and research will long be in his debt.

# CHAPTER 13

# VILFREDO PARETO

Psychological sociology can be as diversified as psychology itself. This proposition is illustrated when the theoretical thought of Thomas is compared with that of Vilfredo Pareto.

### Pareto and His Writings

The distinguished Italian sociologist Vilfredo Pareto (1848–1923) was born in Paris; his father was Italian, his mother French, accounting for his bilingualism. He returned to Italy at the age of eleven and, after classical studies, graduated from the Polytechnical Institute in Turin. For a few years he was employed as consulting engineer by a railway and later on was a superintendent of iron mines. In the course of these occupations, he developed an interest in economic problems. In 1882, he came into an inheritance which enabled him to devote the remainder of his life to study and research.

Pareto published some excellent papers in economics which led to his appointment as professor of that subject at the University of Lausanne in 1892. In the course of the next few years, his contributions to mathematical economics were outstanding. Shortly after the turn of the century, he published *The Socialist Systems*, at that time perhaps the most detailed and profound study of the subject. Shortly thereafter, he began his major work, the *General Treatise on Sociology*, published in 1915 simultaneously in Italian and French. However, the First World War was not a propitious time for the launching of a treatise on theoretical problems; Pareto's study remained unnoticed until some years later.

The *Treatise* contained some caustic statements about democracy (which Pareto knew mainly in its somewhat distorted French and Italian forms). These portions of his work attracted the benevolent attention of

Benito Mussolini who, once in power, offered Pareto a seat in the Italian Senate. To his credit, it may be claimed, Pareto declined this offer.

In 1936, an English translation of the *Treatise* appeared under the title *Mind and Society*. In many regards, it was superior to the original: all quotations were tracked down to their sources (a matter which Pareto had neglected) and an excellent index was compiled, highly useful because of the diffuse and unsystematic character of the *Treatise*. This translation accentuated the wave of interest in Pareto which had started in the United States in the late 1920's. The vogue was especially strong among certain scientists of nonsociological training, notably Professor L. J. Henderson of Harvard University, a physiologist, who stimulated the interest of younger sociologists in Pareto's theory, among them Parsons and George Homans (see Chap. 18).

### Sociology and Its Methods

Pareto's approach to sociology is first of all characterized by his insistence on its scientific (empiric) nature. The *Treatise* contains numerous biting remarks about the pseudoscientism of Comte and Spencer and scathing references to the secular "religions" of progress, humanity, and democracy. If it is to avoid these nonscientific pitfalls, Pareto holds that sociology should use a "logico-experimental" method [1] based entirely on observation and logical inference, presumably according to the strict canon of induction as stated by J. S. Mill. In Pareto's opinion, the experimental (observable) world consists of things and relations that can be perceived by sense organs and usually can be measured.

In the *Treatise*, however, Pareto treats at length of phenomena which do not belong to this "experimental world" but nevertheless play a large part in social life, such as ideas, abstractions, opinions, beliefs, and sentiments. He conceived his main task to be the reduction of such phenomena to observable facts belonging to the world of reality as he defined it. He consequently warns against merely verbal procedures: "natural sciences were never built up by studying and classifying the terms of ordinary language, but by studying and classifying facts. Let us try to do the same for sociology" (No. 396).[2]

Pareto also insists that scientific procedure must explain the unknown by the known. Therefore the past is better explained by the present than the present by the past, a principle often violated in sociological monographs and textbooks. Finally, he stresses that the fundamental concepts of a science must be precisely defined and its theories formulated in precise terms. It is dubious, however, whether Pareto's own treatise complies with these methodological premises.

[1] In French and Italian, the term experiment connotes also controlled observation.

[2] In compliance with Pareto's desire, quotations from his *Treatise* are made by reference to the numbered paragraphs therein.

## The Social System: Its Structure and Dynamics

Pareto's most important contribution to sociological theory is his conception of society as of a system in equilibrium. This formulation allows sociology to forsake crude organicism without abandoning certain of organicism's sound propositions.

If society is a *system*, it is a whole consisting of interdependent parts; change in some part affects other parts and the whole. The "material points or molecules" of the system, according to Pareto, are individuals who are affected by social forces which are marked by constant or common properties. The state of a social system at any given time is determined by the following conditions: first, the extrahuman environment; second, other elements exterior to the society at the time, including other societies and the given society's previous states; and third, inner elements of the system, namely, interests, knowledge, and "residues" and "derivations" which are manifestations of "sentiments." Of these determining conditions, only the residues and derivations are submitted to a detailed study by Pareto.

In this general formula of equilibrium no place seems to be given to such cultural phenomena as law, politics, religion, or art. But lack of explicit treatment does not mean that Pareto failed to recognize their importance. They all play their part in maintaining social systems, but, in his view, only inasmuch as they manifest basic *sentiments*. The role of sentiments is then essential in the maintenance of social equilibrium.

For Pareto, society is a system in equilibrium. This means that there exist, within every society, forces which maintain the form (or configuration) which the society has achieved or which guarantee even and uninterrupted change; in the latter case the equilibrium is dynamic. An important corollary follows: if the social system is subject to pressure of outward forces of moderate intensity, inner forces will push toward the restoration of equilibrium, returning the society to its undisturbed state.[3] These inner forces consist chiefly of the sentiment of revulsion against anything that disturbs the inner equilibrium. Without this sentiment, every incipient alteration of the social system would meet little or no resistance and could grow with impunity. This situation may in fact occur, but its likelihood is minimized by the sentiment of resistance regardless of the number of individuals directly affected positively or negatively by the proposed changes.

This theorem of the restoration of equilibrium of social systems has been confirmed, to some extent, by the study of social reaction to crime, of the outcome of revolutions, and of the impact of war on societies. In these cases, as well as others, a large amount of evidence indicates the

---

[3] More exactly, in Pareto's theory, equilibrium is defined by the presence of forces eventually restoring it.

frequently temporary nature of social upheavals and the persistent quality of fundamental social arrangements.

The analysis of inner forces is based on the distinction between logical and nonlogical action. According to Pareto, an action is logical if its end is objectively attainable and if the means used are objectively united with the end in the framework of the best knowledge available; all other actions are nonlogical (which does not mean that they are illogical, or contrary to logic). Presumably logical actions are rather rare. In Pareto's treatise appear only a few examples, including the formulation of scientific theory, economic action (which by no means, in fact, is always logical), and the behavior of trial lawyers. But even judicial activity is nonlogical because the role of the judge involves more than the mere logical application of abstract legal rules to concrete cases. Pareto argues that judicial decisions to a great extent manifest the sentiments of the judges (which they share with other group members) and that reference to written law is an ex post facto explanation of a decision gained in another way. "Court decisions," he writes, "depend largely on the interests and sentiments operative in a society at a given moment; and also upon individual whims and chance events; and but slightly, and sometimes not at all, upon codes or written law" (No. 466). This illustration is one of many used by Pareto to demonstrate his basic theorem: the predominance of nonlogical action in social life.

Nonlogical action is related to residues and derivations. Both of the latter are manifestations of sentiments which are indefinite but seemingly basic biopsychic states. Although Pareto admits that these states are not directly knowable, he indicates the presumably specific nature of their expression in residues, derivations, and human conduct. Pareto seems to believe that the sentiments are instincts or innate human tendencies; for example, he names one of the most important sentiments "the instinct of combination." On the other hand, he admits that residues are correlated with the changing conditions under which human beings live, that actions in which the sentiments express themselves reenforce such sentiments and may even arouse them in individuals lacking them, that sentiments are engendered or stressed by the persistence of groups and, in their turn, may help such groups to survive. These qualities are not properties of innate and immutable instincts but rather characteristics of learned behavior. The theory of learned behavior was just being developed in psychology in Pareto's day, a fact, no doubt, accounting in part for the ambiguity of his terminology.

Some of the sentiments, according to Pareto, urge men to justify their actions by formulating nonlogical theories which their advocates consider to be highly logical. Examination of these "theories" reveals the distinction between deep, constant, and therefore important elements, the *residues,* and superficial, variable, and therefore less important elements, the *derivations.* Residues can be discovered by studying diverse statements bearing on the same subject and abstracting from them the constant elements. Knowledge of the residues which are closer to the sentiments than the derivations permits deeper penetration into the causation of human actions. Yet residues are also manifestations, and ultimately causation must be sought in the depths of the sentiments. However conjectural or questionable this particular formulation, we must agree with Pareto that to explain actions by accepting at face value what men say about their behavior is, of course, a procedure void of scientific validity—a principle long recognized by students of human life.

Pareto emphasizes the difference between his view of human actions and rationalistic explanation. The latter assumes that men first think, first formulate ideas or theories, and then act accordingly. In Pareto's opinion, behavior follows the reverse process: commission precedes rationalization. For example, he concludes the discussion of popular doctrines of the emergence of private property by declaring: "A family, or some ethnic group, occupies a piece of land . . . The fact of the perpetuity of occupation, of possession is in all probability antecedent . . . to any concept of law of inheritance" (No. 256). For Pareto, there is no direct causal relationship between theory and action. Both are caused by basic sentiments which are revealed in action in a rather constant manner, but in theory or justification, sentiments are manifested almost at random. Every mode of conduct is justified by some theory, to be sure, but in each concrete case the theoretical justification is determined by the accident of invention and therefore is of no great importance in analyzing behavior. This conclusion is another major theorem of Pareto's sociology.

According to Pareto, there are six classes of residues (and several subclasses in each): one, the instinct of combination, the faculty of associating things; two, the residue of the persistence of aggregates, the conservative tendency; three, the residue of the manifestation of sentiments through exterior acts (among them, the formulation of justifications; in simple terms, self-expression); four, the residue of sociability, or the drive to compose societies and to impose uniform conduct; five, the residue of personal integrity, leading to actions that restore lost integrity, such as those forming the source of criminal law; six, the sexual residue. In social life, these residues may combine in different ways. For example, through a combination of the residues of equilibrium and of group persistence compound forces of great social importance are built up, corresponding to vigorous and powerful sentiments of the type vaguely designated by the term "ideal of justice."

Pareto's classification of residues is nowhere explained or justified. Class six, the sexual residue, is heterogeneous and logically would seem to require a complement, like hunger. Classes three to five are related to the tendency of social systems to remain in or to restore a state of equilibrium. Classes one and two are shown in their distribution among people, as indicated below. A great admirer of Pareto concedes that this classification was "the spade work of a pioneer." [4] Although additions and improvements to this spade work have been suggested, it seems improbable that scholars will attempt to develop this phase of Pareto's work because of its conspicuous shortcomings.

Pareto's classification of residues is in part based on his study of material taken predominantly from classic authors. He held that a great literature roughly reflects actual life, that concentration on classic literature precludes bias, and that since the residues remain constant universal propositions can be derived from careful analysis of classic literature. (Notwithstanding these claims, in his writing newspaper releases were interspersed among selections from the classics.) Each item selected from these sources was first interpreted as the manifestation of a particular sentiment; then the individual items were compared and large numbers of similar items were formed into classes and subclasses. This procedure (hardly a forerunner of present-day content analysis used in the empirical study of communications, though similar in purpose) is the closest approximation to the inductive method to be found in Pareto's work.

Pareto's analysis of derivations is less detailed than his treatment of residues. Derivations, as pointed out above, are conceived as surface manifestations—as explanations—of underlying forces in social life. Pareto first considers derivations from the viewpoint of the subjective character of such explanations and thereafter outlines four principal classes of derivations: one, derivations of assertion, including affirmations of fact and sentiment; two, derivations of authority, whether of individuals, groups, custom, or divinities; three, derivations that are in accord with (and therefore serve to maintain) common sentiments and principles; four, derivations of verbal proof, for example, various metaphors and analogies. Pareto's many illustrations of these different kinds of verbal explanations of conduct show the categories to be overlapping. However, there is no close connection between the classes of residues (outlined above) and of derivations; each crosscuts the other.

### The Circulation of Elites

In Pareto's view, although the residues are common to all societies and times, they are unevenly distributed among individuals, and their relative frequency in various societies and epochs is subject to change. Social change, as it is related to the first two classes of residues (the instinct of combination and the persistence of aggregates), is discussed at length. This study results in the formulation of the theory of the circulation of *elites*, which forms one more basic theorem in Pareto's sociology. Elites consist of individuals of highest performance in their respective fields. There are two principal classes of elites: a governing elite comprising

[4] L. J. Henderson, *Pareto's Sociology: A Physiologist's Interpretation* (1935), p. 58.

individuals who directly or indirectly play an important role in the manipulation of political power; and a nongoverning elite consisting of capable men not in power positions. The differential distribution of residues among the members of elites is much more important for social affairs than their distribution in the masses.[5] Depending on the dominance of residues respectively of class one and class two, two types of men are depicted, designated by the terms *speculator* and *rentier*.[6] When the governing elite is dominated by speculators, society is subject to relatively rapid change; when rentiers dominate, change takes place slowly. Pareto holds that a natural tendency exists for the elites of the two types to rotate in positions of political power. When an elite of one type has ruled for some time, superior elements accumulate in the governed classes and, conversely, inferior elements develop in the ruling classes. Consequently, an elite consisting, say, of speculators commits mistakes which open the way to ascent of rentiers; but after the latter are consolidated in power positions, they also commit mistakes, opening the doors for the speculators.

A cyclic theory of social change is thus introduced, the two phases of the cycle being characterized by the dominance respectively of conservative or of progressive attitudes. History, therefore, asserts Pareto, "is a graveyard of aristocracies" (No. 2053). This theory, which closely resembles Saint-Simon's view of the necessary recurrence of organic and critical periods, is illustrated from ancient history and classical literature. But illustration (as we noted in the case of Spencer's theory) is not systematic demonstration. In absence of the latter, there seems little reason to ascribe universal validity to this theory on the basis of Pareto's work itself.

It should be noted, however, that Pareto's analysis of the circulation of elites (and quite apart from the larger context of his work) has had a lasting interest among social scientists concerned with the nature and functions of the "ruling class" and other elite groups. This concern is represented, for example, by Saint-Simon, Pareto's compatriot and contemporary; Gaetana Mosca, author of the still influential *The Ruling Class;* and such present-day scholars as Harold D. Lasswell, the late C. Wright Mills, T. B. Bottomore, and Suzanne Keller. Pareto's views about elites, although largely "intuitive" and out of keeping with his own scientific admonitions, continues to be a source of stimulation for both political scientists and sociologists.[7]

[5] This is a point of view which especially appealed to the Fascists.

[6] *Rentier* connotes in French a person seeking security and therefore investing his savings in bonds (*rente* in French).

[7] See especially James H. Meisel, *The Myth of the Ruling Class: Gaetona Mosca and the Elite* (Ann Arbor: University of Michigan Press, 1962); Harold D. Lasswell, *et al., The Comparative Study of Elites* (Stanford: Stanford University Press, 1952); T. B. Bottomore, *Elites and Society* (New York: Basic Books, 1964); Suzanne Keller, *Beyond the Ruling Class: Strategic Elites in Modern Society* (New York: Random House, 1963); and S. E. Finer, *The Sociological Writings of Vilfredo Pareto* (New York: Praeger, 1966).

## Summary and Appreciation

What, in summary, are Pareto's answers to the fundamental problems of sociological theory? He conceives society to be a system in equilibrium, the material reference points of which are individuals who are exposed to a limited number of so-called forces. These forces, first of all sentiments and residues, determine the condition of the social system. In this conception, the role of culture seems to have little place.

The basic unit for sociological analysis, in Pareto's scheme, is a single manifestation of these persistent underlying forces. Analysis should be primarily concerned with residues, themselves manifestations of unknowable biopsychic phenomena.

For Pareto, the problem of the relationship between individual and society is an aspect of the general problem of the relation between part and whole in any system. His viewpoint on this question is essentially functional: any changes in parts of a system affect the whole, and vice versa.

The latter view is consistent with Pareto's rejection of any version of sociological monism which would reduce explanations of social life to single factors or causes. Nevertheless, he outlines a limited number of factors which he believes determine the state of society and social change. In the case of change, he stresses the nature and distribution of specified residues, or tendencies to act in certain ways, in the ruling elite. Changes in elites seem to occur by immanent necessity.

Pareto does not define the relationship between sociology and the other social sciences. But he insists that sociology must be based on the logico-experimental method, a method requiring disciplined observation and logical inference from such observation. His strong admonitions in this respect are weakened by his own inclination to substitute the collection of others' statements about facts for observation itself and to forsake inductive procedure for seemingly intuitive classification schemes.

These characteristics help to make the study and interpretation of Pareto's theoretical writings exceedingly difficult. His *Treatise,* to be sure, contains a large number of plausible propositions about various phases of social and cultural reality which represent a source of suggestion and hypothesis in present-day study of social structure and change. Yet relatively little use has been made of Pareto's work in this respect, notable exceptions being the landmark research in industrial sociology, *Management and the Worker* by F. J. Roethlisberger and W. J. Dickson [8] and some very recent theoretical analyses of elites.[9]

[8] F. J. Roethlisberger and W. J. Dickson, *Management and the Worker* (New York: Science Eds., 1964). This study of a Western Electric Company plant at Hawthorne, Illinois, makes use of Pareto's equilibrium theory especially; see particularly pp. 272 (note), 567–68.

[9] For example, Bottomore, *op. cit.,* especially Chap. 1, and Keller, *op. cit.,* especially Chaps. 1 and 10.

Pareto's main contributions are the insistence (though not the practice, as we have seen) that sociology must be governed by strictly scientific canons and the conception of society as a system in imperfect equilibrium. With respect to the latter conception, Pareto's propositions concerning the tendency of social systems to restore disturbed equilibrium, the various factors contributing to the condition of social systems, the significance of nonlogical action in social life, and the intermittent nature of social change, marked by successive periods of slow and rapid alterations, are suggestive formulations which approximate observable conditions.

Much less useful is Pareto's analysis of inner forces operating in social life, especially the reduction of these forces to residues. In the final account, Pareto's explanation (a derivation itself?) of social facts rests on a biopsychic theory of something closely akin to instincts. Today we know that any such explanation of individual or social behavior is misleading because of the ubiquitous role of cultural and institutional factors in human conduct.

But even if we identify Pareto's sentiments and residues with learned behavior rather than with instincts, his procedure in establishing these forces is highly questionable. In the first place, to quote the philosopher F. S. C. Northrop, "instead of being the first-hand psychic states given immediately to the trained introspective psychologist," Pareto's psychic traits are "second- or third-hand characteristics assigned to people . . . who, at the time Pareto makes his 'observations,' exist only in his imagination . . . Not once in getting his 'facts' does Pareto leave the armchair in his study." [10]

In the second place, Pareto set for himself the difficult task of sifting presumably fundamental residues from innumerable and admittedly deceptive derivations. The accomplishment of this task requires the identification of derivations associated with "the same subject"; yet criteria for distinguishing subjects are nowhere made clear. Nor are the procedures used in determining the particular residues manifested in the derivations specified. Obviously, Pareto's own work falls far short of the scientific demands he himself voiced so strongly and clearly.

His treatment of residues and derivations which occupies a large part of his *Treatise* is, then, the weakest aspect of his work. Yet diffused throughout this part of the work are many penetrating insights and suggestive leads for further investigation. And, as we have seen, the remainder of Pareto's theoretical formulation, particularly his conception of the social system as a dynamic equilibrium, remains an important contribution to the cumulative development of sociological theory.

[10] F. S. C. Northrop, *The Logic of the Sciences and the Humanities* (New York: Macmillan, 1949), p. 270. See all of Chap. 15 in this volume for evaluation of Pareto's work.

# CHAPTER 14

# MAX WEBER

In the first quarter of the twentieth century, the most remarkable event in the growth of sociological theory was the blossoming of psychologically oriented sociology. This trend developed independently in various countries and, at its theoretical best, was represented by three scholars. The contributions of two of these have already been considered: Thomas' moderate behaviorism coupled with the "cultural approach"; and Pareto's work, including his psychology, which is akin to the instinctivist brand. Now we must turn to the last but by no means the least of the three, the German scholar Max Weber, whose sociology is also subjectivist though it stresses the rational elements of man's mental activity.

### Weber and His Work

Max Weber (1864–1920) was born in a well-to-do family and received excellent training in law and economics. His father, active in German politics, was for many years a member of the *Reichstag*, belonging to the National Liberal Party. In 1893 Max Weber was appointed professor of economics at the University of Freiburg and soon thereafter moved to a similar post at the University of Heidelberg. In 1900 Weber suffered a severe breakdown and was forced to give up academic activity; he did not return to teaching until 1918, when he went to Vienna and subsequently to Munich. In 1920 he died at a time when his talent had reached full maturity.

During the years in which Weber was academically inactive, he was not idle. His private means allowed him to travel extensively—in 1904 he visited the United States—and to concentrate on research. He published an amazing number of studies and essays; many of them appeared in the *Archiv für Sozialwissenschaft und Sozialpolitik* which Weber made prominent among German social-science publications. He also contributed numerous articles to newspapers and actively engaged in politics. His political opinions were liberal, reflecting the point of view which had prevailed in his parental home. He protested against unrestricted submarine warfare in World War I and advocated negotiated peace. After the war, he served on the committee which prepared the memorandum about war guilt submitted to the Paris peace conference, and on the committee which drafted the Weimar Constitution. His life may be said to have been equally divided between science and politics on a high level.

A large number of Weber's writings do not belong to the field of sociology; of the sociological writings, the majority deal with concrete problems, not with questions of general theory. But Weber's mind was highly analytical, and even when he was treating problems not primarily oriented to theory he made important contributions to the latter.

When he died, Weber's major work in the field of sociological theory, a monumental treatise on *Economics and Society,* was left unfinished. It was a large task to prepare for publication (in 1922) the several fragments of this work that were advanced beyond the preliminary stage. At about the same time his contributions that had appeared in various journals and his other writings were collected and published in the form of "Collected Papers." Of these collections, three volumes deal with the sociology of religion, one with social and economic history, one with sociology and social policy, and one with what we call today the sociology of knowledge. This enumeration illustrates the exceptionally wide range of Weber's scientific interests.

## The Background of Weber's Sociology

Max Weber's contribution to sociology cannot be understood without reference to the intellectual, especially the philosophical and scientific, climate of Germany at the beginning of the twentieth century. Marxist theory formed part of this climate. But it was more dominated by the revival of Kantian philosophy, asserting the existence of an insuperable gulf between the world of material phenomena and the world of "spirit" manifested first of all in values. Concerning the material world, it was held that the natural sciences can and must formulate "laws of nature," statements about invariant uniformities. While science can acquire knowledge of the states and processes of the human mind by "understanding" them from within, it cannot perceive uniformities in the world of "spirit" and must limit itself to accurate description and evaluation of events and their sequences in their unique and nonrecurring manifestations.

This approach had not prevented Toennies and Simmel, as we have seen, from constructing sociological systems of the natural science type as described above. Neither of these writers, to be sure, was inclined to formulate "laws"; both were satisfied with the establishment of typologies—in Toennies' case of social groups, in Simmel's of social relations and processes. But Simmel's work, if not Toennies', implies the idea of order in social reality.

Weber himself made a valiant effort to overcome the opposition between natural and "spiritual" science, and to create a sociological system retaining the most valuable elements of the two approaches. He shared the belief that the social and natural sciences are quite different. In the natural sciences, human interest is directed toward control: he who knows the uniformities can control the forces of nature. On the contrary, in the social sciences human interest is directed toward valuation. The concept of culture itself is a value concept. Empirical reality becomes culture to us because, and in so far as, we relate it to values. The validity of values is a matter of faith, not of knowledge, according to Weber; therefore the social sciences must investigate values but cannot provide binding norms and ideals from which directives controlling practical activity can be derived. Accordingly, in Weber's opinion, the social sciences (including sociology and history) must be *value-free.*

When Weber was writing, the variability of value systems in time and space was well known. Since the cultural processes are constantly forming and reforming, the subject matter of the cultural sciences is subject to change; therefore, Weber held, a systematic or generalizing science of culture is out of the question. Social science must be an empirical science of concrete reality.

This was a conclusion that had a profound effect upon Weber's research and scientific thought. Possessing one of the most brilliant theoretical minds in sociology, he rarely allowed himself to make broad generalizing statements transcending concrete culture systems. His main interest lay with the society and culture system in which he lived; his principal effort was therefore given to painstaking studies of the origin and development of the political, economic, legal, and religious institutions of the Western world. But he did not confine himself to these matters. Having come to certain conclusions about the interconnections between the rise of modern capitalism and the growth and nature of Protestantism, he decided to test the validity of these conclusions by examining situations comparable in some but not in all respects in other civilizations. In this endeavor he carried out brilliant investigations of the Chinese, Hindu, and Judaic civilizations (where the religious and philosophical systems greatly varied), studies, he believed, that confirmed the findings he had derived from the study of Western developments. This comparative study prompted him, perhaps, to overcome his original skepticism concerning the possibility of general sociology. Toward the end of his life, he began writing the treatise mentioned above, *Economics and Society.* The first part of this work, to a considerable extent, is a general sociological theory in the direction of an abstract theoretical science as Comte himself had understood it.

There are, as we would expect, differences between the views expressed in Max Weber's most mature work and in his earlier writings, but these are not differences in principle. The earlier works were precursors of the later ones; therefore, Weber's thought-system can be described on the basis of his sociological works taken together.

In his sociological system, Weber tried to take advantage of the possibilities offered both by the natural and the "spiritual" sciences. The highest level of the understanding of social phenomena, he taught, is reached if this understanding is both causally adequate and adequate on the level of meaning. This proposition requires analysis of three questions: What is causally adequate understanding? What is meaningfully adequate understanding? How are the two interrelated?

## Causal Understanding and the Historical Process

In answer to our first question Weber replies: An interpretation of a sequence of events is causally adequate if careful observations lead to the generalization that it is probable that the sequence always will occur in the same way. Such generalizations, in Weber's view, should be derived statistically as far as possible. For phenomena which cannot be statistically described and interpreted, there remains the possibility of comparing the largest possible number of similar historical or contemporary processes which differ only with respect to the factor whose role is being investigated.

The main achievement of Weber's scholarship was an impressive inquiry of the latter type. But this series of studies began along somewhat different lines. In his younger years, Weber wished to test the basic contention of Marxism, according to which all cultural phenomena, including religion, are fundamentally determined by the evolution of economic forces. For Marx, the Protestant Reformation was a by-product of the rise of capitalism. Weber decided to test this hypothesis: he came to a different conclusion. His research and reasoning form a major part of his work and require our attention.

Capitalism in general, Weber holds, is a system of profit-making enterprises bound together in market relations which has developed historically in many places and at various times. But modern mature capitalism is distinguished from capitalism in general by its rational character and the rational organization of free labor. How did this modern type emerge? Weber emphasizes that the problem of initial emergence is distinct from that of later growth since, once fully developed, a social system becomes self-supporting. Weber contends that the rise of mature capitalism was affected by the emergence of Protestant, especially Calvinist, ethics. In a preliminary way he established that in contemporary Germany areas predominantly Protestant were wealthier than primarily Catholic sections of the nation, and he went on to show the correlation between the growth of mature capitalism and Protestantism.

This was reasoning along the line of the method of concomitant changes often employed by the social scientists of his day. But Weber wished to extend this concomitance to *causal* relationship by applying the method of agreement and, as we shall see later, offering an explanation adequate on the level of meaning. Modern or mature capitalism, he asserts on the basis of painstaking historical study, emerged not simply by inner economic necessity, but as if it were pushed by another rising force, the religious ethic of Protestantism, again especially Calvinism. In his further discussion, the terms of comparison are the *spirit* of modern capitalism and the *spirit* of Protestantism. The term spirit, in this context, means a system of maxims of human conduct.

Mature capitalism is not based on simply the acquisitive urge. It is a rational activity, emphasizing order, discipline, and hierarchy in organization. It regards the performance of acquisitive behavior as a kind of calling. It lays stress on success as such, not on the joys which economic success can purchase.

The Protestant ethic does not sanction acquisitiveness directly, but stresses salvation. In its Calvinist form, salvation is assumed to depend on predestination, on an immutable decision of God, and therefore one can do nothing to achieve salvation. However, since salvation is the focus of a person's religious life, he is necessarily interested in knowing whether he is among the chosen. Success in one's secular or worldly calling is believed to be an almost infallible indication of being one of these. Whatever the calling, moreover, the individual should conduct himself in a disciplined and orderly manner.

These maxims of religious and secular conduct, Weber believed, were so far in agreement that the rise of the Protestant ethical orientation can be considered a necessary, though not sufficient, condition of the emergence of modern capitalism. In other words, the maxims of action grounded in Calvinist ethics directed the believers to behave in the spirit of mature capitalism. (Modern science, as well as capitalism, was stimulated by this ethical orientation, a relationship brought out clearly by the American sociologist, Robert K. Merton.[1]

This contention, supported by extensive research, was, however, not enough for Weber. Therefore he decided to study situations which, otherwise similar, differed in the particular factor under investigation: religion. He posed the question: What takes place if general conditions are as favorable to the rise of mature capitalism as they were in Europe about the time of the Reformation, excepting the religious ethic? This question called for investigation along the lines of the method of difference. Consequently, Weber carried out the detailed studies of China and India mentioned above. However, he did not assume that Europe on the eve of mature capitalism, on the one hand, and China and India at certain

[1] See especially Merton's *Society, Technology and Society in 17th Century England* (Bruges, Belgium: St. Catherine Press, 1938).

epochs, on the other, differed *only* with respect to the presence or absence of a religious ethic favorable to the rise of mature capitalism. This admission of the possible causal significance of other factors substantially weakens his argument.

Nevertheless, Weber makes clear that the combination of nonreligious social and economic conditions were propitious to the rise of capitalism in China but that the ethical system of Confucianism was not. In India, while general conditions, especially the caste system, were not so favorable as in China, they were still sufficient background for the rise of capitalism, except for traditional Karma, belief in the transmigration of souls, which was hostile to economic development in the Western manner. On the basis of these and other studies Weber could affirm: Specific economic conditions do not guarantee the rise of capitalism; at least one other condition is necessary, one that belongs to man's inner world. There must be, in other words, a specific motive power, the psychological acceptance of values and ideas favorable to the change.

Social scientists continue to debate whether Weber proved this central contention. Whatever the answer, his lifework shows us the kind of scientific operations that are necessary to reach a causally adequate understanding of historical sequences which are not reducible to statistical treatment. In doing so, he led the way to what is today sometimes known as "sociological experiment," more exactly called "quasi-experiment."

Weber realized that this systematic comparative method is not always possible in sociohistorical study. In this case there remains the "dangerous and uncertain procedure of the 'imaginary experiment' which consists in thinking away certain elements of a chain of motivation and working out the course of action which would then probably ensue in the absence of factors 'thought away.'" [2] To illustrate this procedure, he pointed to the work of one of the outstanding historians of his day, Eduard Meyer (1855–1930), who made this kind of mental experiment with respect to the battle of Marathon, drawing the consequences of an imaginary victory of the Persians and comparing them with the real events.[3] Using Weber's own work as an illustration of this method, one could ask, what would have been the consequences for Western society *without* Protestantism? Or, to cite a more recent situation that has preoccupied several scholars, can we "think away" Lenin from Russian history and still envision the modern Soviet system? These examples illustrate, it should be noted, a mental experiment, exceedingly difficult and demanding logical analysis and imaginative reconstruction of events, one which is nevertheless frequently employed by historians and others.

[2] Max Weber, *The Theory of Social and Economic Organization,* T. Parsons, ed. (New York: Oxford University Press, 1947), p. 97. This volume is a translation by Parsons and A. M. Henderson of Part I of *Wirtschaft und Gesellschaft* (*Society and Economics*).

[3] E. Meyer, *Geschichte des Altertums,* vol. III (1901), pp. 420 ff.

## Understanding on the Level of Meaning and Human Action

Much more difficult to grasp is Weber's conception of understanding on the level of meaning. As we noted above, Weber hoped to preserve for sociology the advantage of the spiritual sciences over the natural sciences. This advantage, he argues, lies in the possibility of a kind of understanding which is based on the fact that human beings are directly aware of the structure of human actions. In the study of social groups, for example, we are able to go beyond mere demonstration of functional relationships and uniformities; we can *understand* the actions—and the subjective intentions of actors—of the individual members. But in the natural sciences we cannot understand in this sense the movements of atoms, molecules, and the like, but can only observe or deduce uniformities present in such movements. The contrast between the social and natural sciences has been expressed vividly by another sociologist, Robert M. MacIver, in the following words:

> Social facts are all in the last resort *intelligible* facts. When we know why a government falls or how a price is determined or why a strike takes place or how a primitive tribe worships or why the birth-rate declines, our knowledge is different in one vital respect from the knowledge of why a meteor falls or how the moon keeps its distance from the earth or why liquids freeze or how plants utilize nitrogen. Facts of the second kind we know only from the outside; facts of the first kind we know, in some degree at least, from the inside. Why did the citizens turn against the government? Why did the union call a strike? To answer these questions we must project ourselves into the situations we are investigating. We must learn the values and the aims and the hopes of human beings as they operate within a particular situation. There is no inside story of why a meteor falls or why a liquid freezes. We comprehend it as a datum, as the expression of a law and nothing more. It is because on the other hand there is always an inside story, or in other words a meaning, in human affairs that we never attain more than partial or relative truth. Here is the paradox of knowledge. The only things we know as immutable truths are the things we do not understand. The only things we understand are mutable and never fully known.[4]

Emphasis on subjective understanding led Weber to a scientific decision of highest importance. He defines *action* as human behavior, whether overt or not, to which the acting individual attaches subjective meaning. Behavior devoid of subjective meaning belongs to the periphery of sociological study. Sociology, in Weber's view, as will be shown later, is

[4] Quoted in M. Berger, T. Abel, and C. H. Page, eds., *Freedom and Control in Modern Society* (New York: D. Van Nostrand, 1954), p. 290 (in Chapter XIII, "Robert M. MacIver's Contributions to Sociological Theory," by H. Alpert).

primarily the study of action which is oriented to the behavior of others. Emphasis upon such orientation of behavior serves to distinguish between sociology and psychology. More important, however, is Weber's stress that social action is a species of behavior involving meaning for the actor himself. This position, it should be noted, stands in opposition to the teachings of American behaviorism, the approach of which precludes study of subjective meanings on the ground that the latter are neither observable nor communicable. Behaviorism, it will be recalled, influenced social science in this country, especially during the 1920's and 1930's, but declined in influence during the more recent period when the views of such writers as Weber, MacIver, and Znaniecki underscored the role of meaning in social action.

For Weber, "understanding on the level of meaning" takes place in two ways. First, there is direct observational understanding of the subjective meaning of another's act. We understand what a person means when he states that $2 \times 2 = 4$, or the subjective meaning of the irrational actions of an obviously angry man, or the meaning of the act of aiming a gun at an animal. We can grasp these meanings because we are aware of the subjective intentions which we attach to our own like actions.

Second, there is understanding of *motive*. We can reproduce in ourselves the purposive reasoning of the actor or, if his action is not rational, we may, through sympathetic participation or empathy, comprehend the emotional context in which the action takes place. (Here we see a close parallel between Weber's methodology and Cooley's stress on sympathetic understanding; see Chap. 12.) The observer need not share the theoretical views or the ultimate ends or values of the actor, but intellectually he understands the situation and the behavior involved. In other words, the particular act is placed in a sequence of motives, the understanding of which can be treated as an explanation of the actual course of conduct. This procedure is possible because motive has a subjective meaning which seems to the actor himself and to the observer adequate ground for the conduct in question.

Theodore Abel has ingeniously recast Weber's subjective approach into a more objective psychology. According to Abel,[5] "the operation *verstehen*" (understanding) consists in the internalization of the factors observed, one being stimulus and another response, and in the finding of a commonly accepted maxim of conduct which links the two together—a procedure applicable to observations of single cases, generalizations, or statements about statistical regularity. Thus, for example, "competent statistical research has established a high correlation . . . between the annual rate of crop production and the rate of marriage in a given year . . . We use as items of information the fact that failure of crops . . . materially lowers the farmer's income . . . and the fact that one is mak-

[5] T. Abel, "The Operation Called *Verstehen*," *American Journal of Sociology*, LIV (November, 1948), 211 ff.

ing new commitments . . . when one marries . . . We then internalize [the first fact] into 'feeling of anxiety' . . . and [the second fact] . . . into 'fear of new commitments' . . . We are now able to apply the behavior maxim: 'People who experience anxiety will fear new commitments' . . . Since we can fit the fact of fewer marriages when crops fail into this rule, we say we understand the correlation."

Weber, to be sure, had in mind cases less simple than this one when he presented "the operation *verstehen.*" But in more complex cases the procedure remains essentially the same. We must imagine the emotions aroused in people by the impact of a given situation or event; we must imagine the motive behind the action of a person or group, and we must find or construct a plausible maxim of action which would show "that the feeling-state we ascribe to a given human action is *directed* by the feeling-state we presume is evoked by an impinging situation or event." [6] Put in the words of MacIver, in analyzing human conduct we must engage in "imaginative reconstruction." [7]

Does this procedure of understanding on the level of meaning call for a sociology which is undistinguishable from psychology? Weber denied this implication, stating that the procedure he recommended is by no means psychological. The confusion, he asserts, is based on the error of assuming everything to be psychic which is not physical. In addition to the physical and the psychic worlds is the world of meanings or ideas. When a man believes that $2 \times 2 = 4$, this is a psychic phenomenon; but the idea that $2 \times 2 = 4$ is independent of the content of any particular person's thought. Although we agree with this view, it must be pointed out that the initial question is left unanswered. For, in Weber's opinion, the meaning which is a necessary attribute of action is *subjective*—a meaning which is present in the mind of the actor himself or at least thought to be present. Otherwise, action is not understandable and its study does not belong to the field of sociology.

Weber overcomes this difficulty in part by stating that in addition to the meaning of an act for the individual, there is also an "average meaning" attributable to a plurality of actors, or even meaning for hypothetical actors in particular *types* of activities. (Here Weber uses the concept of "pure type" discussed below.) However, average meaning and hypothetical typical meaning are not the same as subjective meaning. If sociology is concerned merely with the former its problems are distinct from the problems of individual motivation. But if average meaning or hypothetical meaning differ from the concretely experienced meanings of individuals and still belongs to the province of sociology, then the latter cannot be viewed as the science of social action as Weber defined it. This difficulty or inconsistency must be pointed out; it is not necessary to try to resolve it here.

[6] *Ibid.,* p. 216.

[7] R. M. MacIver, *Social Causation* (Boston: Ginn, 1942), Chapter IX.

## The Relation of Causation and Meaningfulness

How are Weber's conception of causation and his treatment of meaning interrelated? His answer to this question refers less to concrete behavior than to abstract typical actions. Thus he states: "A correct causal interpretation of typical action means that the process which is claimed to be typical is shown to be both adequately grasped on the level of meaning and at the same time the interpretation is to some degree causally adequate. If adequacy in respect to meaning is lacking, then no matter how high the degree of uniformity and how precisely its probability can be numerically determined, it is still an incomprehensible statistical probability . . ." [8] On the other hand, the most adequate explanation in terms of meaning has no causal significance if there is no proof of the probability of the action in question; at best it remains a plausible hypothesis.

Satisfactory sociological explanation, then, must be both subjectively meaningful and factually probable. However, it has been shown that causal explanations are not always available—nor are meaningful explanations. The latter situation, which often occurs, is one of which Weber was fully aware. He acknowledges that considerable social conduct is marked by the actor's inarticulate half-consciousness or even unawareness of its subjective meaning (a situation presumably depriving behavior of the character of "action"). Lack of awareness of meaning is quite common, in fact, when behavior is *traditional*, that is, determined by social custom, or when it is *affective*, that is, determined by emotion.

Weber does not consider similar actions of several persons exposed to the same stimulus, or behavior consisting of mere imitations, as social. (Here he disagrees with Tarde and his followers.) However, he does not exclude these modes of behavior from sociology. Processes and uniformities in human conduct which are not understandable (because they lack subjective meaning) and therefore not immediate subject matter for sociology, on that account should not be neglected in the study of social life, although they should be studied by different methods. In other words, the focus of sociology should be upon social action involving subjective meaning (or at least average or hypothetical meaning), while objective or psychological conditions that influence social action are peripheral, though often significant, considerations for the discipline.

## The Ideal or Pure Type: Its Nature and Applications

The study of social action, as Weber conceived it, calls for the method of the ideal or pure type. As the latter term appears only in *Economics and Society*, "ideal type" is more commonly associated with Weber's name. But "pure type" is perhaps the more adequate term, since

[8] Weber, *op. cit.*, p. 99.

it points up more clearly Weber's meaning of this methodological concept. (Weber, it should be made clear, did not claim invention of the ideal or pure type; rather he sought to make explicit a procedure commonly used in scientific study.)

The ideal or pure type is a mental construct. It is formed by exaggeration or accentuation of one or more traits or points of view observable in reality. The type thus constructed may be called ideal because it exists as an idea. Seldom if ever, says Weber, can there be found in life itself phenomena which correspond exactly with the mentally constructed type. But the type may also be called pure in the same sense in which a chemist thus designates an element after having freed it of the materials with which it was combined in the natural state preceding analysis. An ideal or pure type differs from a statistical average, which, to be sure, is an essential tool in social analysis, as we have seen, but for different purposes.

The ideal type is not a hypothesis. It is a tool for analysis of concrete historical events or situations. Such analysis requires concepts which are precisely and unambiguously defined—standards which can be met with ideal types. An ideal type is a limiting concept with which life situations or actions are compared in the process of investigation. When concrete reality is studied in this manner, Weber holds, it becomes possible to establish causal relationships between its elements.

Weber's *Economics and Society* provides us with a frequently cited illustration of his use of the ideal type and also brings out the difficulties in this procedure. Here Weber formulates a pure type of rational action (the nature of which is discussed below) and argues that for the purposes of a typological scientific analysis it is possible to treat nonrational and irrational behavior as deviations from the rational ideal type. Hence the sociologist is enabled to study the ways in which actual human conduct is influenced by irrational and nonrational elements. This method, Weber concludes, does not imply that rational behavior predominates in social life.

This procedure, however, encounters large difficulties, brought out in Weber's four-fold classification of social action, based in each case on the mode of orientation of behavior. Thus two classes of action are rational, one making use of appropriate means for the attainment of rationally chosen ends, the other utilizing similar means to fulfill such "absolute values" as religious and ethical ends. The other two classes of action are the traditional and affective types mentioned above. Now, if the ideal type in this case is a construct resting on the foundation of rational action, how is it possible to construct ideal types of nonrational or irrational action? This difficulty or inconsistency is not resolved by Weber's interpretation.

Weber made abundant use of the ideal or pure type procedure in his sociological writings. In the process, his sociology, which he intended to be centered around the concept of social action involving subjective meaning, became in large measure a study of types of human conduct found in average or even hypothetical circumstances.

*Economics and Society* to a considerable extent is an attempt to construct a system of ideal types. Their definitions are, so to say, "imposed" by the author: [9] he formulates them more or less dogmatically and then explains them attribute by attribute, sometimes presenting long and detailed descriptions of concrete historical situations which presumably illustrate the definitions. Weber does not construct his types by means of a rigid inductive process; rather he derives their characteristic traits by informal induction based on extensive study of relevant materials and intuitively, it seems, selects the traits to be included in his ideal types.

Among Weber's numerous definitions of ideal types the following are often cited: [10] *Social relationship*, a concept logically close to that of social action, is the behavior of a plurality of actors in so far as, in its meaningful content, the action of each takes account of that of the others. An *organized group* is a social relationship in so far as specific individuals regularly perform the function of enforcing order in the group. An organized group the governing order of which is in principle concerned with territorial validity is a *territorially organized group*. An organized group the members of which are by virtue of their membership subjected to the legitimate exercise of imperative control is an *imperatively coordinated group*. An imperatively coordinated group is a *political group* if its administrative staff enforces order within a given territorial area by application and threat of physical force. A political group is a *state* if its administrative staff successfully claims a monopoly of the legitimate use of physical force in the enforcement of its order. This is a sequence of concepts in which the extension of each successive concept is narrowed by the addition of one or more traits not contained in the definition of the previous concept. The one exception to this procedure occurs in the definition of the organized group, which is narrowed in two directions, to become either a territorial group or an imperatively coordinated group. When an organized group is both territorial and imperatively coordinated, it is a political group of which the state is the typical example.

The definitions of certain of the ideal types reproduced above sometimes contain attributes which are defined separately, often as additional ideal types. Thus one subtype of the organized group is defined by the addition of the attribute of imperative control. This, in turn, is defined as the *probability* that a specific command will be obeyed by a specified group of persons. In this connection, Weber asserts that each organized group endowed with imperative control attempts to establish and cultivate the belief in its *legitimacy*.

[9] Cf. N. S. Timasheff, "Definitions in the Social Sciences," *The American Journal of Sociology*, 53, pp. 206–208.

[10] In some cases, definitions have been somewhat simplified and rendered in a translation at variance with the one appearing in *The Theory of Social and Economic Organization*.

One of the most famous illustrations of the ideal type procedure is Weber's depiction of three types of legitimate authority, each resting on a distinct mode of claiming legitimacy. Thus there is authority on rational grounds, based on the belief in impersonal rules or norms and in the right to command of those who gain authority in keeping with such rules; this *rational legal* type is approximated in modern Western society. *Traditional* authority is based on the belief in the sanctity of traditions and legitimacy of the status of those possessing authority according to tradition, as in the case of established monarchies. *Charismatic* authority, finally, rests on devotion to the specific and exceptional sanctity, heroism, or exemplary character of an individual person and of the normative patterns or order revealed or ordained by him;[11] this type is illustrated by such charismatic leaders as Gandhi and Hitler. These three ideal types in all likelihood do not exhaust the possibilities of types of legitimate authority, a probability which Weber recognized. His intention here, as elsewhere, is to formulate, in a conceptually precise form, some sociologically important types. Moreover, these pure types of authority, it should be remembered, are abstract constructs; concrete systems of political authority incorporate two or more elements of the three types. (Thus political authority in the United States, while predominantly rational-legal, at times reveals charismatic traits and, especially in established political machines, is marked by traditional elements.)

The majority of Weber's ideal types do not refer directly to actions, but to social collectivities (a term he preferred to social group). This emphasis may seem to be a departure from the view of sociology as primarily concerned with social actions. However, *social relationship*, the ideal type forming the foundation of the pyramid of types discussed above and of many others, is defined by Weber as the probability that there will take place a course of social action. This behavioral definition is related to the fact that Weber was keenly aware of the danger of the "reification" of social relations and of all the types of social groups. "A State, for example, ceases to exist in a sociologically relevant sense whenever there is no longer a probability that certain kinds of meaningfully oriented social actions will take place." [12] Action, Weber insists, exists only as the behavior of one or more individual human beings, and social collectivities must be treated solely as resultants and modes of organization of acts performed by individuals. For sociology, such concepts as state, association, kinship, and the like designate categories of human interaction. Hence it is a task of sociology to reduce these concepts to the understandable actions of participant individuals. This position approaches extreme sociological nominalism, the opposite of Durkheim's sociological realism which we encountered in Chapter 9.

[11] Weber, *op. cit.*, p. 328.
[12] *Ibid.*, p. 118.

### Probability

There is one more aspect of Weber's definitions that requires attention: his frequent use of the concept of chance or probability. For Weber, a causal explanation is essentially a statement of probability that things will recur in a specified manner. The concept of probability is involved in the definitions of social relationship, of organized group, and of imperative control. It also appears in several other definitions, including two which are often reproduced (at times without reference to the source): the definitions of convention (very similar to Sumner's *mores*) and of law. *Convention* is the probability that deviation from the social norm will result in a relatively general and practically significant reaction of disapproval, while *law* is the probability that deviation from the legal code will be met by physical or psychic sanction applied by a group especially empowered to carry out this function. Weber's definition of *class*, to cite an illustration from a far different context, also stresses the concept of probability: "We may speak of a 'class' when (1) a number of people have in common a specific causal component of their life chances, in so far as (2) this component is represented exclusively by economic interests in the possession of goods and opportunities for income, and (3) is represented under the conditions of the commodity or labor markets." [13]

Weber's emphasis upon probability, as revealed in these illustrations and elsewhere in his writings, and in spite of the pervasive "idealism" in his work, has helped to bring Weber's theory to the attention of empirically and statistically oriented sociologists in the United States. For his definitions, in their reference to probabilities of behavior, are "operational" and may be applied to the operations of empirical research.[14]

### Weber's Sociology: In Principle and Practice

What was Weber's conception of sociology? The answer to this question involves the difficulties which were discussed in the earlier parts of this chapter. On the one hand, Weber began his final treatise by defining sociology as a "science which attempts the interpretative understanding of social action in order thereby to arrive at a causal explanation of its course and effects." [15] He adds that the specific task of sociology is the interpretation of action in terms of subjective meaning and that the focus of the discipline should be subjectively understandable phenomena. On the other hand, Weber claims that sociology's specific function is the under-

[13] From *Max Weber: Essays in Sociology*, translated and edited by H. H. Gerth and C. W. Mills (New York: Oxford University Press, 1946), p. 181.

[14] Cf. H. Alpert, "Operational Definitions in Sociology," *American Sociological Review*, Vol. 3, No. 6 (Dec., 1938), esp. 861.

[15] Weber, *op. cit.*, p. 88.

standing of typically differentiated individuals—that it should seek to formulate type concepts and generalizations of empiric processes.

The first formulation, if consistently carried out, would seem to make sociology a branch of psychology. But the second conception calls for the development of a typology of meaningfully oriented actions supplemented by exploration of "understandable processes" which affect conduct. Weber's concrete work was more in accordance with the latter conception of sociology than with the former.

Whatever inconsistencies exist between Weber's formal definitions of the field (which he considered in no sense "final"), his investigations of several concrete areas have had a continuing impact on sociology and on other social sciences. We have already referred to his comparative studies of religion, including his treatment of the interconnections between Protestantism and capitalism, and to his analysis of political authority. At least three other subjects—economic history, social stratification, and bureaucracy—have been illuminated by Weber's theoretical and research efforts (though his work in these areas was never completed). His *General Economic History*,[16] based upon students' notes of his final series of lectures, has been available in English since 1927, but it neither does justice to Weber's wide researches nor is it of especial sociological interest. But his writings on class and status—phenomena which he clearly distinguishes—and their interrelations are widely read today in the United States, particularly since the publication in 1946 of *From Max Weber: Essays in Sociology* (translated by Hans Gerth and C. Wright Mills) and, in the following year, of *The Theory of Social and Economic Organization* (translated by A. M. Henderson and Talcott Parsons). The former also contains a large part of Weber's systematic study of bureaucracy. Bureaucracy, with its formalization and hierarchy and standardization, is a mode of social organization especially congenial to the money economy and rationality of the modern world, as Weber stresses. Not confined to the political and economic spheres nor to "capitalistic" societies, this "greatest social invention" of man, bureaucracy, has inevitably captured the attention of many social scientists. It is a tribute to Weber's pioneer work that his analysis of bureaucracy remains a theoretical guide in this field.

## Summary and Appreciation

Max Weber's sociology is so different from other sociological systems that it is not easy to single out from it answers to the basic questions we have chosen as guides in our study of the growth of social theory.

Though Weber never defined society, it may be inferred that he considered society to consist of a complex of human interrelationships charac-

---

[16] Max Weber, *General Economic History*, translated by F. H. Knight from *Wirtschaftsgeschichte* (London: George Allen & Unwin, 1927).

terized by meaningful behavior of a plurality of actors. He made penetrating studies of what we today call culture, but he did not define it. He was anxious to avoid "reification," the ascription of concrete existence to mental constructs such as ideal types; in this respect his views are congenial to America's neo-positivists.

The fundamental element of sociological investigation for Weber is "typical social action," or even the single individual, whom he called the basic unit or the atom of society. The problem of the relationship between the individual and society was not posed by Weber since he conceived society in the final analysis to be the probability of specified human actions.

Weber consistently and convincingly denied the existence of any single predominant determinant of society or social change. But the subjective character of his sociology with its emphasis on rational action inclined him to stress the role of ideas in social life.

As we have seen, Weber defined sociology ambiguously both as the study of social action in its subjective meaning and as the study of typical social action. In practice, he worked along the line of the second definition, employing the method of the ideal or pure type. He also stressed the procedure of *verstehen,* or the internalization by the observer of the actions of his fellow men.

The most important question, perhaps, concerning Max Weber's sociological theory has always been this: Does the concept of *verstehen* give us a complete understanding of the processes through which events in the social world are understood and organized by human minds? Until recently, this seemed to be a yes or no question; that is, is the concept of *verstehen* to be accepted or rejected? Now, after the illuminating statement on the problem by Alfred Schütz (1899–1959), a thoughtful German social philosopher, a *rapprochement* has been accomplished. The two positions, which seemed to be polarly opposed to each other, have been subjected to a synthetic treatment by Schütz,[17] whose solution takes the following form: What social scientists wish to express when they speak of *verstehen* as a technique of dealing with human affairs is that this is not primarily a "method," but rather the particular form in which human-sense thinking takes cognizance of the social-cultural world. *Verstehen* has nothing to do with introspection: it is as much a result of processes of learning and acculturation as is the common-sense experience of the so-called natural world. Nor is it by any means a private affair of the observer. Predictions based on *verstehen* are continuously made on the "common-sense" level with high success.

Both defenders and critics of the process of *verstehen* maintain with

---

[17] See Schütz's "Concept and Theory Formation in the Social Sciences" in Maurice Natanson, ed., *Philosophy of the Social Sciences: A Reader* (New York: Random House, 1963), pp. 231–49.

good reason that it is subjective. Unfortunately, however, each party employs the term in a different sense. Its critics call *verstehen* subjective because they hold that understanding the motives of another man's action depends upon the private, uncontrollable, and unverifiable intuition of the observer or refers to his private value system. Its defenders, however, call *verstehen* subjective because its goal is to discover what the actor means in his action, in contrast to the meaning which his action has for the actor's partners or neutral observers. Clearly, the latter was Weber's own goal.

Max Weber is justifiably considered to have been one of the greatest sociologists of the twentieth century for the following reasons. First and most importantly, his work provides magnificent examples of the kind of painstaking study of concrete social situations and processes that must form the foundation of any adequate sociological theory. The wealth of material contained in his writings could well be used by generations of sociologists to come. Second, as in the case of Durkheim, he helped to make clear the significant role of values in social life, while emphasizing the necessity of keeping social science value-free. Third, he demonstrated that much can be achieved by using the ideal-type procedure in social science. Finally, he contributed enormously to the understanding of social causation and its inseparability from the problem of meaning in human affairs.

We have already criticized certain aspects of Weber's work. His tendency to explain social reality in terms of individual motivation blurred the line between sociology and psychology. A view which he seems to have changed toward the end of his life is that of the insuperable variability of value systems and the resulting impossibility of constructing a sociological system of general validity. In contrast to this viewpoint, it may be maintained that there are universally valid values, on the one hand, and, on the other, that social and cultural variability can be studied in a generalizing manner.

Max Weber was a prolific author and a remarkable thinker. The major part of his work, however, is not really sociology but pertains to the social sciences as a whole. To a large extent, it belongs to social history, or to the discussion of historical phenomena in terms established by sociology. The truly sociologically relevant discussions in Weber's work are concerned with a few subjects, of which probably the most important are bureaucracy, religion, and the sociology of law, to which Weber has given a new start by his very pointed definitions.

Despite his achievements, Weber did not leave a "school" of followers. This may be attributed in part to the fact that his ill health prevented a normal teaching career at institutions of higher learning, and in part to the fact that Weber's mature work was published (posthumously) in a Germany looked upon with suspicion, especially in the realm of social ideas. The absence of a Weber school may also reflect the fact that such a development was of no concern to Weber himself. In keeping with the norms of science and scholarship, he sought the truth, not followers.

However, Weber has something of a convert among American sociologists, Talcott Parsons of Harvard University. Parsons has translated some of Weber's works into English, including *The Protestant Ethic and the Spirit of Capitalism* and *The Theory of Social and Economic Organization* (Part I of Weber's *Economics and Society*), and thus has made these contributions more accessible to Anglo-American scholars. (Other translations have also appeared in recent years, so that Weber's ideas are no longer a mystery to be penetrated only by those who have command of German.) In addition, Parsons has published outstanding interpretations of Weber's work,[18] work that has greatly influenced Parsons' own theoretical contributions, as we will see in Chapter 18.

The availability of Weber's writings in translation, the important place that former European, especially German, scholars have established in American intellectual and academic circles in recent years, the influence of Parsons and of his students (several of whom are now among the leading figures of American sociology), and, most significantly, the theoretical and research developments in this country since the late 1930's have converged to give Max Weber's sociology a prominent position in the United States today.

[18] See especially *The Structure of Social Action,* Part III (New York: McGraw-Hill, 1937).

CONCLUSION TO | *Part Four*

The sociologists of the early twentieth century in one important respect were less fortunate than those of the preceding generation. The latter had shared a set of propositions, which they regarded as scientific, that gave considerable unity to available knowledge and direction for further research—namely, the theory of evolution. Evolutionism, it should be remembered, was not only a theory of social change but also provided an approach to the study of social "statics" since, by reference to evolution, any aspect of social structure seemed to receive scientific significance. Evolutionism was also, at least implicitly, a normative theory because the normatively right was usually identified with the inevitably emergent.

Early in the twentieth century, as we have seen, evolutionary theory fell to pieces. This collapse was by no means without precedent in the history of social thought. But, in the social realm, it was unusual for a general approach to be abandoned on the basis of conflict with concrete evidence and not because of victorious competition on the part of another unsubstantiated general theory. One result of this development was that, for the first time since its emergence, sociology lacked a general theoretical orientation. But the sociologists of this period began working toward other types of theory. The major efforts in this direction reveal two common lines of thought.

First, many sociologists strove to build their theory on a more solid empirical ground than had their predecessors. They hoped to construct theory in a genuinely scientific manner. Of the sociologists of the time, Pareto was the most explicit in this respect: like every science, he insisted, sociology must be rooted in observation and logical inference on the basis of observation. Similarly, Thomas emphasized the necessity of using in sociology the categories of thought which are employed in the natural sciences; he stressed the search for causal relations in his earlier works but this viewpoint gives way to the determination of probabilities in his later writings. Emphasis on probability also permeates Max Weber's work.

This central position was flanked, on the one hand, by the rising neo-positivism which underscored quantitative, especially statistical, methods and made of their use a condition *sine qua non* of true science and, on the other hand, by the view expressed by Max Weber and others that the distinction between the natural and the human sciences makes the use of special methods, in addition to those of the natural sciences, imperative for the understanding of social phenomena.

The concern to make sociology scientific, it should be noted, was not shared by one well-known writer of this period, Oswald Spengler. Though Spengler was not himself a sociologist, his *Decline of the West* (1917–21) was highly influential in some circles in both Europe and the United States and is a sociologically relevant work. (Its main conclusions are briefly considered in Chap. 20.) In it Spengler, going far beyond the characteristically German distinction between the natural and social sciences, denied the possibility of a science of society and culture by claiming that the concept of causation is inapplicable to events in the social world. But Spengler's pessimistic views were not representative of the sociologists themselves, who were moving in the direction of an empirical science of man and his group life.

The second principal development of this period was the belief shared by most of its major representatives that significant sociological theory would necessarily be based on the study of the individual's participation in social life. This conviction inclined many sociologists to accept psychology as the foundation of sociology, in place of the physics or biology of the preceding period. The figures of the early twentieth century did not, however, initiate the psychological trend in sociology. The preceding period, it will be recalled, had given rise to the psychological evolutionism of Ward and Giddings and to Tarde's reduction of the social process to invention and imitation considered mainly on the level of individual action.

The greatest difficulty met by their twentieth-century successors was the absence of a commonly accepted psychological theory, a situation that still exists. Therefore, each attempt to develop a general social theory was apt to be based on a different psychological approach. While the neo-positivists adopted behaviorism and rejected introspection, Cooley wrote in the style of "common-sense" psychology centered in introspection. Pareto's psychology was midway between instinctivism and the emerging theory of learning with which he, at best, was only superficially familiar. Thomas fluctuated between a mild behaviorism, psychoanalytical theory (which he finally rejected), and a situational psychology emphasizing the determination of human conduct by objective conditions including the norms and values ingrained in culture and one's personal life history. Max Weber denied that his theory was psychological; he claimed that sociology should be concerned with the world of ideas or meanings but, as we have shown, he had in view the actual or hypothetical experience of meanings by individuals. Thus it may be claimed that Weber's theory is essentially psychological, stressing especially rational elements in behavior. In contrast, Pareto emphasized the nonlogical or irrational aspects of human conduct.

Acceptance of these two guiding ideas, that sociology must be an empirical science and that it must develop a theory of human action in society, does not constitute by itself a general sociological theory. Nevertheless, on these foundations, the major figures of the period set in place a few building stones for such a theory.

Perhaps the most important single contribution was Pareto's theorem that society is a system, a whole consisting of interdependent parts and marked by inner forces working toward the restoration of equilibrium against mild disturbances. In less precise language, the same proposition was stated by Cooley, the author of the organic (not organismic) approach to society. But the interdependence and integration of the social system was asserted rather than explored by these authors. Concrete study was left to the next generation of sociologists, some of whom developed a "functional school" and one, Sorokin, a theory of sociocultural integration. (See Chaps. 17 and 18.)

Another important contribution was the *rapprochement* of sociology and ethnology, or, more exactly, the application of the ethnological type of survey to the study of modern society. This method was used by Thomas, who was also one of the first sociologists to understand the paramount importance of culture in the determination of human conduct.

Finally, a number of valuable sociological concepts were either formulated or rediscovered. Cooley, for example, specified the nature of the primary groups, a concept that has become a standard part of contemporary sociology, as well as a number of concepts concerning personality formation that have greatly influenced modern social psychology. Thomas and Znaniecki clarified the meaning of social and personal organization and disorganization and gave precise definitions to the concepts of attitude and value. Values, though in a somewhat different sense, were also emphasized by Max Weber and by Durkheim in his later works (chronologically belonging to the period under review).

Important methodological advances were made. As noted above, the neo-positivists and Max Weber assigned respectively a dominant and a significant role in sociology to the statistical method. Thomas (influenced by Dr. William Healy [1]) brought to the forefront the case-study method, thus reviving an emphasis of Le Play. Max Weber demonstrated the art of using the quasi-experimental method; he was seconded by Thomas, whose advocacy of using control groups in social research was based on similar logical considerations. Moreover, Max Weber suggested the some-

---

[1] Dr. William Healy's *Individual Delinquent; A Textbook of Diagnosis and Prognosis* (Boston: Little Brown, 1915) is commonly considered to be the first American book based on the case-study method.

what questionable method of the mental experiment and made explicit the operation *verstehen,* which may provide an answer to the difficult question: Under what conditions can a statistical generalization be considered to be a valid sociological proposition? Weber also made explicit a procedure commonly used by historians and social scientists, that of employing ideal or pure types (a method that had been anticipated by Comte). Finally, Thomas and Znaniecki in their landmark study, *The Polish Peasant,* on an unprecedented scale made use of human documents, including life histories, letters, and case records, thereby stimulating the employment of such materials in social research.

Looking back, we can see some unity in the efforts of the early twentieth-century sociologists, directed toward the development of a general social theory. But this partial unity derived from the similarity of the conditions, especially the scientific background shared by these scholars, rather than from any concerted efforts. In fact, their efforts to build sociological theory were almost as unrelated as those of the earlier pioneers had been. At the time even the influence of the imposing works reviewed in this part of our study was largely limited to the countries of their origins. One of the reasons for the lack of contact between the leading sociologists of the period was the violent disruption of the universe of scientific discourse by the catastrophe of World War I. Not only technical barriers, which were only temporary, but emotional obstacles inhibited the wide circulation of ideas throughout Western society so common until 1914. Moreover, the challenging problems posed by the war and its aftermath diverted attention from theory-building to immediate concrete concerns. Only in the most recent period, since the 1930's, has the view gained widespread recognition that substantiated and systematic theory is of the utmost practical importance.

It is a great tribute to the giants of the early part of the century— Cooley and Thomas, Pareto and Weber (and Durkheim of still an earlier stage of sociological growth)—that many of their formulations guide sociological work today. Separated from one another in their day, these writers move toward one another in the convergencies of the present. We turn to these convergencies in Part Five.

# Contemporary Convergence
# in Sociological Theories

# CHAPTER 15

# NEO-POSITIVISM AND
# MATHEMATICAL SOCIOLOGY

Since the beginning of the second quarter of the twentieth century, sociology has advanced rapidly, both in the United States and in western Europe. Some of the trends which appeared earlier have come to maturation. Such is the case of the neo-positivist school, which had been anticipated in Giddings' later work, as we discussed in Chapter 11; of systemic (called analytical) sociology, which had originated in the later nineteenth century, as brought out in Chapters 8 and 9, and had gained momentum in the works of the foremost sociologists of the early twentieth century (their views were presented in Chapters 12, 13, and 14); and of dynamic sociology, which can be traced back to Comte, Spencer, and Danilevsky, considered in Chapters 2, 3, and 4, and, in the early twentieth century had gained some vogue through Spengler's writings, referred to in Chapter 20.

To these older trends, several new lines of inquiry and of emphasis have been added in recent decades; among the most important are the ecological, the sociometric, the functional, the institutional, and the phenomenological. The ecological and the sociometric approaches may be considered as modifications, perhaps specifications, of the neo-positivist school. Functionalism has been taken over largely from cultural anthropology, but can also claim sociological ancestry in the works of Durkheim and Thomas (see Chaps. 9 and 12). The institutional and phenomenological schools are alike in their belief that sociology must be based on a definite philosophical foundation; their beginnings can be detected in earlier periods, but only in the second and still more in the third quarter of the twentieth century did they become important members of the family of trends which constitute contemporary sociological theory.

By now, however, the term "neo-positivism" is employed less and less; "mathematical sociology" is used in its place to cover what was previously called "neo-positivism."

On the other hand, the sociometric school has merged with "microsociology," which arose as an outgrowth of systemic sociology, and neo-evolutionism and historical sociology can now be considered as merging into a dynamic sociology, after having passed through a period of rejection and neglect by most sociologists.

Sociological theory, then, seems to have become more divided than ever. In some respects, this is true. But the relationships among the various trends are no longer the same as in the late nineteenth century. Factual knowledge about society and culture has gradually accumulated. Moreover, a substantial number of inferences and generalizations have been accepted and are employed in research by most sociologists, although the variations in their formal expression often obfuscate their agreement in content.

The trends differ widely, however, concerning the choice of the most useful methods of obtaining and arranging empirical knowledge, the appropriate procedures to increase it, and the conceptual schemes to be used as tools for analysis. But even in these respects, a gradual convergence of views is apparent. As compared with the period of the battle of the schools in the last quarter of the nineteenth century, the present period may be called one of convergence, though marked by competition between frames of reference.

### Lundberg

Perhaps the most influential of the neo-positivists has been the late Professor George A. Lundberg (1895–1966), of the University of Washington, where he taught for many years before his retirement. Lundberg had been a member of various faculties in this country, served as president of the American Sociological Society in 1943, and published widely. Most of his writings vigorously forwarded his "positivistic" approach. *Can Science Save Us?* (1947) is a popular presentation of his views; his major work still is *Foundations of Sociology* (1939).

For Lundberg, all science, social and nonsocial, is essentially an adjustment technique. Every inquiry begins with an experienced tension or imbalance of some sort in the inquiring organism. This view is in the spirit of behaviorism since it avoids any reference to mental facts. Moreover, all adjustment in human life approximates a situation of equilibrium (or maximum probability), which is the normal state of affairs. This conception appears to be in line with theory in contemporary natural science, for example, biochemistry.

The particular "adjustment" forming the social sciences, including sociology, Lundberg depicts as follows. All phenomena of scientific concern consist of energy transformations (motion) in the physical cosmos.

Any "movement" takes place in time in a "field of force," the latter consisting of that segment of the universe which, for the purpose of study, one finds it convenient or relevant to define as the situation. This formulation is consistent with characteristically American pragmatic philosophy, while the concept of "field," when applied to social phenomena, is analogous to the description of the "total situation" in the earlier work of Thomas. Those movements (behaviors) of men, Lundberg continues, which determine their position in social situations form the subject matter of the social sciences. Sociology, he concludes, is differentiated from the other social sciences in accordance with Sorokin's formula, which was outlined in Chapter 1.

Reciprocal or interdependent behavior between or among any number of components (among them, men) in a situation, Lundberg tells us, is *interaction*. Most human interaction involves the development and use of symbols and is designated as communication. The two basic types of communication are association and dissociation, a distinction remindful of the theory of Simmel. Both fundamental types of communication denote movement toward or away from a position, and are described as analogous to attraction and repulsion among the particles of an atom.

Thus it can be seen that Lundberg's approach to sociological theory is based on a double analogy—with the biochemical stress on restoration of equilibrium and with subatomic physical theory. This approach is an expression of the tendency of certain neo-positivists, and many other writers as well, much in the manner of Spencer, to adopt as models the natural science theories currently in vogue.

The three historical roots of neo-positivism, which were discussed in Chapter 11, are conspicuously evident in Lundberg's work. We have already referred to two of these, behaviorism and pragmatism. The latter, as will be shown below, takes the form of operationalism. But his foremost emphasis is on quantitativism.

In one of his earlier papers (1936) Lundberg wrote that scientific generalization is always and necessarily quantitative.[1] In a later paper he decries the frequently made separation between qualitative and quantitative methods of study.[2] In his well-known textbook, *Social Research,* Lundberg states that "for the more exact description required by science, the quantitative statement is necessary." [3] This work stresses the measurement of attitudes and the construction of attitude "scales" for this task. In this connection, Lundberg denies that the manipulation of artificial units of measurement (commonly based on consensus among experts) differs fundamentally from manipulation of interchangeable physical units, con-

[1] G. A. Lundberg, "Quantitative Methods in Social Psychology," *American Sociological Review,* vol. 1 (1936), p. 44.
[2] G. A. Lundberg, "Operational Definitions in the Social Sciences," *American Journal of Sociology,* vol. 47 (1942), p. 736.
[3] G. A. Lundberg, *Social Research,* 2nd ed. (New York: Longmans, Green, 1942), p. 24.

tending that all measurement is "artificial." Moreover, his operationalism holds that "attitude" (like "intelligence," "opinion," and so on) must be, for scientific purposes, defined as *that which* is measured by such research tools. This view stands in sharp opposition to that of many sociologists and other scholars.

Lundberg's views on measurement have been ventilated in a controversial exchange with Paul Furfey who, in his article "Value Judgments in Sociology," cites the fact that there are nonquantitative *natural* sciences, for example, biology and geology.[4] Lundberg rejoined that biology is essentially quantitative since its generalizations rest upon a number of confirmed observations. Furfey replied that the kind and degree of quantification which Lundberg advocates in his writings (and which is applied by his disciple Stuart Dodd) is not an essential mark of all science. In a further letter Lundberg reiterated his earlier claim that generalizations which constitute the sciences of biology, geology, and so on, are the result of the observation of many cases and that this has always been his basic contention regarding quantification in science. In his final critique, we believe Furfey convincingly shows that Lundberg speaks of quantification in two different meanings: first, science is quantitative since it is based on multiple observations—a rather weak contention that does not meet the criteria set down by Lundberg in his major works; second, science is quantitative in that its *results* must be stated quantitatively— Lundberg's consistent position. This line of reasoning may be reduced to the syllogism: because all science is quantitative in the first sense, it *should be* quantitative in the second.

As noted above, Lundberg considers quantitativism as almost inseparable from behaviorism. His opposition to introspection is outspoken: such terms as will, feelings, ends, motives, and values, he claims, are "the phlogiston of the social sciences." He contends that the scientific canon of parsimony requires, for example, the development of a single principle for the explanation of all flying objects, be it a leaf flying before the wind or a man flying from a pursuing crowd.[5]

It is noteworthy that Lundberg's uncompromising position supporting behaviorism does not prevent him from considering the study of values and ideals to be an important task of sociology. He defines value operationally as that toward which people behave so as to retain or in-

---

[4] Paul Furfey, "Value Judgments in Sociology," *American Catholic Sociological Review,* vol. 8 (June, 1946); the subsequent discussion appears *ibid.,* vol. 9 (Oct., 1946, and March, 1947).

[5] This illustration (the flying leaf and the flying man) is drawn by Lundberg from the work of R. M. MacIver. MacIver stresses the qualitative difference between physical and social relations, a position Lundberg views as nonscientific. This dispute, in which the above illustration plays a chief role, may be followed by consulting R. M. MacIver, *Society: A Textbook of Sociology* (New York: Rinehart, 1937), pp. 476–677; G. A. Lundberg, *Foundations of Sociology* (New York: Macmillan, 1939), pp. 12–14; R. M. MacIver, *Social Causation* (Boston: Ginn, 1942), pp. 299–300; and R. M. MacIver and C. H. Page, *Society: An Introductory Analysis* (New York: Rinehart, 1949), p. 628.

crease their possession of it or, negatively, as that toward which people respond so as to decrease or avoid the "value" in question. On the other hand, institutions are defined at one point as mechanisms which men have established in order to secure or achieve their primary ends—and here we see the intrusion of the presumably unscientific concept of "end." Lundberg proposes various empirical procedures to study values and institutions, favoring especially attitude questionnaires which incorporate quantitative techniques.

In agreement with Max Weber, Lundberg stresses that science as such cannot and should not formulate value judgments; moral and scientific statements are irreducible to one another. And sociology must be a science. He rejects a functional analysis of values that rests upon their significance for the survival of individuals or groups; but he rather inconsistently derives values from "the whole evolutionary and social history." In his long experience "man has found that certain forms of conduct are to his advantage, on the whole and in the long run, and that other behaviors are disadvantageous from the point of view of his objectives." This formulation is consistent with the view of Sumner, but, in contrast with this apostle of *laissez faire,* Lundberg concludes: "The great contribution of science to ethics should be in providing man with a more reliable record and interpretation of his experience." [6]

The third component of Lundberg's neo-positivist sociology is his insistence on operational definitions, an emphasis, as we noted earlier, in keeping with his pragmatist epistemology. In this view, phenomena are "objective" to the extent that the criteria of agreement, corroboration, and prediction are satisfied. Therefore, a priori definitions of the "essential nature" of "society," "culture," "institution," and the like, in Lundberg's judgment, are manifestations of outmoded Aristotelian logic and are scientifically useless. The basic question for science, he holds, is: What are the most "useful" definitions of such phenomena? These, he believes, are *operational* definitions which specify the procedures or operations used to identify and measure the phenomena under study. For Lundberg, accordingly, space is *that which* is measured by the ruler or other instruments; time, *that which* is indicated by, say, a clock; intelligence, *that which* is measured by I.Q. tests.

We might ask: Is human population that which is measured by the Census? Moreover, what are these standardized instruments—rulers, clocks, "intelligence" tests, and so on? Such devices have been developed to measure specified aspects or phases of total reality. But the conceptual definitions that lead to these highly useful technical developments, we maintain, are themselves formed in other, nonoperational ways.

Nevertheless, moderate operationalism performs an essential scientific task in demanding that definitions refer to empirically verifiable attributes of whatever science studies. But in the extreme form advocated by Lund-

[6] G. A. Lundberg, "Can Science Validate Ethics?" *Bulletin of the American Association of University Professors,* 36 (1950), 274-75.

berg and certain members of his "school," operationalism often results in giving awkward and cumbersome form to propositions which are well known and about which there is little dispute.

Lundberg's vigorous espousal of quantification, behaviorism, and operationalism marked an impressive number of articles, to a lesser extent his textbooks *Social Research* and *Sociology* (1954), and especially the first few chapters of *Foundations of Sociology*. However, as several critics have noted, the greater part of *Foundations*, his most developed systematic work, differs very little from other general treatises on sociology. Thus, in his treatment of "societal dynamics," social groups, and social change, frequent use was made of the contributions of such (prescientific?) writers as Sumner, Veblen, Cooley, Park, Mead, Thomas, and Sorokin. This is to say that Lundberg, like most contemporary sociologists, recognized and employed a variety of developments in the discipline—in keeping with a general characteristic of the present period of convergence in sociological theory. Moreover, as his friend and intellectual opponent Furfey has put it, as one of the very few "among American sociologists, Lundberg . . . tried to state his definitions, his postulates and his methods frankly and clearly and to follow them out consistently." [7]

### Dodd

A second foremost representative of neo-positivism is Professor Stuart C. Dodd, who was Lundberg's colleague at the University of Washington for several years. Prior to World War II Dodd had taught and conducted extensive research in the Middle East, where he had also developed the principles which were incorporated in his major work, *Dimensions of Society* (1942). This volume, claims Lundberg, elaborates the "methodological implications" of his own theoretical position and thus constitutes a companion to Lundberg's *Foundations of Sociology*.

The purpose of *Dimensions*, according to Dodd, is to construct a quantitative systematic theory of society. The theory in its original form is called S-theory, the symbol S representing *situation*. Situations, Dodd explains, may be analyzed into four classes of components: *time; space,* which is common to all sciences; *population,* which is found in all classes of social phenomena; and finally, *characteristics* of people or of their environment—the last a residual category covering "all else." As defined by Dodd, the classification is exhaustive: nothing can escape it. To designate these four basic components, Dodd employs the symbols $T$ (time), $L$ (space), $P$ (population), and $I$ (indicator). The indicator, by definition, may stand for almost anything, for example, Buddhist philosophy, city noise, or the extent of human desire.

These symbolic designations represent the first step in Dodd's proce-

---

[7] Paul Furfey, *American Catholic Sociological Review,* 9 (March, 1947), p. 48.

dure. The second step ascribes to every social situation a "quantic formula," consisting of the four basic symbols and exponents. If, in a concrete situation, one of the basic components is absent or is not measurable, the exponent is designated as zero, which, following algebraic principles, converts any magnitude into 1. In other cases, exponents 1, 2, 3, −1 and −2 are used in the manner suggested by the following illustrations.

$L^0 =$ situations involving no space, $L^1 =$ those involving lines, $L^2 =$ those involving area, $L^3 =$ those involving volume. $T^0 =$ no time involved; $T^1 =$ duration, $T^{-1} =$ change, $T^{-2} =$ acceleration. $P^0 =$ no population, $P^1 =$ plurels, $P^2 =$ groups. $I^0_d =$ kind of things called dollar, $I^0_B =$ I.Q. of an individual, $I^0 =$ qualitative characteristics, $I^{\pm 2} =$ correlated characteristics.

Along these lines, then, quantic formulas are elaborated. For example, a social force is symbolized as $T^{-2} I P$ because, presumably, it involves acceleration, no space, and a population, a characteristic peculiar to each particular force. Dodd insists that with this type of formulation he is charting the way for the quantification of qualitative characteristics. The latter are treated *as if* their magnitude is 1.

A quantic formula may be transformed into a quantic number simply by producing a four-digit figure repeating the exponents of the quantic formula. For the sake of simplification, if −2 is replaced by 8 and −1 by 9, the quantic formula for "social force" results in the quantic number 8011. Dodd apparently believes that all social situations which can be symbolized by the same quantic number must have "something" in common.

Dodd's third procedural step is the establishment of an "interrelational matrix," matrix being the mathematical name for an arrangement of numbers in rows and columns. This technique is claimed to be the most adequate one for describing a social group. Thus, in every cell (composed by the intersection of a row and a column) an observed magnitude of an indicator (for example, positive or negative attitude of one person toward another) would appear. The matrix can be three-, four-, or five-dimensional, possibilities beyond the reach of conventional graphic presentation.

The description of the S-theory thus far presented makes it appear to be merely a classificatory system. But Dodd claims that the theory has analytic and predictive uses. He believes that the application of the interrelation matrix may greatly help in improving the operational definitions of such concepts as ingroup, outgroup, isolation, contact, interaction, leaders, stars, plurel, group, community, the economic process, societal control, and so on. For example, a column of large entries when the cell indicator is one of prestige identifies a star, and the degree of stardom becomes measurable; while if both the row and corresponding column contain large entries, the leader is specified. An interrelation matrix permits precise definition of a group; while an aggregation of such matrices, one for each characteristic held in common, defines a community. The exploration of quantic formulas in unoccupied cells permits one to predict in advance properties of situations not yet observed (in the way that Mendeleyev's periodical table of elements allowed him to predict the chemical properties of elements not yet isolated).

However, these alleged advantages of the S-theory can be gained only if the sociologist strictly limits himself to operational definitions. According to Dodd, a definition is "operational" to the extent that it both specifies the procedure for identifying or generating the phenomenon in question and meets the test of high reliability. Whereas the first part of the definition is similar to the formulation of Lundberg, the second requirement refers to the degree of agreement among successive observations of the same phenomena using the same operational definition. This degree of agreement must be measured statistically, which, for Dodd, is a necessary condition of any scientific statement.

Dodd notes that his presentation of the S-theory may appear to be predominantly an exercise in deduction. But he insists that the theory grew out of a large amount of inductive study. The inductive process is invoked by his singling out from a number of sociological texts and monographs basic concepts concerning social situations and assigning them quantic formulas. Only 13 per cent of the concepts appearing in these sources are not capable of symbolic presentation (among them the concept of "reality," which the author believes to be unreal). But he was able to translate into his quantic formulas, we learn, 1,600 social situations chosen from most diversified fields.

Dodd claims that his theory is inclusive, reliable, precise, parsimonious, and fruitful. It is inclusive because of its open-ended residual category, designating "all else" by the symbol $I$. Reliability is presumably established by the fact that the classifications made by two carefully instructed graduate students agreed with those of their mentor. The theory is assumed to be precise since it is expressed in operationally defined concepts and symbols. And it is declared to be parsimonious because only sixteen symbols are used: four for the basic components; four symbols for arithmetical operations; four more referring to aggregation, cross-classification, correlation, as well as the exponent; and four final symbols designating the number and nature of classes, class intervals, and cases. But the parsimony thus obtained is, we believe, illusory. The residual symbol $I$ is used with a very large number of "prescripts" and "postscripts," needed to concretize the "characteristics," for example, as noted above, to differentiate between Buddhist philosophy, city noise, and extent of a desire. It must be stressed, however, that there is no more justification for performing mathematical operations with the $I$'s endowed with various prescripts and postscripts than there is, as in arithmetic, for adding the number of feet separating two points and the number of packages one is carrying between them. Dodd himself concedes that the fruitfulness of his theory can be proven only after numerous sociologists have used his system for some time and have accumulated abundant material. It is noteworthy that, during the years which have elapsed since the publication of *Dimensions of Society*, no large work along these lines has appeared.

In a long article entitled "The Transact Model," [8] published in 1956, Dodd attempted to prove that his system provided reliable knowledge. Despite this effort, the basic weakness of the whole enterprise, the fact that the major part of the universe remained covered by *one* residual factor, has not been eliminated. Dodd has replaced his fourfold classification of the components of situations with a sixfold one; the new elements are behavior or action (A) and objects of value (V). The theory, now termed "transact theory," is said to encompass the probable behavior and the values of people in a context of time, space and other circumstances, and has been applied by Dodd to experimental studies of the diffusion of messages. He is satisfied that the findings substantiated his theoretical predictions, but the hypothesis tested was *not* derived from his "dimensional formula" which merely calls attention to the questions who? does what? when? where? why and how?

In later years Dodd has leaned toward sociometry and microsociology. In a personal letter to this writer, he has stated that the focus of his interest is no longer sociology, but the behavioral sciences in general. Dodd has continued to contribute articles to diverse publications, but the idea that he had discovered the key to an absolutely reliable notation of all social phenomena remains as highly questionable as ever.

### The Mathematical Sociology of Zipf, Rashevsky, and Hart

Among the neo-positivists, Dodd and the late George A. Lundberg are probably the most systematic and articulate theorists. But neo-positivism or rather certain of its emphases tend to dominate the scene of present-day American sociology. An examination of the form and content of articles appearing in the leading sociological journals in this country bears out this proposition. However, in the work of the majority of the contributors whose writings and researches meet this description, theoretical features are scarce. The writings of three scholars whose works are mathematically oriented and theoretically developed deserve special attention. These authors are George K. Zipf, Nicholas Rashevsky, and the late Hornell Hart.

Zipf's work is designed to "integrate theoretically a number of social measurements" and to offer "considerable insight into the mainsprings of human behavior" viewed as a purely natural phenomenon. The work rests on a postulate drawn from mathematical reasoning which is assumed "to govern the behavior of individuals and the collective group" and is supported by empirical material which presumably corroborates this reason-

[8] Stuart C. Dodd, "The Transact Model," *Sociometry and the Science of Man*, vol. 18 (1956).

ing. Zipf's theory is developed in the volume *Human Behavior and the Principle of Least Effort* (1949), the misleading subtitle of which is "An Introduction to Human Ecology." The "ecological" nature of this work is to be found in the type of concrete problem which it treats rather than in Zipf's methodology. (For a discussion of ecological theory, see Chap. 16.)

The guiding postulate of Zipf's theory is the "principle of least effort." This principle, in simplified form, declares that in situations allowing alternatives men choose those procedures which result in the "least average rate of probable work." In other words, human beings strive to minimize output of energy, not with respect to immediate tasks but rather in terms of the average work required in order to attain their goals. Men construct highways or tunnels, for example, because in this way they minimize the rate of work they probably will expend on transportation.

This principle is shown to be applicable in the distribution of people among various communities. Population may be distributed in either of two ways. First, people may choose to live in a number of small communities each close to the sources of raw materials, as is commonly the case when there are few kinds of raw material. Men make this choice because of the "force" of the diversification of their habitat. Alternatively, the population may gather in a few large centers, which occurs when the number of types of raw materials is large and transportation to places of work is essential; in this case economy in work expresses itself in minimizing the efforts expended in conveying finished goods to consumers. The force behind this second choice is called "unification." Zipf acknowledges that no methods are known at present to enable investigators to calculate the absolute magnitude of these two forces. But the ratio of their magnitudes can be empirically established, he believes, in a manner to be described shortly.

According to Zipf, the impact of the forces of diversification and unification (both derived from the principle of least effort) compels men to gather in communities of a pre-established size. The size of every community formed in a large area such as a nation is expressed by the formula [9]

$$P_n = \frac{P}{n^q}$$

$P_n$ represents the population of the community occupying the $n$th rank on the list, $P$ is the population of the largest community in the area, and $q$ is the ratio of the magnitude of the force of unification divided by the force of diversification. The formula can be also expressed in the following way:

$$C = \frac{P}{1^q} + \frac{P}{2^q} + \frac{P}{3^q} + \ldots + \frac{P}{n^q}$$

[9] This and the next formulas are presented with some simplifications and with certain changes in symbols.

Here $C$ represents the total population of the area and the other symbols have the same meaning as in the preceding formula. This formula is of the type called in mathematics a generalized harmonic series.

The theoretically expected magnitudes of the sizes of the communities may be graphically represented. Zipf applies this procedure to the populations of the 100 largest metropolitan areas of the United States, according to the census of 1940, and finds that the positions of the dots on his graph corresponding to these populations are very close to a straight line inclined to the horizontal at 45°. This finding means that in his country the two forces of unification and diversification are almost equal.

Zipf continued his analysis by "predicting" the number and diversity of service establishments, manufacturers, and retail stores in the cities of the United States according to their population. The numbers vary in the ratio of population size, the diversity in the ratio of their square roots. He also "predicts" the size of gross receipts, number of full-time employees, and total pay rolls of service establishments, when these establishments are ranked in the order of their decreasing size of membership. Zipf recalculates data collected by others concerning the circulation of newspapers, number of trips, deliveries by railway express, the intervening distances between the residences of persons asking for marriage licenses, and residential movements, always with results seemingly satisfactory to the author of this mathematical approach.

However, when he applies his formulas to other countries, he meets trouble. Germany, Austria-Hungary, the British Commonwealth, and Europe as a whole are declared to be areas of "unstable equilibrium" since they do not fit his scheme. The greatest difficulty appears when Zipf treats the dismemberment of the Austro-Hungarian Empire after the First World War. Populations which might have fitted into his mathematical formula prior to the dismemberment no longer do so. Zipf "explains" this difficulty in the following manner: "Many repressed persons seceded from the Empire to found independent countries with the neurotic resuscitation of cultures that had lost effective economic meaning centuries ago," [10] and did this in the twentieth century when (according to his theorems) nations should have increased in size and decreased in numbers. The author does not attempt to apply his formula, for example, to the population of the Soviet Union, marked by an enormous difference between the size of the second and third largest communities, or to France where the city second in rank to Paris is five times smaller than the French capital, while the next ranking city is only 40 per cent smaller than the second. These cases—and perhaps many others—would hardly fit into Zipf's mathematical scheme.

One source of Zipf's trouble is that the "principle of least effort" supposes that men always act rationally and that their patterns of behavior

[10] G. K. Zipf, *Human Behavior and the Principle of Least Effort* (New York: Hafner, 1949).

can be analyzed accordingly. This supposition has colored social theory for 150 years or more, most clearly in classical political economy, but it represents a curious anomaly in present-day analysis of human conduct. Moreover, Zipf's work shows a sort of "mathematical obsession"; the author seems to take it for granted that very complex phenomena must, by some inner necessity, obey a rather simple mathematical formula. The probability of such a coincidence, we would estimate, is approximately the same as that of the expectation that the sky line that one admires in the Alps or in the Rockies would follow a mathematical curve.

In works of the type of Zipf's *Human Behavior* we cannot expect to find answers to the basic queries of sociological theory, except perhaps the question concerning the basic determinants of social phenomena. Zipf's theory, it would seem, implies that the state of a society is determined by the play of a mathematical law. Nevertheless, his work is marked here and there by "answers" to questions about society and the relationship between society and the individual. Thus we read that "Human society can be viewed as a field which both influences the individual members and is influenced by them . . ." [11] And again: "The social system is a group of individuals who cooperatively pursue like objects by means of like rules of procedure, under the assumption that everyone gives the same amount of work and receives the same reward, with a minimum of work." [12] This, we maintain, is a highly unrealistic assumption indeed.

Zipf's mathematical preoccupation is surpassed by Rashevsky's *Mathematical Theory of Human Relations* (1947), a work we cite here merely to illustrate this orientation. But Rashevsky is fully aware that, for the time being, mathematical treatment of complex social phenomena is possible only if imaginary oversimplified cases and situations are constructed. In other words, what is explored mathematically are mental constructs which, in contradistinction to Max Weber's ideal of pure types, consist of traits necessarily at variance with those observable in social life. In spite of this recognized limitation, Rashevsky's analysis of such constructs often results in systems of equations which are mathematically insoluble. Contrary to Zipf's work, there is no central postulate.

The postulate of mathematical order in social life was shared by Hornell Hart († 1967), professor of sociology at Duke University. Whereas Zipf and Rashevsky treat phenomena of "social statics" mathematically, Hart, in contrast, attempted to give mathematical expression to a theory of social dynamics. Hart did not, like Zipf, ground his work in a single postulate but tried to integrate numerous findings of his own and other researchers. For example, various studies in the field of population, reports of the number of inventions and patents, of speed records, of recorded sizes of empires, and so on are said to demonstrate that such phenomena

---

[11] *Ibid.*, p. 347.
[12] G. K. Zipf, "The Hypothesis of the Minimum Equation," *American Sociological Review*, 12 (1947), 627.

may be expressed by an appropriate logistic curve. Thus, in diverse areas of social and cultural change, after a slow beginning, there is acceleration, then inflection and slowing down, all according to a precise mathematical formula. Other processes, such as the number of technological inventions and especially the increase of the destructive power of explosives, follow another curve (the so-called "loglog curve"), which, unlike the preceding time-pattern, shows no inflection and deceleration; in other words, acceleration continues until the physical limit is reached.

While other exponents of mathematical theories are often satisfied with formulas and mathematical laws, Hart, as if following Max Weber's advice, tried to discover *why* certain curves are likely to obtain in social life. This effort is illustrated by his general explanation of "the acceleration of culture development": Cultural progress has depended upon inventions, that is, new combinations of older cultural elements. The larger the number of cultural units, it follows, the greater the possibility of inventions. Thus a general tendency should be found of geometrical multiplication of inventions. But Hart was aware that setbacks occur in cultural change; these may be interpreted as survivals of elements poorly integrated in the whole culture. He noted the tendency (which he did not explain) of destructive agents to increase in their effectiveness with an acceleration outdistancing that found in any other type of cultural change. Hart denied the possibility of explaining the conformity of certain social processes with mathematical curves as a matter of pure chance, claiming that behind logistic and other trends something in the nature of underlying law is present.[13]

But laws of nature are always hypothetical propositions of the type "if A then B." A demographic law, for example, which asserts that the growth of population follows the logistic curve requires a statement of the *conditions* under which the ascending movement begins, as well as explanation of the conditions under which the logistic curve is "broken." Hart himself, it may be noted, reported several cases of the latter type. No mathematical reasoning as such, we maintain, can yield knowledge of these conditions.

While Zipf and Rashevsky generally neglect the operational aspect of neo-positivism, Hart did not. But the latter's advocacy of the "operational method" is cautious and considered. This method, Hart wrote, "consists in stating verifiably the specific observations and operations by means of which variables are to be produced, identified or measured, and in determining, to the closest attainable approximation, the specific sets of selective and causal operations by means of which variables can be altered in desired directions, the extent to which variables can thus be

[13] H. Hart, "Logistic Social Trends," *American Journal of Sociology*, 50 (1945), 350. The law of acceleration is confirmed by the recent development of the science of microphysics. Whereas some populations seem partly to corroborate the law, many populations do not conform at all.

controlled and the margins of error probably involved in the foregoing conclusions." [14] No doubt most sociologists would go along with this statement as a guiding principle in empirical research.

Hart, moreover, was not, in the manner of Zipf, a "mathematical determinist." It has been fashionable, he declares, "to talk about technological determinism." But "the Industrial Revolution had its roots in a series of inventions which, in turn, had their roots in antecedent ideas. Technology itself has been ideationally determined. If we seek to control the direction of cultural evolution, we need not be deterred by any notion that technology is the master-cause of everything." [15] The remedy against the dangers presented by the arrival of the Atomic Age, he believed, is to be found in an accelerated development of social science, and here he stood in agreement with Lundberg. One may doubt whether this development would prove altogether efficacious. But, by suggesting its use, Hart placed himself among those sociologists who believe that man is no mere object moved by impersonal social processes and not in some degree their master. It is not surprising therefore that Hart was fully aware that his sociological ancestry went back to Comte, who hoped to build an empirical science of society to save mankind from disaster.

### Moderate Neo-Positivism: Ogburn and Chapin

Preoccupation with "higher mathematics" marks the work of only a few of the sociologists we include in the neo-positivist group. Most of the scholars in this group are not mathematicians. But all of them strongly emphasize the need to measure social phenomena wherever possible and the strategic role of statistical analysis in social research. Most of them also stress the importance of developing empirical research techniques and are apt to be skeptical of "armchair" social theory. These traits characterize the writings of the moderate neo-positivists, including the influential contributions of the late William F. Ogburn, of the University of Chicago, and F. Stuart Chapin of the University of Minnesota. Both Ogburn and Chapin, it should be noted, won their doctoral degrees at Columbia University early in the second decade of the century where at that time Giddings, a precursor of modern neo-positivism (as explained in Chapter 11), was the dominant figure.

Alone or in cooperation with other scholars, Ogburn carried out an impressive number of studies of social phenomena, especially featured by the establishment of coefficients of correlation between their various aspects, with conspicuous emphasis on technological and economic matters. Ogburn's well-known *The Social Effects of Aviation* (1946) has brought him closer to the mathematical wing of neo-positivism than his

[14] H. Hart, "Operationism in Sociology and Psychology," unpublished MS, p. 3.
[15] H. Hart, "Social Science and the Atomic Crisis," *Journal of Social Issues*, Supplemental Series, No. 2 (April, 1949), 13–14.

previous works. One of the themes of this volume is the emphasis on the necessity of working out methods with which reliably to predict future social developments.

Ogburn's major contribution to sociological theory, however, is contained in his early work, *Social Change* (1923), which appeared simultaneously with Giddings' last writings and prior to the recent formulations of the more extreme neo-positivists. *Social Change* can be considered as a prelude to Ogburn's later contributions in the neo-positivist style, an important and thoughtful prelude which significantly affected later sociological thought.

This volume has been given the credit for replacing the term social evolution with "social change." In a 1950 edition of *Social Change*, Ogburn stresses this point and explains the choice of the title by his interest in overcoming the psychological evolutionism which, at the time of his writing, still was strong. The book is also described at times as the first sociological study to use systematically the concept of culture as referring to "the accumulated products of human society." [16] This interpretation, however, is questionable, since Thomas used "culture" in this sense many years earlier (see Chap. 12), though not so consistently as Ogburn.

Among the volume's several theoretical generalizations about social and cultural change (the relationship between the two is not clearly stated by Ogburn), one in particular has gained attention and provoked much criticism: the hypothesis of *cultural lag*. (The author states in the 1950 edition of *Social Change* that the hypothesis is not at all fundamental to his work.) This hypothesis is sometimes interpreted as an expression of economic or technological determinism, an interpretation which is explicitly denied by Ogburn.[17]

The cultural lag hypothesis starts with the fact that a large part of man's social heritage is material culture. To use the latter, cultural adjustments, which Ogburn calls adaptive culture, are necessary. Changes in material culture precede changes in adaptive culture; adjustments cannot start before change requiring them has taken place. But old customs (parts of the previous adaptive culture) persist, bringing about "lags" which may be quite harmful. Hence—and this is where the neo-positivist position of the author reveals itself—the extent of the lag and the severity of the maladjustment should be measured in each instance. This calculation is the more important because adaptive culture is connected with other parts of culture, and social tensions reflecting cultural lags may ramify throughout the social order. Thus many problems are rooted in the relative slowness of change of the adaptive culture—the lag of protective legislation for workers behind the developing factory system, the lag of legal arrangements for political representation behind population shifts,

[16] Cf. A. L. Kroeber and C. Kluckhohn, *Culture* (Cambridge, Mass.: Harvard University, 1952) p. 15.

[17] For an interpretation along these lines and a critique of the theory of cultural lag, see MacIver and Page, *Society*, pp. 574 ff.

perhaps today the lag of decentralization of cities behind the growth of nuclear weapons, and so on. This interpretation of social problems has been employed by a number of sociologists and others, following Ogburn's original formulation, most extensively by Harry Elmer Barnes.

The theory of cultural lag, as various scholars have noted, raises the questions: "What lags behind what?" and "Is the material culture always in advance of the nonmaterial?" Ogburn carefully avoids strictly one-sided answers, stating in the original edition of *Social Change* that change may be made in nonmaterial culture, even adaptive, though the material culture remains constant. In the 1950 edition, the cultural lag hypothesis is stated especially cautiously; the significance of inventions in any part of the culture is recognized and their ramifying consequences are stressed. Such a position clearly should not be construed as economic or technological determinism. Ogburn's emphasis is rather on the necessity of measuring "lags" and their effects.

The other moderate neo-positivist whose views are discussed here, F. Stuart Chapin, has devoted his major volume to *Contemporary American Institutions* (1935). There he poses the question of how social institutions may be described and defined in a more precise manner than in popular language. For Chapin, institutions are essentially patterns of human behavior: networks of conditioned responses, individual habits, and attitudes.

One method of defining institutions precisely is graphic symbolism. Many pages of Chapin's work are occupied by graphs which the author believes help to visualize patterns of invisible relations. But these relations must be also measured. In sociology, Chapin regretfully states, studies of social force comparable to research in physical sciences utilizing units of weight are yet extremely few.[18] The reason for this situation, he believes, is that the problem to be studied consists of psychological attitudes, conditioned responses, interactions, and culture traits. The sociologist must invent units and standardized instruments of measurement; these will render institutional phenomena more susceptible of accurate recording and transmission than they are now. Accordingly, for several years, Chapin and his students have devised a number of scales for the measurement of various forms of "institutional behavior," for example, social status, effects of housing, family environment, and "personality." More recently, especially since the 1950's, scaling techniques have reached a high degree of technical sophistication, notably in the works of Paul F. Lazarsfeld, Louis Guttman, and many of their students. Chapin may be considered a major forerunner of this development.

---

[18] Chapin distinguishes two types of institutions, nuclear and symbolically diffused; here he comes very close to the ideas of Maurice Hauriou, a French student of institutions, conceiving them along the lines of Platonic philosophy (see Chap. 21). Like Hauriou, Chapin has chosen to study only the institutions of the first type in which the personal element is conspicuous, while in institutions of the second type the normative element dominates.

To the techniques of graphic symbolism and measurement by scales Chapin has added a procedure which he calls experimental, but which, at the most, is quasi-experimental. The basic idea behind this procedure, as presented in *Experimental Designs in Sociological Research* (1947),[19] is that of using the logic of laboratory experiment. In his laboratory, the physical scientist holds constant or controls all conditions but one and, varying this one, observes the effects of changes in the variable factor. Since the social scientist cannot control social change for the sake of study, he must observe two or more states of a social system or two or more social situations that differ by the presence or absence of the condition, the causal significance of which is being studied. Thus, one can observe a population before and after rehousing and ascertain the impact of the latter on morbidity and criminality. Or, to cite a more complex case, two populations with the same distributions of age, sex, race, parents' nationality, and father's occupational status, but differing in the numbers of years of schooling, may be studied; if the two populations show a significant difference in earnings or communal adjustment, the experimenter can consider that he probably has established a causal relationship.

Several ingenious applications of this experimental procedure are described by Chapin. But they hardly open new horizons. The concomitance of variations in all likelihood could be predicted on the basis of participant observation. Furthermore, the validity of the measurements of institutional phenomena, or more exactly, of their expression in mathematical symbols, remains, we believe, subject to serious doubts, although substantial work along this line is now part of the sociological enterprise.

In keeping with the neo-positivist emphasis, Chapin endorses the importance of operational definitions in social science. However, he takes a rather moderate position. "The so-called operational definition," he writes, "is not set up as any final or absolute solution, but merely as a useful development in the direction of objectivity." [20] Most sociologists today would subscribe to this view.

Unlike most neo-positivists, Chapin has shown considerable interest in the problem of long-range movements occurring in civilizations as wholes. This phase of his work will be discussed in Chapter 20 on dynamic sociology.

## A Note on Contemporary Neo-Positivism and Quantification

The work of the neo-positive school may be considered as a vigorous attempt to solve a problem that has confronted sociology since its incep-

---

[19] The idea of the experimental approach appears in an article published by Chapin as early as in 1917, but there no technique is offered. The decisive article appeared in 1940. In 1945, Ernest Greenwood published *Experimental Sociology* (New York: King's Crown Press), in which one of the modalities of Chapin's approach is greatly elaborated.

[20] F. Stuart Chapin, *Experimental Designs in Sociological Research* (New York: Harper, 1947), p. 155.

tion. The task of making the discipline fully scientific was a major pre-occupation of Comte, Durkheim, Gumplowicz, Ratzenhofer, Thomas, Giddings, and Pareto, among others. This goal, we believe, is shared by most sociologists. But the problem of whether quantification, behaviorism and operationalism are the best, or even the only, means to this end, is subject to debate.

In very recent years, as noted above, the kind of quantification that permits statistical tabulation and analysis has been supplemented by a rapidly expanding literature on "mathematical" sociology. Aided by the rapid development of sophisticated computational technology, a growing number of sociologists, in keeping with one aspect of the positivistic tradition, have been applying the analytical logic of mathematics to propositions concerning social life. This trend has been highlighted on the methodological side by the writings of Professors P. F. Lazarsfeld of Columbia University, James Coleman of Johns Hopkins, and, perhaps most notably, by Herbert A. Simon in *Models of Man* (1957). To date, however, mathematical sociology has produced few substantive propositions concerning traditional sociological problems. One such attempt is Harrison White's *The Anatomy of Kinship* (1963), in which the author treats mathematically the kinship structure of several primitive societies, but produces propositions about structural alternatives that appear to add little to our substantive knowledge of this subject.[21]

The mounting trend of mathematical sociology, sometimes hailed as the "wave of the future," calls for critical comment in a book on sociological theory. Particularly vulnerable, we believe, is the postulate that social phenomena contain latent continua to the study of which mathematical procedures can be validly applied, a postulate that has been severely criticized by Sorokin in his *Fads and Foibles in Contemporary Sociology* (1956) and, more recently, by Don Martindale.[22]

Criticism of this postulate does not mean, however, that mathematics cannot be faithfully used in sociological studies. To cite only two large-scale instances of such research, work in criminology and demography is heavily dependent upon both statistical and mathematical analysis, but this type of investigation is possible because certain behavioral and collective phenomena may be treated as units subject to mathematical manipulation which permits more or less reliable prediction, as in the case of population projections. We can foretell trends in fertility and death rates, for example, within certain limits of time and space *and* always with the reservation of "other things being equal." But unexpected and frequently unpredictable changes in the social world may take place, as they often

---

[21] See Harrison White's "Uses of Mathematical Sociology" in James C. Charlesworth, ed., *Mathematics and the Social Sciences*, Annals of Political and Social Science (Philadelphia, 1963), in which White summarizes and comments upon *The Anatomy of Kinship*.

[22] See Martindale's "Limits of the Uses of Mathematics in the Study of Sociology" in Charlesworth, ed., *op. cit.*

do in fact, and thereby defeat predictions of future developments. In this way population projections made in the 1930's of probable future trends in the United States and Europe were more often than not far off the mark. For, in historical fact, "other things" did not remain the same.

More significant than these apparent hazards of prediction, the mathematical method in sociology is based on the assumption that by replacing *real units* with corresponding quantified units and proceeding by ingenious mathematical operations, we reach mathematical values which can safely be reconverted into real units permitting the prediction of real events. This assumption, however, is dangerously ambitious. For there are three languages—the mathematical, the operational, and the causal (real)—and these are not easily translatable into each other. Equations used operationally often express asymmetric (that is, irreversible) processes, whereas mathematical equations are symmetric (or reversible). Consider, for example, the equation which expresses the transformation of two gases, oxygen and hydrogen, into water: $2H$ plus $O$ equals $H_2O$. If we were to add to both sides of this equation two other symbols—E for electric force and T for time (perhaps infinitesimal)—we would face the difficulty that time is irreversible and therefore cannot be transferred to the right side of the equation with the minus $(-)$ sign; minus T does not correspond to any reality. A similar illustration of this difficulty refers to the well-known proposition that no velocity higher than that of the propagation of light is really possible. Consequently, if we have before us an equation which expresses the production of velocity, both sides of the equation cannot be multiplied by N, a magnitude which could "produce" on paper a velocity untranslatable into "real" language, since it would be larger than the possible maximum. These examples point up the fact that mathematical data are more flexible than equations pertaining either to operational language or causal language, the latter of course of crucial importance in sociological analysis.

We may conclude this brief, and somewhat technical, discussion of present-day mathematical sociology by comparing it with Comte's original positivism. Mathematical sociologists and other modern neo-positivists are generally faithful to the positivistic tradition that tends to ascribe truth to science alone. Like Comte, the neo-positivists strongly stress observation and inference in sociological analysis. But Comte's historical method is replaced by statistical and mathematical methods, Comte's moderate realism has given way to extreme nominalism, and Comte's tempered organic analogy and his "social physics" have been replaced by a much greater reliance upon the largely mathematical methodology of modern physics. Finally, for the thesis of social progress of Comte and the other founding fathers of sociology has been substituted the aspiration of cumulative growth within scientific sociological theory itself—again, with the perhaps misleading model of physics as the goal.

# CHAPTER 16

# HUMAN ECOLOGY

Quantification, though an essential attribute of neo-positivism, is not confined to that orientation. In present-day sociology, at least two other orientations also emphasize quantification—the ecological and the sociometric. Representatives of these orientations do not necessarily share the behavioristic and operationalistic views of the neo-positivists; in fact, the sociometricians are inclined to concentrate their attention on specific mental processes.

However, the two approaches differ from neo-positivism not so much because they do not subscribe to all of its views but because each focuses upon specific phases of human life for investigation. Human ecology is primarily concerned with social phenomena which are rooted in the dependence of men on limited supplies of the necessary means to satisfy their needs. More will be said about sociometry in Chapter 19.

Human ecology, in one sense, may be viewed as a revival of biological determinism which, in the late nineteenth century, was best represented by social Darwinism, although the particular type of biological phenomena emphasized by the ecologists is quite different from the "tooth and claw" inhabitants of the latter's social world. Moreover, ecology combines biological and geographical approaches by establishing correlations between the biological background of social phenomena and the geographical environment.

The term *ecology* was introduced in 1869 by a German biologist, Ernst Haeckel (1834–1919). Biological ecology is the science of the interdependence of plants and animals living together in a natural area. The main concepts developed by that science are habitat, gradient, symbiosis (or "living together"), competition, food-chain, invasion, and succession. The idea of applying the ecological approach and these concepts to human relations first appeared in the early twentieth century in the work of Charles Galpin, *Social Anatomy of an Agrarian Community* (1915).

Galpin, who did not use the term ecology, collected data about families living in an agrarian county in Wisconsin pertaining to such questions as where they bought their supplies, where they banked, what church they attended, and what school their children attended. The findings were plotted on a map—the cartographic technique was to become quite common in ecology. Although the various areas of activity studied by Galpin did not exactly coincide spatially, nevertheless his evidence justified the claim that determinable "natural areas" exist in human society.

During the same year (1915) as the publication of Galpin's investigation, Robert E. Park (1864–1944), of the University of Chicago, which was to become the main center of ecological research, published an article on the city, again without using the term ecology. Park stated that the city is a natural phenomenon, a product of undesigned and largely uncontrollable forces, organized into areas of manufacturing, commerce, and residence. He also pointed out that people with similar economic and cultural traits tend to aggregate in specific areas of the city, and that the social and cultural characteristics of each area tend to be imposed on the lives of the inhabitants. Park's writings and his teachings were the main stimulus of a new trend of determinism, this time ecological in nature. From 1921 until 1923, R. D. MacKenzie, with Park and Ernest W. Burgess, the third founder of modern ecology, carried out an investigation of the areas of a city in the manner of Galpin; Burgess was perhaps the first sociologist to use the conceptual terminology of human ecology in systematic empirical research. The term *human ecology* was employed by Park in collaboration with Burgess, his colleague at Chicago, in their general textbook, *An Introduction to the Science of Sociology* (1921).

Burgess' classic article, "The Growth of the City," appeared in 1923. In this work, the basic hypothesis of urban ecology was stated, namely, that the city characteristically developed as a series of concentric circles located around the core zone of the central business district. Moving outward from this central area are the zones of transition, marked by physical and social deterioration, of workingmen's homes, of "middle-class" residence, and, finally, the commuters' fringe. This basic or ideal type pattern, however, in concrete cases is distorted by local topography, the transportation system, and other conditions.[1] The existence of the zone of transition was explained by the expansion of the central area; aware of this growth, owners of property in the next concentric circle, the zone of transition, do not keep their buildings in good repair, thereby providing deteriorated but relatively inexpensive dwellings for the economically and socially least privileged strata of society. The view of the spatial and social structure of the city probably holds for the earlier growth of most or at least many growing metropolitan areas in the United States, as indi-

[1] See Walter Firey's *Land Use in Central Boston* (Cambridge, Mass.: Harvard University Press, 1947), for a revealing study of extreme distortion of the concentric circle hypothesis as well as a critique of the hypothesis itself.

cated by a large number of ecologically oriented investigations.[2] However, the concentric zone pattern lacks the universal validity which sometimes is ascribed to it or is implied by urban ecologists.

In the second quarter of the twentieth century works along ecological lines began to multiply so that one could legitimately speak of an ecological "school." In the 1930's, the distinction between strictly ecological interaction and social interaction began to be emphasized; at the same time mere description of human phenomena in terms of spatial distribution was declared not to be truly ecological. Strictly ecological interaction, declared James A. Quinn, an outstanding representative of the school, operates through dependence upon some limited supply of environmental resources; each living organism necessarily affects others by increasing or decreasing the supply of resources on which the others depend. The process is impersonal and since no exchange of meanings is involved, it is subsocial; but its study is an important part of sociological analysis.[3] Park, one of the founders of the school, on the other hand, by the 1930's was arguing that, in human societies, one should distinguish two ecological (or sociological) levels: the symbiotic, rooted in impersonal competition; and the cultural, based on communication and consensus. This inclusive view, however, is not accepted by Quinn, who conceives human ecology as providing only one of the possible modes of abstraction from the indivisible network of human relations within an area of common life.

Beginning with the earlier work of Park and Burgess, the ecologists have correlated various social and cultural phenomena with the "natural areas" of the city. They have singled out for special study the zone of transition, the "slum" area, as the special breeding ground of crime, prostitution, disease, suicide, family disorganization, and other types of deviant behavior. In several works, the role of the local habitat probably has been exaggerated, sometimes even being designated as the main determinant of human conduct in society. When, for example, it is emphasized that the population of a depressed and deteriorated area displays the same deviant tendencies (manifested in delinquency, crime, and so on) despite successive changes in its ethnic composition (through "invasion-succession"), one often has the impression that, in the authors' minds, the very walls and roofs of the dilapidated buildings and the unsightly dirt of the streets themselves shape patterns of behavior. Crude environmentalism of this sort no longer marks the work of sociologists, whether they utilize an ecological approach in their investigations or other methods. Moreover, there are today few exponents of an extreme ecological posi-

[2] Among American cities the ecological patterns of which have been reported are Chicago, St. Louis, Minneapolis-St. Paul, Philadelphia, New Orleans, Seattle, Los Angeles, Boston, New Haven, and Rochester, New York.
[3] Cf. J. A. Quinn, "Human Ecology and Interactional Ecology," *American Sociological Review*, vol. V (Oct. 1940); for full treatments of the subject, see Quinn's *Human Ecology* (New York: Prentice-Hall, 1950), and A. H. Hawley, *Human Ecology* (New York: Ronald Press, 1950).

tion, which has been under attack for some years for ignoring or de-emphasizing the role of cultural and subcultural factors in patterning human conduct and character. Despite such refutations of ecological doctrine in its radical variety, the school has made important contributions to our understanding of the social structure—as well as the spatial pattern —of the modern American city, the processes of growth and movement which feature urban (and, to some extent, rural) life, and the role of these phenomena in helping to bring about characteristic forms of conventional as well as deviant behavior. Thus such studies as Ernest R. Mowrer's *Family Disorganization* and Frederick M. Thrasher's *The Gang*, both published in 1927, Clifford Shaw's *Delinquency Areas* and Harvey Zorbaugh's *The Gold Coast and the Slum*, in 1929, and *Mental Disorders in Urban Areas* by R. E. L. Faris and H. Warren Dunham, published in 1939, all applying an ecological approach to materials drawn from Chicago, not only provide revealing descriptive information about various phases of the social life of that Midwestern metropolis but are important monographs in specialized fields of sociological study.

Since World War II several good surveys of the history and present state of ecology have appeared. The most important among these are Amos H. Hawley's *Human Ecology* (1950) and *The Study of Human Ecology* (1952) by Philip Hauser and O. P. Duncan. Professor Hawley of the University of Michigan formulates a new credo for ecology: that the key determinant of social organization and behavior is the impact of the urban community, characterized by size, density, and heterogeneity; and that the main traits of social organization in cities are secularization, development of secondary associations, increased segmentation of roles, poorly defined norms, and, particularly, marked physical and social mobility. The theory of concentric zones in urban areas (the business center, the circle of areas of transition involving slums, poverty, and high delinquency), which originally was the central ecological focus, in recent years has been greatly modified or perhaps refuted by numerous studies of cities in the Americas, France, Scandinavia, and elsewhere. The study of human ecology has gradually become one of the chapters of urban sociology, that is, of a particular branch of sociology, like the sociology of law, of knowledge, or of religion.

Although urban sociologists, as in the case of other specialists, often make extensive use of propositions and insights from general sociological theory and indeed at times contribute to general theory, discussion of such special sub-disciplines is beyond the scope of the present volume. It should be remembered, however, that the modern sociological enterprise owes a substantial debt to the detailed, empirical, and, as in the studies of Park, Burgess, and Hawley, the truly creative work of the human ecologists.

# CHAPTER 17

# THE FUNCTIONAL APPROACH

In germ, the functional approach to the study of social phenomena can be traced back to the founding fathers of sociology, and then forward, particularly through the works of Durkheim, Cooley, Thomas, and Pareto. But it was only in the second quarter of the twentieth century, under the influence of cultural anthropology, that this approach achieved a definite status in sociology.[1] Functionalism displays conspicuous affinity with some characteristics of systematic sociology, another important trend in mid-twentieth century sociology (see Chap. 18); many recent works could perhaps be classified both as functional and systematic.

### The Genesis and Scope of the Functional Approach

What is functionalism? This is a question which cannot be easily answered because the terms function and functional, in sociology and cultural anthropology, are given different and uncorrelated meanings. Sometimes, especially in Sorokin's work, the term function is used in the mathematical sense, connoting a variable the magnitude of which is determined by the magnitude of another. More often, function refers to the contribution made by a part to some whole, to a society or a culture, for example; this is the meaning often ascribed to function by such leading anthropologists as A. R. Radcliffe-Brown, Ralph Linton, and Bronislaw Malinowski, and also, germinally, in the writings of Durkheim. (We use the term function in this sense when we say that the function of government is to secure peace and order in society.) As a modality of this second meaning, function is sometimes expanded to designate also the contributions made by the group to its members (for example, by the family to the survival of babies), or by larger to smaller groups. Again,

[1] Illustrative of the growing influence of functionalism are many textbooks, perhaps most notably Kingsley Davis, *Human Society* (New York: Macmillan, 1949).

the functional approach frequently refers to the emphasis upon the integration of parts into wholes or, what is almost the same thing, the interdependence of parts; one also meets this usage in the works of the authors just mentioned. Finally, the expression functional analysis is used to designate the study of social phenomena as operations or effects of specified social structures, such as kinship systems or class systems; therefore, it commonly appears in the compound form, *structural-functional*. This phrasing can be found in the works of Parsons and his followers (whose views will be presented in Chap. 18) but may be traced back to Spencer. This terminological situation is confusing indeed, and the confusion is increased when one takes into consideration the fact that, to designate the various meanings of function, other terms are often used.[2]

Nevertheless, observation of recent developments both in sociology and cultural anthropology shows that the movement known as functionalism is centered around the second and the third of the four meanings of function noted above. Functionalism, then, may be interpreted as maintaining the hypothesis that all social phenomena covered by these two meanings go together and that sociological theory should be focused upon them. In a form which is not explicitly stated in any particular writing, the basic functional theorem reads as follows: A social system (the term is often used by the functionalists) is a real system in which the parts perform functions essential for the persistence (eventually, the expansion or strengthening) of the whole and therefore are interdependent and more or less completely integrated.

The functional approach is older in biology, psychology, and cultural anthropology than in sociology. Biology as a science is organized around the idea that each organ, or part of the system called an organism, performs a function or functions essential for the survival of the organism or of the species to which it belongs, or both; as a corollary, the principle of the interdependence of the organs is stressed. In brief, an organism is perceived as a system of functionally interrelated components.

In psychology, during the late nineteenth and early twentieth centuries, various analytical schools painstakingly described the component parts of the mental process (such as cognition, emotion, and volition) but were unable to grasp its unity. Beginning earlier but developing in the 1920's and 1930's, there arose the influential *Gestalt* (configuration) school, maintaining that any element of the mental process, if realistic understanding is to be achieved, must be studied in the context of the whole, because the meaning of every element varies in accordance with the total configuration of which it is a part.

In ethnology or cultural anthropology the functional approach was anticipated by Franz Boas (1858–1942) who, in 1887, wrote: "The art and characteristic style of a people can be understood only by studying its

---

[2] Cf. R. K. Merton, *Social Theory and Social Structure* (Glencoe, Ill.: The Free Press, 1949), pp. 22–27.

products as a whole."[3] But functionalism in anthropology developed much later, in opposition both to evolutionism and to diffusionism. Evolutionism was described in earlier chapters, as well as its collapse as new theories, including functionalism, emerged. Diffusionism is a position taken by some ethnologists which emphasizes the spreading or diffusion of inventions from a relatively small number of culture centers and its significance in cultural growth. Contrary to the historical orientation of both of these schools, which explain every culture item by locating it either in the evolutionary scheme or in a concrete historical process of diffusion, the functionalists declare that the explanation of every culture item is to be found in what it does for the whole and, correlatively, in terms of its interdependence with the other items which form the culture. As frequently is the case with innovators, the functionalists were guilty of exaggerations, sometimes seeming to claim that *every* culture item is functional in the sense of contributing positively to the whole culture and disregarding clearly harmful customs, in the manner of Sumner. Similarly functional anthropologists sometimes implied that every social system is perfectly integrated, disregarding the well-known fact of social disorganization.

The rise of functional sociology was greatly stimulated by the trends in biology, psychology, and cultural anthropology. But functional sociologists can trace back their genealogy within their own discipline as well. The ideas of the integration of parts into wholes and of the interdependence of the different elements of a society appeared in Comte's *consensus universalis,* in Spencer's preoccupation with integration compensating for differentiation, in Cooley's organic theory, and especially in Pareto's conception of society as a system in equilibrium. The emphasis upon the contributions made by particular social structures to the whole was made by Durkheim and by Thomas. The latter's (and Znaniecki's) *The Polish Peasant* can be considered as the first major work in modern sociology written in the functional spirit.

### Some Major Works in the Functional Style

In 1929, Robert S. and Helen M. Lynd published *Middletown,* which has become a classic in American sociological literature. This study is a well-planned and well-executed attempt to understand a more or less representative American community (Muncie, Indiana) as a relatively closed social and cultural system satisfying the basic needs of its members. These needs are stated in dynamic terms: getting a living (acquiring the means of subsistence); making a home (including marriage and child-rearing); training the young; using leisure; engaging in religious practices; participating in community activities, especially operating the government; taking care of public health; caring for the indigent; providing information.

[3] Franz Boas, in an article in *Science,* vol. 9, pp. 485 ff.

The investigation was carried out largely by participant observation, in the manner of modern ethnological studies, though historical documents and statistical data were also used.

The findings convinced the Lynds that the modalities of need satisfaction appearing in Middletown point to a definite type of social structure, namely, the basic division of the population into business and working classes, each of which performs the essential social functions somewhat differently. The hypothesis of full integration of the social-cultural system was not verified, the community life being marked by a maze of interlocking, often contradictory, institutional activities. Side by side, the authors found attempts to employ nineteenth-century psychology in child-training and twentieth-century psychology in business, reliance on eighteenth-century *laissez faire* and use of twentieth-century machines, and so on. However, some uniformities in social change were established, for example, the fact that material innovations were accepted more willingly and rapidly than new ideas concerning the relations between husbands and wives, between parents and children, or between social classes. This finding seemed to corroborate Ogburn's cultural lag hypothesis.

*Middletown*, hailed by some commentators as the first important demonstration of the applicability of anthropological methods and theory to modern complex communities and cited by others as a "new kind of history," was widely read in American universities in the 1930's. In 1937 the Lynds published *Middletown in Transition*, a follow-up study of Muncie during the early depression years, which, while maintaining the holistic point of view of the earlier work, focused more sharply on the class structure and the economic and political power relations in Muncie. These volumes have stimulated a number of similar studies, both in this country and elsewhere.

The best known of these is the Yankee City series, directed by William L. Warner, a six-volume report of a small New England city, which stresses its class and status structure, its changing ethnic patterns, and its industrial system. The first volume, *The Social Life of a Modern Community*, presents Warner's functional viewpoint in terms of the following ideas: When reciprocal interaction is organized into defined relationships, it produces systems of informal and formal groupings called social structures which regulate the social behavior of individuals. Each of these structures (the family, the economic organization, the church, and so on) is manifested by patterned rules enforced by formal and informal sanctions. Finally, the various social structures are so interrelated that they form a dynamic totality. This integrated interrelationship of the social system in all societies is brought about by the emphasis given one structure which gives form to the total society and integrates the other structures into a social unity in much the same way in which the skeleton provides a framework for the other parts of the body. In Yankee City and throughout American society, the role of the skeleton is played by the structure of social class.

A large part of the Yankee City series, as well as several other volumes undertaken by Warner or making use of his theory and method, depict in detail the systems of social class and their interrelations with economic, genealogical status, and ethnic factors in communities in various parts of the United States. Thus, this phase of functional sociology is represented, for example, by *Deep South* (1941), directed by Warner, James West's *Plainville, U.S.A.* (1945), and A. B. Hollingshead's *Elmtown's Youth* (1949).

In Robin M. Williams' *American Society* (1951, revised 1960) a much more ambitious objective is pursued, that of describing and explaining, in sociological terms, the social relations and the concomitant beliefs and values that characterize the people of the United States. Williams distinguishes social organization (defined as a web of recurring social interactions) and culture, especially normative culture understood as "blueprint for behavior." Complexes of norms backed by intensive social sanctions, enjoying wide support and associated with major needs or value orientations, are *institutions*. The major part of the work is devoted to a survey of major institutions in contemporary America. But perhaps the outstanding feature of this study is Williams' treatment of the question of how the partially autonomous institutions are integrated. He answers this question in terms of a tentative but general theory of social and cultural integration. The means of integration, he explains, are, first, mutual dependence of individual gains and interests; second, explicit mechanisms of cohesion, including agreement about the rules under which interests may be pursued, the existence of extensive organizations which link together smaller organizations and primary groups, and finally, systems of representation and imperative control; third, reaction to external pressures, such as war or threat of war; fourth, common acceptance of values and symbols. Using these analytical tools, we are able, Williams believes, to understand "the daily miracle of society in being." Knowledge of these integrative mechanisms is not sterile: in our day, says Williams, most errors in public and private life result from a failure to foresee the repercussions of particular acts taking place within the total social system.

Whereas the works surveyed above are concerned with whole societies or communities, there are others in the functional style, which are devoted to particular aspects of social life. A case in point is Albert K. Cohen's *Delinquent Boys* (1956). The author unfolds the idea that, within American society, there exists a "delinquent subculture," nonutilitarian, malicious and negativistic; this subculture is met primarily among young males of the working class. Cohen poses the question of the causes of such a subculture, and answers it in functional terms by demonstrating how this "subculture" meets actual needs of youth from working class families. The boys of that class are exposed to difficult adjustment problems, especially at schools run largely according to the middle class tradition. The evaluations of this tradition encourage the ascription of a low status to working class boys, which hurts them all the more because of the egalitarian ingredient of American culture. The delinquent gang is one response to this situation: in its midst, boys are rated according to standards quite at variance with those of the middle class, and the latter are negated. Isolated delinquency is not an adequate response to these circumstances (except on the psychological level of frustration-aggression), whereas group activity, in this case delinquent conduct, operates within the gang to confer and to enhance status. Put in functional terms, Cohen's explanation of the formation and the activities of delinquent gangs is that they contribute to the solution of one of the major problems of young male members of America's working class. Of course, there are "functional alternatives" (see next section): a "corner boy" may try to become a "college boy" (which is easier said than done), or he may accept the situation while refraining from delinquent behavior. Members of delinquent gangs, of course, are not ordinarily aware of the social functions of the gang, but this is a frequent situation encountered in functional analysis—a point to be developed shortly.

While Cohen's *Delinquent Boys* may be interpreted in terms of functionalism, W. J. Goode's *Religion Among the Primitives* (1951) is explicitly functional. The author states that his analysis is sociological (which he identifies with analysis in terms of common value orientation), functional and comparative. Goode's general discussion of functionalism identifies this approach with a view of society as a unitary process, going so far as to claim that society has goals which are not identical with individual ends. In his theoretical discussion, the author stresses the parts-into-whole integration aspect of functionalism. But most of his work is devoted to a painstaking study of the interdependence of the religious phase of social life in five primitive societies with their economic, political and familial activities. He shows, for instance, how economic production for the Dahomean is intermeshed with the latter's use of the supernatural; and, more generally, claims that, among the societies studied, the supernatural and sacred interact with the economic realm—by defining concrete behavior, by shifting the ends to be achieved and by furnishing motivation. The religious system supports the political not only explicitly, but also implicitly and symbolically, especially by stressing institutional patterns for avoiding conflicts. And the structure and statuses of the family are often reflected in religion, the gods forming families along human lines. In these societies, at least—Goode is not inclined to extrapolation—religious rules serve as instruments of integration, offering common, societal values which help to direct the society as a whole. But the elements of the religious system are not necessarily entirely functional

—for they may inhibit other areas of action which enhance the welfare of the society; several such illustrations appear in the detailed studies of the economic, political and familial activities.

## Toward a Systematic Functional Theory

These studies constitute a small but representative sample of the functional approach now often used in sociology. However, until very recently theoretical codification of this approach had not been developed. One attempt was that of the anthropologist Bronislaw Malinowski (1884–1942). His *Scientific Theory of Culture* (1944) claims for cultural anthropology the role of the generalizing social science (see Chap. 1), presents an undeveloped definition of functionalism, and illustrates the use of functionalism in research. Malinowski dismisses the rough approach to functionalism that reduces it to the almost useless proposition that everything is related to everything else. To avoid this pitfall, the procedure of isolation is advocated by Malinowski, who states that "the functional isolate is Institution." (In Malinowski's usage the term institution refers to a social group as well as to established methods of procedure.) Each institution carries out at least one social function, which is to say it meets an established social need. Malinowski presents two axioms which, he declares, must underlie every scientific theory of culture. First, every culture must satisfy man's biological needs, such as nutrition, procreation, protection against damaging forces of climate, dangerous animals, and men; but culture must also provide for occasional relaxation and the regulation of growth. Second, every cultural achievement is an instrumental enhancement of human physiology, referring directly or indirectly to the satisfaction of a bodily need. Malinowski expresses the conviction that it is possible "to link up functionally the various types of cultural response, such as economic, legal, educational, scientific, magic, and religious," to biological needs, elementary or derived. Thus "the functional explanation of art, recreation and public ceremonial might have to refer to directly physical reactions of the organism to rhythm, sound, color, line, form and to their combinations." [4]

As presented by Malinowski, who, with Radcliffe-Brown, is commonly believed to be the outstanding exponent of functionalism in cultural anthropology, functional theory—though not his famous field studies of the Trobrianders—almost seems to become a partial revival of biological determinism, which few of its contemporary exponents conceive functionalism to be.

Functionalists today are developing a type of theory, especially applicable to the study of social structure and cultural diversity, which may be briefly depicted as follows. In the first place (and this starting point is

[4] Bronislaw Malinowski, *Scientific Theory of Culture* (Chapel Hill, N.C.: University of North Carolina, 1944), pp. 174–75.

often obscured in the writings of functionalists), the maintenance and the possible extension of a group and its social system, as well as the persistence and the possible improvement of the group's culture, are defined, at least implicitly, as the group's objectives or goals. Empirical study should reveal a given system's *functional requisites,* that is, the conditions under which these objectives can be achieved. It can then be shown that specific parts of the group's social structure and culture operate as mechanisms that satisfy (or do not satisfy) the functional requisites. Further propositions follow as broad theoretical guides. First, universal functional needs can be met in different ways, illustrated by social and cultural variation; and individual societies, so to speak, have "selected" their particular procedures from a wide range of cultural possibilities. But, second, the number of such "choices" is always limited, limited by the biological characteristics of man and by his social and psychic needs; hence the prevalence of independent and parallel inventions in different societies (a phenomenon which served the evolutionists as one of their strongest arguments). Third, the range of "choices" for a specific society is further limited by the interrelationship and, in some measure, the interdependence of the choices themselves; thus, the adoption of one type of kinship system, for example, restricts the number of possibilities in other institutional areas. (More concretely, as it has often been noted, modern industrial growth in traditionally agrarian societies no doubt limits, but does not determine, the number and type of possible political and other institutional developments.) A major task of functional analysis is to discover the number and type of cultural possibilities under diverse social conditions. An ambitious effort in that direction may be seen in *The Structure of Society* (1952) by Marion Levy, Jr., influenced also by the "structural-functional" lines of T. Parsons' theory (see Chap. 18).

The further advance of functional theory requires a clear understanding of the concept of *function* itself as well as the development of a methodology which can be used to establish the functional interrelations of various segments of a sociocultural system and their significance for the persistence (or eventual expansion) of the whole system or of subsystems within it. Conceptual analysis of function and its subconcepts has been provided by Professors Levy [5] and Merton.

Merton defines function as "those observed consequences which make for the adaptation and adjustment of a given system." [6] This definition, we believe, is somewhat misleading. The function of a partial structure, that is, a culture trait, custom, institution, or subsystem (A), more exactly, of its *operation,* is not identical for system N with the consequences of the operation of A, but with the *meaning* of these consequences or of the specific contribution of these consequences for N. Let

[5] Marion Levy, Jr., *The Structure of Society* (Princeton, N.J.: Princeton University Press, 1952), Chap. 2.

[6] R. K. Merton, *op. cit.,* p. 50.

us designate them by M. Then we can say that the specific contribution which A makes for the persistence of N is M. Or, expressed in another way: a contributive cause of the persistence of N (say, the family) is A (for example, the incest taboo) because of M (prevention of confusion in family roles). It would not be functional, but teleological reasoning, however, if one claimed that the prevention of confusion of roles in the family is the cause of the incest taboo. The problem of the origin of functionally relevant traits is beyond the scope of functional analysis.[7]

What procedures may be used to apply and test functional hypotheses? Mental experiment is one possibility. We can sometimes calculate, at least within broad limits, what would happen in a society if a partial structure were eliminated or interrupted in its operation. Thus, a specific economic institution, say, or a sociocultural pattern such as organized sport may be "thought away" (Weber's conception) and the probable consequences for the society may be estimated. But we should not forget the words of caution of Max Weber concerning mental experiment which he proposed as a legitimate tool of causal analysis, to be sure, but nevertheless stressed its limitations (see Chap. 14).

The comparative method is another possibility. Comparison can be performed on the qualitative and on the quantitative levels. Qualitatively, if two social situations could be found differing by the presence or absence of a particular trait or partial structure, the differential consequences of this dissimilarity for the survival and prosperity of the total system may be established. One way to quantitative comparison is set forth in the works of Sorokin (a bitter foe of the functional approach, though in one sense an extreme functionalist, as we shall see in Chap. 20). Sorokin suggests methods to quantify the proportions of functionally contradictory or consistent elements in a culture, for example, religious art in a secular or in a religious culture. Sorokin holds that, first, fluctuation of such magnitudes in time and their distribution in space can be established; second, if these fluctuations and distributions follow the pattern of concomitant change, functional interrelationship of the traits is thereby established; but, third, functional interconnection is refuted if the fluctuations and distributions follow random patterns. These propositions are incorporated in Sorokin's dynamic sociology.

Another procedure available to functional analysis is observation and analysis of the consequences of various types of disturbance to a society brought about by internal or external events or both. Thus, study of the effects of a declaration of war, for example, or of a revolutionary invention such as atomic power may reveal hitherto unsuspected persistencies or functional relations (or weaknesses) in a social system. Indeed, an enormous amount of research along these lines is being conducted today and, while most of it is not explicitly functional, it no doubt will contribute to the further development of functional theory.

[7] These propositions have been developed in H. C. Bredemeyer's article "The Methodology of Functionalism," *American Sociological Review*, 20 (1955), 173 ff.

These procedures represent only some of the methodological possibilities of potential use in functional analysis. (Mental experiment, comparative method, and study of the effects of disturbance, of course, have been and are employed by representatives of other approaches.) The interdependence and interplay of empirical research of various types and the growth of functional theory have recently been stressed by several scholars, perhaps most effectively by Merton in his *Social Theory and Social Structure.*

In this same volume, Merton makes some important contributions to functional theory. He attempts to codify systematically a protocol or paradigm for functionalism, an effort designed to present "the hard core of concept, procedure and inference in functional analysis."[8] In this effort, Merton makes explicit the distinction between *manifest* and *latent* functions, a distinction found in implicit form in the works of numerous scholars. Manifest functions refer to the objective consequences of a specific social or cultural unit which contribute to its adoption or adjustment and were so intended by the participants; latent functions refer to unintended and unrecognized consequences. Thus, to cite a well-known illustration of Merton's, a manifest function of economic consumption is use, while one of its latent functions is (or was, at one time), as Veblen stressed, the maintenance or enhancement of prestige. In the few years since the publication (1949) of Merton's work, this distinction has been employed extensively by American sociologists. The distinction, as Merton himself stresses, and as he illustrates in a short but masterful essay on the urban political machine in which this organization is portrayed as meeting existing needs of various groups that are not efficiently fulfilled by official institutions, is especially valuable because it calls attention to latent functions that are apt to be overlooked in social analysis.

Merton's discussion of the political machine also illustrates the concept of functional alternatives, essential for analysis "once we abandon the gratuitous assumption of the functional indispensability of given social structures"; it should not be assumed, for example, that the machine provides the only way of meeting the needs of such groups as businessmen and ambitious members of deprived segments of the population. The concept of functional alternatives "focuses attention on the range of possible variation in the items which can, in the given instance, subserve a functional requirement. It unfreezes the identity of the existent and the inevitable."[9]

Finally, Merton cautions against preoccupation with the "statics of social structure," a tendency of certain representatives of the functional school. In this connection, he employs the concept of dysfunctions: "those observed consequences which lessen the adaptation or adjustment of the system." (Ethnic discrimination, for example, may be said to be

[8] Merton, *op. cit.,* p. 49.
[9] *Ibid.,* p. 52.

dysfunctional in a society that stresses values of freedom and opportunity.) The concept of dysfunction, Merton declares, "which implies the concept of strain, stress and tension on the structural level, provides an analytical approach to the study of dynamics and change." [10]

Recently a symposium, *Functionalism in the Social Sciences*, edited by Don Martindale, appeared. Of its nine papers, only two pertain strictly to the field of sociology, those by Jan Whittaker (of the University of Cardiff) and by the editor. These two authors appear to be in full accord. They deal at length with the division of functionalism, opposing *holism* to *elementarism*, which Martindale defines as follows:

> Holism is the view that the basic social reality consists of interrelated wholes which are superior to the individual and his actions in the whole, but one cannot reduce the whole to the actions of the individual . . .

> Elementarism is the view that the basic social reality is constituted by individuals and their acts. Social events consist solely in their interaction. Any notion that interaction possesses new or emergent properties such that some sort of whole with irreducible properties of its own arises is a pure product of reification.[11]

Martindale believes that a useful classification of types of theoretical analysis can be achieved by crossing one dichotomy, in this case the epistemological distinction noted above, with another, which in his presentation is derivable from the opposition of mind (soul) to matter (body). The second dichotomy appears to be that which exists between positivism (ascribing reality only to matter or acknowledging both mind and matter) and anti-positivism. In this way he develops a fourfold classification: positive holism, anti-positive holism, positive elementarism, and anti-positive elementarism.

To what extent this classification will be helpful in scientific discussion in obtaining new insights into facts to be explained remains to be seen. (It is neither all-inclusive nor necessarily correct.) However, the ontological dichotomy of holism and elementarism is applicable perhaps to the essential difference between what are now often termed "macrosociology" and "microsociology." (Microsociology is illustrated primarily by the emerging—and somewhat fashionable—"small group theory." This development is not treated in the present volume, however, because we believe it to be of ephemeral interest only to the study of sociological theory as such. Small group theory, necessarily concerned in substantial measure with the explanation of individual behavior, overlaps widely with psychological theory, which in turn raises basic questions of a philosophical nature, including those involving the mind-body distinction. These are beyond the scope of the present discussion.)

[10] *Ibid.*, p. 53.
[11] Don Martindale, "Limits of and Alternatives to Functionalism in Sociology," in Don Martindale, ed., *Functionalism in the Social Sciences*, The American Academy of Political and Social Science Series (Philadelphia: 1965), pp. 150–51.

More generally, opinion about functionalism remains divided. An excellent article, both critical and sympathetic, by Alvin W. Gouldner, convincingly emphasizes that the functional approach offers insights additional to the causal approach: to the "Why?" of the latter it joins the former's "What for?" [12] Although not explaining the genesis or precise makeup of social systems, functionalism allows us to understand why certain elements of these systems are, or at least tend to be, persistent and why some elements occur so frequently. Modern functionalists have not fallen into the error of earlier sociologists denounced by Durkheim; they do not derive the persistence of specified types of social systems from their utility, but treat the utility with the same importance as the problem of causality.

## Functionalism in Larger Perspective

Functional theory and research represent a new but rapidly growing approach. Its accomplishments are promising but still tentative. Functionalism's position concerning the basic problems of sociological theory may be summarized as follows:

The trend takes over the conception of society as a social system, as stated, say, by Pareto. Most functionalists imply, if they do not explicitly emphasize, that a social system operates meaningfully. The operations of the system are oriented toward the needs of the members. The term culture often appears in functional literature as interchangeable with social system.

The units of observation vary from writer to writer. For example, Malinowski, unfortunately, chose the social group (which he called institution). The Lynds focus upon human needs to be satisfied by a society conceived as a going concern. Merton (and Levy) outlines an inclusive scheme for sociological observation, but his own studies are primarily concerned with social structures.

The problem of the relationship of individual and society is not explicitly discussed, though Thomas, as we pointed out in Chapter 12, pioneered important work in the functional interrelations of personality and culture.

The questions of the determinants of social structure and of social change are answered emphatically in favor of multiple causation. Many, but functionally interrelated, factors determine the configuration of a society as well as its changes; this view seems to be widely shared.

But the functionalists share no preferred definition of sociology. Some of them, especially those who are not sociologists, would incorporate sociology in cultural anthropology.

The methodology of the functionalists has been weak, often resting

[12] "Reciprocity and Autonomy in Functional Theory," in Llewellyn Gross, ed., *Symposium on Sociological Theory* (Chicago: Row, Peterson, 1959).

on intuition or the ability of the observer to "see" functions performed by partial structures, correlations, integrations, and so on. We have suggested a few ideas about more precise procedures. More thorough treatments of methodological problems can be found in the works of Merton and Levy.

The relatively short experience of functionalism seems to point to the fact that a meaningful description of social structures and culture in functional terms requires a "central theme" around which the rest of the socio-cultural system can be intelligibly organized.[13] Moreover, as Sorokin, Merton, and others have stressed, it must be recognized that societal integration is never complete, and that every society and culture contains elements which are misfits within the whole. The failure to conceive of society as a dynamic and imperfect equilibrium unfortunately characterizes the work of some functionalists, especially in cultural anthropology.

Finally, there are good reasons to believe that the hypothesis of extreme functionalists, according to which all parts of a culture have positive functions, has been misleading. The more cautious and more realistic formulations of the anthropologist Ralph Linton, who assumes the existence of "functionless items," [14] and of Merton and Levy, who hypothesize non-functional consequences [15] and dysfunctions, should encourage the development of a more sophisticated functional theory.

Functionalism is perhaps more promise than achievement. But it is an important promise. Mathematical sociology would reduce sociology to measurement. Functionalism does not preclude measurement (or other research techniques). But functional analysis directs attention toward meaning; it strives to answer the question: What do specific and diverse phenomena mean from the point of view of the whole social order?

Sometimes, functionalism becomes quasi-philosophical by identifying function with objective, that is transpersonal finality. This shows up for instance in Goode's statement that societies have goals of their own. Still stronger is the expression of the same idea by a Belgian scholar, H. Janne. Janne envisions a new type of general theory, integrating into a coherent whole the main trends of contemporary sociology.[16] Who speaks of function, he argues, admits unconscious and objective finality; in other words, social phenomena or processes are viewed *as if* they were unfolding toward the achievement of definite ends. This situation is conspicuous in education. In communicating knowledge, educational institutions pursue ends of their own, while children and young persons strive for personal goals. But at the conclusion of formal education young people are often

[13] Cf. W. L. Warner and P. S. Lunt, *The Social Life of a Modern Community* (New Haven: Yale University Press, 1941). See also Ruth Benedict, *Patterns of Culture* (Boston: Houghton Mifflin, 1934), and P. A. Sorokin, *Social and Cultural Dynamics*, 4 vols. (New York: American Book, 1937–41) for larger-scale efforts to establish central themes of whole cultures.

[14] R. Linton, *The Study of Man* (New York: Appleton-Century, 1936), p. 406.

[15] Merton, *op. cit.*, pp. 50–51; Levy, *op. cit.*, esp. Chap. 2.

[16] "Fonction et finalité en sociologie," *Cahiers internationaux de sociologie*, vol. 16 (1954).

well prepared for adjustment to social life—much as if there were a center consistently directing the activities of the groups and individuals involved and balancing their particularistic tendencies; similarly with the economic system based on free enterprise, and with the invention of tools which is determined by the functional exigencies of the dynamic adjustment of group members to the environment. The historical process, as shown by Henri Pirenne, can be interpreted as possessing objective finality, goal directedness toward specified aspects of the present.

Such extensions of the meaning of functionalism are by no means necessary. A functionalist may remain on safe ground by confining himself to answering questions about ascertainable contributions of parts to wholes (or *vice-versa*), and about the kind and extent of integration of the elements of a social system.

# CHAPTER 18

# SYSTEMATIC SOCIOLOGY

The central phenomenon in the midcentury development of sociological theory is a trend we shall call systematic. It dominates the field in the United States and has also been acknowledged by many scholars in Europe and Japan. Semantically, *systemic* would have been preferable to denote this trend; but this is an artificial term and it is highly desirable not to plant into sociology too many neologisms that allow its denigrators to speak of a sociological "jargon."

The term *system*, designating a whole of which the parts are interrelated and integrated around a central core, is not new in sociology. Spencer had already used it, and in Pareto's teaching it occupied a central position. But Pareto employed a faulty approach to the study of society as a social system; for him the latter was to a large extent psychological, in the sense of the reduction of social phenomena to mental processes, which met the devastating critique of Durkheim.

In the treatment of the concept *system* and its application to society by today's protagonists of the systematic trend, "system" refers to human behavior in society. The systematic sociologists assert and demonstrate that social phenomena, though closely connected with certain mental phenomena resulting in behavior, are interconnected in the most complex ways, which differ from their grouping by psychologists. However, before presenting the views of prominent systematists of our time, it is important to eliminate a possible confusion with the term *systematic sociology* as it is used by some German sociologists, particularly Leopold von Wiese. Von Wiese has employed *system* to characterize a treatment of social phenomena resulting in propositions that can and must be treated as forming a system (note: not the facts themselves but their reflection in the minds of sociologists) in contradistinction to the study of their genesis and development; this contradistinction is quite similar to that conventionally drawn between static and dynamic sociology. Static sociology, however, should not be confused with an approach that would consider social facts as immutable. All major representatives of present-day systematic sociology are concerned, though in varying degrees, with both social structure and social change.

### Sorokin

Having defined systematic sociology, we can consider the works of a leading sociologist, who may be designated as a protagonist of the systematic trend, one who must be singled out, we believe, and given first rank in creative ability, erudition, and command of the prerequisites of a system of scientific thought. This scholar is Pitirim A. Sorokin (1889–      ).

Sorokin was born in a remote village of northeastern Russia. He studied at the University of St. Petersburg and early in life embarked on a career of teaching, scientific research, and writing, as well as political activity. In 1914 his monograph *Crime and Punishment, Heroic Act and Reward* was published and in 1919 his *System of Sociology* (two volumes, in Russian), a work somewhat behavioristic in orientation.

Sorokin in 1917 acted as secretary to Alexander Kerensky, head of Russia's provisional government, and, after the latter's fall, actively participated in the struggle against Communism. He was arrested, tried, sentenced to death; but the penalty was commuted to exile. After two years in Czechoslovakia, he came to the United States.

In this country, Sorokin became professor of sociology at the University of Minnesota, where he wrote two outstanding works, *Social Mobility* (1927) and *Contemporary Sociological Theories* (1928). The latter volume is a systematic study and criticism of the main "schools" of sociology, emphasizing their different approaches to the problem of the determinants of the structure of society and of social change. In 1930, Sorokin became professor of sociology at Harvard University and there established the first Harvard department of sociology, of which he was chairman for a decade. During his Harvard years his publications were prolific. His major writings include his magnum opus, *Social and Cultural Dynamics* (four volumes, 1937–41); the monograph *Sociocultural Causality, Time and Space* (1943), which may be considered a supplement to the *Dynamics;* and a systematic treatise on sociology, unique in American sociology in terms of comprehensiveness and integration, *Society, Culture, and Personality* (1947). In 1950, he made a substantial addition to his *Sociological Theories* by publishing *The Social Philosophies of an Age of Crisis*. In 1956, he published *Fads and Foibles in Contemporary Sociology*, a critical appraisal of mid-twentieth century sociology and in 1966, *Sociological Theories of Today*.

In 1959, Sorokin celebrated his seventieth anniversary. His admirers and former students brought out two volumes in honor of that event: one, edited by Professor Philip A. Allen, appeared under the title *Sorokin in Retrospect* (1962) and consisted of articles discussing various aspects of Sorokin's contributions; the other, edited by Professor Edward A. Tiryakian, entitled *Sociological Theory, Values, and Sociocultural Change* (1963), contained unrelated monographs in the style of a *Festschrift*.[1] Sorokin himself recently has published a very readable autobiography under the title *A Long Journey*. These publications helped to restore Sorokin's name to the limelight of American sociology. Always a candid critic and a rather controversial figure, this great scholar was elected president of the American Sociological Association for the years 1964–1965.

Sorokin's outstanding reputation here and abroad is suggested by the many translations of most of his numerous books, the recent republication of *Social Mobility* and *Contemporary Sociological Theories*, and the current project in England to condense the latter volume and to combine it with the recently completed *Sociological Theories of Today* (1966). The last-named work is a large-scale survey and critique of major publications in sociology, as well as of contributions in other disciplines of particular sociological relevance. In this ambitious study, the latest revision of Sorokin's own theories are presented in the introductory section and the main classes of sociological theories are discussed under the categories: 1) nominalistic-singularistic, 2) theories of cultural systems, 3) theories of social systems, 4) taxonomies of sociocultural systems (including their changing patterns). Sorokin does not locate his own theories in this scheme, but we may infer from certain comments that he sees his own work as a special case of "integral sociology" in the tradition of Aristotle.

Sorokin's publications may be divided into those which contribute primarily to systematic sociology proper and those dealing with dynamic sociology. In this chapter, we will consider the former; dynamic sociology will be discussed in Chapter 20.

In Chapter 1 it was pointed out that Sorokin has defined sociology in a way that seems acceptable to sociologists of various trends and in a way that describes accurately the scope of theoretical sociology. Thus, sociology, he declares, is the study of the general characteristics common to all classes of social phenomena, of the relationship between these classes, and of the relationship between social and nonsocial phenomena.[2] In *Society, Culture, and Personality* Sorokin provides another delineation of the field, pointing more precisely to the appropriate areas of sociological investigation: Sociology is the generalizing theory of the structure and dynamics of *a*) social systems and congeries (functionally inconsistent elements), *b*) cultural systems and congeries, and *c*) personalities in their structural

---

[1] The present writer contributed to both volumes, with an article discussing Sorokin on war, revolution, and social calamities for the first, and an essay on the sociology of Luigi Sturzo for the second.

[2] Pitirim A. Sorokin, *Contemporary Sociological Theories* (New York: Harper, 1928), p. 760.

aspect, main types, interrelationships, and personality processes.[3] Some of the terms used in this definition require explanation, which is developed in the following pages.

In accordance with the view of many sociologists, going back to Simmel, Sorokin chooses *interaction* as the unit into which social phenomena should be analyzed. "In its developed forms," he explains, "the superorganic [a term that had been employed by Spencer] is found exclusively in the realm of interacting human beings and in the products of their interaction."[4] Interaction in this context refers to "any event by which one party tangibly influences the overt actions or the state of mind of the other."[5] The subjects of interaction are either human individuals or organized groups of human beings.

Sorokin limits the concept of interaction by holding that "the most generic model of any sociocultural phenomenon is the meaningful interaction of two or more . . . individuals."[6] The reason for this limitation is to be seen in Sorokin's conception of sociocultural interaction. The latter includes three inseparably interrelated components: "1) *personality* as the subject of interaction; 2) *society* as the totality of interacting personalities; and 3) *culture* as the totality of the meanings, values, and norms possessed by the interacting personalities and the totality of the vehicles which objectify, socialize, and convey these meanings."[7] Each of these three components is subject to extensive analysis in Sorokin's work. The treatment of culture, however, is by far his most important contribution.

Society is crystallized into *social groups* or *systems*. Depending on the character of interaction, groups may be organized, unorganized, or disorganized. Sorokin states:

> A social group, as a totality of interacting individuals, is organized when its central set of meanings and values, as the reason for their interaction, is somewhat consistent within itself and assumes the form of the law-norms precisely defining all the relevant actions-reactions of the interacting individuals in their relationship toward one another, the outsiders, and the world at large; and when these norms are effective, obligatory, and, if need be, enforced, in the conduct of the interacting persons.[8]

This rather complicated statement may be analyzed into four interrelated propositions: 1) Each organized group is characterized by "a central set of meanings and values"; here the term "meaning" is almost synonymous with "idea." This proposition is similar to the institutionalists' view (see Chap. 21) that a social group is built around a "directive idea," that

[8] Pitirim A. Sorokin, *Society, Culture, and Personality* (New York: Harper, 1947), p. 17.
[4] *Ibid.*, p. 4.
[5] *Ibid.*, p. 40.
[6] *Ibid.*, p. 40.
[7] *Ibid.*, p. 63.
[8] *Ibid.*, p. 70 (original in italics).

is, an idea which expresses some value to be achieved by the group.[9] 2) The central set of ideas and values must be consistent within itself: a principle closely approximating a theorem held by many functionalists. 3) These consistent ideas and values assume the form of norms to be followed by the group members. 4) These norms, which Sorokin calls "law-norms," must be effective and therefore eventually enforceable.

The identification of group norms of conduct with law, it should be noted, is tenable only if the term "law" is used in a much broader sense than is usually the case. Following the Russian scholar Petrazhitsky,[10] Sorokin defines a law-norm as one which ascribes rights to one party and corresponding duties to another party. This formulation gives the concept a more inclusive meaning than that assigned to legal norms, which require enforcement by politically organized society.

Sorokin holds that from his definition of interaction, which focuses upon human conduct that influences others, one may derive the proposition that "any group of interacting individuals is first of all a *causal-functional unity* in which all components are mutually and tangibly interdependent."[11] In other words, for Sorokin, every social group, even an unorganized one, is a *social system*.

How does Sorokin treat *culture,* which, as we noted earlier, is such an important part of his theory? In *Social and Cultural Dynamics,* culture is defined as "the sum total of everything which is created or modified by the conscious or unconscious activity of two or more individuals interacting with one another or conditioning one another's behavior."[12] Culture, in *Society, Culture, and Personality,* as we have seen, is depicted in terms of its component parts; in this work the meaning of culture is incorporated in the definition of social interaction and each of its components is carefully defined and shown to be interrelated with the others. First, there are "pure culture systems," which are systems of meanings or ideas in the most elementary sense, for example, the proposition that $2 \times 2 = 4$. Such systems are independent of their acceptance or rejection by men. Second, a culture system may be "objectified" or expressed so as to make it knowable to human beings. Third, culture systems may be "socialized," becoming operative in social interaction. A system of meanings which is expressed in communicable terms and which constitutes an important element of an area of interaction is a *sociocultural* system, a key concept in Sorokin's sociological theory.

The most important property of cultural and sociocultural systems is

[9] This proposition is an important part of the theory of R. M. MacIver, among others. Thus, MacIver's analysis of groups, as indicated later in this chapter, is largely based on the types of interests (or values) they promote.

[10] Petrazhitsky's magnum opus, *Theory of Law and the State* (2 vols., 1907) is now available in abridged English translation under the title *Law and Morality* (Cambridge, Mass.: Harvard University Press, 1955).

[11] Sorokin, *Society, Culture, and Personality,* p. 147.

[12] Pitirim A. Sorokin, *Social and Cultural Dynamics,* 4 vols. (New York: American Book Co., 1937–41), vol. I, p. 3.

their tendency to become integrated into systems on ever higher and higher levels. The problem of culture intergration is treated somewhat differently in the first volume of *Social and Cultural Dynamics,* on the one hand, and in the fourth volume of the same work, as well as in *Society, Culture, and Personality,* on the other. In the earlier treatment, "the numerous interrelations of the various elements of culture," Sorokin declares, "are reducible to four basic types. Thus cultural interrelations are marked by spatial or mechanical adjacency, by association due to some external factor, by causal or functional integration, or, finally, by internal or logico-meaningful integration.[13] Here causal-functional integration of sociocultural phenomena is identified with causal-functional relations in the realm of natural phenomena, indicated by uniformity of relations between variables. The criterion of "logico-meaningful" integration, however, is identity of central meaning or idea.

In his more recent treatment of cultural interrelations, Sorokin shows some tendency to deny or to minimize the applicability of the concept of causation (at least as used in the natural sciences) to sociocultural phenomena and to identify sociocultural causality and logico-meaningful integration. Thus, in *Society, Culture, and Personality* Sorokin states that "cultural phenomena, in their relationship to one another . . . can be either integrated (solidary), unintegrated (neutral), or contradictory (antagonistic). They are *integrated* . . . when two or more interacting, that is, causally connected cultural phenomena stand in *a logical or, for art phenomena, aesthetic consistency with one another.*" These, then, constitute sociocultural systems. Sorokin continues: "Not only the meanings, values, and norms can stand to each other in the relationship of logical or aesthetic consistency, unrelatedness, and contradiction, but also the overt actions and the other material vehicles, so far as they articulate and express the respective meanings, values, and norms." [14]

His theoretical writings reveal Sorokin's concern with the hierarchy of sociocultural systems and the degree of their integration. He conceives the total sociocultural system of a "population" as a "supersystem" which may be more or less integrated. Each supersystem consists of the five basic and functionally essential systems of language, religion, the arts, ethics, and science. Each of these in turn is subdivided into systems, subsystems, sub-subsystems, and so on, which also are more or less integrated.

Sorokin emphasizes that his "supersystem" is by no means identical with the sum total of culture items to be found in a given society. For a society's total culture includes, in addition to a supersystem, a certain number of *congeries*. Congeries are related to one another and to the supersystem itself in terms of mechanical adjacency or of association brought about by external factors. Sorokin, in developing this point,

[13] *Ibid.,* vol. I, p. 10.
[14] Sorokin, *Society, Culture, and Personality,* p. 314.

strongly and convincingly opposes the view held by certain radical functionalists that all culture items necessarily have positive functions in a given system.

Sorokin, however, is primarily concerned with large supersystems. Each supersystem is characterized by a central theme or idea, which is the predominant view of truth in a specific culture. Thus, men may ascribe ultimate validity to the testimony of their senses, in which case Sorokin terms the supersystem *sensate*. If men generally accept the truth of faith, believing that behind sense impressions lies another, deeper reality, the supersystem is *ideational*. These two approaches may be combined. If the combination of sensate and ideational is harmonious, a third system of truth is invoked, that of reason, which indicates an *idealistic* supersystem. If the two basic systems of truth, the sensate and ideational, are merely juxtaposed, the system is "mixed."

The classification of the four basic culture styles (a term not used by Sorokin)—sensate, ideational, idealistic, and mixed—forms the foundation of his theory of social change, a subject we shall discuss in Chapter 20.

Sorokin's main theorem, which is developed and extensively illustrated in the four volumes of *Dynamics* and in other volumes, may be described as follows. The central theme of the sociocultural supersystem permeates the fabric of society and culture. If one knows the system of truth that prevails in a society, one should be able to deduce the general nature of its art, literature, music, philosophy, and ethics, as well as the predominant types of social relations. In this way, according to Sorokin, the *style* of a culture, a subject treated by other scholars in a rather impressionistic way, can be approached scientifically and can even be studied quantitatively. (Sorokin's methodological views are discussed below.)

We noted earlier that Sorokin defines sociology as the generalizing theory of the structure and dynamics of social systems, cultural systems, and "personality." The study of personality is the least developed and perhaps the least influential aspect of his work, although two full chapters of *Society, Culture, and Personality* are directly concerned with this subject, as well as numerous passages in this and other volumes. The following quotation suggests Sorokin's fairly conventional sociological approach:

> Personality is a microcosm reflecting the sociocultural macrocosm wherein the individual is born and lives. The life of an individual is a great drama determined first by his social universe and then by the biological properties of his organism. Even before the organism is born, the sociocultural universe begins to influence and to determine the properties of the organism, and it relentlessly maintains this molding process till the individual's death and beyond.[15]

[15] *Ibid.*, p. 714.

Although he strongly stresses the influence of the sociocultural environment in shaping personality, Sorokin, like most sociologists today, avoids a one-sided "sociologistic" interpretation of human behavior. He sees the individual and personality, on the one hand, and society and culture, on the other, as interdependent and interacting elements of a totality. Nor does he assume a one-to-one correspondence between culture and personality. But Sorokin emphasizes the "pluralistic" nature of personality structure, viewing the pluralism of "selves" in the individual as a reflection of the pluralism of groups and the multiple "social egos" of the individual as a consequence of his various group memberships.[16] In his earlier *Social Mobility* as well as in his more recent works, Sorokin also brings out interconnections between sociocultural patterns and changes and personality disorganization. Similarly, he holds that each of the broad sociocultural systems—the sensate, ideational, and idealistic—produces characteristic personality types.

While Sorokin uses the expression "empirical soul" (which he identifies with "self" or "ego"), he wisely points out that analysis of the "superempirical or transcendental soul" lies outside of sociological discussion: "its analysis belongs to religion and metaphysics." [17]

Sorokin's methodological views are most fully developed in the fourth volume of *Dynamics* and in *Sociocultural Causality, Time and Space*. He declares himself to be an adherent of an "integralist school" in sociology which investigates social phenomena in three ways. In their empirical aspect, social phenomena are studied through sense perception and sensory-empiric observation. Second, the "logico-rational" aspect of sociocultural phenomena must be comprehended through the discursive logic of human reason. Finally, "sociocultural reality has its supersensory, superrational, and metalogical aspect. It is represented by the great religions, absolutistic ethics, and the truly great fine arts. . . . This . . . phase of sociocultural reality . . . must be apprehended through the truth of faith, that is, through a supersensory, superrational, metalogical act of intuition or mystic experience." [18]

This is a dubious statement indeed. Intuition is not tantamount to an act of faith, which involves the acceptance of some revelation. Sorokin's conception of intuition is very close to the phenomenological procedure of "ideational abstraction," to be discussed in Chapter 21. Therefore, Sorokin's methodological pluralism is not as inclusive as it first appears. Moreover, his methodological position, we contend, does not transform his sociological theory (in the meaning defined in Chap. 1) into a philosophical theory.

One of the most disappointing aspects of Sorokin's methodology is

[16] See especially *Society, Culture, and Personality*, Chaps. XIX and XLVIII.
[17] *Ibid.*, pp. 345 ff.
[18] Pitirim A. Sorokin, *Sociocultural Causality, Time and Space* (Durham: Duke University Press, 1943), pp. 227–28.

lack of precision concerning what he calls the *logico-meaningful method*. Insofar as this method is purely *logical* it is understandable; and when art phenomena are compared with each other it is perhaps also understandable (though some authorities dispute this point). But the correlation of intellectual and esthetic phenomena raises a serious question. How can it be firmly established, on the basis of concomitance in time and space, that certain configurations of intellectual phenomena are "innerly" or meaningfully integrated with specified configurations of esthetic phenomena? Sorokin's illustrations of such integration are often quite plausible, but cogent proof is conspicuous by its absence.

Although Sorokin strongly disagrees with the pretensions of the extreme exponents of quantitativism in sociology, he makes abundant use of quantitative methods. Thus, in order to establish the style of a particular sociocultural subsystem, for instance, philosophy, he computes lists of those cultural phenomena which most clearly manifest the subsystem (in the concrete case, the works of the philosophers of the time), distributes each item among the three major types of culture, and ascribes to each a weight (depending on the number of philosophers' followers, later editions and translations, and other objective criteria). Simple arithmetical calculations result in findings that take the following form: In the $N$th century, $A$ per cent of Western philosophy was sensate and $B$ per cent was idealistic. Such findings support Sorokin's theory of social change, but they also demonstrate a limited possibility of quantifying data on culture style. In a similar manner, the varying intensity of such phenomena as war and revolution is measured. The measurements are crude, to be sure, a fact recognized by Sorokin himself. But, with rare exceptions, they do not lead to conclusions that deviate greatly from the views expressed in qualitative terms by many historians. Moreover, Sorokin's correlations sometimes open unexpected perspectives into unexplored regions of man's sociocultural past.

### Parsons

From Sorokin's work we turn to that of Talcott Parsons (1902–    ), for many years Sorokin's colleague at Harvard, also a highly influential systematic sociologist. Although there are important similarities between the theories of these two scholars, as we shall see, they are nevertheless often regarded as sociological opponents.

Parsons, though born in this country and a graduate of Amherst College, where biology was his primary interest, was greatly influenced by European scholars. As a graduate student at the London School of Economics, he studied with the sociologists L. T. Hobhouse and Morris Ginsberg and the anthropologist Malinowski, who aroused his interest in the functional approach. Subsequently, at Heidelberg, he turned to the German social scientists, writing a doctoral dissertation on *The Concept of Capitalism in the Theories of Max Weber and Werner Sombart;* within a few years he translated Weber's *The Protestant Ethic and the Spirit of Capitalism.* In 1926–27 Parsons was an instructor in economics at Amherst, and the following year he assumed the same rank at Harvard, later to become a member of the newly created department of sociology under Sorokin's chairmanship. As professor of sociology, Parsons became head of Harvard's interdisciplinary department of social relations in 1946, an office he held for several years.

At Harvard, Parsons early came into contact with a group of distinguished economists and became a close student of the work of the classical theorist Alfred Marshall (1842–1924). He also studied the writings of Durkheim, opponent of Spencerian individualism and exponent of a science of society as a reality *sui generis* (see Chap. 9), and came under the influence of the physiologist L. J. Henderson, an admirer of the writings of still another major European sociologist, Pareto. Of these various scholars, the works of Weber, the economists, Durkheim, and Pareto were especially important in shaping Parsons' theoretical views, indicated in his first major work, *The Structure of Social Action,* published in 1937. Starting about this time, Parsons has become increasingly interested in psychoanalytical theory, evidenced in many of his recent volumes.

For many years Parsons has consistently emphasized the necessity of developing a systematic, general theory of human behavior. He views the development of abstract theory as a principal index of the maturity of a science. Such theory facilitates description, analysis, and empirical research. These pursuits, Parsons stresses, require a general frame of reference (such as tridimensional space and force in mechanics) and demand understanding of the structure of the theoretical system as such. Sociological theory, he holds, should be *structural-functional.* (The term "functional" is often used by Parsons, as noted below, in a meaning at variance with that of other functionalists.)

Parsons' early contributions were based on the conviction that the appropriate subject matter of sociology is *social action,* a view reflecting the strong influence of Max Weber and perhaps, to some extent, the work of Thomas.[19] In *The Structure of Social Action* Parsons presents an extremely complicated theory of social action in which it is held to be voluntaristic behavior. The analysis is largely based on the means-ends scheme. This complex formulation of a theory of social action, representing an ambitious but early effort by Parsons, is interwoven with a detailed analysis of the theories of Weber, Durkheim, Pareto, and Alfred Marshall (and as such constitutes an important secondary source on these scholars), and, moreover, frequently has been regarded as too difficult or overly abstract

---

[19] Znaniecki, coauthor with Thomas, Parsons, R. M. MacIver, and Howard Becker have been treated as the leading "social action" theorists by R. and G. Hinkle in *The Development of American Sociology,* Studies in Sociology (New York: Random House, 1954).

for utilization in research. Under the influence of Henderson, Parsons restated his theory in a form more appropriate for presentation here.

The restated theory was first formulated in a series of papers brought together in *Essays in Sociological Theory, Pure and Applied* (1949), but later underwent further change in *The Social System* (1951). And while writing this book, certain of Parsons' theoretical views were in the process of modification, partly under the influence of cooperation with several colleagues.[20] Parsons' next work has been especially close to that of Edward A. Shils, with whom he wrote a lengthy paper entitled "Values, Motives, and Systems of Action," published in a symposium edited by the two and entitled *Toward a General Theory of Action* (1951). The theoretical viewpoint expressed in this paper [21] in comparison with the original *Structure of Social Action*, in certain respects is even more complicated; nevertheless, in many aspects it comes closer to widely held sociological opinion. However, here *social action* is again emphasized in contrast to the stress given the title-subject in *The Social System*.

According to Parsons, the frame of reference of "action" involves an actor, a situation, and the orientation of the actor to the situation. The focus of his theory is the actor's orientation (a conception similar to Thomas' "definition of the situation"). Two orientational components can be distinguished, *motivational* and *value* orientations. Motivational orientation, which supplies the energy to be spent in action, is threefold: (1) *cognitive*, corresponding to that which the actor perceives in a situation, in relation to his system of need-dispositions (which, perhaps, in Parsons' thinking, overlap with attitudes; (2) *cathectic*, involving a process through which an actor invests an object with affective or emotional significance; (3) *evaluative*, by means of which an actor allocates his energy to various interests among which he must choose. Value orientation, on the other hand, points to the observance of certain social norms or standards, in contradistinction to "needs" which are focal in the motivational orientation. Again, there are three modes of value orientation: the cognitive, the appreciative, and the moral.

This scheme serves as background for the construction of three analytical systems: the *social system*, the *personality system*, and the *cultural system*. Parsons emphasizes that, though all three modes are abstracted from concrete social behavior, the empirical referents of the three types of abstraction are not on the same plane.

The meaning Parsons gives to *social system* varies from place to place in his analysis. Social system is first defined as a plurality of individual

[20] See T. Parsons, *The Social System* (New York: The Free Press, 1951), pp. 537–38.
[21] Parsons subsequently published further modifications of his views, particularly T. Parsons, E. A. Shils, and F. Bales, *Working Papers in the Theory of Action* (New York: The Free Press, 1953); T. Parsons, "Some Comments on the State of the General Theory of Action," *American Sociological Review*, vol. 18 (1953); and T. Parsons, F. Bales, and others, *Family, Socialization, and Interaction Process* (New York: The Free Press, 1955).

actors interacting with one another. Elsewhere it is said to be a network of relations between actors or a network of interactive relationships. This diversity of definition raises the important conceptual question: are the "material points" of the social system the actors themselves or social relationships?

Again, the social system is described as a plurality of individuals who are motivated by a tendency to optimum gratification and whose relation to this situation is defined in terms of a system of culturally structured and shared patterns. This proposition, as so many in Parsons' work, requires lengthy explanation guided by continual reference to the preceding analysis of social action. Individuals are "motivated by a tendency to optimum gratification" of needs which, as noted above, dominate *motivational orientation*. Moreover, the relation of individuals to their social situations is defined in terms of specified cultural patterns. Probably the term "relation" refers to what is elsewhere called "orientation"; in which case, this part of Parsons' proposition points to the other major component of the actor's orientation to the situation, the value orientation. At this place, in the analysis, the term "value" does not appear explicitly; but one may assume that patterns involve values. These patterns are culturally structured and shared. This aspect of the social system may serve as a kind of bridge between social and cultural systems: the social system includes something which belongs to culture.

Social system in the meaning described in the preceding paragraph and social system as a plurality of interacting individuals are two different things. Many pluralities of interacting individuals do not possess the traits depicted in the former, more involved statement. It may be claimed that Parsons has not yet firmly designated the elements of a social system, a lack that prevented a sharp focus for sociological study. Every case of human interaction may be viewed as a social system in terms of Parsons' simpler definition. He frequently refers to "stable social systems;" in fact, his theory of *the* social system might be said to be rather a theory of the *stable* social system.[22] This criticism, voiced by several commentators, however, does not detract from Parsons' large-scale and perhaps promising effort both to distinguish conceptually and to bring together in one theoretical scheme social systems, culture, and personality.

Parsons views *culture* as "on the one hand the product of, on the other hand a determinant of, systems of human social interaction."[23] In keeping with conventional anthropological emphasis, he stresses that culture is transmitted, learned, and shared. Following his three modes of

[22] Stable systems are also referred to by Parsons as "structures" at certain places, a term he also uses to designate more or less stable clusters of social roles, as will be shown below. He also uses the term "collectivity" (which he prefers to the more frequently employed "social group") to refer to actors who share common value patterns, a sense of responsibility for the fulfillment of (role) obligations, and group solidarity.

[23] T. Parsons, *The Social System*, p. 15.

motivational orientation (described above), Parsons distinguishes three major classes of culture patterns: (1) systems of ideas or beliefs, characterized by the primacy of cognitive interests; (2) systems of expressive symbols, such as art forms, characterized by the primacy of cathectic interests (attachment or rejection of objects); and (3) systems of value orientations or "integrative patterns." Culture patterns tend to become organized into systems on the basis of the logical consistency of belief systems, the stylistic harmony of art forms, or the rational compatibility of a body of moral rules. The analysis of cultural systems is not pursued by Parsons, who seems to consider this task as one belonging to cultural anthropology. He is concerned primarily with cultural systems in so far as they affect social systems and personality.

The central theme of Parsons' sociological theory as it appears in earlier works is "the functioning of structures." Structural-functional analysis requires systematic treatment of the statuses and roles of actors in a social situation as well as the institutional patterns involved. *Status* refers to the place of the actor in a social relationship system considered as a structure; *role*, which in any concrete instance is inseparable from status and represents the dynamic aspect of status (hence the concept of status-role), refers to the behavior of the actor in his relations with others, when viewed in the context of its functional significance for the social system. Institutional patterns are conceived of as patterned (or "structured") expectations which define culturally appropriate behavior of persons playing various social roles. A plurality of interdependent role patterns forms an *institution*.

In another formulation Parsons identifies "institutions" with a complex of institutional patterns which is "convenient" to analyze as a structural unit in the social system. This formulation transfers the concept of institution from the level of a symbol representing social reality to that of the *study* of social reality, because such convenience is scientific, not social. But this apparently nominalistic view seems to have been modified in Parsons' more recent writings. For, in the latter, an "institution" is declared to be of strategic significance in any social system being studied. This statement probably means that the existence and more or less efficient functioning of the institutions are prerequisites of that stability which singles out a structure or a stable system from the social system at large.

Institutions, Parsons holds, are the focal point of sociology. He defines sociology or social theory (in contradistinction to anthropology which he views as the theory of culture) as that aspect of the theory of social systems which is concerned with *institutionalization*.

"Institutionalization," Parsons stresses, "must be regarded as the fundamental integrative mechanism of social systems." [24] For institutionali-

---

[24] T. Parsons and E. A. Shils, eds., *Toward a General Theory of Action* (Cambridge, Mass.: Harvard University Press, 1951), p. 150.

zation involves *both* the structuralization or patterning of value orientations in the social system and the "internalization" of value systems in the
human personality. Institutionalization, then, is the integrative and
stabilizing process par excellence; it forms a firm link between society and
culture on the one hand and personality and motivation on the other. "Put
in personality terms this means that there is an element of superego organization correlative with every role-orientation pattern of the individual
in question. In every case the internalization of a superego element means
motivation to accept the priority of collective over personal interests,
within the appropriate limits and on the appropriate occasions." [25] This
statement, the substance of which is illustrated at length in both "Values,
Motives, and Systems of Action" and *The Social System*, provides an example of why Parsons' recent theory is often described as being as much
psychological (and, in some measure, psychoanalytical) as sociological.

Of course, Parsons is clearly aware that his treatment of the social
system brings sociology very close to psychology. The following statement
indicates his view on the relationship of the two sciences: "The relation of
psychology to the theory of social systems appears to be closely analogous
to that of biochemistry to general physiology. Just as the organism is not a
category of general chemistry, so a social system is not one of psychology.
But within the framework of the physiological conception of what a functioning organism is, the *processes* are chemical in nature. Similarly, the
*processes* of social behavior as of any other are psychological. But without
the meaning given them by their institutional-structural context they lose
their relevance to the understanding of social phenomena." [26]

Among the many ramifications of the theory outlined above, one has
perhaps caught most attention on the part of Parsons' fellow sociologists.
This is what he calls "the pattern variables." Their discovery, he believes,
has been the core of his theoretical contribution.

The pattern variables denote the *alternatives* which appear both in
norms, or role expectation patterns, and in individual choices. In *The Social System*, Parsons presents five pairs of alternatives, viewing these, on a
certain level of generalization, as exhaustive. But in a later paper (cited in
footnote 20) he notes the possibility of constructing a sixth pair, but this
line of development has not been pursued in his later works.

Five pattern variables are delineated, as follows: (1) *Affectivity versus affective neutrality:* the pattern is affective if it permits the immediate
gratification of the actor's interest, but affectively neutral if it imposes discipline, demands renouncement in favor of other interests; (2) *Self-
interest versus collective interest:* social norms may define as legitimate

[25] *Ibid.*
[26] T. Parsons, *Essays in Sociological Theory, Pure and Applied* (Glencoe,
Ill.: The Free Press, 1949), p. 38. In his later *The Social System*, Parsons stresses
that his sociological theory is not based on psychology but rather on a general theory
of action, the outlines of which are presented by Parsons and associates in Part I of
*Toward a General Theory of Action.*

the pursuit of the actor's private interests, *or* obligate him to act in the interests of the group. (3) *Universalism versus particularism:* the former refers to value standards that are highly generalized, the latter to those having significance for a particular actor in particular relations with particular objects. (4) *Performance versus quality* (originally "achievement versus ascription"): stress may be given either to the achievement of certain goals (performance), *or* to the attributes of the other person, to the fact that he is such and such; for example, the actor's father, a physician, and so on. (5) *Specificity versus diffuseness:* an interest can be defined specifically so that no obligation is assumed to exist beyond the boundary thus indicated, *or* in a diffuse manner so that obligations going beyond the explicit definition may be assumed to exist.

Since, in principle, these alternatives are independent of each other, there are, one could argue, thirty-two possible combinations of "role expectation patterns." In *The Social System,* Parsons himself has examined sixteen such combinations; here the second alternative, because of its special significance for integration, has been "placed in the middle." In *Working Papers,* the same alternative is applied only to relations *between* systems and not to the internal constitution of systems, whereas the other alternatives are paired in such a way that only four combinations remain, namely specificity and universalism, affectivity and performance, diffuseness and particularism, and affective neutrality plus quality.

This revised scheme of pattern variables is used in *Family, Socialization and Interaction Process,* a work concentrating on the socialization of the child in the family. Here is unfolded a theory of successive "binary fissions" through which a fully socialized personality emerges. This development, it is claimed, is marked by preëstablished and universal phases—a claim in conformity with Freudian theory. During the highest developmental stages, when socialization within the family is supplemented by other experiences, the binary fission process is affected by those pattern alternatives depicted in *The Working Papers.* The empiric background of this study seems to be participant observation of the normal middle class family, which is perhaps somewhat more authoritarian than most American families. In a special chapter written by Morris Zelditch, Jr., a cross cultural comparison is made of 56 societies of role distribution in the "nuclear family." He concludes that in 46 societies socialization takes place in keeping with Parsonian theory. This finding, if valid, of course invalidates the hypothesis that the differentiation process as described by Parsons has universal validity.[27]

It is not easy to locate Parsons' theory in the universe of contemporary sociological theories. He is not a neo-positivist and definitely not a behaviorist. He emphasizes a functional approach, which is perhaps best illustrated by his view that partial social structures operate as mechanisms

[27] P. M. Blau in *American Journal of Sociology,* vol. 61 (March, 1956) makes this point.

through which the functional prerequisites of the continuity of social systems are secured. But Parsons often seems to identify this meaning of function with function as the social action itself, from which the observer infers the existence of a social structure.

Parsons' theory, as we have seen, emphasizes the *normative* aspect of social life. Social action is viewed as behavior involving value orientation and as conduct patterned by cultural norms or social codes. Society is thus essentially a "moral order" in the sense that it is rooted in morally sanctioned norms. With respect to this normative approach, Parsons' ancestry may be traced back to Durkheim, Thomas, and Sumner.

Parsons has already produced a body of theoretical writing that has stimulated extensive—and intensive—comment in sociological circles. Criticisms of his work which we believe to be especially in order include the following. First, Parsons' theory is based on the arbitrary (and, from our viewpoint, incorrect) assumption that sociological theory is a partial aspect of a general theory of human behavior. Second, Parsons' sociological theory, in spite of his qualifying explanations, as we have noted above, is inseparable from psychological theory. Third, while Parsons' theory of culture meets these objections, like many cultural anthropologists, he views culture as patterned systems of *symbols* which are objects of the orientation of actors and interprets culture not as an empiric system, as he depicts both personality and society, but as a kind of abstraction of elements from these systems. But if we reduce culture to symbols, "there remains nothing for the cultural symbols to symbolize." [28] On the other hand, culture is more than a mental construct (as are all abstractions). Culture, as Parsons stresses frequently, is internalized by those who share it; and when a culture pattern is internalized it becomes a learned behavior tendency which is as real as any kind of potential energy. Thus there is no substantial difference between culture and social system if, as Parsons argues, the latter is identified with a network of role expectations. Finally, Parsons' theoretical works are written in a style often exceedingly difficult for the reader, especially the uninitiated student, and marked by word usages in which old concepts are given new terms and fairly simple matters are sometimes obfuscated.

It is not quite clear whether Parsons intends to present a general theoretical system of sociology (if not of all the "behavioral sciences") or merely a program for the construction of such a theory. In *Working Papers* we read: "We conceive the conceptual scheme of the theory of action to be applicable over a range running all the way from the behavioral systems of elementary organisms to the most complex social and cultural systems, and on the human level, from the elementary learning processes of the infant to the processes of development of historical change in most complex societies." This statement, of course, may be interpreted to mean

[28] David Bidney, *Theoretical Anthropology* (New York: Columbia University Press, 1953), p. 157.

that the general theory of action, only in a more developed form than that presented by Parsons and his associates, will possess the generality described in the quotation.

In *Structure and Process* (1956) Parsons did not further develop his theory of social systems but sought to establish its analytic utility. In this volume, he describes a number of contemporary American institutions in terms of his complicated terminology, among them the military establishment, the big business firm, and the universities (sometimes referring to schools in general). Presumably supported by these depictions of concrete organizations, he claims that the applicability of his general theory to these systems functioning on the intermediate level increases confidence in the generality of the theory derived earlier from the study of total societies and of small groups. Unfortunately, the analytical usefulness of Parsons' classification and terminology is not established by this exercise in application. His classification is logically impeccable; Parsons is too well trained in the scientific method to commit the mistakes which often appear in the works of beginners. The difficulty is that this terminological and applicational labor appears to yield few dividends: Parsons' analyses of the various institutions provide little or no more knowledge about them than studies using quite different approaches and seem to give no greater understanding of them (in the sense of Weber's *verstehen*). This low yield, we believe, is largely the consequence of the violation of the principle of parsimony in formulating definitions and developing classifications.

Moreover, Parsons not only limits himself to the study of modern societies, a phrase he does not explain, but in much of his work he narrows this restriction to contemporary American institutions. But English, French, or German universities, for example, differ substantially from American ones, and the system of educational institutions and procedures are also at great variance. Thus Parsons' effort of working toward a universally valid theory of action and of the social systems is enormously handicapped.

Another limitation of his writings is the vagueness of Parsons' treatment of primary concepts. For instance, he offers a definition of values— one of the basic concepts in his thought system—which does not help to understand the role of values in social systems. The definition begins with a substantive proposition, namely, the statement that a system of value orientations held in common by the members of a social system can serve as the main point of reference for analyzing structure and process in social systems. Values are here understood as commitment of individuals to support certain directions or types of action for the collectivity and hence derive their roles in the collectivity. But what about other meanings of values? What is commitment—a vague term meaning what? Would it not have been preferable to say: social values are repeated objects of efforts of a mass or collectivity (groups)?

A few years ago an honor was bestowed on Professor Parsons by a group of scholars—not only sociologists but also psychologists, economists, political scientists, and philosophers, all members of the faculty of Cornell University. During the academic year 1957–58, the group met regularly for discussion of Parsons' social theories. The following year a series of public seminars was held, culminating in a session at which Parsons himself answered the criticisms of the Cornell scholars. The papers delivered at the seminar (including Parsons' contribution), revised and expanded, were publised in the form of a symposium in 1961, with the philosopher Max Black (also a contributor) as editor.[29] Since many of the papers were based on Parsons' earlier works only (through *The Social System* and *Toward a General Theory of Action,* both published in 1951), this symposium, as emphasized by Parsons himself, should not be considered a codification of his theories in their present state. Let us hope that this aim will be attained by a sociologist in the years to come.

Of the several criticisms (some of which have been made above) contained in the Cornell volume, Professor Black's paper deserves special note. Black attempts to translate Parsons' principal formulations into common English. This has resulted, we believe, in a simplification of Parsons' thought system. Black's claim that his version of the theoretical scheme of the Harvard scholar faithfully reproduces Parsons' formulations is highly questionable: Kant's views reduced to common language do not express his original thought. But this comment is not meant to soften the frequently made observation that Parsons' use of language is often obscure and inexact.

These critical remarks carry no implications concerning a great deal of Parsons' work. He has published deeply penetrating analyses of the American kinship system; the professions, and particularly the doctor-patient relationship; the "radical right" in the United States; and of other subjects of sociological concern.

Until recently Parsons has argued that the formulation of a general theory of social change must await the full development of the structural analysis of social systems. On this score, however, his current writings appear to represent a change of view, a matter which will be discussed in Chapter 20.

Many sociologists make use of Parsons' theoretical leads. This is illustrated by such volumes as Kingsley Davis' *Human Society* (1949); R. M. Williams' *American Society* (original edition, 1951), discussed in Chapter 17; Marion J. Levy's *Structure of Society* (1952); Bernard Barber's *Science and the Social Order* (1952); and, possibly, *Character and Social Structure,* by Hans Gerth and C. W. Mills (1953). Parsons' influence is also reflected in recent German publications and in the fact that some of his writing has been translated into French. Yet Parsons' thought system

[29] Max Black, ed., *The Social Theories of Talcott Parsons* (Englewood Cliffs, N.J.: Prentice-Hall, 1961).

is by no means an entirely unique innovation in present-day sociology, for it possesses, in fact, several affinities with the works of other contemporary writers, among them Sorokin.[30]

### Znaniecki

A third major representative of the systematic trend in American sociology is Florian Znaniecki (1882–1958), already known to the reader as coauthor of *The Polish Peasant in Europe and America* (see Chap. 12). Znaniecki was born in Poland, beginning his academic activity in his native country as a philosopher as well as a sociologist. He came to the United States during World War I, collaborating with Thomas on their famous study. Thereafter he returned to Poland, but in subsequent years he visited this country as a professor at Columbia and Chicago Universities. He settled here permanently during World War II, joined the faculty of the University of Illinois, and in 1953 became president of the American Sociological Society. His major contributions to general sociology, in addition to *The Polish Peasant,* include *The Laws of Social Psychology* (1925), *The Method of Sociology* (1934), *Social Actions* (1936), *Cultural Sciences: Their Origin and Development* (1952), and the posthumous volume *Social Relations and Social Roles* (1965). The following brief survey is based largely on *Cultural Sciences,* representing Znaniecki's mature thought in his final completed work.

Znaniecki's theoretical system may be best understood as an unfolding of the postulate of *universal cultural order.* Acceptance of this postulate is essential for sociological comprehension of social and cultural phenomena.

This proposition presupposes precise and generally applicable conceptual definitions of social and cultural phenomena. *Culture,* according to Znaniecki, is an inclusive concept symbolizing religion, language, literature, art, custom, mores, laws, social organization, technical production, economic exchange, philosophy, and science. *Societies* are viewed as separate wholes, territorially located, including both human beings and systematically integrated cultures.

Znaniecki, like Parsons, specifies the unit of sociological analysis as *action.* Action is defined as "conscious" conduct, a view contrasting with the behavioristic position and, in this respect, Pareto's. However, not all human actions are sociologically relevant. *Social* action of primary concern for sociology is behavior which tends to influence conscious human beings or collectivities. Elsewhere the term "interaction" is used to connote approximately the same class of phenomena. Social actions are classified into creative, reproductive, and destructive types, a classification based on Tarde's much earlier work.

Interacting individuals are often related by consensus or mutual

[30] A long table of similarities appears in Sorokin's recent book *Sociological Theories of Today* (New York: Harper, 1966), pp. 420–31.

agreement. This fact indicates that the values on which are based the judgments of individuals related in this manner are shared in some degree. Such agreement may be rooted in common acceptance of ideological models in which case actions are "axionormatively ordered." Observation shows that most actions of the participants in every collectivity follow definite cultural patterns. Znaniecki explains this ubiquitous patterning of social conduct by showing that cultural patterns of action tend to satisfy basic human needs. In other words, actions are culturally patterned in such a way that, if the patterns are followed, their respective purposes will be regularly realized. This explanation serves to account for the "universal cultural order" postulated at the outset of Znaniecki's discussion. This order is crystallized into "limited systems (a term which Znaniecki came to prefer to the term "closed systems" used in his earlier works). Functionally interdependent social actions of human beings or of "agents" become integrated into axionormatively organized systems. Thus, cultural order has a double meaning: it is an order of conformity (with the social norms) and an order of functional interdependence.

This view is consistent with Znaniecki's conception of the nature of sociology (which is similar to Simmel's). Sociology, he stresses, concentrates on social or human relations and on groups within or between which such relations exist.[31] The limitation of sociology to social relations and groups in large part is the result of the rapid advance of social research. For research findings now enable sociologists to generalize about the common social foundations of all categories of cultural order. The importance of sociology for the other social sciences, Znaniecki holds, has increased in proportion as it has limited itself to the study of the social systems upon which the existence of every realm of culture depends.

Znaniecki's methodological position is not spelled out in his *Cultural Sciences*. However, his earlier publications, especially *The Method of Sociology*, place him in a group of sociologists that includes Weber, Cooley, and MacIver. Like the latter two scholars, Znaniecki strongly opposes behavioristic psychology in sociological analysis, regarding extreme behaviorism as a kind of scientific superstition. He made this view conspicuous in *The Method* and repeats his argument in *Cultural Sciences*. According to him, those who condition human behavior do so in order to make the objects of their conditioning activity behave as if they themselves were conscious agents, and such activities often are effective to a high degree. The success of such conditioning activities, implies Znaniecki, is a strong argument in favor of the basic proposition that the human objects of conditioning are themselves conscious beings with ability to comprehend symbolic actions directed toward them.

Znaniecki's methodology, as well as his conception of the nature of the social order, incorporates his concept of the "humanistic coefficient"

[31] See Znaniecki's "Social Groups in the Modern World," in M. Berger, T. Abel, and C. H. Page, eds., *Freedom and Control in Modern Society* (New York: D. Van Nostrand, 1954), Chap. V.

which marks social relations and points to the significance of human consciousness in the lives of both the individual and society. This conviction gives support to Znaniecki's advocacy of the use of autobiographies and other personal documents—which reveal the attitudes and evaluations of people—in research; it also supports his opposition to an undiscriminating reliance upon quantitative methods. Finally (and here too his views are similar to those of Cooley and MacIver), Znaniecki's emphasis upon conscious and selective human action leads him to the opinion that sociology and social psychology are necessarily very closely related, if not interdependent, disciplines. His own work represents an important contribution to both fields.[32]

During the last years of his life, Znaniecki began to write a book which would have crowned his work, a treatise on systematic sociology. But at the time of his death in 1958 he had accomplished no more than half of his plan. The volume, published in 1965, contains only two parts; parts three and four, "Social Groups" and "Social Systems," were to follow. The two completed parts appeared under the title *Social Relations and Social Roles: The Unfinished Systematic Sociology*. To a certain extent, the book anticipates studies which are frequently covered by the term "contemporary" sociology and exemplified in the works of Hans Gerth, C. Wright Mills, and David Riesman. It is not based on statistical or mathematical investigations and abounds in examples from the most diversified phases of social life, in the presentation of which Znaniecki was indeed a master. The unfinished condition of this theoretical treatise, particularly the missing treatment of social systems, represents a great loss, for Florian Znaniecki was one of the most thoughtful and insightful twentieth-century sociologists.

### MacIver *

Znaniecki's sociology, as indicated above, in several respects resembles that of his friend and former colleague, Robert M. MacIver (1882–    ). Of Scottish birth and training, MacIver has taught in his native country, in Canada, and, from 1927 until his retirement several years ago, at Columbia University. Like Sorokin, Znaniecki, and Parsons, he has served as president of the American Sociological Association.

MacIver is the author of a long list of distinguished volumes in political theory, economics, and applied social science and philosophy as well as sociology. In the latter field his most systematic works include *Community* (1917), *Society* (1931)—revised in 1937, and again in 1949 in collaboration with Charles H. Page—and *Social Causation* (1942). One ex-

---

[32] This point, as well as the methodological similarities among Weber, Cooley, Znaniecki, and MacIver, are briefly discussed by George Simpson in *Man in Society, Studies in Sociology* (New York: Random House, 1954), Chap. IV.

* This section on Robert MacIver was written by Charles H. Page.

cellent evaluation of MacIver's sociological writings describes his contributions as fourfold:

> First, . . . he has systematically developed and fruitfully explored an impressive network of fundamental sociological concepts. Secondly, he has helped stem the tide of excessive positivism and raw empiricism. Thirdly, he has reaffirmed the view of man as a creative human being with subjective hopes, feelings, aspirations, motives, and values. Finally, he has positively demonstrated that sociological writing can be beautiful, clear, artistic, and literate.[33]

MacIver's major strength is synthesis, the ability to interpret and reintegrate diverse materials from the large heritage of social science and to construct a clear-cut system of sociological theory. Insistent that a mature sociology requires thorough understanding of the organizing concepts which guide its efforts, MacIver precisely defines such key concepts as society, community, association, institution, attitudes and interests, social codes, social class and crowd, culture, and civilization. These and other concepts are utilized throughout his works with unusual consistency. Moreover, the sharp conceptual distinctions he draws between different aspects of empirically related phenomena—for example, between like (individualized) and common (shared) interests, state and society, the "inner" (involving human consciousness) and "outer" (biological, geographical, and technological) orders of phenomena—form the basic framework of his theory of social structure and social change.

Most of his fundamental concepts can be traced back to earlier sociologists, though in MacIver's hands they become refined and logically interrelated with one another. Thus his understanding of *society* as a network of social relationships, the subject matter of first importance for sociology, is similar to the conception of Simmel and others. Toennies' much earlier distinction between *Gemeinschaft* and *Gesellschaft* (see Chap. 8) provides the basis for MacIver's contrast between *community*, the most inclusive social group and territorially rooted, and *associations*, organizations promoting a limited number of specific interests. Following this distinction, community is the matrix of all social organization, while the state and family, as well as numerous lesser associations, are necessarily limited in their range of activities. MacIver's conception of social *interests* and of their essential role in helping to shape patterns of relationships and group organization has affinities with the views of several theorists including Spencer, Giddings, Small, and Durkheim; yet his classification of interests and his analysis of their social implications go beyond the work of these earlier scholars. To take a final illustration (there are many others), MacIver's distinction between objective *interests*, the "objects" toward which people are oriented (for example, "friend," "enemy," peace,

---

[33] Harry Alpert, "Robert M. MacIver's Contributions to Sociological Theory," in Berger, Abel, and Page, eds., *Freedom and Control in Modern Society*, Chap. XIII, pp. 286-8ɣ.

money), and subjective *attitudes,* "states of consciousness *within* the individual human being, with relation to *objects*"[34] is conceptually very close to Thomas' distinction between objective values and subjective attitudes (see Chap. 12). Both Thomas and MacIver stress that complete definitions of social relationships must always include attitudes *and* interests or values, and that consequently a full theory of human behavior necessarily involves the two disciplines of sociology and social psychology.

We noted earlier that MacIver's sociology also bears resemblances to the views of Cooley. Not only are there methodological similarities between the two, but MacIver stresses and develops Cooley's theme of the interdependence of individual and society, without, however, making this fundamental and reciprocal relationship one of complete harmony. Thus, in his discussion of the often neglected normative aspect of social life, he analyzes in detail not only the nature of social norms and the "major social codes" (religion, morals, custom, law, fashion) but both the positive and negative relations between normative social control and the life of the individual.[35]

In *Society,* which most fully presents his general sociological theory, MacIver's treatment of social norms forms one part of the lengthy discussion of *social structure* (norms are referred to as "the sustaining forces of code and custom"). The remainder of the analysis of social structure is largely concerned with various types of social groups, including the family, community, social class and caste, ethnic groups, crowd, and the political, economic, and "cultural" *great associations.* While much of this discussion, especially in the most recent edition of *Society,* is designed as a general textbook in sociology, nevertheless MacIver's theoretical system is utilized throughout and his basic conceptual definitions are applied consistently to a large variety of materials drawn from modern social research. Moreover, MacIver's stress upon the fundamental role of subjective feelings, aspirations, and attitudes in social life is woven into his interpretation all along, together with his firm conviction that man is a creative as well as socially and culturally created being.

This conviction is revealed sharply in *Social Causation,* until recent years a neglected, but perhaps MacIver's most mature, theoretical work. In this volume MacIver, we believe, has found the golden mean between the position of many neo-positivists, who identify social causation with natural causation, and the skeptical view, voiced by Sorokin among others, that denies the applicability of the concept of *cause* to social phenomena. MacIver does not maintain that we can learn the determining conditions or causes of *all* of man's behavior. However, he does insist that it is possible to develop a general conception of causation that encom-

[34] R. M. MacIver and C. H. Page, *Society: An Introductory Analysis* (New York: Rinehart, 1949), p. 24.
[35] This analysis includes a brief but seminal essay on "The Problem of Moral Liberty"; see MacIver and Page, *op. cit.,* Part II.

passes psychological and social as well as nonsocial relationships. But the latter—for example, the causal relationship between wind and wave or soil and growth—must be understood as relationships of "invariant order" of external nature, reflecting natural not social laws. The propositions and methods used to study these relationships (by physical and biological scientists) are not, as neo-positivists such as Lundberg argue, sufficient to comprehend the causation of social phenomena. For these incorporate a psychological element: there is a fundamental "distinction between the type of causality involved when a paper flies before the wind and that revealed when a man flies before a pursuing crowd . . . 'the paper knows no fear and wind no hate, but without fear and hate the man would not fly nor the crowd pursue.'" [36]

MacIver stresses that human behavior is influenced by a large variety of circumstances, both social and nonsocial. He distinguishes three "great dynamic realms": that of the *physical,* that of *organic being,* and that of *conscious being.* Though each has its own distinctive attributes (requiring distinctive methods of investigation), they are ultimately interrelated. But the "realm of conscious being," consisting of the cultural, technological, and social orders, is MacIver's primary concern; it is here that the peculiarities of social causation are discoverable. MacIver writes:

> In all conscious behavior there is . . . a twofold process of selective organization. On the one hand the value system of the individual, his active cultural complex, his personality, is focused in a particular direction, towards a particular objective. . . . On the other hand certain aspects of external reality are selectively related to the controlling valuation, are distinguished from the rest of the external world, are in a sense withdrawn from it, since they now become themselves value factors, the means, obstacles, or conditions relevant to the value quest. The inner, or subjective, system is focused by a dynamic valuation; and the outer, or external, system is "spotlighted" in that focus, the part within the spotlight being *transformed from mere externality into something also belonging to a world of values,* as vehicle, accessory, hindrance, and cost of value attainment.[37]

This statement suggests the meaning of MacIver's strategic concept, *dynamic assessment,* the conscious act by which human beings relate means to ends and weigh alternatives. Men's dynamic assessments bring into a single focus "all the factors determining conscious behavior," social and nonsocial; they represent the uniqueness and the inevitable variance of social action. The study of *social* causation (unlike that of psychological motivation) is centered on "like or converging assessments that underlie group activities, institutional arrangements, folkways, in general the phenomena of social behavior." [38]

Converging assessments underlie three distinct types of dynamic so-

[36] R. M. MacIver, *Social Causation* (Boston: Ginn, 1942), p. 299.
[37] *Ibid.,* pp. 292–93.
[38] *Ibid.,* pp. 300–301.

cial phenomena. First, *distributive* changes, such as shifts in mores and styles of life and fluctuations in rates of birth, crime, marriage, and so on, represent an "aggregate of many individual actions," but no conscious group objectives are involved. The latter are central in the second type, *collective* phenomena, such as organized social movements, administrative policies, and political revolutions. Finally, *conjunctural* phenomena are large-scale persistencies or changes in the social structure, for example, fluctuations of the business cycle or the shift from an agrarian to an industrial society, which are not planned by men but nevertheless represent important consequences of myriad individual assessments. To be sure, the mode of analysis of these three types of phenomena varies, but the fundamental role of conscious selective action in all three must be studied if we are to grasp the dynamics of social causation. In keeping with his emphasis on the interdependence of individual and society, MacIver states his key thesis:

> The individual assessment cannot be separated from the group assessment. Each has nevertheless its own coherence. There is the individual personality on the one hand, there are the group-sustained mores on the other. The evaluational scheme is imperfectly coherent on both levels, deviates on both levels from the professed norms, and is forever subject to change. But these interdependent schemes of valuation together constitute the assessing system by means of which the diverse factors are brought within the single order of social causation.[39]

MacIver's analysis of social causation is closely related to his treatment of social change and social evolution. His contributions to these subjects will be discussed in Chapter 21.

In these various areas of sociological inquiry—social control and normative regulation, social structure and social groups, social causation and social change—MacIver writes with unusual skill and sensitive awareness of the complexities of social life. Yet his enviable literary style sometimes obscures the march of his argument. Moreover, his sociological writings are highly diffuse, constituting a problem for the reader who is intent upon following the scheme of MacIver's sociological system. The sociology itself (though less so than his equally well-known political theory, which we do not discuss here) is clearly colored by his social and political convictions, especially by his strong advocacy of political democracy, and by his idealistic social philosophy. Whatever the shortcomings of his work, however, MacIver stands as a major figure in present-day systematic sociology.

Finally, it should be noted that MacIver's theoretical concepts, distinctions, and propositions have enriched his numerous publications in a large variety of fields, including, for example, the control of ethnic discrimination (*The More Perfect Union*, 1948), higher education (*Academic Freedom in Our Time*, 1955), literary comment (*Great Moral*

[39] *Ibid.*, p. 310.

*Dilemmas in Literature,* 1956), international relations (*The Nations and the United Nations,* 1959), the nature and use of power (*Power Transformed,* 1964), and juvenile delinquency (*The Prevention and Control of Delinquency,* 1966). These are not studies in sociological theory, of course, but they reveal the way in which diverse areas of human activity can effectively be analyzed with the help of a systematic theoretical apparatus. But the extent to which *others* similarly can put to use MacIver's theory remains to be demonstrated.

## Other Systematic Theories

Several sociologists, in addition to the four major scholars whose views have been presented above, recently have made provocative contributions to systematic theory. These include, among others, George C. Homans, Peter Blau, Hans Gerth, and C. Wright Mills (in collaboration) and Charles P. Loomis. Some comment upon their writings is in order, especially because of the affinities between certain aspects of their work and that of Sorokin, Parsons, Znaniecki, and MacIver.

### HOMANS

The starting proposition of *The Human Group* (1950) is that this group which, for Homans, is the focal point of sociology, is a *system.* The concept of system is fundamental to scientific theory and thus sociology is conceptually linked to the older and more advanced theoretical sciences. Homans, viewing sociology's task as the study of group behavior, first analyzes it into a number of mutually dependent elements. He then proceeds to study the group as a social system surviving in an environment. The group is defined operationally: A, B, C . . . form a group if, within a given period of time, A interacts with B and C more often than with M, N, and so on, and if similar statements are possible about the behavior of B and C.

Homans explains that the elements of group behavior are, first, *activities*—what men do, muscular movements; second, *interaction,* which takes place if activity follows or is stimulated by some activity of another (a dubious definition since mere sequence in time is an insufficient criterion of interaction); third, *sentiment,* or the internal state of the body of the actor. "Sentiment" suggests one of Homans' principal theoretical sources, namely Pareto, whose views form the subject of an earlier volume by Homans. Sentiments may be inferred, Homans reasons, from tones of the voice, facial expressions, bodily postures and from what men say about their inner feelings—such statements have meaning because we can recognize in ourselves the conditions to which others refer. (This view recalls the approaches of Max Weber and C. H. Cooley and, similarly, is not behavioristic.)

These three elements and their interrelations constitute the *social system*, other phenomena being part of the social environment. Homans draws a distinction between external and internal segments of the social system. The external system is the state of activities, interactions and sentiments plus their inter-relationships insofar as this state contributes to the solution of the problem of how the group survives in its environment, a formulation clearly calling for analysis in the functional style. And study of the internal system, composed of detailed group behavior beyond functional requisites, but simultaneously arising from the external system and reacting upon it, also involves functional analysis.

Homans demonstrates these theoretical propositions in an analysis of a number of selected case studies, in which other propositions concerning group life are also employed. Particular emphasis is given to norms and social control. Social control is almost identical with Pareto's conception of restoration of equilibrium, being understood as the process by which if a person's conduct deviates atypically from a norm (Homans notes that *slight* departures from norms are quite common), his behavior is brought back to the typical degree of conformity.

Homans' *Social Behavior,* which appeared ten years after *The Human Group,* is constructed according to an altogether different plan. In *The Human Group* the study was based on the findings of five detailed research projects concerning social groups of different size and complexity followed by an inductive construction of general propositions which seem to fit the data. But in *Social Behavior* deduction comes to the forefront. The first three chapters present general propositions based mainly on animal psychology and now commonly accepted in behavioral psychology, as well as propositions taken from elementary economic theory but held to be relevant for explanation of social behavior in general. For each of the main empirical propositions adequate research evidence, forming the major part of the volume, is presented. This research has been carried out mainly experimentally, that is, in the rather artificial climate of the laboratory, in which, Homans claims, valid explanations for specific situations in real life can be discovered. This part of Homans' study may be considered a highly valuable codification of contemporary research in small groups theory (a subject to be discussed in Chap. 19).

The general propositions on which Homans' recent work depends are set forth in Chapters 2 to 4 of *Social Behavior.* First, a few basic terms are defined, taken largely from the psychologist B. F. Skinner, but are often renamed. Thus, for example, Skinner's *operant behavior* becomes activity; *reinforcement* is used to designate rewards and punishments for specific activities, and so forth. But some terms remain undefined, among them, the elusive concept of value, although several generalizations concerning values are presented.

Chapter 5 sets forth Homans' basic propositions. In somewhat abridged formulation, they run as follows:

1. If in the past the occurrence of a particular stimulus situation has been the occasion on which a man's activity was rewarded, then the more similar the present stimulus situation is to the past one, the more likely is the actor now to emit that or some similar activity.
2. The more often within a given period of time a man's activity rewards the activity of another, the more often the other will emit that activity.
3. The more valuable to a man a unit of another's activity, the more often he will emit activity rewarded by the activity of the other.
4. The more often in the recent past a man has received a rewarding activity of another, the less valuable any further units of that activity become to him.

These propositions are not offered as proven; they are theorems to be demonstrated by empirical research. Homans discusses them in some detail (which cannot be reproduced here) under the headings Influence, Including Social Power, Conformity, Esteem, and The Nature of the 'Givens' which are taken to be constant during the period of time under consideration.

In returning to more general propositions, the propositions explicated in the major part of the work are used by Homans to explain the processes marking "practical equilibrium," but not group dynamics. The final three chapters treat the latter subject and "demonstrate" the theorems in the same way as in the earlier part of the volume. It appears, for example, that not only men of low status but also those of high status tend to display nonconformity; a situation found not only in small groups studied by empirical methods but also in large societies (for instance, the South of the United States at the present time and seventeenth-century England). Yet in the concluding summary chapter, Homans denies that propositions based upon the study of small groups can be automatically applied to large groups because in some cases they differ quite substantially.

## BLAU

Homans' systematic theoretical work is somewhat similar to the equally ambitious recent volume by Peter Blau, *Exchange and Power in Social Life* (1964)—both Homans and Blau are greatly concerned with exchange in social life. This study belongs to systematic sociology, but is quite at variance with Parsons' treatment of the subject. Blau, although he does not refer to Sorokin, similarly considers interaction to be the basic unit of sociological analysis. At the same time, Blau's approach is very close to that of Simmel, whom he often cites.

Such is the genesis of *Exchange and Power*, whose title fits only the first half of the book. Blau argues that social exchange (of which economic exchange is only one of the species) represents the major part of human institutions in collectivities (social groups) and societies, while norms and values remain in the background (they are treated in the second half of the volume). Social exchange is a mechanism based upon the principle of reciprocity, presumably ingrained in human nature or, at least, essential.

Another basic concept in Blau's treatise is social power. He defines social power as control of others by negative sanctions, which also may be called the "punitive consequences of noncompliance with orders emanating from a holder of power." Power is derived from such situations within a collectivity. Blau holds that the use of physical violence is a rather poor instrument for maintaining social order (again a term which Blau does not define). Nevertheless, violence often is employed as a social deterrent and a procedure.

Blau discusses several additional concepts necessary for the understanding of the functioning of social groups, including explanation, position, norms, and values. He compares expectations of social rewards with real experience of rewards and disappointments concerning the individual's own participation in particular associations and from learning what benefits (or disappointments) are experienced by others in comparable situations. Social norms play a large part in assessing the value of various associations. Social sciences develop in societies that stipulate rates of exchange between social benefits and the impact of work or natural material things as well as nontangible nonmaterial values. Here Blau seems unduly influenced by economic thought; in this regard he differs from Parsons who seems to imply that the principle of distributive justice is a natural sentiment. But the question thus posed seems more philosophical than sociological.

In the second half of *Exchange and Power* Blau analyzes secondary groups as consisting of primary groups. He takes the fact of the existence of such primary groups for granted, but has little to say about them (he might have made note of their spontaneous coalescence by imposition of the will from above). As to the inner life of associations, Blau uses the same categories as in the analysis of collectivities, namely, social exchange, power, social norms, and values. The processes on the higher level are often reduced to those on the primary level. This part of the tentative theory of social systems offered by Blau deserves further elaboration.

The main question about this ably reasoned work which should be addressed to the author is this: How does he know the facts he reports, which are often presented on a level of high generality but are sometimes greatly detailed? Most of Blau's generalizations are plausible and may be correct. References to the results of research and concrete problems relative to limited time and space are especially frequent in the earlier chapters. The question, however, is one of the major problems of contemporary sociology, belonging rather to the methodology to be used in research than to theory itself.

Methodologically and theoretically, Blau's work is in the style of Simmel, but lacks the latter's synthetic and insightful qualities. Simmel remains unsurpassed in bringing together diverse social situations and processes; Blau commonly limits his horizon to economics and political life and rarely uses facts from everyday experience. Moreover, Blau's references are largely limited to contemporary American life (this defect is most conspicuous in an otherwise brilliant examination of love— Europeans might not recognize their own ideas and feelings on the subject).

### GERTH AND C. WRIGHT MILLS

*Character and Social Structure* (1953) by Hans Gerth and C. Wright Mills is noteworthy because of the attempt to use *social role* as a central concept unifying the psychological and the sociological outlooks, an enterprise in the style of Parsons. Character (the *first* word in the title) connotes the individual as a whole entity, in which one may distinguish the organism, the psychological structure, and the person or man as player of roles. The importance of *role* is brought out in the view that society as a structure is composed of numerous institutional roles. The total social structure, according to the authors, may be analyzed into institutional orders, for example, the economic, political, and religious. Such orders are recognizable as combinations of institutions (as frequently the case, a vaguely defined term) which have similar consequences, ends or functions. The degree of autonomy of institutional orders is a matter for investigation in any given society. But everywhere several aspects or spheres of social conduct characterize all institutional orders, namely technology, symbols, status and education. On the other hand, some aspects of social life are not identifiable in terms of structure or institutional order: there are also amorphous or ephemeral modes of interaction.

Given this theoretical background, Gerth and Mills consider a problem that preoccupies both functionalists and systematic sociologists: how is society integrated? Four alternative principles are presented: (1) *Correspondence* refers to the unification of society by the development of a common structural principle which operates in a parallel manner in each institutional order, illustrated by the case of American society in the first half of the 19th century. (2) *Coincidence* obtains if different structural principles developed in various orders result in a partial, though never complete, unity, exemplified by the rise of modern capitalism through the combination of the breakdown of feudal privileges and the development of legal and administrative frameworks (an interpretation somewhat at variance with that of Max Weber). (3) *Coordination* involves the integration of society by one or more institutional orders which become dominant, as in modern totalitarian societies. (4) *Convergence* takes place when two or more institutional orders coincide to the point of fusion (this process seems to be a kind of reversal of social differentiation).

*Character and Social Structure* provides interesting insights, especially since theoretical propositions are interwoven with the presentation of historical materials (in this respect, the volume differs substantially from Homans' *The Human Group* which employs case studies). To be sure, the historical method involves the danger of concentrating upon the concrete and unique, which is not the purpose of sociological study. Gerth and Mills, however, pursue the sociological goal of formulating propositions of general applicability.

## LOOMIS

In addition to the sociologists whose purpose is to analyze social groups and to explain the integration of elements forming them, Charles P. Loomis, who is persuaded of the importance of such study, has attempted to formulate a pattern of correlated concepts providing the possibility of investigating scientifically any social system, actual or possible. In place of real social systems, Loomis presents a paradigm for a fruitful study of the verbal systems of those sociologists who have tried to penetrate into the mystery of social systems on the level of universality. This unique effort is presented in twin volumes: *Social Systems* (1960) and *Modern Social Theories* (with Zona K. Loomis, 1961). The second volume includes a chapter summarizing the findings stated in the opening essay of the first book; the other essays in *Social Systems* demonstrate the theoretical utility of studying concrete social phenomena. Most of *Modern Social Theories* is devoted to the dissection of the theoretical writings of the prominent sociologists: Howard Becker, Kingsley Davis, Homans, Robert K. Merton, Parsons, Sorokin, and Robin Williams. Loomis brings out similarities and differences among the views of these writers, but his comparative analysis is sporadic and by no means exhausts the analytical possibilities provided by the theoretical material that he has assembled and meticulously portrayed. Moreover, the comparative analysis is rather disappointing, the present author believes, in that it offers little more insight into the complicated theories which are dissected and later reconstructed than do the original writings themselves.

What, however, is the content of Loomis' paradigm? He has constructed a "Processually Articulated Structural Model" (referred to as PASM), which is the central theme of both *Social Systems* and *Modern Social Theories*. Loomis employs this model in analyzing the theoretical contributions of the seven sociologists named above, and suggests that PASM is applicable to the study of all viable theories of social systems. Fruitful analysis of such theories, he contends, should include the conceptual categories or "elements" of belief (knowledge), sentiment (goal objective), norms, status-role (position), rank, power, sanction, and facility; these more or less standard sociological concepts, in the study of systematic theory, should be viewed with reference to patterns of communication, "boundary maintenance," functions, socialization, and social control, as well as to such "conditions of social action" as territoriality, size, and time.

The details of this complicated and highly abstract scheme do not require elaboration in the present context. Students of sociological theory, however, should be aware of the following characteristics of Loomis' work: First, and most importantly, his analysis of contributions by other sociologists does not represent a new theory of social systems, but rather a conceptual system which *may* prove to be useful in comparing and assessing theoretical writings. Secondly, as Loomis makes clear, his scheme derives in large part from the theoretical contributions of Parsons and those of several of his former students (Davis, Merton, Williams, as well as Loomis himself), illustrating the continuing influence of Parsonian formulations. Thirdly, and consistent with this derivation, the PASM model strongly emphasizes such psychological processes as knowing, feeling, achieving, and normative behavior, an emphasis that makes Loomis' work (as it has that of Parsons) vulnerable to the charge of being concerned as much with psychological as with sociological theory. Finally, and in this respect again showing a characteristic of Parsons' writings, Loomis' scheme appears to relegate the study of social change to a secondary position as a kind of appendix to the analysis of social structure.

### Summary: Convergence in Systematic Sociology

Do the theories discussed in this chapter form a "congeries," to employ a term often used in Sorokin's works? Or do they represent converging efforts in the direction of the goal of a unified sociological theory?

These questions, with relation to the theories of Sorokin and Parsons, have stimulated a very unusual document. Following the publication of Parsons' *The Social System* and *Toward a General Theory of Action* in 1951, Sorokin circulated a memorandum on "Similarities and Dissimilarities between Two Sociological Systems" (part of which has been reproduced, in German translation, and commented upon by Leopold von Wiese, a long-distinguished sociologist, in the *Kölner Zeitschrift für Soziologie*). Here Sorokin claims that there is a striking concordance between the basic scheme of Parsons and his associates and his own conceptual framework developed in a series of works predating the theoretical publications of Parsons. This claim is supported by a synopsis of excerpts from the writings of both scholars. Sorokin concludes that the similarities between the two systems are greater than those between the views of Parsons and the theories of Weber, Pareto, Durkheim, and Freud—which are strongly acknowledged by Parsons, whereas Sorokin's works are cited but once in *The Social System*. This volume's basic framework, it is also pointed out, is notably different from that of Parsons' earlier *Structure of Social Action*, the change being in the direction of Sorokin's theoretical scheme.

We are not concerned here with the justification of Sorokin's claims. But the trend of convergence in contemporary sociology is a central theme of this volume. There seems little doubt that this trend is illustrated by significant similarities between the theories of these two rival scholars. These are partly the result of the fact that Sorokin has spent many years reformulating and testing the theories of numerous earlier eminent social thinkers; he has systematized them and enriched them with valuable contributions of his own. Parsons more recently has been engaged in a like enterprise and presents theoretical propositions which are often similar in content to Sorokin's, though clearly different in form (and decidedly contrasting in style). Parsons' own creative contributions, while not as spectacular as those of Sorokin, are, as we have indicated, considerable. But the theoretical affinities between Sorokin and Parsons—and to some extent between their views and those of Znaniecki and MacIver—require closer study than they have been given. The following summary paragraphs briefly indicate the direction that such a study might take.

In the first place, most of the scholars whose systematic works have been surveyed in this chapter agree on a basic problem for sociological theory, namely, the question of the nature of *society*. For systematic sociologists, and many others, conceive of society as a system or, more exactly, a system of systems.[40] The ultimate components of social systems are actors, human personalities, whose social conduct necessarily involves selectivity or assessment but is also patterned by the expectations of others and by cultural values. However, the basic unit for sociological analysis is not the actor himself but his "action," as Parsons puts it, or, perhaps more accurately, interaction; MacIver's "social relationships" also imply an interactional approach.

Sorokin, Parsons, Znaniecki, and MacIver likewise agree that *culture* is a system of systems. But the concept of culture does not refer to social interactions as such, but to their durable products, whether material or non-material. (MacIver identifies "culture" with human products marked by end values, distinguishing culture in this sense from utilitarian or instrumental products, such as technology, which he terms "civilization"; this distinction, though the terminology varies, also appears in the writings of Sorokin and Parsons.)[41]

The two systems of society and culture stand in a complicated relationship of interdependence. While this relationship has been partially clarified by the systematic sociologists, especially by the conceptual theory of Sorokin and Parsons, a large problem remains for other analysts of social and cultural matters.

[40] Gerth and Mills hold a somewhat particularistic view on the connotation of the term social system.

[41] Homans and Gerth and Mills discuss culture only incidentally.

The systematic sociologists seem to be in fundamental agreement concerning the problem of the relationship of society and individual. The individual, on the one hand, is an active and creative agent in the systems of society and culture and, on the other, is a product of these systems. It is noteworthy that Sorokin, Znaniecki, and MacIver explicitly acknowledge their basic agreement with Cooley's much earlier but closely similar view of the interdependence of individual and society.

Of our major systematic sociologists, Znaniecki in *The Method of Sociology* and MacIver in *Social Causation* have pursued methodological problems extensively. But all, explicitly or implicitly, oppose crude behaviorism; and three of them, Sorokin, Znaniecki, and MacIver, take strong issue with extreme neo-positivism. However, all of these proponents of systematic sociology agree that abstract theory must be tested by empirical research; in this endeavor Sorokin has made ample use of historical and quantitative procedures, Homans infers many of his theoretical propositions from case histories and laboratory experiments, Blau links most of his theoretical formulations directly to his own empirical research and that of others, while Gerth and Mills make considerable use of historical materials. In keeping with the designation—systematic—we have given to their works, all demonstrate the virtues of logical reasoning, as well as sensitive awareness to social complexities. In a very broad sense of the terms, all are superior "participant observers" in the world about them.

# CHAPTER 19

# SOCIOMETRY
# AND MICROSOCIOLOGY

Some of the characteristics of systematic sociology, the subject of the preceding chapter, are to be found in the approaches of sociometry and microsociology, themselves interrelated, as we shall see. The leading proponents of these approaches, although principally concerned with the structure and dynamics of small groups and their interconnections with psychological processes, are similarly attempting to develop a body of empirically based, general propositions about social life. Their effort, in some of its aspects, might be described as "microsystematics."

### Sociometry

Modern sociometry may be traced back to Toennies' penetrating study of the community, to Simmel's analysis of the elementary social processes, and to Cooley's treatment of primary groups. Sociometry has also taken over some features of modern psychiatry. These various elements have been interwoven with a strong emphasis on measurement, the latter of neo-positivist inspiration.

"Sociometry," a very confusing term, seems to follow the terms "biometrics" and "econometrics," though the content of sociometry itself is quite at variance with these. According to its chief promoter, Jacob L. Moreno (1892–     ), sociometry seeks to give an exact and dynamic meaning to the laws of social development and social relations. It deals with the inner structure of social groups and studies the complicated forms emerging from the forces of attraction and repulsion among group members. It is claimed, moreover, that sociometry studies the human group as a totality: each part is considered in relation to the whole and the totality is viewed with relation to each part. It concentrates on relations *between* individuals, leaving the investigation of individuals, as such, to psychology. Significantly, the major findings of sociometrists such as Moreno are frequently expressed in a quantitative manner, often shown in graphic form, but not by equations.

Sociometry maintains that social groups are a reality *sui generis,* irreducible to the elements of which they are composed. As will be shown later, one of the problems attacked by sociometry is concerned with the degree of group reality.

As the term sociometry indicates, the advocates of this approach concentrate on measurement. However, they do not seek to measure social phenomena in general but restrict themselves to interpersonal relations based on attraction and repulsion. The sociometrists note that the systems of human preferences which are rooted in these processes cannot themselves be discovered by statistical methods. Nor can they be investigated satisfactorily with sole reliance upon methods which prevail in the physical sciences, because, to obtain valid results, the sociometrist must solicit the assistance of the subjects under his investigation.

Born in Rumania, Moreno began his professional work in Austria. He published (in German) the volume *Invitation to a Meeting* in 1914 and thereafter participated in the reorganization of a community near Vienna where social difficulties were mounting. In 1925 he migrated to the United States. In this country, after having conducted several sociometric investigations in public and correctional schools, his best-known work, *Who Shall Survive?,* appeared in 1934. This work received the favorable attention of several neo-positivists, among them Lundberg and Dodd. In 1942, Moreno and his colleagues opened a Sociometric Institute in New York where his methods were frequently demonstrated. Moreno's followers, though few in number, seem to be devoted disciples. One of them, Helen Jennings, is the author of *Leadership and Isolation* (1943), a volume giving clear insight into the techniques and procedures of sociometry.[1]

Sociometry can be considered as a combination of a theory about the informal structure of human societies and groups and a method of investigating that structure. The basic propositions of the theory may be stated briefly.

Human society, according to Moreno and his followers, is more than a network of intermental relations; it has an objective existence of its own—a view quite at variance with the extreme nominalism of the neopositivists. The structure of society is not identical with the "social order" or the form of government. The state, for example, may vanish, but the underlying "sociodynamic structure" of society must persist. This structure is evidenced by the process of positive and negative choices made by people, based on attraction or repulsion, that is, some sort of selective affinity

[1] Under Moreno's guidance, the journal *Sociometry* was published from 1937 for over twenty years; subsequently *Sociometry* became a general journal in social psychology, published under the auspices of the American Sociological Association.

among individuals. These selective relations between individuals give social groups their reality. By the measurement of choices and selective patterns the degree of reality of social configuration may be determined.
Some groups have a structure that places them nearer to the chance level
than others; which is to say that the attraction and withdrawal relations
between the individuals concerned are not more frequent or intensive
than among individuals picked up at random. Other structures, however,
approximate the level of optimum social cohesion.

To establish the *tele*, a term used in sociometry to connote the forces
of attraction and repulsion between individuals, a procedure is used
called the sociometric test. The test calls for each subject in an investigation to indicate his choices of companions in various situations, such as
play or work or study. The number of selections or rejections of the subjects may be restricted or unlimited, depending on the scope of the research.

In order to obtain a total and genuine picture of a group or society
all individuals composing it must be observed as active agents. An important task of the sociometrist is to stimulate the people being studied to act
and to choose and to reject one another according to sociometric procedures. If this task is accomplished, every domain of human relationships
—economic, ethnic, cultural—will be "stirred up" and brought into the
research picture. Therefore, sociometrists advocate a warming up procedure, used to provoke the highest possible spontaneity of the subjects' responses to the observer's questions and suggestions. The investigator also
must coact with the group; in other words, he must act as a participant
observer.

Tests using these techniques provide material for graphs called *sociograms*. A sociogram is a kind of group map on which, by appropriate
symbols, positive and negative choices of the group members are represented. Sociograms permit the plotting of social atoms, defined as the sum
total of relations surrounding every individual, numerous in some cases
and fewer in others. Social atoms however are only parts of a larger pattern, the psychosocial network, represented by the interlocking of a number of social atoms. This graphing procedure reveals a limited number of
typical configurations: the isolate, or a solitary figure in terms of choices
made by him of others and of choices made of him by others; the pair; the
self-sufficient triangle; the chain (A chooses B, but B chooses C, and so
on); and the star with its cluster. In addition to these configurations,
characteristic of small groups, more extensive structures are noted by the
sociometrists: the community composed of psychosocial networks, and
humanity consisting of communities. Though Moreno or other leading
sociometrists have not studied the subject, others, including Lundberg,[2]

²See G. A. Lundberg and M. Lawsing, "The Sociography of Some Community
Relations," *American Sociological Review*, vol. 2 (1937) and G. A. Lundberg and
M. Steele, "Social Attraction Patterns in a Village," *Sociometry*, vol. 1 (1938).

have employed sociograms to chart patterns of social relationships in small American communities.

In addition to the construction and analysis of sociograms, the sociometrists use the method of the cultural atom, schematically presenting the various social roles in which individuals participate, actively or passively, as well as the interrelation matrix suggested by Dodd.

The findings of numerous sociographic studies have encouraged the sociometrists to come to the following conclusions: In social life there is concentration of human choice upon a few individuals, this acting to reduce the amount of choice expended toward others. This situation produces a sociometric proletariat, the isolates, the oldest and most numerous proletariat of human society. Moreover, a correlation exists between the individual's proclivity to make positive choices and the ability of becoming the object of others' choices. Those who are overchosen in choice-making easily assume the position of leadership.

A further conclusion of Moreno is that social conflict and tension increase in direct proportion to the sociodynamic difference between official society and the sociometric matrix (expressing relations of attraction-repulsion). The sociometrists have studied disturbances developing in groups, for instance, in correctional homes, and have ascertained the relations between various forms of group organization and different types of disturbance. For example, if the emotional interests of the majority of the members of a home group are directed mainly to individuals outside of the group, the functioning of the group will be disturbed through lack of precision in work, superficiality of performance, and so on. If, on the contrary, the group is largely introverted, but many of the members reject one another, disturbance of another type will arise, expressed in friction and conflict between the members concerning the execution of necessary actions. If many members reject the housemother, on the other hand, but attract one another, regression in work and open rebellion may ensue.

On the basis of several studies of intragroup conflicts, the sociometrists have worked out techniques for reducing such tensions, especially the *psychodrama* and *sociodrama*. These techniques may also be used for other purposes, such as training individuals for group leadership.

Moreno and his followers, like many innovators, have been inclined to overestimate the significance of their findings. They often write as if they have found *the* key to the understanding of interpersonal relations. In all likelihood, the selective affinity among group members which they emphasize operates in combination with an affinity based on kinship, spatial propinquity, and other factors. Moreover, interpersonal relations are affected by traditional customs and institutions and coercion. Nevertheless, the sociometrists have opened up a promising field of study. Their ideas have found ground in France where a Sociometric Institute was established some years ago. In that country, Georges Gurvitch has indicated a striking similarity between the basic views of the sociometrists and his own microsociology (see Chap. 21). The two trends began independently, and their similarity may be considered another example of the converging tendency in contemporary sociology.

## Microsociology

During the past two decades the term *microsociology* has been heard more and more as a newly opened field, the study of small groups, has been developed. The opening up of this field of study testifies to the fact that quite a few contemporary sociologists believe that substantial differences exist between small groups and other groups, for which no commonly accepted term exists. In contrast to the small group is of course the "large group," but this uncommon phrase covers many collectivities with many different traits: for example, all-inclusive societies such as nations on the one hand and on the other large ethnic groups which may but do not necessarily coincide with political units. Present-day students of small structures or groups generally seem to neglect the conventional distinction between primary and secondary groups, and concentrate upon the artificial groupings formed in laboratories. These temporary units brought together for experimental investigation are not, of course, the primary groups of Cooley (see Chap. 12) and most contemporary sociologists, nor are they, because of their small size and face-to-face nature, impersonal secondary groups. In the hands of the sociometrists they correspond to the temporary laboratory groupings of the experimental social psychologists. Indeed, the approach and methods of sociometry itself are found in both sociology and social psychology—and, we believe, are more appropriate to the tasks of the latter than to the pursuit of sociology's principal objectives.

The development of a type of general sociological theory along sociometric lines, as suggested above, began in the 1930's with the publication of Moreno's *Who Shall Survive?* Quite independently of the latter, but closely associated with Parsons' theories concerning social groups, small or large, several research programs, generally consistent with sociometry's approach, have been established in recent years at Harvard and elsewhere. (Some of the findings of this research have been codified by George C. Homans, as noted in Chap. 18.) Probably the most influential work in microsociology is that of Professor Parsons' colleague at Harvard, Robert F. Bales, a principal contributor to the well-known *Working Papers* of Parsons and his associates.[3]

---

[3] Talcott Parsons, Robert F. Bales, and Edward A. Shils, *Working Papers in the Theory of Action* (Glencoe, Ill.: The Free Press, 1953). See especially Chapter 3, "The Dimensions of Action-Space," by Parsons and Bales, and Chapter 4, "The Equilibrium Problem in Small Groups," by Bales; the latter paper describes the empirical study cited in the text. Bales' studies are also reported in A. Paul Hare, E. F. Borgatta, and Robert F. Bales, eds., *Small Groups: Studies in Social Interaction*, rev. ed. (New York: Knopf, 1965).

The major aim of Bales' studies is the development, on the basis of observation and experiment, of logically related general propositions—that is, a body of *theory*—about behavior within small groups. As noted above, however, the collectivities studied by Bales and his associates are the short-lived and "artificial" laboratory groups (mostly Harvard students) typical of social psychological experimentation, and it is doubtful, this writer believes, that propositions concerning them are applicable to the actual microsociological world. Nevertheless there appears to be, in some of Bales' research findings,[4] support of certain of Parsons' analytical categories, particularly the pattern variables discussed earlier (see Chap. 18). Of greater sociological significance, perhaps, are Bales' systematic observations concerning equilibrium patterns, role differentiation, and types of leadership that emerge in small groups, but again the question of applicability of these findings, based upon laboratory observation, to small groups in general remains problematic. Moreover, as various critics have pointed out,[5] the tentative propositions of the microsociologists do not yet constitute a body of viable theory.

These reservations and criticisms should not obscure the fact that a very large number of sociologists (and social psychologists) are engaged in the study of small groups—microsociology has become an established specialization of the discipline. From this increasingly extensive and intensive research should emerge, as systematic codification of findings and their theoretical implications develops, a fuller theoretical understanding of small groups. In the larger view, it is quite possible, as the collaboration of Bales and Parsons suggests, that the affinities and interconnections between the "macro" and "micro" areas of social life will be brought together in a single theoretical system.

## Summary and Appreciation

To conclude, we can say that society is interpreted by the sociometrists as a network of selective affinities among individuals—affinities to which reality is ascribed that transcend the intermittent interactions among them. Though the term system is rarely used by sociometrists, they treat the relationship between society and individual systematically: each individual is the center of a "social atom" in which other individuals are involved through the processes of attraction and repulsion, while society is a complex network of such atoms.

Both sociometry and microsociology aim at the construction of a gen-

[4] See, for example, Robert F. Bales and Philip E. Slater, "Role Differentiation in Small Decision–Making Groups," in Parsons and Bales, *Family, Socialization and Interaction Process* (Glencoe, Ill.: The Free Press, 1955), Chap. 5.

[5] See, for example, Michael Olmsted, *The Small Group Studies in Sociology* (New York: Random House, 1959); and P. Sorokin, *Sociological Theories Today;* Sorokin severely condemns this mode of work as productive of "platitudes."

eral theory of small groups comparable with the theories of larger groups, as offered by different systematic sociologists. But sociometric and micro-sociological research is largely descriptive, and one finds only rare attempts to generate a system of theory as such. The work of such scholars as Homans and Bales, however, probably is a portent of the eventual development of a rigorous systematic theory of small groups.

# CHAPTER 20

# DYNAMIC SOCIOLOGY

The second quarter of the twentieth century was a period of intensive activity in the field of dynamic sociology, an activity which has continued into the current third quarter. Dynamic sociology designates the attempts to discover uniformities in, and principles of, the movements of whole societies, cultures, or civilizations. Although sociology had begun its existence as dynamic sociology in this sense—as in the work of Comte and such predecessors as the eighteenth-century Vico—the task was largely abandoned with the great decline (though not the demise) of theory.

## Spengler and the Study of Cyclical Change

Preceding the rise of neo-evolutionism (to be considered later in this chapter), a trend in theoretical orientation developed which could be termed dynamic macrosociology. This trend is rooted historically in Danilevsky's *Russia and Europe,* a volume now one hundred years old (see Chap. 4). The most influential work of this style in the 1920's and 30's was that of Oswald Spengler (1856–1936), *The Decline of the West* (1918); during those years it was perhaps the most widely discussed work on one of the major problems of sociology, the problem of uniformities in the life-course of cultures or civilizations. Translated from the original German into several languages, the temporary success of this ambitious work was due in large part to the fact that its gloomy prognosis was congenial to the disheartened mood of a generation overwhelmed by the catastrophe of the First World War.[1]

[1] Careful examination reveals that the thought system of Spengler reproduces, in embellished form, that of Danilevsky (see above Chap. 4). The resemblance is so striking that, in H. E. Barnes' and H. Becker's opinion, "the parallelism is too close to be accidental" (*Social Thought From Lore to Science,* 1938, Vol. II, pp. 1032–33). Spengler never mentions or quotes Danilevsky. But he could have read his work in the abridged French translation, perhaps also in Russian. In any case, a Russian sociologist informed Sorokin that he saw Danilevsky's book in Spengler's library in

Spengler's views, put in terms more or less adequate to the study of sociological theory, may be expressed as follows: The history of humanity *as a whole* has no discoverable meaning whatsoever. Moreover, the conventional division of universal history into ancient, medieval, and modern is highly misleading and has no interpretative use. Great significance resides in the life histories of *separate* cultures, while their interrelationships are relatively unimportant and accidental. Each such independent culture is the possession of a people (or of a group of peoples) who share a common *Weltanschauung* (philosophy of life).

Spengler insists that every culture possesses its own style or ethos which is irreducible to the style of any other culture (a situation which means that men belonging to different cultures cannot in fact understand one another). However, Spengler characterizes the styles of only a few cultures, and then in a highly impressionistic manner. For example, the symbol of Classical culture is the naked statue, for the Arabian (Magian, early Christian) culture the basilica, and for the Faustian (Western) culture the symbol is instrumental music and calculus.

Culture itself is depicted as an organism. Its development is less a matter of causation than one of "destiny." Cultures pass through the same stages of growth and decline as individuals; each has its own childhood, youth, maturity, and old age. For this image of four ages, Spengler at times substitutes that of the four seasons—spring, summer, autumn, and winter. He also conceives of both a prelude to the life cycle of a culture and an epilogue. Thus before the awakening, or the beginning of springtime, peoples live in a precultural stage; in fact, most people never emerge from this stage. Once the culture is launched, however, the four stages follow in order. The last of these stages, winter, imperceptibly becomes a dying "civilization," a derogatory term in Spengler's vocabulary. Civilization is thus the epilogue of every culture: death following life, rigidity succeeding intellectual creativeness.

Spengler's lengthy discussion is confined largely to eight cultures: Egyptian, Mesopotamian, Hindu, Chinese, Classical (or Apollonian), Arabian (or Magian), Mayan, and Western (or Faustian).[2] (He also considers a ninth, the rising Russian culture, but makes no claim that his treatment is exhaustive.) Each culture, according to Spengler, possesses a life span of approximately one thousand years. To fit the facts into this phase of his organismic conception of culture, Spengler arranges the cultures in a very artificial way. The Arabian or Magian culture, for example, is described as beginning at the time of early Christianity, continues in Byzantium, and comes to an end in the Arabian Khalifate, thereby depriving Western culture of any continuity with early Christianity.

1921. (See P. A. Sorokin, *The Social Philosophies of an Age of Crisis* [Boston: Beacon Press, 1950], p. 349.)

[2] Spengler's Apollonian and Faustian categories are used by Ruth Benedict to depict the "ethos" of different types of nonliterate cultures in her well-known *Patterns of Culture* (Boston: Houghton Mifflin, 1934).

Only one of these cultures, the Mayan (in its Mexican phase), was destroyed by external forces. The others died or are now dying from the senility of urban civilization. Spengler claims that the Classical culture was not destroyed by Germanic invasions since, at that time, Greco-Roman civilization had been dead for many centuries. Western culture, he holds, emerged about A.D. 900; therefore its end must be close, since the lifetime of a culture is commonly a millennium. Hence the title of his work, *The Decline of the West,* and the sensation provoked by it.

The popularity of Spengler's volumes reached its height in the 1920's. Since then, with the accumulation of sociological knowledge, new attempts have been made by sociologists, cultural anthropologists, and historians to formulate large-scale theories of the fluctuations of whole cultures or civilizations. Two of these attempts have received world-wide attention, those by Toynbee and Sorokin, though several somewhat similar efforts have been published as well.

### Toynbee

The English historian Arnold Toynbee (1889– ) published six volumes of his *Study of History* in 1934–39, followed in 1954 by four more volumes completed in 1963. Toynbee's dynamic sociology is an attempt to depict uniformities in the growth and decline of civilizations and to explain the principles of this pattern of change. He bases his conclusions on the study of twenty-one civilizations which he assumes have run through their natural and complete, or almost complete, life histories, plus five "arrested" and a number of "abortive" civilizations. The fully developed civilizations are the Western, two Orthodox Christian, Iranic, Arabic, Hindu, two Far Eastern, Hellenic, Syriac, Indic, Sinic, Minoan, Sumerian, Hittite, Babylonian, Andean, Mexican, Yucatec, Mayan, and Egyptian; while the five "arrested" civilizations include the Polynesian, Eskimo, Nomadic, Ottoman, and Spartan.

Toynbee's unit of study, *civilization,* he regards as an intelligible and essential field of historical study. Similar to Danilevsky's and Spengler's "culture," the concept civilization refers to a certain number of peoples who possess numerous common traits. Civilizations may be "original," having arisen spontaneously from a precivilizational level, or "affiliated," when they have been stimulated by already existing civilizations. Toynbee concludes that four or five original civilizations have emerged and flowered: the Egyptian, Sumerian, Chinese, Mayan, and possibly the Indic; the others have been affiliated to earlier civilizations. The recognition of "affiliated" civilizations separates Toynbee's view from Danilevsky's theory and especially Spengler's. Some of the civilizations, Toynbee holds, are marked by a definite style—esthetic in the case of the Hellenic, technical in the Western, religious in the Russian; as in Spengler's work, however, the concept of style is not elaborated.

But Toynbee's answer to the question of uniformity in the movement of culture is generally similar to that of his two predecessors. At a certain time and in a certain place, he notes, a civilization emerges. Under particular conditions (the nature of which is described below) the civilization grows, if it is not arrested or is not one of the abortive types, such as the Spartan or Polynesian. This growth ultimately brings with it a "breakdown," followed by decline. Unlike Spengler, Toynbee does not use the rather poetic images of the four seasons or the four ages of men to depict this cycle. But Toynbee joins Spengler in believing that the course of every civilization (with the exceptions mentioned) is uniform, that it passes through predetermined stages and dissolves. Unlike Spengler, he does not ascribe a definite length of life to civilizations.

The study of the origin and growth of civilizations is the most brilliant part of Toynbee's work. One of his principal theses is that the processes of origin and growth are dominated by the pattern of *challenge-response*. A challenge may derive from natural forces, such as severe climate, or from men, especially from warlike neighbors. A civilization emerges and grows if, on the one hand, the challenge is not too severe, and, on the other, an intelligent minority or elite exists and finds the adequate response to the challenge.[3] This view represents a substantial improvement over Spengler's conception of destiny as the explanation of the origin of civilizations.

Growing civilizations, according to Toynbee, display definite characteristics. Each contains a *creative minority*, which is followed by the majority of people. The latter consists of an "internal proletariat" of the same society as well as an "external proletariat," barbarian neighbors who are influenced by the growing civilization. Each growing civilization expands as a whole, more in qualitative terms than numerically; large size is by no means a symptom of developing *civilization*. The growth process includes the important traits of progressive integration and self-determination of the civilization and its differentiation from others through the acquisition of a unique style.

But civilizational growth is interrupted by breakdown, which occurs when the minority does not find the response adequate to a serious challenge. This development is inexorable: in no historical case has the creative minority found appropriate answers to all the challenges faced by its civilization. Commonly, the breakdown takes place only a few centuries after the emergence of a civilization. Thus, the major part of history covers declining civilizations.

Breakdown, Toynbee continues, is followed by disintegration and dissolution. Decline and death develop as an "inner necessity," through

---

[3] An interesting application of his conception to America is Toynbee's explanation of the rise of New England: the colonists, faced with the challenges of fairly severe local climate, limited resources, and an unsettled land, but possessed of an intelligent minority, developed a civilization that ultimately dominated an entire continent.

the operation of the internal forces of the civilization itself, such as dissent between the elite and the proletariat, not by action of enemies or by decline of technique or by any cosmic necessity. During the period of civilizational disintegration culture develops no longer as a whole but in decomposed parts, bringing about, for example, developments in art, religion, and economics. The minority, no longer capable of adequate responses and losing its creativity, becomes a ruling elite, imposing itself by force. The size of political units grows, for example, empires emerge, a process Toynbee believes to be rather detrimental to civilizational welfare. And wars are now frequent. The internal proletariat, however, secedes from the elite and opposes it; external proletariats are apt to attack the declining civilization, a point Gumplowicz had made much earlier, as noted in Chapter 5. After a "time of troubles," which may be prolonged, the ruling minority creates a "universal state," universal in the sense of controlling the whole area of the particular civilization; at the same time the proletariat may create a "universal church." Here we see Toynbee's use of classical history (his professional special field of study), the Roman political empire representing a universal state and rising Christianity a universal church.

In this phase, a civilization may live centuries or even millennia. Thus, the mortal blow was inflicted on the Hellenic civilization 600 years before its death; on the Sumerian, 900 years before; on the Minoan, 500 years before. Between the date of the breakdown and the date of the death, these civilizations existed in a petrified state.

During the final stage of the civilizational cycle, four types of personalities emerge: the archaic, looking for salvation in the return to the past (the "savior with the time machine"); the futurist, who appears as the "savior with the sword"; the indifferent stoic; and the religious savior. At this stage, the only way of salvation is by means of transfiguration, on the basis of religion. A widespread religious orientation does not save the declining civilization, but it may prepare the way for the emergence of a new successful way of life, affiliated with the foredoomed civilization itself.

In the last volume of *The Study of History*, appropriately entitled "Reconsiderations," appeared several substantial changes in historical reconstruction, interpretation, and prediction, but these do not affect significantly Toynbee's general theory of change. For example, the possibility of repeated cultural blossomings within the framework of a single civilization is recognized, as is the possibility of the absorption of one civilization by another. Similar flexibility is brought to the scheme summarizing the genesis, transfiguration, and extinction of civilizations. And, in keeping with much of his recent writing, Toynbee now gives greater emphasis to the role of religion in historical change than he had in earlier volumes of the series.

Toynbee's brilliance and erudition and the suggestive quality of his work are widely acknowledged. However, this ambitious interpretative scheme raises some crucial questions. First, what is *a* culture or a civilization? Toynbee provides no objective criteria for this basic concept which designates his very unit of study. Why, for example, is Russia viewed as forming a civilization of her own? Is it not arbitrary to consider Sparta as having developed a separate civilization and to interpret Roman history in its totality as almost entirely a part of the declining phase of the Hellenic civilization? Is "Nomadic" really a civilization or, as sometimes claimed, merely a nominal group? Questions of this order have been raised by Toynbee's critics, both sociologists and historians.

A second type of question pertains to his conception of civilizational breakdown and the succeeding period of decline and death. How can we be sure about the "moments" of breakdown in viewing the past? And, after a breakdown, why, *exactly*, is a civilization not able to resume its ascending movement? It is hardly a virtue of his general theory that Toynbee finds it necessary to catalogue two distinct Chinese and two distinct Hindu civilizations to explain the undeniable fact of successive blossomings.

Finally, Toynbee's uniformities in the development of civilizations are "substantiated" largely by examples drawn from Hellenic and Western history. His broad generalizations could probably not have been derived from Egyptian or Chinese history; in fact, Toynbee presents only scattered statements about the majority of civilizations, which neither confirm nor refute his theory (in the case of Arabic civilization he acknowledges that it departs from the general pattern). It is apparent that Toynbee's theory has not emerged (or been tested) by inductive study but is essentially the product of insights gained from the investigation of Hellenic and Western civilizations. We may conclude that this theory was arbitrarily superimposed on the history of other civilizations.

These criticisms extend in some measure to most attempts to develop a general and inclusive theory of social change. The very immensity of this task prevents most scholars from undertaking it. It is to Toynbee's everlasting credit that he has produced a serious effort to plot the pattern of cultural change. The same comment applies to the other major historical sociologist, Sorokin.

### Sorokin's Cultural Dynamics

Sorokin's cultural dynamics is based on his systematic theory, which was described in Chapter 18, particularly as developed in the four-volume work, *Social and Cultural Dynamics*. He agrees with the historians that there are unique, nonrecurrent aspects of social change. But the social processes are not woven of entirely unique materials. They display recurrent and repeated elements, which should be isolated and studied by sociology.

The general trend of social change, Sorokin holds, is that of straight-line advance up to a certain limit; when this limit is almost reached, a reversal of the linear trend (or, in some cases, cultural stagnation) takes place. The reversed development advances toward still another limit, and is once more subject to reversal. Thus the pattern of change is a fluctuation between what Sorokin names (as we explained in Chap. 18) *ideational* and *sensate* cultures, marked by swings in one direction through the mixed type of culture and in the other through the idealistic type.

This pattern is shown to have characterized the whole history of Western culture which, according to Sorokin, can be traced back to the days of ancient Greece. Greek culture is described as ideational from the eighth century until the end of the sixth century B.C.; for the succeeding century and a half, including the Golden Age of Athens, it was idealistic. From the later part of the fourth century B.C. to the fourth century A.D., during which the Roman Empire emerged and flourished, culture was sensate. The subsequent two centuries of mixed culture were followed by a long period of ideational culture. From the end of the twelfth century to the early fourteenth, culture was idealistic; this is the age of Gothic cathedrals, of Dante, and of St. Thomas Aquinas. Since the end of the fourteenth century, culture has become more and more sensate, reaching the climax in recent decades. Today some symptoms can be perceived of a coming change in the direction of the ideational pole.

This description, based on painstaking study carried out with the help of twenty collaborators, Sorokin supplements with brief excursions into Egyptian, Chinese, and Hindu history. The latter materials, however, are not central to Sorokin's theory, forming the basis for only very cautious statements. Finally, Sorokin assumes that the polarity between the ideational and the sensate can also be traced back to primitive culture.

The moving spring of the pattern of change described above, Sorokin stresses, is located in the culture system itself: it is the nature of culture to change because change is the law of all life. This does not mean that culture change is not affected by such external factors as climate and terrain, but these play a minor role. *Immanent change* is a kind of destiny or life career of any sociocultural system; it is an unfolding of the immanent potentialities of the system. Though the main direction and the main phases of this unfolding process are predetermined by the inner forces of the system, there remains a considerable margin for variation.

As we have seen, Sorokin declares that historical movement in one direction comes close to the limit which it would attain if the culture were to become perfectly ideational or perfectly sensate. But this extreme situation never develops: every cultural supersystem is incompletely integrated. When cultural development approaches the theoretical limit, the trend is reversed (although cultural stagnation is a possibility). However, culture, as such, never dies; some parts may be rejected, but others are absorbed by different cultures and survive. Here Sorokin shows himself to be much more optimistic than Spengler or Toynbee.

Sorokin's theory of cultural dynamics, only a brief outline of which has been presented, is open to several criticisms. To begin with, the theory seems to oversimplify the facts to be explained. For example, the Golden Age of Greece and the era of Dante both presumably were idealistic; but they differed sharply in many respects. In such cases, additional and contrasting elements should be considered, so that concrete cultural situations can be determined by the coincidence of specified phases in different processes. This point is not ignored by Sorokin, but remains backstage in his presentation.

In the second place, the distinction between cultural elements which change or fluctuate together or interdependently and those which do not is Sorokin's criterion of sociocultural "systems." When he ascribes the property of interdependent fluctuation to the elements of such systems, Sorokin, at least in part, is reasoning in a circle.

Thirdly, the choice of the cultural conception of *truth*, defined in sensate, ideational, or idealistic terms (as explained in Chap. 18), as the basic determinant of sociocultural development is not very convincing. It may be argued that it is possible to rewrite Sorokin's work, selecting alternative elements as the fundamental determinants of cultural growth, with almost similar results.

Other works discuss the problems of dynamic sociology in a tone of lesser certainty than the "big three"—Spengler, Toynbee, and Sorokin— reported above.

### Chapin and Kroeber

F. Stuart Chapin in *Cultural Change* (1928),[4] stresses that a primary responsibility of the sociologist is a keen awareness of the "main stream of culture" which marks human history from the Stone Age to the present Machine Age. However, this is not a single stream, but rather consists of a number of separate currents corresponding to "group cultures," in which cycles of national growth and decay may be established. Each cycle, finally, must be understood as the product of a complex of forces, consisting of the individual phases of culture, such as the economic, political, religious, and intellectual. These individual components of culture are themselves characterized by a cycle of growth and decline. When the cycles of several cultural forms are chronologically correlated, when they grow together and reach a high point of development at the same time, the result is an era of maturity of the nation or group.

[4] Chapin's contributions to neo-positivist sociology are discussed above in Chap. 15.

In presenting this conception of cultural maturation, Chapin concludes that it is impossible to determine the particular culture traits or the number of social forms, composing the whole complex, that are required to produce the blossoming of a national culture. However, he applies his theory to a few concrete developments, for example, to the advance of the civilization of Greece, to class struggle and agrarian problems in Rome, to some changes in the material culture of medieval England, as well as to some aspects of the Western civilization of our day. Nevertheless, in the absence of further testing, Chapin's theory remains rather a brilliant guess.

In 1944, Alfred L. Kroeber (1876–1960), a prominent anthropologist, published *Configurations of Cultural Growth,* an investigation of the manner in which the high-level cultures change. This work is based on a painstaking study of both the growth and decline of individual phases of culture within a number of cultures and, additionally, within selected nations having participated in these cultures.

Kroeber's conclusions, however, do not support a general theory of cultural change. He states that there exists no "law" according to which the growth (or decline) of a culture can be predicted. In opposition to the views of Spengler and Toynbee, Kroeber declares that the same culture may flourish many times. He finds no strict correlation between the growth of different aspects of a culture, though he holds that periods of a high level of cultural creativity may be established in which several cultural strands show mature development at the same time. Kroeber argues that the determination of cultural growth or decline cannot be attributed to any specific single factor or set of factors except, perhaps, the general tendency of movements to exhaust themselves.

### Alfred Weber

Of studies in dynamic sociology written in languages other than English, perhaps the most important is that of Max Weber's brother, Alfred Weber. His major work in dynamic sociology is *Cultural History as Cultural Sociology* (1935). The basic ideas contained in this volume (and in earlier scattered publications) may be summarized as follows:

Life is fundamentally historical. The dynamic character of history depends on the immanent urge to give existence to a spiritual form which Weber designates the "cultural will." The latter is taken to be a fact which the sociologist must accept. (Sociology, for Weber, is a cultural not a natural science.) The cultural sociologist is faced with this question: What is our place in the stream of history? His answer will be *sociological* if he is able to grasp the historical process in its totality.

This accomplishment, according to Weber, is brought within reach if the total complex of history is divided into three fundamental processes: the *social,* the *civilizational,* and the *cultural.* Each of these processes follows different laws of development and movement, but nevertheless they are closely interrelated.

The *social process* is revealed in the unfolding of concrete events taking place in societies. It is propelled by the human forces of impulse and will, though it is partly limited and determined by physical conditions. It is manifested in the formation and social organization of families, tribes, and nations, and in their struggles. Although the social process consists of specific and distinct events, typical general patterns of form and growth can be established within these events. The latter task is simplified by using the ideal-type approach: Alfred Weber held in high esteem the theories of his brother Max.

Civilization consists of man's arsenal of weapons in his struggle for mental and material existence; the civilizational process is tantamount to the subduing and exploitation of nature. It is manifested especially in the development of technology and of the natural sciences. It is dominated by purposefulness, rationality, and considerations of utility. Since the products of civilization are transferable and cumulative, the civilizational process is unilinear and progressive. Moreover, in Weber's view, the civilizational process is irreversible and ultimately will lead to a unified civilization.

But *culture* is a different matter, in many ways diametrically different from civilization. The cultural process is characterized by creativeness. Cultural products are exclusive and unique and thus not easily transferable from one historical period to another. Fundamentally, culture is a synthesis of the world and of individual personality. It is expressed in art, religion, and philosophy—fields of genuine creativeness. In these realms, there are no predetermined patterns, no universally valid and necessary criteria (as in the technology of civilization), no generally applicable laws of growth or decline.[5] However, periods of productivity and other periods of inertia may be observed in the realm of culture, as well as distinct cultural "ages" and cultural conflicts.

Nevertheless, the social and the civilizational processes are invariably intertwined with and influence cultural movements; in fact, the creativity and spontaneity of the latter are characterized by man's realization of his place in the social and civilizational scheme of things and by his diverse individualized efforts to interpret and often to change and control the social process. The cultural patterns of specific historical and social organizations are fixed very early in their history. This creates a unity of cultural

---

[5] Alfred Weber's distinction between *civilization* and *culture*, originally presented in an article published in 1920, is closely akin to that of MacIver and his followers. As we noted in Chap. 18, MacIver, like Weber, identifies *civilization* with man's instrumental activities, especially technology; his concept of culture, however, is broader than Weber's, referring to all human products and processes that man endows with end value. Again, like Weber, MacIver employs this conceptual distinction in the analysis; of the affinities between it and Weber's works, see R. M. MacIver and C. H. Page, *Society: An Introductory Analysis* (New York: Rinehart, 1949), Chaps. XXI and XXII.

style which permeates religion, philosophy, and art and, in turn, helps to shape both men and societies.

In a later work, *Principles of Historical and Cultural Sociology* (1951), Weber has elaborated and elucidated these views. He also develops the theme that culture unfolds according to a pattern of recurring waves. This conception is somewhat similar to the theory of cultural dynamics of Sorokin, though, in Weber's usage, culture connotes a much narrower class of phenomena than in Sorokin's. The cultural process, continues Weber, is only indirectly affected by the two other basic processes, the social and the civilizational. The products of the social and civilizational processes continuously provide man as a culture-creator with new materials which can and must be "overcome" (*bewältigt*) spiritually.

## The Challenge of Dynamic Sociology

The views of the dynamic sociologists of our day seem to diverge widely. To a large extent, however, their principal conceptions can be reconciled.

The leading proposition can be taken from Alfred Weber's theory. This is the theorem that the development of "culture" (as it is usually conceived) in its totality is governed by more than one type of uniformity of principle. Weber holds that, relative to the command of man over nature, especially in technology and the sciences upon which technology is based, the main uniformity is *accumulation*. The "civilizational" (to use Weber's and MacIver's term) accumulative process, however, is eventually interrupted by setbacks and human catastrophes and is modified in its course by culture contact and diffusion. This principle of cumulative growth represents a partial and qualified version of evolutionism, as we shall see shortly.

The more specifically creative aspects of human activity, such as religion, philosophy, humanities, and the fine arts (Weber's "culture") as well as political and economic organization, the dynamic sociologists agree, do not reveal unilinear evolution toward progress. Nor is the pattern of growth-breakdown-decline as formulated by Spengler and later by Toynbee applicable in these areas. But variations between periods of cultural blossoming and breakdown, between economic efficiency and inefficiency, are observable. The general pattern of change in these instances is perhaps the one formulated by Chapin and Kroeber: semi-independent curves of activity in various social and cultural fields which may or may not be synchronous, but which suggest, during periods of high development, an interdependent flourishing of culture in general. However, the conditions under which trends of growth of the various phases of culture are initiated and under which they become synchronous are still to be established. Considerable insight into these problems is manifest in the work of Toynbee.

On the other hand, Sorokin has opened up a new field, by shifting attention to the qualitative point of view in dynamic sociology and by establishing a theory of wave-fluctuation between major culture styles. His theory needs refinement and, like all scientific theories, is subject to corrections. But the objectives of his cultural dynamics and the frame of reference of his investigations are a significant departure from those of Danilevsky, Spengler, and Toynbee.

If the conjectures of these various scholars are correct, a theory of social and cultural development may evolve which will permit the analysis of every concrete sociocultural configuration by locating it in a tridimensional scheme involving, first, the phase of technological evolution; second, the phase of cyclical movement in creative activities and political and economic organization; and, third, the phase of wave-fluctuation of broad culture styles. The second of these processes may be discovered to be a cluster of related processes. Most probably, interdependence among the various processes will be found; Sorokin has already shown that different phases in the fluctuation of culture style in all likelihood determine the intensity of creative activity in specified fields of human endeavor.

Unfortunately, relatively few scholars today are working along the lines suggested by the investigations of the dynamic sociologists. This fact is especially regrettable in a world as dynamic as our own. Sociology, to be sure, and society as well, are in need of an empirically verified general theory of social and cultural change, a theory that is related to and supplements a general theory of sociocultural structure and organization. This need probably has stimulated some of the recent developments in neo-evolutionism.

### Neo-Evolutionism

Social evolutionism in its classic form is dead: probably no social scientist nowadays holds the theory of unilinear development of human society toward progress according to preestablished stages. While it was fashionable at one time to reject the evolutionary idea in its totality, there always have been sociologists and cultural anthropologists who advocated a moderate evolutionism. At the present time, their influence is so increasing that some detailed comment is in order on this trend of neo-evolutionism.

Among sociologists, Charles A. Ellwood (1873–1946), whose general sociological views are quite close to those of Cooley,[6] continued well into the second quarter of the twentieth century the tradition of psychological evolutionism (see Chap. 6), modified with regard to objections raised against that doctrine and enriched by the incorporation of the concept of culture. In his *Cultural Evolution* (1927), Ellwood holds that the theory

[6] Especially in *Sociology in Its Psychological Aspects* (1912).

of culture would be a psychosociological explanation of culture in terms of distinctly human traits. Cultural evolution, he declares, proceeds by invention which, whether physical or social, is impossible without the formation of mental patterns or concepts. It follows, according to Ellwood, that the stages through which culture passes are necessarily tantamount to stages in the process of learning. He acknowledges, contrary to the teaching of the early evolutionists, the absence of a single typical line of cultural evolution, but he assumes the existence of inevitable stages of learning. Thus, early man was not only illiterate but had not yet discovered the art of cultivation; in the next stage he still was illiterate but had discovered that art; in the most recent stage, he has become literate. Ellwood holds at the same time that cultural evolution is a product of social evolution, itself a distinct phase of universal evolution. He identifies the rise of culture with a "mutation" in social evolution, a process that exists among nonhuman animals. These formulations are somewhat consonant with Spencer's theory of cosmic evolution.[7]

Much more limited is the evolutionary ingredient in the somewhat later sociological theory of Robert M. MacIver, whose views on social structure and causation were outlined in Chapter 18. In his *Society* (1931),[8] MacIver restates Spencer's doctrine of differentiation, liberating it however from the founding father's references to cosmic laws, to parallelism with organic evolution, and to inevitable progress. According to MacIver, evolution is the unfolding of the nature of a thing, a process in which it becomes better adapted to the environment, but it is not necessarily progress, which is the approach of reality to some human ideal. Each belongs to different categories of thought: evolution to science and technology, for example, where cumulative growth is marked and indeed measurable; progress to the humanities or the realm of human ideals. Thus one can trace the differentiation of religious associations from religious institutions and the evolutionary development of the former organizations (as does MacIver in an extended illustration[9]), but to speak of the "evolution" of religious ideals is misleading and is not a scientific quest. For MacIver, then, *differentiation* is the strategic process in social evolution—and this process can be observed in various realms of human enterprise—and, historically, *continuity* is social evolution's essential characteristic.

MacIver, like most modern sociologists, is highly critical of the inclusive evolutionary models of Spencer and Ward and Giddings, and of the search for the origins of institutions stimulated by these earlier views. But he is also an advocate of what he calls "the reality of social evolution," in the modified sense noted above, and today such moderate evolutionists as

---

[7] In later years, Ellwood published a number of articles in which he modified his position, making symbols the distinctive characteristic of culture. See, for example, "Culture and Human Society," *Social Forces*, 23 (1944), 6 ff.

[8] Robert M. MacIver, in collaboration with Charles H. Page, *op. cit.*

[9] *Ibid.*, pp. 601 ff.

Wilbert E. Moore (see below) find in MacIver's analysis important leads for their own work.

Among cultural anthropologists, Malinowski, although a main exponent of the functional school (see Chap. 17), has strongly supported a moderate evolutionism. The main assumptions of evolutionism, he contends, are not only valid but indispensable to the ethnologist. And the concept of stages also remains useful. "Certain forms definitely precede others; a technological setting such as expressed in the terms 'Stone Age,' 'Bronze Age,' 'Iron Age,' or the levels of clan or gentile organization, of numerically small groups thinly scattered, as against urban or semiurban settlements, have to be viewed from the evolutionary point of view. . . ." [10] However, Malinowski himself has not developed a theory of evolution.

But two other authors, Leslie A. White (1900–    ) and V. Gordon Childe (1892–1957), have done so. In a challenging volume, *The Science of Culture* (1949), White attempts to carry on the evolutionism of Spencer, Tylor, and Morgan from where it broke down about 1900. Cultural anthropologists and many sociologists, in his opinion, have abandoned the philosophy of evolutionism along with the errors of certain evolutionists.[11] A new start must be made by focusing evolutionism on culture, which must be carefully defined. Culture should be defined as symbolic behavior, a symbol being a "thing the value or meaning of which is bestowed upon it by those who use it." [12] It is noteworthy that symbol thus defined is almost identical with "value" as conceived by Max Weber, Thomas, and Sorokin, among others, and with "culture" as conceived by MacIver, Alfred Weber, and, to some extent, Parsons. Here again is an illustration of convergence in modern social theory.

Culture, according to White, constitutes a suprabiological and suprasociological class of events; it is a process *sui generis* that distinguishes men from other animals. Culture can and must be described in terms of principles and laws of its own; psychological explanations and interpretations are inadequate because they explain almost nothing. Throughout the demonstration of this thesis, copious references to Durkheim are made by White.

To trace the evolution of culture from the very beginnings to the present time, three cultural subdivisions must be recognized: *technological, sociological,* and *ideological*. The technological subdivision is composed of material instruments together with the technique of their use; the sociological system is made up of interpersonal relations expressed in patterns of behavior; the ideological system is composed of ideas, beliefs, knowledge, all expressed in symbolic form. The primary evolutionary role

[10] B. Malinowski, A *Scientific Theory of Culture* (Chapel Hill: The University of North Carolina Press, 1944), p. 16.
[11] L. A. White, *The Science of Culture* (New York: Farrar, Straus & Young, 1949), p. 20.
[12] *Ibid.,* p. 25.

belongs to the technological system. Sociological systems are secondary and depend on the technological; ideological systems express technological forces and reflect sociological systems. Thus, the key to an understanding of the development of culture is technological. It is clear that White's neo-evolutionism is marked by economic and technological determinism.

The degree of culture development, White continues, can be measured by the amount of energy harnessed by men per capita and by the efficiency of the technological means. The first source of energy exploited by the earliest culture systems is the energy of the human organism itself. No great advance could be made until men domesticated plants and animals; subsequently, in a few thousand years, the great ancient civilizations came into being, both in the Old and the New World. But following a period of rapid growth, the upward curve of progress leveled into a plateau, until a new technological revolution took place which initiated the Fuel Age, about 1800. Again, after a rapid rise, the curve of cultural development began to slow down. Finally, atomic energy was harnessed, which might—or might not—herald a new technological era.

Each technological stage, White declares, corresponds with particular features of the social system. If people are nomadic hunters, they must have one type of social system; if they lead a sedentary life, they will have another. Social institutions, to be sure, are related to technology rather indirectly; and the institutions of peoples who have reached a fairly high technological level vary tremendously. But all social systems resting upon human energy belong to one common type; all societies of pastoralists and agriculturalists in the early stages of technological development belong to another type. White presents a cursory review of the main lines of the later evolution of social institutions, stressing their dependence upon technological achievements.

This presentation hardly overcomes the numerous and serious objections which have been made against earlier evolutionism, especially criticism of the belief in the existence of necessary and well-correlated stages in the development of societies and cultures. Moreover, White makes no attempt to correlate ideological developments and technological advance. White insists that ideology is an important part of culture. But if this essential part of culture does not obey any evolutionary law, his claim to offer a unifying view on cultural evolution remains unwarranted.

Childe, in *Social Evolution* (1951), disagrees with White's suggestion to revive in a new form the theories of Spencer and Tylor, but nevertheless finds value in some of Morgan's propositions (see Chap. 4). The only reliable type of evidence about social and cultural evolution, namely the archaeological, Childe holds, confirms the idea that at least the technological advance of men passes through identical stages in various places. Savagery, barbarism, and civilization—Morgan's categories—do in fact represent the consecutive stages of human advance. Early civilization, writes Childe, was concretely very different in each case. But everywhere one finds definite evidence of large cities, differentiation among producers, effective concentration of political and economic power, use of conventional symbols for records, time and space measurements, and culture of cereals and breeding of some animals. The author concedes, however, that the intervening stages do not exhibit even abstract parallelism. This fact does not invalidate the use of the concept of evolution to describe social development as an orderly and rational process. Yet there is a great difference between *social* and *organic evolution*. Organic evolution is based on divergence and differentiation; social evolution displays these patterns, but also manifests convergence through culture contacts, a fact without parallel in organic evolution.

Despite this difference, Childe maintains that the Darwinian formula of variation—heredity, adaptation, and selection—can be transferred from organic to social evolution, and even makes more sense in application to the latter than the former. Variation corresponds to invention; social heredity, or the transmission of culture from generation to generation, is a familiar force. Adaptation takes place much more rapidly in human history than in natural history. Selection is expressed in the fact that only a fraction of inventions survive as being beneficial in the long range. In this selective survival, there is affinity with the selection of mutations in nature; but the selective process in society differs significantly because it goes on without destroying or replacing one type of being by another.

The formulations of Childe are very much in the style of A. G. Keller's *Societal Evolution*, published in 1915 (see Chap. 11). Perhaps the earlier criticisms of Keller's interpretation of evolutionism are applicable to Childe's more recent theory as well.

The evolutionary theories of White and Childe do not represent the conventional opinion of today's anthropologists. Margaret Mead, for example, probably speaks for a good many anthropologists when she sharply criticizes the views of these two scholars. In *Continuities in Evolution* (1964), Mead acknowledges the reality of evolution in human societies, but argues that its pattern is directorial (why not directed?) and polycentric, that is, directed by the interplay of many centers of influence. Decrying the sense of inevitability that pervades White's work, Mead, like a growing number of present-day cultural anthropologists, presents a viewpoint somewhat similar to that of certain sociologists whom we designate here as "moderate evolutionists."

### Moderate Evolutionists

"Dynamic sociology," we have indicated, includes large-scale efforts to work out patterns of historical movements of whole societies or cultures (as in the work of Toynbee and Sorokin), interpretations of long-range cultural trends (Chapin and Kroeber), attempts to provide the basic conceptual categories for historical sociology (Alfred Weber), and both sociological and anthropological neo-evolutionary formulations (for example, MacIver and White). Finally, dynamic sociology also is represented by a very recent moderate evolutionism, which to date (1967) has taken as its principal form attempts by a few leading sociologists to specify the "universals" of sociocultural change. These theoretical efforts are by no means definitive formulations, appearing for the most part as fugitive essays, notably several by Talcott Parsons and Wilbert E. Moore.

Several years ago, particularly in *The Social System* (1951), Parsons had argued that the development of a full-bodied and systematic theory of social systems (a goal toward which much of his own work was then aimed), both logically and temporally, must *precede* the formulation of an adequate general theory of social change. Some of Parsons' more recent publications, however, are directly concerned with social dynamics, including especially his paper on "Evolutionary Universals in Society." [13]

These "universals" appear to consist of those developments in social organization that are sufficiently influential to foster further evolutionary growth (an operational definition?). "An evolutionary universal," Parsons declares, "is a complex of structures and associated processes the development of which so increases the long-run adaptive capacity of living systems in a given class that only systems that develop the complex can attain certain higher levels of general adaptive capacity." [14] (This formulation derives from the principles of natural selection, but in *social* evolution, Parsons stresses, "disadvantaged" systems are not necessarily "condemned to extinction.") Evolutionary universals include *religion*, of fundamental importance in adaptive human growth; *language*, clearly an essential ingredient of social life; *social organization* in the form of kinship systems; and *technology*. Supplementing these four universals in the modern era of social evolution are *bureaucracy*, historically associated with emerging social stratification; a *money economy* and the rise of the modern market; and the growth of a general *legal order*, a requirement of modern democracy and perhaps of greater long-range evolutionary significance than the "industrial revolution."

Parsons notes the tentative nature of this depiction of evolutionary universals, especially with respect to the more recent period of human history. But his essay, and most notably the conception of the generalized adaptive capacity of social systems, is an important illustration of the current vogue of moderate evolutionism.

For Wilbert E. Moore, the study of social change and social evolution has been a long-standing major concern. In addition to several papers on this subject, he has recently published *Social Change* (1963), a short

---

[13] T. Parsons, "Evolutionary Universals in Society," *American Sociological Review*, 29, 3 (June, 1964). Presumably the evolutionary theme is developed more extensively in Parsons' forthcoming volume, *Societies: Comparative and Evolutionary Perspectives*.

[14] T. Parsons, "Evolutionary Universals in Society," *op. cit.*, pp. 340–41.

but elegant and illuminating discussion of the nature and direction of change, the roots of both small-scale and societal changes, the dynamics of "modernization" (a subject about which Moore is a foremost specialist), and longer-range social evolution. This volume, together with Moore's paper on "Predicting Discontinuities in Social Change," [15] constitutes a highly suggestive (though in no sense definitive) and currently influential analysis of several of the principal problems in the study of social dynamics.

In historical prediction, for example, Moore notes the assumptions underlying his approach: that there is a measure of order in the part of the universe under study, and that mankind and social organizations will survive the now possible Armageddon. Assuming these conditions, we must as a preliminary step identify the "principal components" of historical prediction, which, Moore suggests, are persistence, continuation of "orderly trends," "recapitulated experience," and planning for the future. Study of these components, in combination and interaction, permits some degree of short-range forecasting, but they are an insufficient basis for predicting shifts in rates of change, longer-term directions of change, or large-scale changes such as social revolutions. Anticipation of major changes of this kind, Moore argues, depend upon careful assessment of the "multiplier effects of innovations" which prompt acceleration of trends and, possibly, radical structural alterations. Moore stresses the well-established proposition that social tensions, though an essential condition of revolutions, are not sufficient to induce them—modern revolutions require a substantial degree of urbanization, centralized government, and effective communications, and are signaled by the polarization of society induced by economic deprivation, relative or absolute, or by curtailment of political rights abetted by the failure of elites to rectify such conditions.

This example of Moore's work indicates his concern with "modernization," a widespread phenomenon that is turning the attention of many social scientists—economists, political scientists, and anthropologists, as well as sociologists—to general theories of social change. Thus Moore himself, after several years of work in this area, has helped to revive what appears to be a mounting interest in neo-evolutionism or, as he puts it, "the broadly sequential fate of mankind generally." [16] But Moore has not himself—nor have other leaders of present-day sociology—produced an inclusive theory of social change in the manner of a Toynbee or Sorokin. His work, as in the case of that of others of his generation, is strongly anchored in systematic empirical analysis, comparative study of contemporary societies, and what, from an evolutionary view, are short-range changes in human history.

[15] Wilbert E. Moore, "Predicting Discontinuities in Social Change," *American Sociological Review,* 29, 3 (June, 1964).
[16] Wilbert E. Moore, *Social Change* (Englewood Cliffs, N.J.: Prentice-Hall, 1963), p. 115; see Chap. 6 of this volume for a brief discussion of social evolution.

# CHAPTER 21

# PHILOSOPHICAL SOCIOLOGY

Since its birth, and continuing today, sociology often has been discussed in philosophical terms; indeed some sociologists, including several whose views are presented in this chapter, are also social philosophers. This linkage, anathema to strict empiricists and others, has long received institutional recognition in France where at the Sorbonne sociology is taught within the department of philosophy, with one of its major spokesmen until recently being Professor Georges Gurvitch.

## Gurvitch: "Sociology in Depth"

Georges Gurvitch (1896–1965) was born in Russia, lived in Germany, Czechoslovakia, and the United States, finally settling in France shortly after World War II. A partial list of his extensive bibliography includes *Essays in Sociology* (1936) and their revision under the title *The Vocation of Sociology* (1950), *Social Determinism and Human Freedom* (1955), *Dialectique et sociologie* (1962), and *The Spectrum of Social Time* (1965). He has published monographs on Saint-Simon, Comte, and Proudhon; during his final years he was preparing an extensive history of sociology; and his *Vocation* was brought out in a revised, two-volume edition in 1963. Translations of his works have appeared in German, Spanish, Dutch, Italian, and Serbo-Croatian. All of this suggests the wide influence of Gurvitch in many countries—with the notable exceptions of England and the United States.[1] The following discussion is concerned principally with ideas presented in the *Essays* (and *Vocation*), *Social Determinism*, and his long paper on "Social Structure." [2]

In the *Essays*, Gurvitch constructs a "sociology in depth," in which

[1] The Dean of the School of Letters at the Sorbonne remarked to me in 1955 that Gurvitch was *the* French sociologist.

[2] Georges Gurvitch, "Le Concept de la structure sociale," *Cahiers internationaux de sociologie*, vol. 19 (1955).

the starting point consists of phenomena that are immediately given and proceeds to deeper and deeper levels. These levels include: (1) the geographic and demographic bases of society; (2) the symbolic level manifested, for example, by the fact that people respond in a definite way to such symbols as flags and traffic signals; (3) the "organized superstructures" of society; (4) social habits (more correctly, customs) and practices; (5) revolutionary or reformistic phenomena (the relationship between this level and the preceding one is the same as that between invention and imitation in Tarde's view); (6) values which underlie the activities observable on the preceding level; and (7) the immediate social reality or *collective mind*—here is indication of Gurvitch's acceptance of certain aspects of Durkheim's theory. The collective mind, he maintains, is felt in the depth of the individual consciousness, operates through individual minds, and provides man the innermost knowledge of the reciprocity of value relationships in social life.

Two classifications in Gurvitch's sociology should be noted. First, his distinction between *microsociology* and *macrosociology* indicates two principal types of sociology, each of which uses quite distinct methods of investigation. (This methodological distinction is denied by many sociologists, including neo-positivists and such functionalists as Merton, who maintain that the same logic of procedure must be used in studying all social phenomena.) Microsociology studies, for example, small informal groups (as indicated in Chap. 19), while macrosociology is concerned with such large-scale phenomena as states and whole civilizations. Second, Gurvitch has constructed a complicated classification of the forms of *sociability;* however, this depiction of no less than 162 types of sociability is essentially an insightful exercise in definitions and offers little for theoretical growth. (In a later contribution Gurvitch argued that the development of microsociology must take place within the framework of macrosociology.)

In *Social Determinism and Human Freedom,* Gurvitch no longer cites phenomenological philosophy as the starting point of his reasoning (in *Vocation of Sociology,* 1950, he had already denied his allegiance to that school of thought). As pointed out, however, by another French sociologist, A. Cuvillier,[3] this change of orientation—now described by Gurvitch as "hyperempiric dialectics"[4]—is not reflected in the substantive content of his sociological views. To a large extent, this comment applies to *Social Determinism.*

In this volume, Gurvitch claims that no causal, evolutionary or functional laws can be established in the realm of sociology. Determinism, if any, can be found only in the form of statistical laws (probability statements), covariation of variables, uniform tendencies in various social

[3] A. Cuvillier, *Où va la sociologie française?* (1953).
[4] A philosophical theory about five possible dialectical relationships, of concepts, expounded by the author in *Cahiers internationaux de sociologie,* vol. 15 (1953). The Hegelian triad thesis-antithesis-synthesis is one of them.

developments, and in the integration of parts into wholes. After examining various definitions, Gurvitch identifies freedom with spontaneous and voluntary actions which tend to modify situations and break resistance. This conception of freedom is used to test sociological forms of determinism—against a background of a sociology in depth reproducing, with slight modifications, the one reported above. None of the levels of depth are found to suppress human liberty unduly, since they interplay and limit each other. A similar situation prevails with respect to the "forms of sociability," a major object of study in microsociology.

Perhaps the most interesting part of *Social Determinism* is the study of determinism and freedom in "all-inclusive societies," that is, those large-scale societies in the framework of which the vast majority of human needs can be satisfied. According to Gurvitch, no universal principle of integration of such societies is known to exist, a lack demanding preliminary typological study. Thus Gurvitch depicts four "archaic" or primitive types, six historical types (for example, enlightened despotism in combination with nascent capitalism and democratic society combined with competitive capitalism), and four modern types (among them, the "organized capitalism" of contemporary United States and the "collective pluralism" of Great Britain and Sweden). With respect to each type, the relative significance of the levels of depth and of the forms of sociability are briefly sketched and these problems are posed: what is the prevailing type of social determinism?, and what is the "chance of liberty"? Gurvitch's general conclusion is that in every type of society there exists plurality of social determinisms while the degree of liberty fluctuates but never disappears entirely. Answers to these large questions are not empirically established in this relatively brief book, but this is a challenging volume, suggesting how much study would be necessary to answer, scientifically, these problems of the relationship between society, culture, and personality.

Gurvitch published in 1955 a lengthy article on "Social Structure," which he considers to be one of the most important concepts in sociological theory, and one attracting more and more attention on the part of sociologists. After a brilliant survey of the causes of this attraction, Gurvitch takes over from the Durkheimian Mauss the concept of the "total social phenomenon" which seems to refer to society as given in immediate experience. Characteristics of this phenomenon include the prevalence of centripetal over centrifugal forces, some regulation of conduct, certain collective attitudes, and accentuation of levels of depth (as treated in *Social Determinism*). Gurvitch attempts to show what is added to this rather amorphous object of experience by *structure* which, he claims, is met only on the macrosociological, never on the microsociological, level. These additions—in other words, the difference between structured and non-structured social phenomena—are contained in the following propositions: (1) there are hierarchies of the levels of depth, of symbols, and of the forms of the regulation of human conduct; (2) the units forming these hierarchies are always in dynamic equilibrium; (3) some collective consciousness of these hierarchies and equilibria exists; (4) there are also "forces" sustaining equilibrium; but (5) the structure is never in fact static for it is always subject to processes of formation, destruction, and reconstruction. Gurvitch warns against any static interpretation of social structures: in his opinion, nothing is stable in society, which is marked by perpetual movement and change. As noted by a friendly critic, Gurvitch's emphasis on incessant movement forces him to concentrate on the unique. If sociology follows this lead, however, it risks losing its subject matter; for sociology, at least general sociology, is a theoretical science, and as such, must deal with recurrent phenomena.[5]

Gurvitch's later work is still centered around "sociology in depth," the mainspring of which is phenomenological. During his final years he worked mainly on refining and redefining his concepts and propositions. In *Dialectique et sociologie* Gurvitch (again) denied his adherence to the phenomenological school, and cited as the main sources of his inspiration the works of Fichte (a philosopher), Marx (a social philosopher if also a social scientist), Durkheim, and Mauss; this denial is repeated in *The Spectrum of Social Time*.

In the recent edition of *The Vocation of Sociology* (1963), Gurvitch cites what he views as two mistakes of his earlier works. First, he rules out such methods as "inversion" or "phenomenological reduction" since sociology as a science should not be tied to any particular philosophical orientation, which he had believed to be possible in the 1930's. Second, he regretfully rejects the use of "cultural models," such as one meets in studies of morality, law, religion, and art, and which he himself had employed in earlier studies. During the last years of his life, Gurvitch declared that his sociology belongs to the trend of "hyper-critical empiricism," a phrase he left unexplained. Literally, the phrase means beyond empiricism, and what is that but speculation on the philosophical level?

It is surprising that so able a scholar as Gurvitch repeatedly denied the very possibility of a static approach to social phenomena because "in society," as he wrote, everything is always moving, that is, always in the process of structuralization and destructuralization. Only once in *The Vocation of Sociology* does he mentally arrest this movement as he puts it, describing the state of social systems at the precise time chosen by the observer. This "snapshot" procedure, of course, is an inevitable and essential part of scientific analysis, whether in the natural or social sciences. This is to say, in the case of sociology, that study of social dynamics and change, in the final analysis, is inseparable from the structural—or "static" —study of that which changes, namely the social order.

Although Gurvitch strongly denied that his sociology is philosophical

---

[5] H. Janne, "Fonction et finalité en sociologie," *Cahiers internationaux de sociologie*, vol. 16 (1954).

and seemed to downgrade the philosophical approach, he gave a great deal of attention to and wrote at length about various philosophical problems. The sociologist's principal task, we believe, is to extricate from such philosophical works empirically valid propositions. An important example of this kind of enterprise is offered in the later section of this chapter on Luigi Sturzo.

## The Phenomenological School

We have noted that as a younger scholar Georges Gurvitch had been influenced by the philosophical outlook of phenomenology. This school reflects the philosophy of Edmund Husserl (1859–1938), whose main work, *Ideas on Pure Phenomenology*, appeared in 1913. The sociological manifestation of Husserl's position was inaugurated by Theodor Litt, whose principal theoretical contribution is *Individual and Society* (1919). According to Litt, phenomenology is applicable to those phenomena of a psychic nature which are so constituted that a structure, or inner arrangement, is perceivable in a single cognitive experience of the observer and points the way to analysis. This is the case of the phenomena studied by the social sciences. In this respect, Litt's approach resembles that of Max Weber.

The best-known work in sociology along these lines is the theory of Alfred Vierkandt (1867–1952). Vierkandt was born in Hamburg, studied in Leipzig under the psychologist Wundt, and published his first work, *Natural and Cultural Peoples*, in 1895. From 1921 to 1934 he was professor of social sciences at the University of Berlin. Vierkandt's *Theory of Society* first appeared in 1922 (revised in 1928) and in later years the views presented in this volume were expanded in numerous books and essays; a new version of the *Theory* was published in 1949.

For Vierkandt, the task of sociology is the construction of a theory of society and culture. Society is defined as the sum total of human interactions—a conception reminiscent of Simmel's theory, which Vierkandt quotes. Of the various possible approaches to sociology, Vierkandt stresses, the most adequate one is based on the phenomenological method. This method, called "ideational abstraction," is oriented toward ultimate concepts which cannot be reduced to other concepts. These basic concepts can be grasped by "a look at" (*Ansicht*) social life, in other words, by clarifying their specific nature through inner contemplation of instances, or even of one instance which may be an imaginary one. Comparison of fundamental concepts derived in this manner with others is a desirable procedure for the phenomenologist.

By means of this inner contemplation, understanding of the inborn dispositions of men is possible. These include both "self-sentiment" and the dependency of people on the judgments of others. Society is thus a "being together" of men who find themselves bound by mutual dependency. This view, Vierkandt emphasizes, is not a psychological conception of society. The latter's individual members experience a kind of inner constraint; but the bonds between the members are based on intercommunication, which can take place in the absence of physical movements or conscious reflections.

Vierkandt stresses the basic properties of human societies. In the first place, each society possesses a *wholeness* in the sense that it is a system, a structure in which every event in any part affects the other segments of the whole. This functional proposition is supplemented by a second theory, namely, that families, tribes, nations, and other social organizations to a certain extent have "lives of their own": how they behave, how they develop, what they achieve cannot be arbitrarily determined by individuals. Societies have their own style, their laws, their orders which shape the behavior of people who often do not feel their dependence on the whole. Individuals come and go, but the structure and order and, indeed, the purpose and achievement of social groups persist.

Social groups, Vierkandt continues, show various degrees of solidarity. In the *Gemeinschaft* or community type the bonds are close and warm; ego-consciousness is expanded beyond the boundaries of the individual. However, there are gradations of such solidarity among different types of communities or *Gemeinschaften*. Moreover, *associations*, in the sense of Toennies' *Gesellschaften* (and closely similar to MacIver's concept of *association* as presented in Chap. 18), also are marked by varying degrees of group cohesion.

Each social group, Vierkandt holds, possesses its own spirit, which is "superior" to the subjective spirit of its individual members. The unconscious purposiveness of group life is almost a "miracle." Yet the individual and the group do not stand in opposition since each person is permeated by group characteristics and the individual's attitude toward the group is basically one of love and admiration. It should be noted that Vierkandt's conception of a fundamental harmony between individual and group and his emphasis on the former's "love" for the group are consistent with a traditional intellectual orientation in Germany, illustrated, for example, in the works of the philosopher Hegel and his followers and the "romantic" movement.

Several other sociologists have been impressed by phenomenological philosophy. One of these is the Frenchman Jules Monnerot, author of *Social Facts Are Not Things* (1946). The title of this volume indicates Monnerot's anti-Durkheimian point of view.

Only phenomena of *attraction*, which form the starting point of sociology, Monnerot maintains, can be really understood (in the meaning of Max Weber's *verstehen*, or, still more, according to "ideational abstraction"). In general, we "understand" certain events while we "explain" other ones. We understand when we are in the presence of evidence which is valid per se. Such evidence is found in immediate experience, and attempts to base understanding on induction distort the evidence itself.

Contrary to Durkheim's view, Monnerot insists that social facts are not things. For social facts present themselves to the mind in a manner distinctly different from the way things do; the former are "human conditions," located and dated. The primary material of sociology consists of sequences of such conditions, which means that sociology's fundamental data are the same as those of history. The aim of sociology itself is to give a new meaning to phenomena already studied by other sciences. Sociology, then, is a manner of looking at other humanistic sciences, of comparing their elements, and of seeking new understanding of social life. But sociology is not the science of society for, according to Monnerot, there are no "societies," but only states of societies, social situations experienced by men.

Social facts or human conditions (which in Monnerot's work seem to refer to the condition of men when faced by immediate experiences) do not in themselves explain such phenomena as social movements. To understand the latter, for example, a person must first feel the grasp of the particular movement and subsequently free himself from it; only then can he achieve objective understanding.

These attempts to describe the act of understanding and its goals are supplemented by Monnerot's survey of what he calls *fundamental representations*. The most important of these is the fact that every individual "transcends his natural boundaries," thereby producing effects in the social order. Such effects meet and oppose one another; they enter into "duels" (reminiscent of Tarde's "logical duels"). But there is no society without attraction. Society, in fact, is said to be primarily a human aggregation that develops ties of coordination and cooperation (a formulation at odds with Monnerot's statement, reported above, denying the very existence of society). Within this aggregation, patterns or structures arise on the basis of spatial propinquity and affinity. Three broad types of social structures are distinguishable, which Monnerot designates by the German terms *Gemeinschaft*, *Gesellschaft*, and *Bund*, the latter being based on affinity and common affective experiences. The first two categories, as we have seen, have become almost standard concepts in modern sociology.

Phenomenological sociology is also represented in the United States, in some of the publications of Friedrich Baerwald (1900–    ), born in Germany, and since 1935 professor at Fordham University. Baerwald's theoretical views may be summarized as follows: [6]

Social reality, Baerwald maintains, is tantamount to society. Society is not a psychological phenomenon manifested in the discovery of

---

[6] Our summary of Baerwald's theory is based largely on two of his articles, "Society as a Process," *American Catholic Sociological Review* (Dec., 1944), and "A Sociological View of Depersonalization," *Thought* (Spring, 1956). His forthcoming article in *Thought* tries to reconcile humanistic and existential sociology.

reciprocity relations in one's own consciousness. Fundamental data of experience include the actual existence of people other than ourselves and our dependency on them. But we must understand not merely the fact of coexistence but its general mode. Human dependency is based on the insufficiency of the individual to secure his own survival. His "time framework" is limited to his own existence and experience; the individual's "space framework" is similarly limited. These limitations are overcome through coexistence.

The process of coexistence in *time*, Baerwald explains, creates patterns of social groups into which individuals are integrated and through which they are placed in a position to link their efforts with those of others. Social participation integrates the individual into a chain of significant past events; by the same token it assigns him a share in the projection into the future of the existence of the group. Through this involvement in a transpersonal framework, the individual experiences a widening of his horizon in time and integrates into his consciousness skills, customs, meanings, and values developed over long periods.

Coexistence is also an interactional process in *space*. It brings about the widening of the individual horizon by setting up transpersonal systems of "space domination" in which individuals participate, to which they contribute, and from which they benefit.

Social institutions do not represent society on the existential level. For institutions must be rooted in the process of coexistence itself, the continuous projection of time-space horizons of individuals into larger transpersonal systems. Coexistence involves continuous transformation of astronomic time into a meaningful past and future as well as a continuous transformation of geographic habitat into social space.

While coexistence is the mode of existence of individuals, Baerwald continues, the actual systems of living and cooperating are neither automatic nor instinctive. Society is a prerequisite for survival, to be sure, but it requires constant activation through the establishment and maintenance of extended social time and space frameworks. Society does not continue of itself as far as specific social formations are concerned. Therefore, inherent in all social structures there exists the possibility of their deterioration and disintegration through a weakening of links in the social time and space frameworks.

These highly abstract propositions of Baerwald's, suggestive as they are, have not yet attracted the attention of many sociologists in this country, nor have they been subjected to empirical test. The latter comment is applicable, in large degree, to the philosophical school in general.

## The Phenomenological School: Summary and Appreciation

When abstracted from the philosophical premises and methodological peculiarities, some interesting insights are to be found in the work of the phenomenological school. In connection with the relationship between society and individual, three emphases are apparent: the independent duration of society, the relative independence of group behavior from the acts and intentions of the group's individual members, and the inherent danger of societal deterioration. As the unit for sociological analysis, the whole or the group is singled out, rather than the individual actor or social interaction. The problem of the determinants of social order and social change lies outside the school's principal preoccupations.

The phenomenological approach is open to several criticisms. In the first place, the phenomenologists claim that the basic concepts of science, including sociology, must be formulated by philosophy (of their own variety). To accept this claim would make impossible a common universe of discourse, a prerequisite for the growth of empirical science. Secondly, the phenomenologists' sociological formulations, which they believe to be the result of "ideational abstraction," in all likelihood are actually based on previous knowledge which they have accumulated through participant observation of social life. Finally, the phenomena which phenomenologists claim to "see" in society seem to be selected in an arbitrary or even biased manner. Vierkandt's description of the individual's attitude toward the group, for example, may fairly accurately portray the German viewpoint, but hardly that of American or French scholars or laymen.

Another philosophical approach which developed almost simultaneously with phenomenological sociology is what we call here the institutional school.

## The Institutional School: Platonic and Thomist Phases

The institutional branch of the philosophical school arose in France in the middle 1920's. This approach is marked by two peculiarities: first, all of its members are Roman Catholics and, with the exception of the founding father of the school, they attempt to construct a system of sociology on the foundation of Thomist philosophy; second, the majority of the members of the school are jurists, the sociological theory they present being a by-product of their attempt to solve a juridical problem, namely, the problem of the nature of corporate personality.

In contrast with the Roman tradition and with Anglo-American thought, which deny the reality of such personalities, and with the ideas of Otto Gierke (1841–1921), the great German jurist of the late nineteenth century who in the realm of jurisprudence professed an extreme social realism (in the manner of Durkheim), they ascribe to social groups, among them corporations, a reality *sui generis*—which may or may not be recognized by law but is independent of such recognition.

The father of this point of view was Maurice Hauriou, one of France's greatest jurists. Traces of what was to become the "institutional theory" may be found in his early works; but *The Theory of the Institu-*

*tion and Foundation,* which appeared in 1925 shortly before the author's death, is an explicit and vigorous formulation of this approach. Hauriou was influenced by Henri Bergson and Claude Bernard to some extent, but he found the core of his theory in rediscovery of a statement by St. Augustine: "A people is an assemblage of reasonable beings bound together by a common agreement as to the object of their love." [7]

Hauriou's starting point is this rather Platonic proposition: "Objective ideas exist in advance in the vast world around us." Among these ideas are those pertaining to tasks to be performed. The latter cannot "wander at large" in amorphous society; they must be captured and embodied in *institutions.*

Hauriou distinguishes two types of institutions, the first consisting of such normative systems as rules of conduct, and the second composed of persons or social groups. Hauriou was primarily interested in institutions of the second type. [8] Therefore his sociological writings are mainly a theory of the social group, a field in his day surprisingly neglected by professional sociologists.

The institution (or social group), according to Hauriou, is comprised of three elements: the organizing idea, the organized government, and intercommunion of the members around the idea. The *organizing idea,* the idea of the task to be performed, enters the minds of an undetermined number of individuals. In truly Platonic style, Hauriou emphasizes that, although the common idea receives somewhat different forms in the various individual minds, "objectively" it remains the same. Organizing ideas confer upon institutions an existence of their own and are significantly different from those of the groups' constituent members.

Hauriou's second institutional element is *organization,* analogous to government in the state. Government is a manifestation of human will. Exercise of will is therefore an essential element of the social reality of an institution, but it is contributed by the individual members and is thus not the "will" of the institution itself.

The third institutional element is *intercommunion* of the members. Hauriou rejects any conception of collective mind. His concept of intercommunion refers to the fact that individuals are similarly affected by contact with the same organizing idea, that they spontaneously recognize the similarity of their mental states, and that in this manner they are induced to common action.

This analysis of the interactive elements of social groups or institutions is supplemented by Hauriou's theory of how institutions are born,

[7] As shown by Moorhouse I. X. Millar in "Hauriou, Suarez and Marshal," *Thought* (March, 1932).

[8] Several contemporary theorists, among them Parsons and MacIver, distinguish sharply between concrete social groups, collectivities to which people *belong,* and institutions, established and socially enforced procedures marking group life. Hauriou, like Sumner years earlier, encompasses both meanings in "institution," though his conception of the first type—systems of conduct—corresponds to the more widely accepted usage.

live, and die. Being a jurist, he identifies the stages of group life with legally relevant processes. Thus, institutions emerge through "acts of foundation" and die by means of "dissolution." Their lives, according to Hauriou, consist mainly of the legal operations of their "governments," group elections and deliberations, and the gradual adherence of new members. The duration of an institution depends not so much on the will of its founders as on the persistence of the essential organizing idea. For the originators of an institution plant a living idea in amorphous society which, once planted, develops by itself.

Despite his Platonic philosophical foundation and his overemphasis on its legal aspects, Hauriou produced a suggestive theory of the social group. Another institutionalist, Georges Renard, developed Hauriou's theory but shifted its basis from Platonism to Thomism in *The Theory of the Institution* (two volumes, 1930–39). For Renard, an institution or social group is "communion of men in an idea." Renard stresses that in his conception institution and social group are identical. However, he frequently expands the meaning of this key sociological concept. Thus, he mentions the possibility of "instituting peace," and in one place even expresses the idea that human nature is a primary institution. But most of *The Theory of the Institution* is confined to an analysis of the social group, constituting the body of propositions that concerns us here.

The "generating idea," according to Renard, produces some degree of solidarity among the persons who support or will support the social group. The group or institution thus unites people—but it does not abolish their individuality as rational beings. The internal structure of an institution is composed of social relations. But whereas other relations link together people as individuals as such in various ways, within institutions the group results from the fact that the members share an entity which dominates them.

In the second volume of his major work, which is more philosophical than the first, Renard develops the following ideas: Each person has both a conception of a distinctive *me* and a belief in the linkage of me with *us*.[9] The link itself is not purely logical; it is real or existential. The purpose of sociological study of the institution is to show how these individual and social elements are mutually adjusted. In Renard's view, the institution, like an organism, integrates its members into a whole, though not so completely as to destroy the individuality of its members. On the contrary, the institution provides individual beings with properties they would not otherwise possess. In other words, the group is not reducible to the sum total of its parts.

The inner life of a social group or institution, Renard holds, is characterized by *intimacy, authority,* and *objectivity.* Institutional intimacy is a "link of confidence," but this confidence is socially patterned or organized,

[9] This view is similar in language and, to some extent, in substance to the theories of Cooley and Mead, discussed in Chap. 12.

and in this respect it differs from individual friendship. Authority of some kind is essential in a social group; it is in fact the condition of its existence, its manner of being, being inseparable from the exigencies of social life. (As noted by some of Renard's critics, he overlooks the possibility of egalitarian groupings in which authority is held by every member according to a principle of justice.) Authority is ingrained in the whole, but it is exercised by individuals in so far as they serve the "common good"; the latter, in this context, presumably is identified with the generating idea of a particular institution. The mutual relations between persons composing institutions are essentially relations between organs of a juristic organism; their stability requires the existence of group rules and sanctions. These essential rules and sanctions form what Renard calls the *objectivity* of an institution.

Finally, Renard considers the question of institutional change. Institutions originate by an "act of foundation" which manifests a communion of wills. Once formed, the institutions escape, so to speak, the will of their founders. Thus, institutions have their own life, developing through time according to their particular nature.

In general, Renard's theory of institutional structure and change is very similar to Hauriou's but is freed from the latter's Platonism. According to Renard, the common will of individuals, the consequence of common support of an idea, is the instigating force in institutional development. But this common will creates a new kind of social being who differs from individuals outside of group life.

The theories of the institutionalists in recent decades have begun to penetrate a few general treatises on sociology. This is the case in the volume *Essay of Sociology* (1946), by the Belgian scholar Jean Haesaert, who, perhaps significantly, like the other members of the institutional school, is a man of legal training. According to Haesaert, social structures that develop from contact and cooperation are "*synergic systems.*" These systems may be simple or complex structures, the latter consisting of a number of simpler systems. The synergic system is an entirely original phenomenon, transcending the individuals whose activities call it into being. It has its own "reality," although a secondary and artificially created one. The basic elements of the synergic system include a directive idea, the means to realize this idea through the activities of the group members, and established patterns of action congenial to the idea.

This formulation of the characteristics of social structures seems to have little influence upon the content of Haesaert's extended sociological essay except in its final part. Here the author discusses the concept of *dysergy*, the sum total of phenomena through which synergy or social structure deteriorates. This deterioration may be partial or total. But elements of virtual dissolution are always present in every synergic system. If the system absorbs these elements, its equilibrium is restored, a concept very similar to that of Pareto (whom Haesaert cites). If the forces of dysergy are not absorbed, the system is dissolved.

Haesaert's work represents an advance over the views of the earlier institutionalists in that it strips away the legalistic façade of the earlier theories. It also identifies institution and group and attempts to depict their nature.

## The Institutional School: Summary and Appreciation

The majority of the members of the institutional school claim that their work has been inspired by Thomist philosophy. But authorities on Thomism doubt whether they have achieved their purpose.[10] But it should be noted that, independently of any philosophical inspiration, the teaching of the institutionalists offers valuable insights into the nature of social groups. The contributions of the institutional school may be summarized as follows:

First, the methodological views of the individual members differ widely. Hauriou's approach is somewhat intuitive, relying upon impressionistic (but *insightful*) observation of social phenomena. Renard and some of his followers employ the deductive method, deriving their most important formulations from Thomist philosophy or what they hold it to be. Renard also advocates induction, but he fails to show how his propositions are derived from experience; essentially his induction is tantamount to Hauriou's intuition.

Second, the institutionalists are in agreement concerning the reality of institutions, which they are all inclined to identify with social groups. But at the same time, they all reject both the crude type of organismic analogy and the conception of a collective mind. They also concur in claiming that the reality of social groups is that of a whole transcending its parts without, however, eliminating the real and independent existence of the latter.

Third, Hauriou's thesis that the organizing or directive idea unites a number of individuals into a collective whole has been adopted by later institutionalists, after having been liberated of its initial Platonic flavor.

Fourth, the institutionalists have contributed to our understanding of the duration of social groups independently of the persistence of the initial conditions which engendered them. They also have suggested a method for the analysis of different types of social groups which are generally not encompassed by current standard definitions of community and association.[11]

[10] See for instance Luigi Sturzo, *The Inner Laws of Society* (New York: Kenedy, 1944), p. 243.

[11] However, as we noted in Chap. 18, the systematic sociologists have developed theories of different types of social groups. See especially R. M. MacIver and C. H. Page, *Society: An Introductory Analysis* (New York: Rinehart, 1949), Chap. X; F.

Fifth, being jurists, the institutionalists tend to overemphasize the legal phase of social life and to identify legal order and social order. This identification, however, does not follow from their basic premises.

Sixth, in general, the works of the institutionalists contain many stimulating ideas. But none among them has succeeded in offering a consistent theory of social groups or social institutions covering all their sociologically relevant aspects and variations.

To complete the survey of contemporary sociological theories of philosophical inspiration, we shall consider some of the theories of three otherwise quite distinctive sociologists: Luigi Sturzo, Pierre Teilhard de Chardin, and Karl Mannheim.

### Sturzo: Social Harmonism

Luigi Sturzo was born in 1871 in a poor district of Sicily, received his education at Catholic institutions in Rome, and became a priest. The abject poverty of large portions of the population in southern Italy pushed him to action: he founded the Popular Party. After Mussolini's ascent to power, Sturzo emigrated first to England, then to the United States. During his twenty-five year exile he wrote and published his main works, including *Essai de Sociologie* (1933) or, in English, *The Inner Basis of Society*. In 1945, he returned to Italy, where he continued his activities until his death in 1959.

Although Sturzo's sociological theory is little known, it is often dismissed out-of-hand primarily because it includes the study of the impact of the supernatural on human society. Yet subtraction of this analysis from his total theoretical system yields a residue worthy of recognition and deserving consideration as a valuable contribution to sociological thought.

For Sturzo, sociology is the science of society in the concrete. By this he means that sociology should be concerned with the study of "the total social phenomenon," that is, as society appears in its entirety, before its analysis into classes of economic, religious, and other partial phenomena. The central question for Sturzo is: What is *a* society, a *concrete* society?

In pursuing this question, Sturzo offers a well-developed analytical definition, a proposition including all the necessary traits of any object of observation that is a referent to the symbol "a concrete society." According to this definition, a concrete society is present whenever the following traits coexist: a plurality of individuals; striving for a common end; a collective consciousness; and a collectivity subject to a temporal process, beyond the limits of individual life. What does it *mean*, Sturzo asks, not

Znaniecki, "Social Groups in the Modern World," in M. Berger, T. Abel, and C. H. Page, eds., *Freedom and Control in Modern Society* (New York: D. Van Nostrand, 1954), Chap. V; and G. C. Homans, *The Human Group* (New York: Harcourt, Brace, 1950).

conceptually, but on the level of reality, that a plurality of men endowed with these traits forms a concrete society?

Sturzo's theory of the relationship between society and the individual is an illustration of "social harmonism," with a certain inclination toward "personalism." Social harmonism is a synthesis of personalism and collectivism. On the level of ideas, a synthesis presupposes a thesis and an antithesis. This dialectical form of presentation is especially appropriate in this case since Sturzo, without being a Hegelian, favored the term "dialectic."

Sturzo believes that the unity of society and the individual is rooted in the fact that man's consciousness is "individual-collective." He conceives of collective consciousness as the composition of specified elements of individual consciousnesses. These elements are not torn away from their roots, that is, from the personalities of individuals.

In every individual consciousness, one may analytically distinguish two components: the pure individual or personal, and the collective or associative. The personal component consists of a specific individual's consciousness inasmuch as it is related to himself, his thoughts, aspirations, and activities. The collective component, centered around "the instinct" [12] of association, by contrast is formed of thoughts, aspirations, and achievements of the individual insofar as they are related to those of other human beings who with him form a society.

True mental communion among those associated is identified by Sturzo with *sociality*, or, more exactly, with the concretization of sociality; the associative tendency of men is inherent in their nature. The irreducible "principle" of sociality is the rational capacity of men to acquire consciousness of their associative nature. Awareness of belonging together, communion, friendship, participation in ideas, and the like are real phenomena incorporated in the associative components of the individual consciousnesses. In different individuals the processes are not parallel, but interrelated. This interrelation is effected through a mechanism which Sturzo calls projection.

In this way, a compound is formed, the collective consciousness, the resultant of the composition of the associative components of individual consciousnesses, and "is not something standing apart from concrete individuality." This compound may, on the one hand, be analytically resolved into individual consciousnesses; on the other hand, it tangibly influences the individual consciousnesses and, through them, human actions.

From Sturzo's emphasis on collective consciousness, one should not conclude that the reality of society is identical with its apprehension by men. Societal reality, according to Sturzo, is not tantamount to the *idea* of the members that the society exists, but to the *fact* that the consciousness of each member, actively or passively or both, is tied to the ideas and actions of others. This is a tangible reality. The fusion of the associative components of individual consciousnesses, for each individual, is part of

[12] The term "instinct" should be replaced by "tendency."

his conditioning, which is as influential as his material and biological conditioning.

Such is Sturzo's theory of social structure. But much more important for him is social dynamics. In Sturzo's words, in addition to the structural dimension, societies possess a processual, or temporal, or dynamic dimension. This means that society as given in immediate experience cannot be understood as something stable; like all else, it is in constant flux, the present being only a spark between past and future. Many elements of the past disappear without a trace; others are instrumental in the structuring of the present.

In applying the time dimension to anything, we employ the three tenses—present, past, and future—to express what we mean. Sturzo himself speaks of "society with the past" (the dead) and "society with the future" (the progeny); he adds: "Every moment of the process is reality inasmuch as it is present." For the sociologist, this is the existence and coexistence of human beings. When studying this "process," we start from the present, seeking in the past the laws of its formation and development.

Organization (together with human ends) gives to any social formation its specific character, which leads Sturzo to depict society as "organico-finalistic." As organs of society, individuals express their consciousness of being in communion with one another and of acting as a whole. This is one of the clearest expressions of Sturzo's sociological harmonism.

In the "past tense," as Sturzo puts it, society is tradition or the impact of the past on the present. Society, he argues, is fundamentally a datum of historical consciousness; a specific society preserves its identity through the consciousness formed among its members that it is the "same" as it was in the beginning. The past is felt in the present as language, custom, and continuity of places and of representative symbols; among the latter are succession of persons endowed with high authority, names of illustrious families, recurring phases of work, and the return of popular festivals. This continuity is reinforced by chronicles, myths, works of poetry, and such "returning" actions as rites, formalities, and legal institutions.

In the "future tense" society is expressed in finality, that is, in the pursuit, by associated men, of common ends. This finalistic element is inherent in every social formation, but it is not superimposed on human nature. As the individual consciousness, when projected, develops on the social plane, so individual ends are extended on the social plane. More precisely, this "finalistic element" both in men and society is the product of the tendency to see fulfillment and perfection, which are construed as rationality.

In conclusion, Sturzo's views on the relationship between society and the individual and, implicitly, on the nature of social reality present a substantial advance along the lines of social harmonism.

### Teilhard de Chardin: Philosophical Evolutionist *

Pierre Teilhard de Chardin (1881–1955) was born in the village of Orcines (Puy-de-Dome). In 1899 he entered the Society of Jesus at Aix-en-Provence and from there he went to Laval to continue his studies. Prior to his ordination in 1911, he taught physics and chemistry in Cairo for a few years; he was also professor of geology at the Institut Catholique in Paris during the early 1920's, studying at the Sorbonne for the license in natural sciences and for the doctorate in geology and paleontology. Due to the boldness of some of his philosophic ideas, he was barred from teaching and spent the bulk of his professional career in exile in China, with some brief interruptions for visits and field trips to Africa, the United States, and France. In 1928 he was a party to the discovery of "Peking" man. His chief works, *Le Phenomène humain* (1955), *L'Apparition de l'homme* (1956), *La Vision du passé* (1954), *L'Avenir de l'homme* (1959) and *Le Groupe zoologique humain* remained unpublished until after his death.

Teilhard's central insight is the essentially evolving (and therefore interrelated) character of all levels of reality. He argues, moreover, that evolution possesses a definite direction, progressing on a "chosen axis"—it appears as a clear line of progress toward greater complexity and consciousness. However, the trend toward what he refers to as "complexity/consciousness" affects only a small part of the universe, for much of life is involved in a process of dispersal similar to entropy among physical things. "Psychism" enters into selection and guides evolution from its earliest beginnings because of some form of consciousness in the "within" of matter and energy. It is man toward whom and for whom the whole of evolution has been directed because only in man is there an entirely new consciousness, the capacity to reflect upon himself.

The process of social and cultural evolution is roughly analogous to the evolution of all natural forms; the former arise out of the dynamic tension of the "radial" and "tangential" forces of living matter in terms of the function complexity/consciousness. While the evolution of life within the biosphere appears to be almost "Darwinian," within the *neosphere* there is a progressive rise of conscious self-determination. Moreover, there is more than one ascent into the final stage of evolution.

Each culture, past or present, simple or complex, represents in a given collectivity a particular solution to the problems of reflective life, a realized form of adaptation of the universal potential of reflective consciousness to a given environment. Each culture is the present stage of a long and complex evolution, psychic and morphological. Adaptation is the total structure of the life of the group and the definite modality of its real

* This section on Pierre Teilhard de Chardin was written by Dr. Josephine Wtulich.

and potential existence within the historical determination of time and place. The future of an evolving culture or society has an indeterminate number of possibilities, but its progressive realization continually limits and orients the subsequent configuration of the possible.

In this process, there can emerge a totally new form of human life, the basis of an altogether new potential of human existence. Each new sociocultural form is a new form of life, and is irreversible. Each new form surpasses any past form in organic complexity and potential intensity. Any radical change involves and necessitates the breakdown of the stability and unifying coherence of the whole mode of life. The past cannot serve as a model. No one stage of a society or culture should be viewed as more or less natural, nor should its disappearance be regarded as more or less unnatural. Progress is movement of socio-cultural forms toward self-determination, self-realization, in the final convergence of humanity into some sort of a superorganism of an "ultrapersonal" nature with the collective development of the human mind. The final success of the processes mentioned above is not necessary, inevitable, or certain.

Much of what Teilhard proposes has been said before. What is new is his *synthesis* of seemingly divergent theories. His evolutionary ideas do not center on those of Darwin—his intuitive theories are of a different order. As in the case of Sorokin, he studies the whole realm of the superorganic, in its general characteristics and main types and especially in its static and dynamic uniformities. Contrary to Marx, he sees human collectivities as arising out of unity and synthesis. Furthermore, he argues, as does Durkheim, that not only does unity differentiate but differentiation unites. He recognizes that collective psychism is especially important in evolution, but at the same time he perceives the significant role of technology. His description of what he terms the law of evolution is similar in some ways to the views of Ward and Spencer, yet significantly different. Like Cooley and Mead he recognizes the compatibility of social forms and individual consciousness, and philosophy more than sociology.

### Mannheim: Social Structure and Meaning

In this chapter on philosophical sociology we have considered some of the principal views of Georges Gurvitch, representative phenomenologists, exponents of the institutional school, Luigi Sturzo, and Pierre Teilhard. The common element in this otherwise markedly "mixed bag" of writers is their preoccupation with philosophical problems—as we noted at the outset, these scholars were, at once, sociologists and social philosophers. This double allegiance, more and more rare today, in substantial measure characterizes the work of Karl Mannheim, the final figure whose theories will be discussed here.

In the case of Mannheim, the limited nature of our treatment should be indicated. His contributions to a variety of fields—the sociology of knowledge, political sociology, culture and personality, social planning, educational sociology, the interpretation of social change and of totalitarianism—continue to be influential among many sociologists and others, notably so in Britain. In this section, however, we shall concentrate on only certain of Mannheim's ideas of essentially theoretical and philosophical or quasi-philosophical relevance.

Karl Mannheim (1891–1947) was a German scholar who, after Hitler's ascent to power, established himself in England, became a leading figure at the London School of Economics and Political Science, and found there new inspiration. Mannheim's best-known works are *Man and Society in an Age of Reconstruction* (1946) and *Ideology and Utopia* (1936), the latter rightly considered to be one of the cornerstones of a special branch of sociology, the sociology of knowledge. More important for general theoretical sociology are two of his several posthumous collections of papers, *Essays on Sociology and Social Psychology* (1953) and *Essays on the Sociology of Culture* (1956).

There is no doubt that Mannheim's sociology is philosophically grounded, though perhaps in a somewhat eclectic manner. In the earlier phase of his work, one may perceive "a metaphysical, quasi-religious belief in the creative function of history" always striving for the harmonization of contending trends.[13] In the later phase, especially during his years in England, he conceded that one could not be guided solely by history; this guidance must be supplemented by such criteria as reason versus unreason and peacefulness versus aggression. This new position clearly introduces value judgments and thus runs contrary to the dominant trend in contemporary sociology, though not in philosophical sociology. For Mannheim, this position resulted in the adoption of the idea of social planning which he briefly but brilliantly unfolded in *Freedom, Power and Democratic Planning* (1950), much of which lies in the field of political sociology. This subject is also well represented in his stimulating *Man and Society*.

For Mannheim, sociology is a science aiming at the coordination of studies in the provinces of the various social sciences. This view seems to hark back to Spencer. But this is not the case, for sociology is defined by Mannheim as a general theory of society or of the total social process (which is essentially Sorokin's definition, as explained in Chap. 1). This theory cannot be confined to the study of the processes of "sociation," or of the coalescence of men into structural groups; it must also include the study of meanings which unite or divide men, in their relationship to social structures. This phase of social inquiry should be performed by a sociology of the mind, or *cultural sociology*.

One of the basic concepts to be used in sociological study is *social structure* which, in Mannheim's view, is the most comprehensive feature

[13] As stated by Paul Keczkemeti in his excellent Introduction to Mannheim's *Essays on Sociology and Social Psychology* (New York: Oxford University Press, 1953).

ial reality. Here Mannheim's approach resembles Gurvitch's, but the
's conception of structure is closer to that of system. For Mann-
...., structure is a concept applicable to any object of a certain complexity which one conceives as formed of items of lesser complexity. A structure may be static, but often is dynamic, presenting a configuration of
antagonistic forces competing for supremacy—for example, a society
marked by developed class conflict. In his earlier works, Mannheim
assumed that structures commonly are intrinsically goal directed; in later
writings he replaced this impersonal direction with conscious planning.

No phase of the social process which, to a large extent, consists of the
building and modification of structures, may be separated from *meanings*.
Socially relevant meanings originate in cooperative situations. But diverse
meanings often emerge, and people may first grasp one and then accept
another—a situation that is facilitated when men easily change their social roles. Under these circumstances, abstract reasoning makes its appearance and finally meditation on "the meaning of meanings" often expressing the struggle between various social ideals. Thus any conception
of social structure as of a principle which inexorably unfolds itself must
be rejected. For this "unfolding" is in fact a succession of limited choices
in which the catalytic role of the personality, especially of the leader,
sometimes plays an important role. We met other, more deterministic
views, when studying dynamic sociology (in Chap. 20).

Like Max Weber, Mannheim advocates a dual study of social phenomena, but disagrees with him as to the composition of the duality.
Weber supplements causal analysis with interpretative study on the motivational level. For Mannheim, the supplement to causal analysis is
functional analysis: what has been causally explained must also be understood in terms of its function in maintaining the equilibrium of the whole
system (this phraseology appears in Mannheim's text as if to corroborate
our identification of his *structure* with *system*). In other words, Weber's
subjective meaning of action or process is replaced by its objective meaning, for the group or system as a whole.

### Postscript

Now we pose a question which may have puzzled the reader of this
chapter. How is philosophical sociology possible? Is not sociology a study
of phenomena on the empiric level while, in philosophy, another level of
abstraction is sought, that of a unifying conception of total reality?

In principle, the question is warranted. Sometimes, however, scholars
use philosophical premises only as a kind of scaffold, after the removal of
which their propositions that are valid on the empiric level remain standing. This was, incidentally, Spencer's idea concerning cosmic evolution
and the organic analogy (see Chap. 3). But Spencer's proposition which
remained after the removal of the scaffold, as we now know, could not be

empirically verified. The *sociological* theories set forth by the exponents of more recent philosophical sociology—by Gurvitch and Sturzo and Mannheim, for example—similarly, in the contemporary empirically oriented social sciences, must face the test of verification.

# PART SIX

*Conclusion*

# CHAPTER 22

# MID-TWENTIETH CENTURY
# SOCIOLOGY: A SYNTHETIC REVIEW

During the first half of the twentieth century, sociology made a decisive advance, from being a tentative program and a cluster of controversies about the scope and method of a science yet to be developed, toward being a firmly established body of knowledge based on a large number of verified observations and inferences drawn from them. However, the goal has not been completely achieved. Disparate sociological viewpoints have not yet merged into sociological theory, a counterpart of the type of theory that forms a part of each of the natural sciences. This goal has not been reached despite the strong exhortations to follow the methods of the natural sciences and the numerous attempts to do so (illustrated, for example, by the works of Thomas, Pareto, and the neo-positivists) and despite the promising contributions of the analytical sociologists.

Nevertheless, several positive results have accumulated.

First, whereas earlier *sociology* contained lengthy discussions of the question of what "sociology" ought to be, today the discussion is about what sociology really is. Of the four basic answers to the former question presented in Chapter 1, the fourth has prevailed, the one which, it will be recalled, defines sociology as the study of the general characteristics of all classes of social phenomena and of the interrelations between these classes. Though the best formulation was by Sorokin, the way to this conception was prepared by Simmel, the founder of the third approach, which identified sociology with the study of the form of social phenomena, and also by Giddings. The ancestry can be traced even farther back to Comte, whose idea that sociology was to become the general theoretical science of social phenomena has been unfolded in Sorokin's widely accepted definition.

Second, *social* phenomena, the subject matter of sociology, are now commonly recognized to be *sui generis,* in other words, to be irreducible to nonsocial facts, for example, psychological or physical. In this respect, Durkheim's view has prevailed against that of the psychological sociologists. The latter, in their turn, were correct in their opposition to those who saw in society the mere interplay of impersonal or, so to say, superhuman forces. Social phenomena are *sui generis* but nevertheless are the result of the composition of human actions.

However, a particularistic view is observable, deriving from Max Weber and Thomas, and now best represented by Parsons. This view reintroduces confusion between sociology and psychology because of its preoccupation with "action."

On the other hand, as a corollary of the irreducibility of social phenomena to any other class of phenomena, common opinion among sociologists rejects biological analogies in all their variations (organicism, social Darwinism, and so on) as well as the understanding of social phenomena in terms of a theoretical model designed for the study of physical phenomena, which played a large part in Spencer's thought system. The late George Lundberg's attempt to understand human society in terms of the structure of the atom is a conspicuous anachronism.

Third, the basic social phenomenon, the unit for sociological analysis, is commonly identified as *interaction* between two or more human beings. Interaction requires intelligible dependency of the action of one human being on the existence or action—past, present, or anticipated—of another human being. Interaction is directly observable, since action is movement in the outside world. The element of dependence is easily inferred either by the interpretation of a participant observer utilizing man's ability to make mental reproductions of processes suggested to him by the actions of other men—this is Max Weber's *verstehen*—or by establishing statistical correlations between universes of actions considered as antecedents and subsequents.

Where there is interaction, the participants are said to be in social relationship. Interaction and social relationship are therefore two points of view regarding the same basic fact; relationship is static (or structural), interaction is kinetic (commonly, but incorrectly, called functional or dynamic).

Fourth, when social relationships endure, they form *social groups* into which men are arranged in manifold ways. The social group is commonly recognized to be one of the major subjects of sociological study, especially and explicitly by the systematic sociologists, the institutionalists, the sociometrists, and microsociologists. In the study of groups the main propositions which have been rather firmly established include the following:

The social group is a *system,* that is, a structure consisting of parts which, without losing their identity and individuality, constitute a whole transcending the parts. In other words, the whole possesses properties which cannot be found anywhere in the several parts. This conception reflects the moderate sociological realism which now prevails; it is best discernible in the works of Pareto, the functionalists, and the institutionalists, as well as in those of the contemporary systematic sociologists except, perhaps, Parsons. This view is not shared by the neo-positivists, whose nominalistic position is closely akin to that of Simmel. It also greatly differs from the extreme sociological realism of the Marxists, Gumplowicz, and Durkheim, all, to be sure, nineteenth-century sociologists.

The individuals who form the social group stand in patterned relationships, so that to each person is ascribed a definite social position, sometimes called *status*. Differential roles are assigned to individuals occupying various social positions—hence the use of the concept "status-role" by Parsons and others.

Interaction within social groups aims at the satisfaction of human needs. The accomplishments of social groups in satisfying needs are their *functions*. The needs which must be satisfied within the framework of the social groups are distributed among various groups; there exists an almost unlimited number of schemes of this distribution arrangement. This aspect of group life has been brought to the forefront by the functionalists, but, as shown in Chapter 17, they have had a number of predecessors.

Interaction within the framework of groups is regulated by *norms*, or propositions defining the conduct expected on the part of the members under specified conditions. The norms of the group are commonly accepted by its members, but they are also enforced by sanctions which are applied in case of violation. The normative view of social phenomena was independently promoted by Toennies and Sumner. Among later sociologists, Thomas, Parsons, and MacIver have laid the greatest emphasis on this aspect of group life.

The system which is the social group possesses the property of restoring its equilibrium, or normal state, if and when disturbance takes place. This proposition goes back to Pareto's theory.

Social groups often form hierarchies in which one group, the all-inclusive society, forms the summit. Within a society, there is a discernible tendency for the smaller groups and their members to be arranged in horizontal strata to which differential participation in wealth, power, and prestige is socially ascribed. But societies vary in the degree of rigidity of the distribution of men and social groups along the social ladder, and in the differential statuses of the groups and persons concerned. Today social stratification, the term given to these phenomena, is a field of intensive research.

Fifth, another basic area of study in sociology consists of the *social processes*. In this type of investigation, the fundamental phenomena of interaction are arranged in keeping with a plan different from the one used in the study of social structure. Social processes are classified according to the goal orientations of the actions composing them.

Among the social processes, *cooperation* is basic in social life. Cooperation is interaction oriented to the achievement of common goals and flows from the very nature of the bonds that hold together the members of social groups. It is manifested in intragroup solidarity, which is usually strengthened by antagonism to other social groups. The basic phenomenon of cooperation was known to Comte; its study was signally advanced by Durkheim and now is being promoted especially by Sorokin. The correlation between intragroup solidarity and out-group antagonism was stressed by Sumner and has become a well-known principle in sociology.

The logical opposite of cooperation, antagonism, appears in two principal forms, *competition* and *conflict*. In some cases, elements of cooperation and conflict are so closely interwoven that the concept of "mixed processes" is required in sociological study.

In addition to these basic processes, a number of secondary social processes are observable. The basic processes have been studied by a number of scholars, including Simmel and the social ecologists. But analysis of the secondary processes is not sufficiently advanced.

Sixth, a third major emphasis of sociological study is *culture*, which is usually taken to be the sum total of relatively stable and standardized ways of thinking and acting operative in a given society (but sometimes is given a more restricted meaning, as in the writings of MacIver and Parsons). At least the following basic propositions are established concerning culture:

All elements of culture are functionally interrelated; in other words, individual cultural items are integrated into systems. However, this integration is never perfect, as has been demonstrated particularly by Sorokin and such moderate functionalists as Merton.

The many determinants of culture include climate, soil, density of population, level of technological advance, and the "social neighborhood," that is, the type of culture prevailing in the society or societies with which the given culture is in contact. But there is no single determinant of culture to which dominance can be ascribed. This viewpoint represents a decisive change from ideas which still prevailed early in the century. The single-factor or monistic sociologies—economic, racial, geographic, demographic, and so on—are now dead, or nearly so. Almost all of these once dominant factors are recognized as playing definite roles in the formation and development of culture; but these roles are carried out in complex interaction with one another. The ecological factor has been added to the various determinants already stressed in nineteenth-century sociology.

However, these several determinants of culture do not imply a strict determination of social life. Societies possess a large margin of freedom, though the choices are not unlimited. Choices made during earlier phases of the development of a culture narrow down the margin of freedom relative to other choices; choices relative to one phase of culture narrow down the margin of freedom relative to the other phases.

The traits constituting a culture are instruments for the satisfaction of socially and culturally recognized needs of the members of the corresponding society and the various groups within it. (However, as Merton and others stress, investigation may reveal certain traits to be nonfunctional or dysfunctional.)

A kind of circular interaction between the individual and his culture (as well as society) is generally emphasized by sociologists. The personality of an individual is molded by the culture marking the society to which he belongs; this molding takes place through agencies of socialization, of which the family is the most important. But socialization is never complete. Moreover, most cultures—if not all, in some degree—leave the individuals a certain margin of freedom and initiative. On the basis of the latter, men perform actions which result in changes in culture.

Seventh, *change* in culture and in social structure constitutes a fourth major area of study developed in sociology. The principal mechanisms of social and cultural change have been well known since Tarde's days, these consisting of invention, acceptance of invention, and diffusion. A number of detailed propositions concerning the conditions of invention and of the acceptance and diffusion of inventions belong to the common domain of contemporary sociology and cultural anthropology.

Every culture may be defined as an accumulation of inventions— technological, ideological, and social. In each society, this accumulation is selective and therefore unique, never exactly repeating the accumulations made in other societies. This is why every culture has its own *style,* as every man has his distinctive personality.

No general agreement exists as to uniformities that characterize long-range trends in social and cultural change. But one point is definitely established: old-fashioned evolutionism, which required the study of one basic and irreversible process consisting of predetermined stages, has disappeared from the sociological effort. However, a fusion of views expressed by various sociologists is possible along the following lines: The technological and economic phases of culture develop according to a pattern of accumulation interrupted by setbacks; other aspects of culture, especially the intellectual and esthetic, are subject both to quantitative fluctuations of the up-and-down type and to qualitative fluctuations in style. These generalizations are suggested by the work of Sorokin, Alfred Weber and others, as discussed in Chapter 20.

The statements above do not form a sociological theory. They merely outline an *area of agreement* which, in some respects, incorporates the views of most of the outstanding present-day sociologists, but which, in other regards, presents only a majority opinion not shared by minorities, sometimes influential minorities.

The existence of an area of agreement or, closely related, of *convergence* among various trends in sociology, has been recognized frequently for some time. The present writer, for example, cited this development in 1950;[1] in 1955 he was seconded by George Lundberg who referred to "the convergence . . . of viewpoints that have until recently been considered by many students as quite irreconcilable."[2] Lundberg's "convergence" is made up largely of propositions worked out by neo-positivists (especially his own and Dodd's), functionalists (particularly Merton), and sociologists influenced by the systematic theories of Parsons. Both Merton and Parsons, he claimed, for some time have been engaged in research—fully comparable with, and contributory to, the position and programs advocated by any informed neo-positivist. Moreover, Lundberg seemed eager to establish a common universe of discourse between himself and such an outstanding Catholic scholar as Paul Furfey;[3] the separation between the two, according to Lundberg, is reducible to the acceptance or rejection of "mind"—which is analogous to, say, phlogiston for Lundberg, but not for Furfey.

The convergence movement may be further illustrated. Thus, at least one attempt has been made to verify, and to expand by mathematical reasoning, some of the hypotheses of George Homans.[4] On the other hand, as emphasized by Lundberg, Parsons and Bales have worked out four "laws" of social action, three of which are practically identical with those of classical mechanics—an accomplishment clearly consistent with "the natural science trend in sociology."

We must, however, view these trends with caution. For even in "the area of agreement," many differences exist in the presentation of the basic findings. The four major areas of sociological study outlined above, and their subdivisions, form an integrated system, so that thorough understanding of any part is impossible without knowledge of the others. However, it is possible to emphasize some phases or areas of the system at the expense of the others, let us say, the interactional (kinetic) or normative or functional or a combination of two of the three; or, as many anthropologists do, one may start with *culture* as the key concept. In these ways, varieties of sociological theory can and do emerge which, at first glance, have little in common, but, without great difficulty, can be reduced to one another.

Moreover, confusion persists in terminology. The same terms are

[1] N. S. Timasheff, "Sociological Theory Today," *American Catholic Sociological Review*, vol. 11 (1950).

[2] G. A. Lundberg, "The Natural Science Trend in Sociology," *American Journal of Sociology*, 61 (1955), 191–202; see also "Some Convergence in Sociological Theory," *American Journal of Sociology* 62 (1956), 21–27.

[3] G. A. Lundberg, *The Scope and Method of Sociology* (New York: Harper, 1953).

[4] Herbert Simon, "A Formal Theory of Interaction in Social Groups," *American Sociological Review*, vol. 17 (1952).

used to designate different aspects of social and cultural reality; in other words, the same terms often stand for diverse concepts. And the same aspect of sociocultural reality is sometimes designated by two or more terms; that is, the same concept is often given different terms. This terminological confusion is to be found even within the writings of the same author. In addition, concepts are rarely defined in full accordance with logical requirements: many redundant traits appear in definitions. In many instances, moreover, it is difficult to decide whether an author is offering a definition to be used as a tool for identification and analysis of sociocultural phenomena or is predicating the properties of phenomena defined in some other place.

These terminological difficulties could be rather easily overcome. More serious seem to be disagreements concerning methods. The quarrel between the quantitativists and their opponents and the related arguments between the behaviorists and their antagonists have not been as yet finally resolved. This impasse, moreover, is accentuated by problems relative to operational definitions and the *verstehen* procedure. However, these differences do not seem to be insuperable.

Very few sociologists today deny that enumeration, measurement and refined statistical procedures are desirable techniques to be used in any investigation—when they can be reasonably applied. The quantitativists, with rare exceptions, would also agree that a mathematical formula or a coefficient of correlation is not a final goal of research. In the social sciences, as in the natural sciences, one must be able to *interpret* findings couched in these terms. Here, we believe, Max Weber's splendid analysis of understanding on the level of causality and understanding on the level of meaning could bring about reconciliation if it were fully understood and more widely known.

Very few sociologists disclaim the importance of behavioristic descriptions of human actions, in so far as they are sociologically relevant. But today only a minority of sociologists disagree with the proposition that, through the process of symbolic communication, mental states are reciprocally open to one another, a point made brilliantly by Znaniecki. Whenever mental states are sociologically relevant and can be unambiguously expressed in verbal form, it seems almost absurd to resort to behavioristic subterfuges.

Extreme operationalism is rare. But many sociologists agree that sociological definitions should be moderately operational, consisting of traits which are directly or indirectly observable ("indicators"), on the level either of outward behavior or of introspection.

It is therefore likely that, with good will and steady effort, a commonly acceptable sociological theory can be formulated in a not too remote future. This does not mean that a day will arrive when all sociologists agree with one another. Such a situation does not arise in the natural sciences—nor is it desirable in any science. But the time should not be far away when all sociologists speak the same language and therefore share a real universe of discourse—which is a requirement of any science.

Even now, despite the fact that it has not yet become a fully mature science, theoretical sociology has advanced sufficiently to provide a much better foundation for research in the specialized fields than was the case fifty or sixty years ago. New specialties have appeared, such as the sociology of knowledge, the sociology of religion, the sociology of law, organizational analysis and industrial sociology. The fact that they have emerged as branches of *sociology* and not as new, concrete social sciences testifies to the existence of a central core of concepts, of a commonly recognized point of view, of a promising perspective. These specialties are held together by sociological theory.

Another view on convergence emerges from a study of the multiform movements which have been prevalent in sociology since approximately 1925. Several "schools" (for example, human ecology) appeared rather early, but were short-lived. To a certain extent neo-positivism, which in the 1940's and early 1950's seemed likely to conquer the whole field, has lost ground—notwithstanding the widespread use of quantification techniques. There are no real successors of Lundberg with respect to the background theory; Dodd apparently has abdicated, and other neo-positivists have few imitators.

Several trends or even schools appear to be merging. In this process, systematic sociology clearly is the predominant model, with such currently influential theoretical sociologists as Peter Blau, George Homans, and Charles Loomis (to mention only certain scholars whose views have been discussed in this volume) publishing contributions in the intellectual style of the more senior systematists: Sorokin, MacIver, and Parsons. Although much of his work consists of "codification" of sociological knowledge and insightful evaluation of the theoretical contributions of others, Robert K. Merton, whose lucid and graceful writings are widely influential, also has high credentials as a systematic sociologist. The dominant position of systematic sociology again is illustrated by numerous volumes written in the functional style, whose authors—for example, A. K. Cohen, William J. Goode, and Robin Williams—often subscribe to the principal features of this theoretical orientation. Finally, sociometry and microsociology, with their emphasis upon small group theory, form an important addition to systematic sociology.

Systematic sociology has not been seriously challenged by dynamic sociology in spite of the latter's vigorous advance in recent years. But these two approaches are closely interrelated, we believe, with systematic sociology's treatment of structural social relations and interaction complemented by dynamic sociology's analysis of process and change. This complementarity is brought out by the fact that important theoretical contributions of the major scholars, Sorokin and Parsons and MacIver, have

been made to *both* areas of study, as indicated in Chapters 18 and 20 (and it may be added that Wilbert E. Moore, certain of whose views were discussed under dynamic sociology is also an exemplar of systematic analysis).

Philosophical sociology, to which we have given a full chapter (21), no doubt will continue to be a part of the discipline, but peripheral to sociology's central interests. Some members of all scientific fields, however, are philosophically minded (or become so with maturity) and this intellectual prospective will be manifested in their contributions.

In conclusion, we make two notations reflecting personal views concerning the present condition of sociology: one the author's comment upon the "science versus humanity" question and the related matter of quantification, and the other a recent discussion of sociological trends by Pitirim A. Sorokin.

A major problem confronting one who studies the present state of sociological theory is posed by the question: has the field actually been captured by the "hard" naturalistic scientists from the "softer" and generally more humanistically oriented sociologists? An affirmative answer to this question is suggested by the (unwarranted) identification of science with quantification and the fact that a very large number, no doubt the majority, of contributions to leading sociological journals are replete with quantified data and their statistical analysis. (These features also mark more and more Ph.D. dissertations and even undergraduate papers.) Many such publications, of course, are very useful in aiding the accumulation of sociological knowledge and in testing hypotheses drawn from both specific and general theories. But many others seem to be featured by what, in quantification oriented circles, often is construed as science itself, but what more accurately might be thought of as scientific window dressing. The reduction of observations to tabular or other quantified forms, correlational testing, factor analysis, and other statistical techniques are part of an increasingly sophisticated research apparatus which is highly useful in many disciplines, including sociology; but all too often quantified data and these research instruments appear to serve a decorative, rather than scientific, function. Accumulations of data, however voluminous, and their statistical manipulation, however technically skillful, contribute little or nothing to science until and unless their *theoretical* relevance is established—and this requires knowledge and understanding and indeed creative imagination that relatively few individuals possess. The contributions of a large sample of theoretically creative sociologists have been reported in this volume.

To close this book, it is appropriate to cite a prediction based upon a plausible hypothesis. Such a prediction is offered by Pitirim Sorokin in his most recent volume, *Sociological Theories of Today*. He advances the hypothesis that theoretical sciences develop according to the pattern of wave fluctuation which, as viewed by Sorokin himself (and as described in Chap. 20), characterizes the long-range changes of whole sociocultural systems. Thus theoretical sociology emerged historically as a kind of speculation about general laws that presumably govern social and cultural dynamics, as illustrated in the broad theoretical schemes of Auguste Comte, Herbert Spencer, Lester F. Ward, and other pioneers. In the twentieth century, most sociologists, especially in the English-speaking countries, shifted their attention to much less ambitious problems and particularly to the gathering of empirical data about social life, a stage that perhaps reached its climax in the 1930's. In recent years, however, the sociological quest once more is becoming focused upon broader generalizations and theoretical systems, a trend, according to Sorokin, that is likely to continue for some time. He sees the next generation of sociologists led by scholars who, on the basis of extensive but currently scattered data, will be concerned with the formulation of general laws of social statics and dynamics.

This prediction may well be an accurate one. But there is no certainty about the future of sociology—the laws of the development of theory (if such there be) have not been established on the basis of careful study. Therefore, it is quite possible that the current division of sociology into two "camps"—one bent upon the accumulation and manipulation of empirical data, the other using these data to undergird broad theory—will continue.

*Appendix*

# APPENDIX

## Note to the Instructor

There exists in academic circles an old and venerable tradition according to which a student must develop a knowledge of the historical development of the discipline in which he is specializing. An objective of this book is to help the student meet this requirement and to help the instructor convey to students this knowledge. Depending in part on the degree sought (A.B., M.A., or Ph.D.), all of the material offered in this volume should be studied or read in selected parts, according to the theoretical preferences of the instructor.

Independently of the level of study, the textbook should be supplemented by assignments of readings in primary sources, that is, in the works surveyed and interpreted in this volume. An effective way of executing this phase of the program is to assign several classic or otherwise representative works in the field.

The number of assigned readings should not be large and again depends on the level of study. The readings should be distributed among works written during the various periods in the history of sociological theory so that every student directly experiences the difference between early and later theories. In addition to reading primary sources, students seeking advanced degrees should be assigned some secondary sources dealing with authors selected for special study. A number of readings, both in primary and secondary sources, are contained in *Suggestions for Further Reading* following this note.

While students seeking higher degrees *must* have read several classic or otherwise representative works *in toto*, for undergraduates assignments from "Readers" may suffice; the same Readers may help to familiarize graduate students with the manner of thinking and writing of those authors whose works they have not studied in the original texts. Readers now available include E. F. Borgatta and H. J. Meyer, *Sociological Theory: Present-Day Sociology from the Past* (New York: Knopf, 1956), which, as the subtitle indicates, concentrates on nineteenth and early twentieth century contributions; L. Coser and B.

Rosenberg, *Sociological Theory: A Book of Readings* (New York: Macmillan, 1957), which presents selections from the pioneers, their successors and our contemporaries; and T. Parsons, E. Shils, K. D. Naegele, and J. P. Pitts, eds., *Theories of Society*, two volumes (New York: The Free Press, 1961), which includes extensive essays by the editors as well as numerous selections from earlier and modern social theorists. None of the Readers is organized according to the plan of this volume; but neither the instructor nor the student will find any difficulty in using them as auxiliary study material.

Since sociological theory is a difficult subject for study, recapitulation is highly desirable. It is sometimes advisable to arrange recapitulation in an order at variance with the one used in the course. The rearrangement may be chronological or systematic. To facilitate such recapitulation a chronological table is included in this volume. This table may be used to organize discussions of such topics as these: what new ideas appeared on the horizon of the sociologists from 1901 to 1905? or from 1946 to 1956?

With advanced students especially, excellent results may be achieved by surveying the historical development of ideas concerning the basic problems of sociological theory which are presented in Chapter 1. To prepare such assignments the index may be used to good effect.

# APPENDIX

## Suggestions for Further Reading

The purpose of the following readings is to aid the student in selecting the works of the masters of sociology which remain especially significant as well as certain secondary sources which are able surveys and pertinent criticisms, or both, of the individual theories. Works amply discussed in the text are not mentioned here, except in the case where several contributions by the same author have been considered, of which only some are recommended for reading by the students. During the past few years a number of these sources have also become available in paperback editions.

CHAPTER 2 (*Comte*). H. Martineau's abridged translation of Comte's *Positive Philosophy* provides insight into the thought system of the founding father of sociology. Some of the surveys of his theory written fifty to one hundred years ago have not been surpassed by later attempts; they include D. Caird, *The Social Philosophy and Religion of Comte* (1885); J. S. Mill, *The Positive Philosophy of Comte* (1887); L. Lévy-Bruhl, *The Philosophy of Comte* (1903). Several contemporary articles consider Comte's work in retrospect, for example: MacQuilkin DeGrange, "Comte's Sociologies," *Am. Soc. Rev.*, vol. 4 (1939); F. von Hayek, "The Counter-revolution of Science," *Economica* (1941); R. A. Nisbet, "The French Revolution and the Rise of Sociology in France," *Am. Jour. Soc.*, vol. 49 (1943); N. S. Timasheff, "Comte in Retrospect," *Am. Cath. Soc. Rev.*, vol. 13 (1952).

CHAPTER 3 (*Spencer*). The student interested in Spencer's theory should read his *The First Principles* and either *The Study of Sociology* or some parts of *Principles of Sociology*. The second founding father's *Autobiography* (1904) illuminates the genesis of his views. Of the many secondary sources, the following are recommended: W. H. Hudson, *An Introduction to the Philosophy of H. Spencer* (1894); J. Royce, *Herbert Spencer, an Estimate and Review* (1904); H. Macpherson, *Spencer and Spencerism* (1900); H. Elliot, *Herbert Spencer* (1916); J. Rumney, *Herbert Spencer's Sociology* (1934); R. Hofstadter, *Social Darwinism in American Thought* (1944), pp. 18–36; T. Parsons, Introduction, Ann Arbor paperback edition of Spencer's *The Study of Sociology* (1961).

CHAPTER 4 (*Other Pioneers*). Knowledge of the works of the pioneers who cannot be considered as "founding fathers" can be gained by reading the following studies: On Quételet: A. Quételet, *Essay of Social Physics* (many English translations available), and F. H. Hankins, *Quételet as Statistician* (1908). On Le Play: Parts of Le Play's *European Workers* are translated by C. Zimmerman in his *Family and Society* (1935), pp. 359–595; see also Sorokin's chapter on Le Play in *Contemporary Sociological Theories* (1928), pp. 63–98. On Marxism: F. Engels, *The Origin of the Family, Private Property and the State;* N. Bukharin, *Historical Materialism;* M. Bober, *Karl Marx' Interpretation of History* (1948); T. B. Bottomore and M. Ruben, eds., *Karl Marx: Selected Writings in Sociology and Social Philosophy* (1956). On Morgan and Tylor: R. Lowie, *History of Ethnological Theory* (1937), chapters on Morgan and Tylor (pp. 54–85). On Buckle: H. T. Buckle, *History of Civilization in England;* M. Robertson, *Buckle and His Critics* (1885); A. H. Huth, *Life and Writings of Buckle* (1887). Sorokin's chapter on Danilevsky in *Social Philosophies of an Age of Crisis* (1950), pp. 49–71, is useful.

CHAPTER 5 (*Social Darwinism*). Bagehot's *Physics and Politics* is short and readable; for evaluations of his work see J. Lichtenberger, *The Development of Sociological Theory* (1923), pp. 279–84, and Floyd House, *The Development of Sociology* (1936), pp. 160–63. Of Gumplowicz's works, *Outline of Sociology* is one to be read; see also Lichtenberger, *op. cit.,* pp. 432–53 and House, *op. cit.,* pp. 163–74. Acquaintance with Ratzenhofer's work (which is not translated into English) can be gained by consulting A. Small's *General Sociology*, which, in chapters XII–XXVII, includes large portions of the Austrian master's work as well as Small's own theory; see also Lichtenberger, *op. cit.,* pp. 453–64 and House, *op. cit.,* pp. 174–77. Sumner's *Folkways* is a classic; however, reading the first two chapters and a few chapters on particular groups of folkways (depending on the student's interest) probably is sufficient for most purposes; see also H. E. Starr, *W. G. Sumner* (1925); A. G. Keller, *Reminiscences of W. G. Sumner* (1933); C. H. Page, *Class and American Sociology* (1940), pp. 73–110; and Hofstadter, *op. cit.,* pp. 37–51.

CHAPTER 6 (*Psychological Evolutionism*). From Lester F. Ward's works, *Dynamic Sociology* is the best written, but *Pure Sociology* the most mature. On Ward also see: E. P. Cape, *Lester Ward, a Personal Sketch* (1922); C. Wood, *The Substance of the Sociology of Lester Ward* (1930); S. Chugerman, *Lester Ward, the American Aristotle* (1939); Page, *op. cit.,* pp. 29–69; Hofstadter, *op. cit.,* pp. 52–67. F. H. Giddings' *Principles of Sociology* can be read with profit; see further H. Odum, ed., *American Masters of Sociology* (1927), pp. 191–228; Page, *op. cit.,* pp. 145–80.

CHAPTER 7 (*Other Evolutionisms and Organicism*). Of the works belonging to the minor evolutionary schools, only Veblen's *Theory of the Leisure Class* has retained full value; on him, see Louis Schneider, *The Freudian Psychology and Veblen's Social Theory* (1948); David Riesman, *Thorstein Veblen* (1953); Odum, *op. cit.,* pp. 231–70. On Coste, see Sorokin, *Contemporary Sociological Theories,* pp. 359–70; on Novicow, *ibid.,* pp. 205–6, 314–16; on Kidd, see Lichtenberger, *op. cit.,* pp. 287–91. The works of the organicists can be consulted only in the French or German originals. Those who read German can learn much about Schäffle from A. Ith, *Die Grundlinien der Gesellschaftslehre A. Schäffle's* (1926). On Lilienfeld, see Sorokin, *op. cit.,* pp. 200–4; on Fouillée, A. Guyau in Barnes' *Introduction to the History of Sociology,* pp. 460–70.

CHAPTER 8 (*Early Analytical Sociology*). Toennies' volume, *Fundamental Concepts of Sociology*, reproduces all of his major contributions; see also the excellent article by R. Heberle in Barnes, *Introduction to the History of Sociology,* pp. 227–48. Large parts of Simmel's work are available in English, K. Wolff, trans., *The Sociology of George Simmel* (1950); Simmel, *Conflict* and *The Web of Group Affiliations,* K. Wolff and R. Bendix, trans. (1955). On Simmel see K. Wolff in the volume entitled *The Sociology of G. Simmel;* N. Spykman, *The Sociological Theory of Simmel*

(1925); Heberle's article in Barnes, *op. cit.*; L. Coser, *The Functions of Social Conflict* (1956), an attempt to build up an up-to-date theory of conflict on the foundation of several propositions selected from Simmel's work; and L. Coser, ed., *Georg Simmel* (1965), which contains evaluations of Simmel by Coser, Toennies, Durkheim, Heberle, Sorokin, and others. Several essays on Simmel are to be found in *Am. Jour. Soc.*, vol. 63 (1958) and *Am. Soc. Rev.*, vol. 24 (1959). Of Gabriel Tarde's works, *Laws of Imitation* presents his theory in the most vivid form, while *Social Laws* gives a more complete knowledge of the theory as a whole; see also the excellent but unfortunately not easily available work by M. M. Davies, *Gabriel Tarde* (1906), which was later incorporated in the same author's *Psychological Interpretation of Society* (1909).

CHAPTER 9 (*Durkheim*). Of Durkheim's major works, which are now available in English, *The Rules of Sociological Method* is most important when concentrating attention on sociological theory, while *The Division of Labor in Society* and *Suicide* are unsurpassed sociological monographs. The best commentary on Durkheim is available only in French, G. Gurvitch's *Essais de sociologie* (1936); other useful secondary works include H. Alpert, *Emile Durkheim and His Sociology* (1939), E. Benoit-Smullian in Barnes, *op. cit.*, pp. 499–537; K. Wolff, ed., *Emile Durkheim* (1960); and R. A. Nisbet, *Emile Durkheim* (1964). Secondary works by Durkheim, published only a few years ago in France but now available in English, based on lecture notes, include *Socialism and Saint-Simon* (1958), *Pragmatism and Sociology, Sociology and Philosophy* (1953), *Education and Sociology* (1956), and *Moral Education* (1961). Several essays on Durkheim are to be found in *Am. Jour. Soc.*, vol. 63 (1958) and *Am. Soc. Rev.*, vol. 24 (1959).

CHAPTER 10 (*Russian Subjectivism*). On the Russian subjective school one may consult J. Hecker, *Russian Sociology* (1915) and M. Laserson, "Russian Sociology" in Gurvitch and Moore, eds., *Twentieth Century Sociology* (1946), pp. 678–81.

CHAPTER 11 (*The Decline of Evolutionism and the Rise of Neo-Positivism*). On the decline of evolutionism, see A. Goldenweiser in Barnes and Becker, eds., *Contemporary Social Theory* (1940), pp. 437–90. On Kovalevsky, see N. S. Timasheff in Barnes, *op. cit.*, pp. 614–53; and H. Caster, *The Social Theory of L. T. Hobhouse* (1927); on Westermarck, House, *op. cit.*, pp. 153–57, and Mills in Barnes, *op. cit.*, pp. 654–67. On the rise of neo-positivism, especially the Galton-Pearson school, see Lundberg in Barnes and Becker, *op. cit.*, pp. 125–30.

CHAPTER 12 (*Cooley and Thomas*). Of Cooley's work, *Human Nature and the Social Order, Social Organization*, and the posthumously published *Sociological Theory and Social Research* (1930) have preserved a fresh quality until the present day; see also Page, *op. cit.*, pp. 183–209; E. Jandy, *Charles Cooley, His Life and Social Theory* (1942); R. Dewey's paper in Barnes, *op. cit.*, pp. 833–52; and R. Gutman, "Cooley: A Perspective," *Am. Soc. Rev.*, vol. 23 (1958). Thomas' theoretical contributions are presented in E. H. Volkhart, ed., *Social Behavior and Personality* (1951); the discussion of Thomas' work in H. Blumer, *Critique of Research in the Social Sciences: I* (1939) is highly illuminating; see, also, *The Contribution of William Isaac Thomas* by Kimball Young (1963).

CHAPTER 13 (*Pareto*). The student should read vol. I, chap. XII in vol. III, and the second half of vol. IV of Pareto's treatise, *Mind and Society*. Of the many secondary sources, see the following: Sorokin, *Contemporary Sociological Theories*, pp. 37–62; L. Henderson, *Pareto's Sociology* (1935); G. Homans and C. Curtis, *An Introduction to Pareto* (1934); M. Ginsberg, "Pareto's General Sociology," (British) *Soc. Rev.*, vol. 28 (1936); N. S. Timasheff, "Law in Pareto's Sociology," *Am. Jour. Soc.*, vol. 44 (1939); M. S. Handman in S. Rice, *Methods in the Social Sciences* (1931), pp. 139–53; A. Bongiorno, "A Study of Pareto's Treatise of General Sociology," *Am. Jour. Soc.*, vol. 35 (1930), pp. 349–70; W. Stark, "In Search of the True Pareto," *British Jour. Soc.*, vol. 14 (1963). See also a short but excellent chapter in

F. S. C. Northrop, *The Logic of the Sciences and the Humanities* (1947), pp. 265–72. Among recent works making use of Pareto's theory one could cite, in addition to Homans, *The Human Group* (discussed in the text); T. B. Bottomore, *Elites and Society* (1964); and especially Suzanne Keller, *Beyond the Ruling Class* (1963).

CHAPTER 14 (*Max Weber*). The following works of Weber (among others) are available in English: *The Protestant Ethic and the Spirit of Capitalism; From Max Weber: Essays in Sociology* (a collection of excerpts from various works, translated and edited by H. H. Gerth and C. W. Mills, 1946); *The Theory of Social and Economic Organization* (a translation by T. Parsons and A. M. Henderson of part of his *Wirtschaft und Gesellschaft*, 1947); *The Methodology of the Social Sciences* (translated and edited by E. A. Shils and F. A. Finch, 1949); *Law in Economics and Society* (a translation by E. Shils and M. Rheinstein, 1954). Of these, *The Theory of Social and Economic Organization* is most important in the study of sociological theory. A useful collection of Weber's writings is S. M. Miller, ed., *Max Weber* (1963). Among secondary sources, Parsons' contributions are very important, especially part IV of his *Theory of Social Action* (1937), his introduction to the translation of Weber's *Theory of Social and Economic Organization*, and his chapter in Barnes, *op. cit.*, pp. 287–308; an excellent recent study is R. Bendix, *Max Weber: An Intellectual Portrait* (1960). See also T. Abel, *Systematic Sociology in Germany* (1929), pp. 116–50; R. H. Tawney, *Religion and the Rise of Capitalism* (1939); A. Salomon, "Max Weber's Methodology," *Social Research*, vol. 1 (1934); A. Salomon, "Max Weber's Sociology," *Social Research*, vol. 2 (1935); T. Abel, "Operation Called Verstehen," *Am. Jour. Soc.*, vol. 54 (1949), pp. 211–19; A. Pierce, "Empiricism and the Social Sciences," *Am. Soc. Rev.*, vol. 21 (1956); P. Munch, "Empirical Science and Max Weber's Verstehende Soziologie," *Am. Soc. Rev.*, vol. 22 (1957).

CHAPTER 15 (*Neo-Positivism and Mathematical Sociology*). Lundberg's theoretical approach may be grasped by careful reading of his *Foundations of Sociology;* see also his popular *Can Science Save Us?* (1947). Dodd's *Dimensions of Society* is almost unreadable for many people, but the author has condensed his views in two articles: "Tension Theory of Social Action," *Am. Jour. Soc.*, vol. 46 (1939), and "A System of Operationally Defined Concepts for Sociology," *Am. Soc. Rev.*, vol. 4 (1939). An excellent criticism of Dodd's work is E. Shanas, "A Critique of Dodd's Dimensions of Society," *Am. Jour. Soc.*, vol. 48 (1942). For the views of Zipf, Rashevsky, Hart, and Chapin, consult the works cited in the text. For a more recent volume in the style of mathematical sociology, see Herbert A. Simon, *Models of Man* (1957), which remains the best of its kind. For a thoughtful criticism of the operational aspect of neo-positivism, see A. C. Benjamin, *Operationism* (1955), while Sorokin's *Fads and Foibles* (1956) sharply criticizes neo-positivism in all its ramifications.

CHAPTER 16 (*Human Ecology*). The present state of human ecology is ably presented in J. A. Quinn, *Human Ecology* (1950) and A. H. Hawley, *Human Ecology* (1950), while a developed criticism is to be found in M. A. Alihan, *Social Ecology* (1938). Among recent presentations, see especially George Theodorson, *Studies in Human Ecology* (1961) and the theoretically sophisticated L. F. Schore, *The Urban Scene: Human Ecology and Demography* (1965).

CHAPTER 17 (*The Functional Approach*). To gain insight into one important version of the functional approach one should read B. Malinowski's *Scientific Theory of Culture* (1944), but to understand the approach in action see Malinowski's *Argonauts of the Western Pacific* (1922); R. Redfield's *The Folk Culture of Yucatan* (1949); or vols. 1 or 3 of W. L. Warner's Yankee City Series: *The Social Life of a Modern Community* (with P. S. Lunt, 1941) and *The Social Systems of American Ethnic Groups* (with L. Srole, 1945). On the strengths and weaknesses of the functional approach, Chapter 1 in R. K. Merton's *Social Theory and Social Structure* (1949) is excellent. Of the many evaluations of the functional approach, see especially K. Davis, "The Myth of Functional Analysis," *Am. Soc. Rev.*, vol. 24 (1959) and G. C. Hawkins, "Bringing Men Back In," *Am. Soc. Rev.*, vol. 29 (1964).

CHAPTER 18 (*Systematic Sociology*). Sorokin's theoretical views are thoroughly developed in his *Social and Cultural Dynamics* (4 volumes) and *Society, Culture, and Personality* (1947); the former is popularly summarized in *Crisis of Our Age* (1941), while Sorokin has approved the excellent condensation by F. R. Cowell, *History, Civilization, and Culture* (1952). An outline of Sorokin's early Russian work has been offered by W. W. Isajew, "Pitirim Sorokin's Sistema Sotsiologii: A Summary," *Am. Cath. Soc. Rev.*, vol. 17 (1956); this outline has been authorized and briefly commented upon by Sorokin. Evaluations of Sorokin's work include L. J. Maquet, *The Sociology of Knowledge* (1951); H. Speier in Barnes, *op. cit.*, and R. L. Simpson, "Pitirim Sorokin and His Sociology," *Social Forces*, vol. 32 (1953). A good survey of Sorokin's work is offered in P. Allen, ed., *Sorokin in Review* (1963). Parsons' views on diverse sociological problems are contained in his *Essays in Sociological Theory* (1949), *Working Papers in the Theory of Action* (with R. F. Bales and E. A. Shils, 1953), *Structure and Process in Modern Society* (1960), and *Social Structure and Personality* (1964), while *The Social System* (1951) remains perhaps his most developed systematic work. Of the many critical evaluations of Parsons' theoretical work, see G. E. Swanson, "The Approach to a General Theory of Action by Parsons and Shils," *Am. Soc. Rev.*, vol. 18 (1953); A. W. Gouldner, "Systematic Sociology, 1945–55," in H. Zetterberg, ed., *Sociology in the United States of America* (1956); H. Black, ed., *The Social Theories of Talcott Parsons* (1961), especially Black's "Some Questions About Parsons' Theories," pp. 268 ff.; P. Selznick, "The Social Theories of Talcott Parsons," *Am. Soc. Rev.*, vol. 26 (1961). Znaniecki's theoretical point of view is most adequately presented in his *Method of Sociology* (1934), *Social Actions* (1936), and *Cultural Sciences* (1952); see also the posthumous *Social Relations and Social Roles* (1965). Of MacIver's many volumes, his sociological theory is most thoroughly presented in *Society* (1931 and 1937; revised with C. H. Page in 1949) and *Social Causation* (1942); while it is discussed by H. Alpert in M. Berger, T. Abel, and C. H. Page, eds., *Freedom and Control in Modern Society* (1954). The views of Parsons, Znaniecki, and MacIver are ably summarized in R. and G. Hinkle, *The Development of Modern Sociology* (1954). Present-day systematic sociology is represented by such diverse theoretical contributions as H. Gerth and C. W. Mills, *Character and Social Structure* (1953); G. C. Homans, *The Human Group* (1950) and *Social Behavior* (1961); P. M. Blau, *Exchange and Power in Social Life* (1964); C. P. Loomis, *Social Systems* (1960) and *Modern Social Theories* (1961); M. J. Levy, Jr., *The Structure of Society* (1952).

CHAPTER 19 (*Sociometry and Microsociology*). J. L. Moreno's best-known work is *Who Shall Survive?* (1934); his views are condensed in *Sociometry*, vol. 6 (1943). A report of sociometric techniques appears in *Am. Cath. Soc. Rev.*, vol. 11 (1950) and vol. 12 (1951). Various contributions are brought together in L. Moreno, *Sociometry, a Reader* (1961). Small group theory is best represented in the works of Homans, *op. cit.*, and R. F. Bales, *Interaction Process Analysis* (1950). See also A. P. Hare, E. F. Borgatta, and R. F. Bales, eds., *Small Groups* (rev. ed., 1965); M. S. Olmsted, *The Small Group* (1959); and C. King, *Sociology of Small Groups* (1963).

CHAPTER 20 (*Dynamic Sociology*). The first four chapters of Spengler's *Decline of the West* are stimulating reading, though sociologically weak. On Sorokin, see the readings for Chapter 18. The first six volumes of Toynbee's magnum opus have been ably condensed by D. C. Somervell into one volume (1947); this work has been continued in *A Study of History*, vols. 7–10, by A. Toynbee, edited by D. C. Somervell (1957). For criticisms of Toynbee's views see M. F. Ashley Montagu, ed., *Toynbee and History* (1957); Sorokin's *Philosophies of an Age of Crisis*, pp. 113–20 and 205–33; and P. Geyl, *Can We Know the Pattern of the Past?* (1949). Chapin's

*Cultural Change* and Kroeber's *Configurations of Culture Growth* should be consulted directly. So should A. Weber's *Cultural History as Cultural Sociology;* for an evaluation, see N. Newman, in Barnes, *op. cit.,* pp. 353–61. An excellent critique of historical sociology of the Spengler-Toynbee-Sorokin variety is H. Becker's chapter on the subject in Barnes and Becker, *op. cit.* MacIver's qualified evolutionism is presented in MacIver and Page, *op. cit.,* Book III; the most ambitious attempts to formulate a modern-day evolutionary theory by anthropologists are L. A. White, *The Science of Culture* (1949) and V. G. Childe, *Social Evolution* (1951); see also the symposium on "Evolution and Man's Progress," *Daedalus* (Summer, 1961). The most systematic recent attempt to develop a theory of social change and social evolution is the brief *Social Change* (1963) by W. E. Moore, who together with T. Parsons, S. N. Eisenstadt, and others are contributors to a collection of papers on social change, *Am. Soc. Rev.,* vol. 29 (June, 1964).

CHAPTER 21 (*Philosophical Sociology*). Gurvitch's major works are available in French only. An able summary of his work can be found in René Toulemont, *Sociologie et pluralisme dialectique* (Louvain, 1955); the title suggests Gurvitch's shift from phenomenology to "Hyperempiric dialectics" mentioned in the text. The views of the French institutionalists have been summarized by N. S. Timasheff in *Thought* (1946), pp. 493–572; the originals are available only in French and deal more with problems of jurisprudence than of sociology. On Vierkandt, see Abel, *op. cit.,* pp. 50–79. On Sturzo, see N. S. Timasheff, *Sociology of Luigi Sturzo* (1962). Mannheim's most influential works are *Ideology and Utopia* (1936) and *Man and Society in an Age of Reconstruction* (1940), while his philosophical bent is best brought out in the posthumous publications, *Essays on the Sociology of Knowledge* (1952), *Essays on Sociology and Social Psychology* (1953), and *Essays on the Sociology of Culture* (1956).

CHAPTER 22 *Mid-Twentieth Century Sociology: A Synthetic Review.* Assessments of developments in various branches of sociology during the last two or three decades include H. L. Zetterberg, ed., *Sociology in the United States of America* (1956); J. B. Gittler, ed., *Review of Sociology: Analysis of a Decade* (1957); R. K. Merton, L. Broom, and L. S. Cottrell, Jr., eds., *Sociology Today* (1959); and R. E. L. Faris, ed., *Handbook of Modern Sociology* (1964). A challenging survey of current sociological trends is P. A. Sorokin's "Sociology of Yesterday, Today, and Tomorrow," *Am. Soc. Rev.,* vol. 30 (1965) and still more his *Sociological Theories of Today* (1966). Also suggestive are W. E. Moore, "Global Sociology: The World as a Singular System" and R. Bierstedt, "Indices of Civilization," both in *Am. Jour. Soc.,* vol. 71 (1966).

# Chronological Table

In this table, the following facts are presented: (1) the death dates, indicated by the symbol †, of prominent sociologists (which, of course, are more important than their birth dates); (2) the years in which important works in sociology were published; and (3) some events of general importance in the unfolding of sociological theory.

*1821–30.* 1822: Comte's "great discovery." 1830: Comte, *Positive Philosophy,* vol. I.
*1831–40.* 1835: Quételet, *Essay on Social Physics.*
*1841–50.* 1842: Comte, *Positive Philosophy,* vol. VI; Spencer's first article in the *Conformist.* 1848: Marx-Engels, *Communist Manifesto.* 1850: Spencer, *Social Statics.*
*1851–60.* 1852: Comte, *Positive Politics,* vol. I. 1853: de Gobineau, *Essay on the Inequality of Human Races,* vol. I. 1855: Le Play, *European Workers,* vol. I. 1857: † Comte; Buckle, *History of Civilization in England.* 1859: Darwin: *Origin of Species.* 1860: Lavrov-Mirtov, *Sketch of Culture Philosophy.*
*1861–70.* 1862: Spencer, *First Principles;* † Buckle. 1864: Le Play, *Social Reform in France.* 1869: Galton, *Hereditary Genius;* Danilevsky, *Russia and Europe.*
*1871–80.* 1871: Tylor, *Primitive Culture;* Le Play, *Organization of the Family.* 1872: Bagehot, *Physics and Politics.* 1873: Spencer, *Study of Sociology.* 1874: † Quételet; Galton, *English Men of Genius.* 1875: Gumplowicz, *Race and State.* 1876: Spencer, *Principles of Sociology,* vol. I. 1877: † Bagehot. 1878: Schäffle, *Structure and Life of the Social Body;* Morgan, *Ancient Society.* 1879: Spencer, *Principles of Ethics,* vol. I. 1880: Fouillée, *Contemporary Social Science.*
*1881–90.* 1881: † Morgan. 1882: Mikhailovsky, *Heroes and the Mob;* † de Gobineau; † Le Play. 1883: † Marx; Ward, *Dynamic Sociology;* Sumner, *What Social Classes Owe to Each Other.* 1884: Engels, *The Origin of the Family, Private Property and the State.* 1885: † Danilevsky; Gumplowicz, *Outline of Sociology.* 1887: Toennies, *Gemeinschaft und Gesellschaft.*
*1891–1900.* 1893: Ward, *Psychic Factors of Civilization;* Ratzenhofer, *The Nature of the State;* Novicow, *Struggles between Human Societies;* Durkheim, *The Di-*

*vision of Labor in Society;* foundation of *Revue internationale de sociologie;* first textbook on sociology by Small and Vincent. 1894: Kidd, *Social Evolution.* 1895: Durkheim, *The Rules of Sociological Method;* foundation of *The American Journal of Sociology.* 1896: Giddings, *Principles of Sociology;* Spencer, *Principles of Sociology,* vol. III; Worms, *Organism and Society;* foundation of *Année sociologique.* 1897: Durkheim, *Suicide.* 1898: Tarde, *Social Laws;* Ratzenhofer, *Sociological Studies;* Ward, *Outline of Sociology.* 1899: Chamberlain, *Foundations of the 19th Century;* Veblen, *Theory of the Leisure Class;* Coste, *Principles of an Objective Sociology;* † Lavrov-Mirtov.

*1901–1910.* 1901: † Coste. 1902: Cooley, *Human Nature and the Social Order;* † Spencer. 1903: † Schäffle; Ward, *Pure Sociology.* 1904: † Tarde; † Mikhailovsky. 1905: Small, *General Sociology;* foundation of the American Sociological Society. 1906: Sumner, *Folkways;* Ward, *Applied Sociology;* Max Weber, *The Protestant Ethic and the Spirit of Capitalism;* Schäffle, *Outline of Sociology* (posthumous). 1907: Huntington, *Pulse of Asia.* 1908: † Ratzenhofer; Ratzenhofer, *Sociology;* Simmel, *Sociology.* 1909: W. I. Thomas, *Source Book for Social Origins;* Cooley, *Social Organization.* 1910: † Sumner; Fouillée, *Psychology of Ideas-Forces;* Oppenheimer, *The State;* Kovalevsky, *Sociology.*

*1911–1920.* 1911: Durkheim, *Judgments of Reality and Judgments of Value;* Graebner, *Methods of Ethnology;* † Galton. 1912: † Novicow; † Fouillée; Durkheim, *The Elementary Forms of the Religious Life.* 1913: † Ward. 1915: Pareto: *Treatise on Sociology* (later translated and expanded as *The Mind and Society*); Keller, *Societal Evolution;* Hobhouse *et al., The Material Culture and Social Institutions of the Simpler Peoples;* Galpin, *The Social Anatomy of a Rural Community.* 1916: † Kovalevsky. 1917: † Durkheim; † Tylor; MacIver, *The Community.* 1918: † Simmel; Spengler, *The Decline of the West;* Thomas and Znaniecki, *The Polish Peasant,* vol. I; Cooley, *Social Process.* 1919: Sorokin, *System of Sociology* (in Russian); Litt, *Individual and Society;* Mackinder, *The Eurasian Heartland;* 1920: † Worms; † Max Weber.

*1921–1930.* 1921: Thomas and Znaniecki, *The Polish Peasant,* vol. V; Bukharin, *Historical Materialism.* 1922: Giddings, *Studies in the Theory of Human Society;* Vierkandt, *The Theory of Society;* Max Weber, *Economics and Society* (posthumous). 1923: † Pareto; Thomas, *The Unadjusted Girl;* Ogburn, *Social Change.* 1924: von Wiese, *General Sociology;* Giddings. *The Scientific Study of Human Society;* Hobhouse, *Social Development;* Park and Burgess, *Introduction to the Science of Sociology.* 1925: Hauriou, *Theory of Institution and Foundation;* † Hauriou. 1926; Malinowski, *Crime and Custom in Savage Society;* † Small. 1927: Ellwood, *Cultural Evolution.* 1928: Sorokin, *Contemporary Sociological Theories;* Thomas, *The Child in America;* Sumner-Keller, *Science of Society;* Chapin, *Cultural Change.* 1929: † Hobhouse; † Cooley; † Veblen; Lynd and Lynd, *Middletown.* 1930: † Kareyev; Renard, *The Theory of the Institution,* vol. I.

*1931–1940.* 1931: † Giddings; MacIver, *Society: Its Structure and Changes. 1934:* Moreno, *Who Shall Survive?;* Znaniecki, *The Methods of Sociology;* Toennies, *Introduction to Sociology.* 1935: † Toennies; Alfred Weber, *Cultural History as Cultural Sociology;* Chapin, *Contemporary American Institutions.* 1936: † Spengler; Toynbee, *A Study of History,* vols. I–III; Gurvitch, *Essays in Sociology;* Pareto's treatise translated into English as *The Mind and Society.* Mannheim, *Ideology and Utopia.* 1937: Sorokin, *Social and Cultural Dynamics,* vols. I–III; Parsons, *Structure of Social Action;* Lynd and Lynd, *Middletown in Transition.* 1939: Lundberg, *Foundations of Sociology;* Lynd, *Knowledge for What?* 1940: Mannheim, *Man and Society in an Age of Reconstruction.*

*1941–1950.* 1941: W. L. Warner, *Yankee City Series,* vol. I. 1942: † Malinowski; Dodd, *Dimensions of Society;* MacIver, *Social Causation.* 1943: † Loria. 1944:

Malinowski, *Scientific Theory of Culture* (posthumous); Kroeber, *Configurations of Cultural Growth;* Delos, *The Problem of Civilization;* Myrdal, *An American Dilemma;* Lundberg-Furfey polemics. 1945: Huntington, *Mainsprings of Civilization.* 1946: Haesaert, *Essays in Sociology;* Monnerot, *Social Facts Are Not Things;* † Ellwood. 1947: † Thomas; Sorokin, *Society, Culture and Personality;* Rashevsky, *Mathematical Theory of Human Relations.* 1948: Quinn, *Human Ecology.* 1949: Zipf, *Human Behavior and the Principle of Least Effort;* Merton, *Social Theory and Social Structure;* MacIver and Page, *Society, An Introductory Analysis;* Parsons, *Essays in Sociological Theory;* White, *Science of Culture.* 1950: Sorokin, *Social Philosophies of an Age of Crisis;* Riesman, *The Lonely Crowd;* Homans, *The Human Group;* Gurvitch, *The Vocation of Sociology;* Hawley, *Human Ecology.*

*1951–60.* 1951: Parsons, *The Social System* and (with others) *Toward a General Theory of Action;* Childe, *Social Evolution;* completion of Stouffer *et al., The American Soldier;* R. Williams, *American Society;* W. Goode, *Religion and the Primitive Man.* 1952: Znaniecki, *Cultural Sciences;* Alfred Weber, *Principles of Historical and Cultural Sociology;* Levy, *The Structure of Society;* Barber, *Science and the Social Order;* † Zipf; † Vierkandt. 1953: Nisbet, *The Quest for Community;* Barnett, *Innovation;* De Grange, *The Nature and Elements of Sociology;* Gerth and Mills, *Character and Social Structure;* Mannheim, *Essays in Sociology and Social Psychology.* 1954: *For a Science of Social Man,* edited by J. Gillin. 1955: Parsons (with others), *Family, Socialization and Interaction Process:* Gurvitch, *Social Determinism and Human Freedom;* † T. de Chardin. 1956: Sorokin, *Fads and Foibles in Contemporary Sociology;* Mannheim, *Essays on the Sociology of Culture;* W. H. Whyte, Jr., *The Organization Man.* 1958: † Znaniecki. 1959: † Sturzo. 1960: Homans, *Social Behavior;* Loomis, *Social Systems;* Parsons, *Structure and Process in Modern Societies.*

*1961— .* 1961: Loomis and Loomis, *Modern Social Theories;* Black, ed., *The Social Theories of Talcott Parsons.* 1962: † C. W. Mills; Gurvitch, *Dialectique and Sociologie.* 1963: Allen, ed., *Sorokin in Review;* Wilbert Moore, *Social Change.* 1964: Blau, *Exchange and Power in Social Life;* Parsons, *Social Structure and Personality.* 1965: † G. Gurvitch; Znaniecki, *Social Relations and Social Roles* (posthumous); Yinger, *Toward a Field Theory of Behavior.* 1966: Sorokin, *Sociological Theories of Today.* 1967:† H. Hart.

# Index

Page numbers set in italics refer to chapters, sections, or paragraphs especially devoted to the author in question.